# In the Shadow of Vitoria: A History of International Law in Spain (1770–1953)

# Legal History Library

VOLUME 22

# Studies in the History of International Law

*Series Editor*

Randall Lesaffer
*Tilburg University, Catholic University of Leuven*



VOLUME 9

The titles published in this series are listed at *brill.com/shil*

# In the Shadow of Vitoria: A History of International Law in Spain (1770–1953)

*By*

Ignacio de la Rasilla del Moral

BRILL
NIJHOFF

LEIDEN | BOSTON

Cover illustration: Bank note of 500 pesetas from 1946, with the image of Francisco de Vitoria.

Library of Congress Cataloging-in-Publication Data

Names: Rasilla, Ignacio de la, author.
Title: In the shadow of Vitoria : a history of international law in Spain (1770–1953) / Ignacio de la Rasilla del Moral.
Description: Leiden : Brill, 2018. | Series: Studies in the history of international law ; volume 22 | Includes bibliographical references and index.
Identifiers: LCCN 2017041675 | ISBN 9789004343221 (hardback : alk. paper)
Subjects: LCSH: International law–Spain–History. | Vitoria, Francisco de, 1486?-1546.
Classification: LCC KZ1242 .R37 2017 | DDC 341.0946/0903–dc23
LC record available at https://lccn.loc.gov/2017041675

Typeface for the Latin, Greek, and Cyrillic scripts: "Brill". See and download: brill.com/brill-typeface.

ISSN 1874-1793
ISBN 978-90-04-34322-1 (hardback)
ISBN 978-90-04-34323-8 (e-book)



This book is printed on acid-free paper and produced in a sustainable manner.

致吾妻郝雅烨子

∵

'Es corona de la discreción el saber filosofar,
sacando de todo, como solícita abeja, o la miel del gustoso provecho
o la cera para la luz del desengaño'

BALTASAR GRACIÁN, EL DISCRETO (1646),
*'Culta repartición de la vida de un discreto'*

# Contents

# Acknowledgements

Every book begins somewhere.

This book's journey into the terra incognita of the history of international law in Spain in the nineteenth and the first half of the twentieth centuries began with a completely disorganized, dusty and barely catalogued set of bibliographical materials that the passing of time and the indifference of generations of Spanish law professors seemed to have deposited with barely any system on the shelves in the locked archives of the departmental library of a Spanish university *the name of which I have no desire to call to mind.*

Over the following years, my research into the history of international law in Spain took me deep into the stacks of other archives and academic libraries. I am grateful to the Spanish Ministry of Innovation and Science, the Spanish Ministry of Economy and Competitiveness, the Harvard Law School's Summer Academic Fellowship Program, the Post-Doctoral Max Weber Programme at the European University Institute, the British Academy, the Max Planck Society and to all the research centres which have welcomed me over these years. These include the Real Colegio Complutense at Harvard University, the Harvard European Law Research Centre, the Watson Institute for International Studies at Brown University, the Institute for Global Law and Policy at Harvard Law School, the Lauterpacht Research Centre for International Law at the University of Cambridge, the Max Planck Institute for European Legal History in Frankfurt, the Max Planck Institute for Comparative Public Law and Public International Law in Heidelberg and the Graduate Institute of International and Development Studies in Geneva.

Before finding its final place in the larger framework of the present book, earlier versions of parts of it have appeared published in peer-reviewed international law and legal history journals. An earlier and far shorter version of Chapter 1 appeared in Spanish as 'El estudio de la historia del Derecho internacional en el corto siglo XIX español' in the Zeitschrift des Max-Planck-Instituts für europäische Rechtsgeschichte (Rg. 23, 2013, pp. 48–65) and in English as 'The Study of the History of International Law in the Short Spanish Nineteenth Century' in the Chicago-Kent Journal of International and Comparative Law (Vol. 13, No. 2, 2013, pp. 122–150). An earlier version of some parts of Chapter 2 appeared as 'The Ambivalent Shadow of the Pre-Wilsonian Rise of International Law' in the Erasmus Law Review (Vol. 7, No. 2, 2014, pp. 80–97) and other excerpts were published as 'The Unexpected Transformations and Reintepretations of Francisco de Vitoria for International Law' in International Community Law Review (Vol. 15, No. 3, 2013, pp. 287–318). A version of a much-extended Chapter 4 appeared as 'In the General Interest of Peace? British International Lawyers and the Spanish Civil War' in The Journal of the History of International Law (Vol. 18, No. 1, 2016, pp. 1–42). A much earlier and shorter version of Chapter 5 was published as 'The Fascist Mimesis of Spanish International Law and its Vitorian Aftermath, 1939–1953' in The Journal of the History of International Law (Vol. 14, No. 2, 2012, pp. 207–236), and as 'The Zero Years of Spanish International Law' in Les doctrines internationalistes durant les annees du communisme reel, Emmanuelle Jouannet and Iulia Motoc (Eds.) Paris, Société de législation comparée (2012) pp. 237–276. Finally, some reworked excerpts from the introduction appeared as 'Beyond the Spanish Classics—The Ephemeral Awakening of the History of International Law in Pre-Democratic Spain' in Monde(s). Histoires, Espaces, Relations (No. 7, 2015, pp. 137–157). All translations contained in the book correspond to the author except if otherwise indicated.

David Kennedy remains a prince of lost causes; he provided me—as well as many others—with undreamt-of opportunities. Martti Koskenniemi's work has inspired hundreds with the intellectually intoxicating spell of his writing over the years. Ramón Soriano supported my first research years in foreign lands. Emmanuelle Jouannet lit the fuse of my interest in the history of international law in Spain with a timely invitation and Yolanda Gamarra walked its sinuous path with me for some time. John D. Haskell and Philip Alston have provided warm support over time. My gratitude also goes to Randall Lesaffer, Jorge Viñuales, Marcelo Kohen, Anne Peters, Luigi Nuzzo, Ben Chigara, Duncan Kennedy, Andrea Bianchi and many others who I cannot mention but who certainly fall into the category of teachers and academic colleagues who I have had the pleasure to have encountered over the years. The assistance of David Frank Barnes to help navigate the modern lingua franca is acknowledged. Also, gratefully acknowledged are the constructive comments provided by two anonymous reviewers of the manuscript and the editorial guidance and encouragement provided by the general editor of the series, R.C.H. Lesaffer. Finally, every author owes a great debt of gratitude to all the authors whose works he has read and pondered. Acknowledging them at the beginning of a book is a reminder that each author's work is but one individual interpretation of an ever-expanding great web of knowledge whose synergetic intellectual and transformative potential is borderless.

This book is dedicated to every member of my large family. A special dedication goes to my wife, Yayezi Hao, my sister, Margarita de la Rasilla del Moral, and to my father, Luis de la Rasilla Sánchez-Arjona, for their love and patience, as well as to my mother, Cristina del Moral Ituarte to whom I am infinitely in debt. The pages of this book are finally dedicated to the memory of my grandfather, Jose María del Moral Pérez de Zayas (1917–2014), in the succinct Latin that he taught me, from my early childhood, to always keep learning from:

*Homo, pater, magister.*

IGNACIO DE LA RASILLA DEL MORAL
London
November 2016

# A History of International Law in Spain, 1770–1953

## Timeline

1770 A Royal Decree of King Carlos III establishes the teaching of public law, natural law and the law of peoples for the first time in Spain.

1771 The first systematic treatise on the law of peoples by a Spanish author is published by Jose de Olmeda y León: Elementos de derecho público de la paz y de la guerra.

1772 The first chair in public law, natural law and the law of peoples at the Royal School of Studies of San Isidro in Madrid is occupied by Joaquín Marín y Mendoza.

1776 The first doctrinal history of the law of peoples in the Spanish language is published by Joaquin Marín y Mendoza: Historia del Derecho Natural y de Gentes.

1794 A Royal decree of Carlos IV suppresses the chairs of public law, natural law and the law of peoples in Spain.

1808 War of Independence (1808–1814) in Spain.

1812 Spanish Constitution Cadiz. In vigour: 1812–1814, 1820–1823 and 1836–1837.

1814 Ferdinand VII reinstates absolutist rule.

1817 Spain signs the Congress of Vienna Final Act and the Declaration relating to the Universal Abolition of the Slave Trade of 18 February 1815.

1820 The study of natural law and the law of peoples is restored at the start of the 'liberal triennium' (1820–1823) in Spain. E. de Vattel's Le droit des gens is translated for the first time into Spanish.

1824 The study of natural law and the law of peoples disappears from the programme of university studies at the onset the 'ominous decade' (1823–1833) of return to absolutist rule by King Fernando VII. The Battle of Ayacucho puts a symbolic end to the Wars of Independence in Latin-America (1810s-1820s).

1827 The Universidad Central of Bogotá establishes the first chair in international law (eo nomine) in the world.

1832 Andres Bello publishes the first treatise on international law in the American continent: Principios de Derecho de Gentes.

1833 Queen Isabel II is crowned aged three years old. Regency of Maria Cristina of Naples (1833–1840). Outbreak of first of the 'Carlist wars' (1833–1840).

1837 The study of natural law and the law of peoples is restored in Spain. The ratification of the Treaty of peace, friendship, and commerce with Mexico initiates the official Spanish practice of developing diplomatic ties with its former colonies in America. Constitution of 1837 (1837–1845) establishes a constitutional monarchy.

1843 José Posada Herrera and E. Moreno López become the first professors to 'officially' lecture on international law in Spain at the Special School of Administration. José María de Pando publishes in Madrid the first book to include the term 'Derecho Internacional' in its title in Spanish language.

1844 The first 'private' chair in international law is established at the Madrid Athenaeum.

1845 The term Derecho Internacional (international law) enters for the first time the Spanish General Plan of Studies. Its teaching becomes separated from the study of natural law. The 1845 Spanish Constitution is enacted. Constitutional monarchy with parliament elected by censitary suffrage. Outbreak of the $2^{nd}$ Carlist War (1845–1849). The first chair in international law is established at the University of Madrid.

1846 Esteban de Ferrater publishes Código de Derecho internacional, o sea, Colección metódica de los tratados de paz, amistad y comercio entre España y las demás naciones.

1852 The term 'Derecho Internacional' enters in the Dictionary of the Royal Spanish Academy. A chair for doctoral studies in 'Philosophy of Law: International Public and Private Law' is established in Madrid.

1854 The term 'international law' appeared for the first time in Spanish in the title of an article published in Revista General de Legislación y Jurisprudencia (RGLJ)

1856 Constitution of 1856. Not enacted. Liberal Biennium (1854–1856).

1868 Queen Isabel II is deposed. 'Revolutionary or Democratic Sexenium' (1868–1873) begins in Spain. Outbreak of the First War of Cuba (1868–1878).

1869 The Spanish constitution of 1869 establishes a monarchic constitutional parliamentary democracy based on the principles of separation of powers and national sovereignty and enshrines the most extensive bill of rights and freedoms until that time in Spain.

1870 C.C. Langdell becomes the first Dean of Harvard Law School.

1871 Amadeo I of Savoy elected King by Parliament (1871–1873).

1872 Outbreak of the Third Carlist War (1872–1876).

1873 First Spanish Republic (1873–1874) is established. Constitution of 1873 (not enacted). Law on the abolishment of slavery is enacted. The Institut de droit international is founded.

1874 Bourbon Restoration (1874–1923). King Alfonso XII (1874–1885) Regency of María Cristina of Habsburg (1885–1902). King Alfonso XIII (1886–1931)

1876 Spanish Constitution. Constitution of 1876 Constitutional monarchy and parliament elected, first by censitary, then universal male suffrage from the 1890s. Founding of Institución Libre de Enseñanza.

1879 Concepción Arenal publishes the first book on international law published by a woman, Ensayo sobre el Derecho de Gentes.

1883 A Royal Order extends the compulsory establishment of courses in public international law and private international law to seven Spanish universities in addition to the Central University of Madrid.

1885 The Berlin Conference recognizes the territories of the Gulf of Guinea as a Spanish Protectorate along with another area in northwest Africa facing the Canary Islands.

1887 Alejo García Montero launches the first specialized international law journal in Spain: Revista Española de Derecho Internacional, Legislación y Jurisprudencia Comparadas (1887–1888).

1898 Spanish-American War. Spain losses Puerto Rico, Cuba and The Philippines.

1899–1900 Spain subscribes to the 1899 Hague Conventions in their entirety.

1905 The Marquis de Olivart launches 'Revista de Derecho Internacional y Política Internacional' (1905–1912).

1906 The Conference of Algeciras is held. The final Algeciras settlement created a de facto Franco-Spanish protectorate under vague international control. The American Society of International Law is founded.

1907 The 'Junta de ampliación de estudios e investigación científica' (Board of Extension of Studies and Scientific Research, known as the JAE) is established. Spain signs nine of the fourteen conventions and the final act of the 1907 Hague Peace Conference. The American Journal of International Law begins publication.

1910 A decree by the Council of Ministers authorises the enrolment of women as official students at Spanish universities.

1911 The first meeting of the Institut de droit international is held in Spain. The Marquis de Olivart's collection is purchased by Harvard Law School.

1912 The 'Spanish Protectorate' in North Morocco is established.

1920 Spain deposits its instrument of adhesion to the League of Nations. The Spanish Office of the League of Nations is created. Rafael de Altamira, a member of the 'Committee of Ten,' which drafted the Statute of Permanent Court of International Justice, becomes a permanent judge of the PCIJ (1919–1946). The British Yearbook of International Law is launched.

1921 The Office of Cultural Relations is established at the Spanish Ministry of Foreign Affairs. The 'Disaster of Annual' is the 'greatest defeat suffered by a European power in an African colonial conflict in the 20th century'. Spanish-Moroccan or 'War of the Riff' (1919–1927).

1923 End of the Restoration period (1874–1923) and beginning of the dictatorship of General Miguel Primo de Rivera (1923–1930).

1925 Quintiliano Saldaña teaches the First Hague Academy Course on 'La justice pénale internationale'.

1926 The Association Francisco de Vitoria is founded. Spain formally withdraws from the League of Nations until 1928.

1927 Spanish National Consultative Assembly (1927–1930) is established. First course on the Spanish School of Ius Gentium at The Hague Academy by Camilo Barcia Trelles: 'Francisco de Vitoria et l'école moderne du droit international'.

1929 Spain accedes to the Briand-Kellogg Pact.

1931 Establishment of the Second Spanish Republic (1931–1936). Spanish Constitution of 1931: Universal Suffrage including female vote. Salvador de Madariaga appointed Permanent Spanish Delegate at the League of Nations (1931–36).

1933 The Spanish Phalanx is founded by Jose Antonio Primo de Rivera. Federation of Spanish Associations of International Studies reunites the Instituto de Derecho Comparado hispanoportugués-americano, the Asociación Española de Derecho Internacional y Legislación Comparada and the Seminario de Estudios Internacionales. The University of Salamanca authorizes the creation of the 'Instituto Francisco de Vitoria'. Japan and Germany withdraw from the League of Nations.

1934 James Brown Scott publishes 'The Spanish Origins of International Law. Francisco de Vitoria and his Law of Nations and The Catholic Conception of International Law'.

1936 Beginning of the Spanish Civil War. The international non-intervention agreement is signed. The London Non-Intervention Committee is established.

**1938** Fundamental Laws of the Realm (1938–1978).

**1939** End of the Spanish Civil War. General Francisco Franco, Head of the Spanish State (1939–1975). The last Hague Academy Course on the Spanish Classics of International Law is taught by Camilo Barcia Trelles: 'Fernando Vázquez de Menchaca. L'école espagnole du droit international du xvie siècle'.

**1940** Establishment of The Council of the Hispanidad.

**1941** Revista de Estudios Políticos, flagship of the Franco regime's think-tank, Instituto de Estudios Políticos, pledges itself to be at the service of the 'whole and radical truth' of the 'Movimiento Nacional'. The book 'Reivindicaciones de España' is awarded the Spanish National Prize for Literature in 1941 for elaborating in extenso on the legal-historical titles that supported the Franco regime's neo-colonialist pretensions.

**1943** The Spanish University Law of 1943 decrees that the Spanish university will have as its 'supreme guidance, Christian dogma and morals'.

**1946** GA Res. 39 (I) of 12 December condemns the 'Fascist Franco Government of Spain'. The introduction by the Bank of Spain of a 500-peseta banknote with the effigy of Francisco de Vitoria completes the official events of the 400th anniversary of the death of Francisco de Vitoria.

**1947** The James Brown Scott Chair (1947 to 1965) is inaugurated at Universidad de Valladolid.

**1948** Revista Española de Derecho Internacional (1948-present) is founded by Phalangist Spanish international lawyers.

**1950** The rehabilitating General Assembly Resolution 386 (V) of 4 November 1950 gives Franco's government the possibility of reestablishing diplomatic relations and joining the UN's specialized agencies. Carl Schmitt's 'Der nomos der erde im Völkerrecht des ius publicum europaeum' is published.

**1951** Spain integrates international institutions (OMM, FAO, OMS, UIT in 1951 and UNESCO in 1952). Carl Schmitt becomes the first foreign author published in Revista Española de Derecho Internacional.

**1952** The first Hague Academy Course by a Spanish author after the Second World War is taught by Antonio Herrero Rubio: 'Le droit des gens dans l'Espagne du XVIIIème siècle'.

**1953** Spain signs Economic-Military Pacts with United States and a Concordat with the Holy See.

**1955** Spain officially becomes a state member of the Organization of the United Nations.

# Introduction

> 'Vitoria's reputation has its own history and requires special treatment'
> CARL SCHMITT, The Nomos of the Earth (1950)

The shadow of the longest personal dictatorship in the history of the Western world, and the ninth longest globally during the twentieth century has loomed large over the study of the history of international law in Spain during the nineteenth century and the first half of the twentieth century. This study has been mysteriously neglected by both Spanish international law scholars and foreigners alike. The almost infant state of scholarly investigation of it contrasts starkly with the archetypical role that the so-called Spanish classics of international law have played in the consciousness of every generation of international lawyers globally for the last hundred and fifty years. The elevation of Francisco de Vitoria and the natural law tradition of the School of Salamanca to the altars of the classics of international law has overshadowed the historical evolution of the study of international law in the country that most contributed to the foundational place the Salamanca School occupies in the imagery of the Western tradition of international law. It is in this sense that the history of international law in Spain remains, as the title of this book suggests, in the shadow of Vitoria.

## 1.

Leaving barely anything written in his own hand, Francisco de Arcaya y Compludo (1483/86–1546), a sixteenth-century Dominican friar and Prima Professor of Sacred Theology at the University of Salamanca, is universally acknowledged as the founding father of international law. Francisco de Vitoria, as he was later to be known, owes this honour to having been the first author to connect the notion of ius gentium with the international community, which, he argued, 'in a certain manner, is a republic' and as such 'potestate ferendi leges aequast et convenientes omnibus, quales sunt in iure gentium'.[1]

1 Francisco de Vitoria, *De Potestate Civili* (1528), in Luis G.A. Getino (ed) *Relecciones Teologicas del Maestro Fray Fr. De Vitoria* (Madrid: Editorial FEDA, 1934), 169–210, 207. See also, Francisco de Vitoria, *Political Writings*, in Anthony Pagden, Jeremy Lawrance (eds.) (Cambridge: Cambridge University Press, 2001).

 | DOI 10.1163/9789004343238_002

Francisco de Vitoria is widely considered to have presided over the School of Salamanca, also variously known as the School of the Spanish Natural Law Classics, the Spanish School of the Law of Peoples, or, as the school was re-baptised in Spain in 1981, the 'Spanish School of Peace'.[2] This school of legal theologians produced an extensive corpus of literature gathered under the titles De Justitia et iure and De legibus, which can be divided, as noted by L. Pereña, the scientific coordinator of the 26 volumes of the Corpus Hispanorum de Pace, in three generations: a 'creative generation, from Vitoria to Soto (1526–1560); a generation of cultural expansion, from Sotomayor to Medina (1560–1584) and a generation of doctrinal systematization from Báñez to Suárez (1584–1617).'[3] The School of Moral Theology of the Seconda Scholastica which flourished in Spain during the Siglo de Oro was the origin of an extensive body of scholarship which included 'more than 125 treatises which can be hierarchized and classified under the epigraphs of social ethics, political philosophy, and jurisprudential commentaries.'[4]

The first renaissance of Francisco de Vitoria and the School of Salamanca among international law scholars took place in the late nineteenth century at a time when the incipient academically organized profession was looking for a genealogy of the origins of the science of international law. Overshadowed by the rise of the natural law of protestant roots, neglected and finally forgotten by Spanish intellectual elites as Spain went through a long historical and intellectual decadence throughout the late seventeenth and eighteenth centuries and the first half of the nineteenth century, the natural law tradition of Francisco de Vitoria had remained largely disregarded and intellectually submerged for almost two centuries. The Salamanca School re-surfaced in this period, as M. Koskenniemi has highlighted, 'as the starting-point of an international law tradition that would continue through Grotius, Pufendorf, Vattel and the later 19th-century public law into the present.'[5]

This historiographical tradition, both deeply Eurocentric and Christian, lay the foundations for an early Western historiography of international law. It did so against the background of the climax of late nineteenth-century European imperialism and the emergence of a positivist method in the social sciences, which gradually came to encompass international law. This historical

2 Luciano Pereña, 'La tesis de la paz dinámica', in Luciano Pereña (ed) *Corpus Hispanorum de Pace*, Vol. VI (Madrid: Consejo Superior de Investigaciones Científicas, 1981), 29–94, 65.

3 Id., 65.

4 Id., 67.

5 Martti Koskenniemi, 'Vitoria and Us', *Rechtsgeschichte—Legal History Rg* 22 (2014), 119–138, 121.

background was completed by the rise of the standard of civilization, which separated the 'family' of European (and/or Europeanized) Christianised civilized nations from non-Christian and non-Europeanised territories, and methodological nationalism in the formation of the modern European nation-state at a time when the disciplines of both history and law started to become professionalized.

Meanwhile, in Spain, at the time a relatively peripheral Western European country clinging to the last remnants of its overseas empire, the academic study of international law had accompanied the troubled emergence of the constitutional liberal state throughout the nineteenth century. The term Derecho internacional had, indeed, already become widely employed, for the first time in the 1820s and 1830s on the occasion of the independence of the Latin-American republics after three hundred years of Spanish colonial rule. It was from this original impulse toward greater self-government, which in both the Thirteen Colonies and later in Latin America turned into independentism under the influence of the eighteenth-century tradition of natural rights, that modern international law would grow up during the nineteenth century. The comparatively early integration of the study of international law in the Spanish official curriculum in the 1840s mirrored the impulse that Latin-American independence had given to the study of the subject in the Spanish language. In 1883, the professional academic organization of international law was further boosted by the establishment of chairs in public and private international law all over Spain. In this context, the rise in prestige of Francisco de Vitoria and the Seconda Scholastica in international intellectual circles coincided with a polarizing debate around the conforming traits of the 'Spanish science.' This contributed to nurturing the soil for the gradual consolidation of a national identity myth around the foundational role of the Spanish tradition of natural law in the law of nations.

The second and definitive 'renaissance' of Francisco de Vitoria, and the ensuing consolidation of the international reputation of the Spanish classics as the forefathers of international law materialized in the mid-1920s and early 1930s. The intellectual updating of the doctrines of Francisco de Vitoria and the Seconda Scholastica was part and parcel of the interwar revival of 'natural law' at a time when the international legal doctrine across Europe, shocked by the horrors of the First World War, was looking in an anti-sovereigntist vein for the natural law-based ancillary stone of the 'international community' to further legitimize the binding force of international legal obligations and the universalism of the League of Nations. A clear example of this theoretical impulse is represented by the constitutional approach of A. Verdross to international law which grounded the theoretical foundations of international law on the normative idea of the 'moral unity of mankind.'[6] The abstract idea of this moral unity upon which was based Verdross' monism, which relied upon his interpretation of the Spanish 'founders' of International Law, found itself associated with the notion of the international community and the constitutional unity of a unique universal legal system. Such a system was originally posited as a hierarchical model constitutionally crowned by 'a series of fundamental principles of international law determining its sources, subjects and execution, and the jurisdiction allocated to states.'[7] For Verdross, the general principles of law were, in its international version, a reflection of the legal conscience of the international community and as such 'a bridge between pure natural law and pure positive law.'[8]

Less well-studied, but ultimately no less relevant for the consolidation of the Spanish classics in the global imagery of international law, is the fact that the second renaissance of Vitoria took place against the background of international codification projects in the Americas and the renewal of cultural, linguistic and diplomatic ties between Spain and the Latin-American nations under the cloak of Hispanidad. The 'Association Francisco de Vitoria' was co-founded by the international law professor, and Minister of Foreign Affairs, Jose Yanguas Messia, in Madrid in 1926. The new association, 'a Spanish institution which could make known the Vitorian doctrine and would put it in contact with the current situation of the legal sciences and with the diverse schools and institutions of these sciences,'[9] was born with the aim of 'spreading knowledge about the legacy of the classic Spanish ius-internationalists' and 'updating their doctrines.'[10] In the following years, supported by the highly influential Secretary of the Carnegie Endowment for International Peace and President of the American Society of International Law, James Brown Scott, the Association became the matrix for

6 Alfred Verdross, 'Le fondement du droit international'. Collected Courses of the Hague Academy of International Law 16 (1927), 247. See also Robert Kolb, *Les cours généraux de droit international public de l'Académie de la Haye*, (The Hague: Brill 2004), 31.

7 For the evolving path of the definition of international constitution in Verdross' successive works, see Bardo Fassbender, *UN Security Council Reform and the Right of Veto. A Constitutional Perspective*, (Leiden: Martinus Nijhoff 1998), 37–45.

8 Alfred Verdross, *Die Verfassung der Volkerrechtgemeinschaft* (Wien: J. Springer, 1926). See, also, Bruno Simma, 'The Contribution of Alfred Verdross to the Theory of International Law', 6 *European Journal of International Law* 1 (1995), 33–54, 49.

9 Estatutos de la Asociacion Francisco de Vitoria (1926). See also James Brown Scott, 'Asociacion Francisco de Vitoria', *American Journal of International Law* 22 (1928), 136–139.

10 Id.

the further institutionalization of the Vitorian cause, including through the establishment of chairs, and numerous publications on the Spanish classics of international law several of which were published by The Hague Academy of International Law.

However, almost absent from the Vitorian historical narrative in the interwar period is the fact that the Association Francisco de Vitoria became an essential centre of legitimizers who relied on the doctrines of the School of Salamanca to justify General Franco's coup d'état against the democratically elected Spanish Republican government during the Spanish Civil War. In the aftermath of the war, during the crudest political repression in Spain, an ideological glorification of the Salamanca School took place, which Spanish international law scholars greatly contributed to, and helped to anchor the Franco regime's preferred strategic portrayal of Spain as the last international bastion of Catholic values after the Second World War.

The first two 'renaissances' in the history of international ideas of Francisco de Vitoria and the School of Salamanca were respectively marked by their rediscovery in the late nineteenth century and their ulterior consolidation in the interwar period. These were followed by remarkably contrasting aftermaths following the Civil War in Spain, and the Second World War internationally. The post-Cold War third 'renaissance' of Francisco de Vitoria 'whose long shadow extends,' as A. Padgen notes, 'over all subsequent discussions on the Law of Peoples'[11] is, by contrast, characterized by the already firmly established status of Francisco de Vitoria and the Spanish School of ius gentium among the 'classics' of international law.

There are, broadly speaking, four main axes of the revitalisation of studies on Francisco de Vitoria and the School of Salamanca in international law today. The first is that which makes the works of Vitoria constantly reappear as a precedent for the discussion of different branches of international law[12] with particular acuity in connection with just war and the laws of war.[13]

---

11 Anthony Padgen, 'Gentili, Vitoria and the Fabrication of a Natural Law of Nations', in Benedict Kingsbury and Benjamin Straussman (eds), *Roman Foundations of the Law of Nations: Alberico Gentili and the Justice of Empire*, (Oxford: Oxford University Press, 2010), 340, 342.

12 Including indigenous rights, see seminally Felix S. Cohen, 'The Spanish Origin of Indian Rights in the Law of the United States' 31 Georgetown Law Journal 1 (1942–1943), 1.

13 See e.g. José Antonio Pastor Ridruejo, 'Francisco de Vitoria y la modernidad de sus enseñanzas: ius ad bellum y ius in bello", in Yolanda Gamarra & Ignacio de la Rasilla (eds), Historia del pensamiento internacionalista español del siglo XX (Cizur Menor: Thomson Reuters Aranzadi 2012), 79–87.

It is customary to retrace modern notions of humanitarian intervention back to the 'duties towards the defence of the innocent,' which Vitoria signalled as one of the possible grounds for a just war.[14] The principle of necessity in the conduct of war,[15] the classification of wars in terms of legal and illegal, and the implicit assessment that the ius gentium does not admit all types of war, but only those associated with the reparation of a received injury, are but some of the numerous examples highlighted as legacies of Vitoria in the Charter of the United Nations.[16]

The second axis of renewal of Vitorian studies fleshes out a narrative of continuity with the past in asserting the foundational role of Francisco de Vitoria and other members of the School of Salamanca, like Bartolomé de las Casas,[17] in providing inspiration for an 'international community' inspired by the universality of human rights as a keystone of the United Nations' system.[18] Such a value-ridden conception of constitutionalism in international law, where human rights are depicted as the 'alpha and omega' of sovereignty,[19] has been summarily captured by B. Simma. This notes that 'in contemporary international law the universalistic blueprint originally drawn up by natural law philosophy is slowly but steadily being turned into a reality. Thus, the positive international law is moving in the direction of the 'ought' delineated by the school to which Verdross adhered. It is currently involved in a fundamental process of transformation from a mere ius inter potestates to a legal order for mankind as a whole.'[20]

The third axis of the renaissance of Francisco de Vitoria, and the one which has been the most influential of the four modern renewals, in contributing to the long list of 'unexpected interpretations and re-interpretations' of Francisco

14 See e.g. Daniel Schwartz, 'The Principle of Defense of the Innocent and the Conquest of America: Save Those Dragged Towards Death', 9 Journal of History of International Law (2007), 263–291.

15 Pastor Ridruejo 'Francisco de Vitoria y la modernidad' 2012.

16 Id.

17 Bartolomé de las Casas, 'Historia de las Indias', in Juan Pérez de Tudela (ed.), Obras escogidas de Bartolomé de las Casas. vol. I (Madrid: Ed. Atlas. 1957).

18 See Pekka Niemela, 'A Cosmopolitan World Order. Perspectives on Francisco de Vitoria and the United Nations', *Max Planck Yearbook of the United Nations* 12 (2008), 301–344. See, also, R.B. Boast 'The Spanish Origins of International Human Rights Law: A Historiographical Review', *Victoria University of Wellington Law* Review 41 (2010), 235–272.

19 Anne Peters, 'Humanity as the Alpha and Omega of Sovereignty' 20 European Journal of International Law (2009), 513–544.

20 Simma, 'The Contribution of Alfred Verdross' 1995, 44.

de Vitoria for international law,[21] is inspired by a critical 'post-colonial' reading of Francisco de Vitoria. This presents itself as a critical reaction to the dark sides of the liberal international order to which Vitoria had been traditionally associated in the history of international ideas. This reinterpretation of Vitoria takes places in the context of post-colonial readings of international law's traditional companionship of imperial projects. Today, the Seconda Scholastica, under the influence of a post-colonial historiographical challenge in a globalizing and multi-polar international legal order,[22] triggers bloody intellectual debates between international legal theorists and historians regarding Eurocentrism, the imperial genealogy of international law, and the extent to which Vitoria's work may have seen as the early precursor of an intellectual pattern pursued by subsequent imperialist projects up to the present day. In this meta-historical context, Vitoria's work has been interpreted as one that can 'be read as a particularly insidious justification of (their) conquest precisely because it is presented in the language of liberality and even equality.'[23]

Finally, the fourth axis of the renaissance of Francisco de Vitoria in contemporary international legal studies is historiographical in nature. This has sprung in the context of what has come to be known as the 'turn to history' in international law[24] over roughly the past fifteen years. It is within this context where M. Koskenniemi highlights that 'it is perhaps above all the person of Francisco Vitoria, a Dominican scholar from Salamanca in the first part of the 16th century, whose role and significance for the history of international law has been the object of the greatest recent interest.'[25] Francisco de Vitoria is, indeed, discussed in academic articles penned by historians of international law and international relations[26] in connection

21 The expression comes from Carl Schmitt Carl Schmitt, *Der nomos der erde im völkerrecht des jus publicum europaeum* (Berlin: Duncker & Humblot, 1950)

22 See Antony Anghie, *Imperialism, Sovereignty and the Making of International Law*, (Cambridge: Cambridge University Press, 2005).

23 Anghie, *Imperialism* 2005, 28.

24 On the 'turn to history' in international law see e.g. M Koskenniemi, 'Why History of International Law Today?' *Rechtsgeschichte*—Legal History Rg 4 (2004), 61–66. R.C.H., Lesaffer, 'International Law and Its History: The Story of an Unrequited Love', Matthew Craven/ Malgosia Fitzmaurice/ Maria Vogiatzi (Eds) *Time, History and International Law* (Leiden/Boston: Brill, 2006) 27–41.

25 Koskenniemi, 'Vitoria and Us' 2014, 121.

26 Chris Brown/ Terry Nardin/ Nicholas Rengger (eds) *International Relations in Political Thought: Texts from the Ancient Greeks to the First World War* (Cambridge: Cambridge University Press 2002)

to new historiographical and methodological debates in historical writing in international law.[27]

The effects that the elevation of the 'Spanish classics', whose authors are heralded as the 'founding fathers' of international law, and of Vitoria, a dominant figure in all textbooks of international law, and every bibliography of the history of international law,[28] had on the Spanish-internationalist identity is an important part of the history of international law. The first two Vitorian 'renaissances', and their Spanish Civil War's aftermath, which are explained in this book, slipped into the international legal consciousness, religious conscience and nationalist professional identity of Spanish international lawyers, and went on to influence the study of international law in the world at large. This book engages with the effects of the first two renaissances of Francisco Vitoria among Spanish international law scholars in their historical context in several senses. First, it analyses the role of Vitoria, a symbolic shorthand for the renaissance of the natural law tradition of the School of Salamanca, in the construction of a Eurocentric globalising historiography of international law. Second, it examines the two renaissances of Francisco de Vitoria in the context of its effects on the 'nationalist universalism' of Spanish international law scholars. Third, it relates them to the deep Catholic cultural substratum of Spanish traditional thought, and its strong purchase over the social elite of international law scholars in different historical periods. Fourth, it examines the political and ideological use that was made of the 'Spanish classics' during the Spanish Civil War and the early period of Franquismo. The Spanish classics, with Vitoria at their head, were glorious reminders of the Spanish imperial past, international emblems of the Catholic tradition, and the essence of an intellectually uncontaminated Spanish thought. These three pillars of historical continuity legitimized the regime of General Franco, who declared himself only to be 'accountable before God and History'.

---

27 See e.g. Martti Koskenniemi, 'Expanding Histories of International Law', American Journal of Legal History 56 (2016), 104–112.

28 See e.g. Ignacio de la Rasilla, 'History of International Law 1550–1700', in *Oxford Bibliographies of International Law* (Oxford: Oxford University Press, 2014), 1–25 (available at http://www.oxfordbibliographies.com/view/document/obo-9780199796953/obo-9780199796953-0036.xml)

**2.**

The lack of critical attention among Spanish international lawyers to the modern history of international law in Spain in the nineteenth and twentieth centuries is partly an offspring on a cumulative array of causes. These also account for its disregard among non-Spanish international lawyers.

The first general reason both in Spain and abroad for the disregard that the history of international law in Spain has suffered is the adaptability that the 'foundational' mythical role of Francisco de Vitoria and the Salamanca School has shown through different historical periods of the discipline. In Spain, often side-lined as a semi-peripheral state among the 'great powers' of the last two centuries, Francisco de Vitoria gradually became enshrined as a national identity myth, and a reassuring emblem of a glorious past throughout the late nineteenth century, the interwar period and the Cold War. Later, after the Spanish Transition to democracy, the Spanish 'classics' were conveniently re-updated to fit a new modern democratic sensitivity, and became known as the Corpus Hispanorum de Pace, or 'Spanish school of Peace'.[29] The occasional engagement of Spanish international lawyers with post-colonial and critical perspectives on Francisco de Vitoria reflects this deeply-rooted cultural nationalist defensive attitude towards the intellectual legacy of the Spanish 'classics'.[30] However, their defense against the 'leyenda negra' has never questioned the political manipulation of the Spanish classics of international law by Spanish international law scholars during the Spanish Civil War and the Franco years.

The second reason for the disregard by Spanish and non-Spanish international lawyers of the history of international law in the nineteenth and twentieth centuries is the only relatively recent interest among international law scholars in the 'darker legacies of law in Europe.'[31] This reluctance of generations of legal scholars 'to glance in the mirror' of the past is particularly acute in an epistemological community which operates as a professionally-driven technical discipline with a particular authority and expertise that makes it less susceptible to interdisciplinary engagement by historians. The discipline's short memory span is compounded by the fact that international lawyers may tend to

---

29 Luciano Pereña (ed) *Corpus Hispanorum de Pace* (Madrid: Consejo Superior de Investigaciones Cientificas 1981)

30 See e.g. Pablo Zapatero, 'Legal Imagination in Vitoria. The Power of Ideas', Journal of the History of International Law Volume 11 (2009), 221–271.

31 Christian Joerges/Navraj Singh Ghaleigh/ Michael Stolleis (eds), Darker Legacies of Law in Europe: The Shadow of National Socialism and Fascism Over Europe and Its Legal Traditions (Oxford: Hart, 2003)

see themselves, as Koskenniemi remarks, 'among the avant-garde of liberal modernity—against conservative nationalism, sovereignty and power politics',[32] or, alternatively, to consider the products of international law scholarship as relatively irrelevant to the actual course of international relations.[33] The sharing of these international collegiate peculiarities among Spanish international law scholars was complemented by what historians often call a 'pact of forgetfulness' in Spanish universities[34] after the Spanish transition to democracy in the mid-1970s. All Spanish international lawyers had sworn their complete adhesion to the principles of the National Movement and other fundamental laws of the Spanish State under Generalissimo Franco for almost four decades.[35]

The third factor behind the disregard among international law scholars and non-Spanish scholars of the modern history of international law in Spain is the neglect of the study of the history of international law itself. Until recently, this was obscured by the weight, as A. Peters and E. Jouannet highlight, of 'the methodological primacy of technicism (doctrinalism) and pragmatism in international legal scholarship.'[36] Over the last roughly fifteen years, contemporary international law has seen a 'turn to history' whereby new historiographies and methodologies have put into question, as M. Koskenniemi notes, the dominant trans-historical methodology that 'viewed international law as a trans-historical conversation over great principles or indeed as a project of global progress.'[37] However, Spanish international law scholars remain latecomers to the 'historical turn' in international law.

Indeed, the weight of a dominant formalist methodological normative approach to international law is an important explanatory factor accounting for a flight from history among contemporary Spanish international law

32 Martti Koskenniemi, 'International Law in a Post-Realist Era' Australian Yearbook of International Law 16 (1995) 1, 1.

33 'To take an analogy, art critics may influence the development of painting in a variety of ways, but it would be misleading to write a history of art by reference to their work. For the most part the product of international law scholarship is a similarly secondary literature', James Crawford 'Public International Law in 20th Century England' in Jack Beatson and Reinhard Zimmermann (eds.) Jurists Uprooted: German-Speaking Emigré Lawyers in Twentieth Century Britain. Oxford University Press, Oxford (2004) 681–701, 687.

34 See, in particular, Michael Richards, *After the Civil War. Making Memory and Re-Making Spain since 1936* (Cambridge: Cambridge University Press, 2013).

35 Ley de 29 de julio de 1943 Sobre ordenación de la Universidad española Boletin Oficial del Estado 212 (31 de julio de 1943), 7406–7431.

36 Emmanuelle Jouannet and Anne Peters, 'The Journal of the History of International Law: A Forum for New Research', 16 Journal of the History of International Law (2014), 1–8, 2.

37 Koskenniemi, 'Vitoria and Us' 2014, 121.

scholars in at least two senses. First, Spanish international law scholars have traditionally tended towards a methodologically homogenous and formalistic approach to international law—understood as a technically-oriented juridical discipline. This mainstream approach to international law—which is also prevalent in academia in other nations—is consonant with the technical-legal specialization of the career-oriented aspirations of Spanish international law scholars. International law in Spain is disciplinarily separated from the distinct area of international relations. This is easily recognisable from the template of parameters of recognition within an area or sub-discipline: methods, assumptions, foci, topoi, key questions, intellectual frameworks, and in most of the cases, a bias against inter-disciplinarity. Second, despite the existence of some 'progressive' precedents in the cultivation of the history of international law in Spain in the 1960s, the sociological history of the profession in Spain has been identified with an uncomfortable past by the 'democratic' generation. This was looking forward to jumping into the green professional pastures of democratic modernity and European and international life to which Spain definitively opened itself in the 1980s.

The fact that a comprehensive study of the history of international law in Spain in the nineteenth and twentieth centuries has fallen between the cracks of the works of Spanish international law academia explains the need to predominantly have recourse to interdisciplinary sources of knowledge in the Spanish language—particularly works by historians of Spain, historians of Spanish international relations, legal historians and contributions to the history of Spanish universities—in this book. Although to the best of this author's knowledge, no single work by any international law scholar directly examines the history of international law in Spain in the nineteenth century and the first half of the twentieth century,[38] abundant use has been made of an extensive array of foreign works to provide international contextualization and, in particular, at crucial turning points in the history of international law in Spain, to engage in punctual excursuses on the evolution of the study of international law in the United States of America and the United Kingdom.

A brief historiographical review of works produced by Spanish international law scholars on which the present book has relied should be divided into three periods. The first two represent two stages during Franco's dictatorship

38 M. Koskenniemi dedicates several pages to deconstruct how opposite ideological positions conditioned the international legal analysis of two French authors, Louis Le Fur and G. Scelle, regarding the Spanish Civil War. See Koskenniemi, *The Gentle Civilizer*, 338–342. However, symptomatically, perhaps, Koskenniemi only dedicates two footnotes to quote the work of two Spanish authors throughtout his whole book.

(1939–1975). The third focuses on the transition and democratic period, in particular since the entering into force of the Spanish Historical Memory Act of late 2007.

After the end of the Spanish Civil War, the opulence of works on the 'Spanish classics' of the Siglo de Oro contrasted with the scarcity of historical reconstructions of the study of international law in Spain before the Spanish Civil War. Those that existed were inspired by the official ideology of 'National Catholicism' of the 1940s and 1950s. A most notable representative of this historiography, which contributed to the ideological glorification of the authors of the sixteenth century and the Spanish School of International Law at a time of Spanish international isolation, is Garcia Arias' 'Adicciones' to the Spanish translation of A. Nussbaum.[39] Contributing to the centennial issue of Revista General de Legislación y Jurisprudencia, A. Quintano Ripolles provided an overview, divided into three historical periods, of the state of the science of international law in Spain.[40] In 1952, A. Herrero Rubio, who was the first Spaniard to be invited to lecture at The Hague Academy of International Law after World War II, devoted a course to the study of international law in the Eighteenth century in Spain.[41]

The first modern attempt to look back at the history of international law in the nineteenth and early twentieth centuries by Spanish international law scholars had to wait until the mid-1960s. Twenty-five years after the end of the Spanish Civil War, a short-lived collective historical project attempted to cast light on the evolution of international law in Spain in the period preceding the civil war. This project, which attempted to 'reflect the new premises and the partially different problems and methodologies of new Spanish 'legal realism,'[42] paid some attention to 'analyzing and reconstructing the Spanish internationalist thought of the nineteenth and twentieth centuries,' not 'merely to square the historical dimension but to decisively influence the present of our own internationalist thought.'[43] This attempt to cultivate an intra-disciplinary historiography of international law in Spain from a new standpoint was part

39 See Luis García Arias 'Adiciones sobre la historia de la doctrina hispánica del Derecho internacional' in Arthur Nussbaum *Historia del Derecho Internacional* (transl. by F.J. Osset) (Madrid: Editorial Revista de Derecho Privado, 1949).

40 See Antonio Quintano Ripolles, 'Cien Anos de Derecho internacional', Revista General de Legislación y Jurisprudencia 100 (1953), 134–197.

41 Alejandro Herrero Rubio, 'Le droit des gens dans l'Espagne du XVIII siècle', *Collected Courses of the Hague Academy of International Law* 81(1952), 309–450.

42 Mariano Aguilar Navarro, *Tareas de la doctrina española de Derecho internacional público, Revista Española de Derecho Internacional* (1964) 501, 502.

43 Id., 504.

and parcel of the methodological renovating spirit embodied by a number of Spanish authors. These, in the words of Aguilar Navarro, were 'looking for an interdisciplinary exposition, longing to put into practice new methodological attitudes, which try to escape all kinds of mutilating monisms, aware of the need to translate in a positive and institutional reality the new international situation' of the mid-1960s.[44]

Their vehicle of expression was Revista Española de Derecho Internacional (REDI). This has been co-founded by F.M. Castiella, by then the Director of the Falangist 'brain trust' Instituto de Estudios Politicos, and later the future longest-serving Minister of Foreign Affairs in the twentieth century, in 1948. Symbolically, the image of Francisco de Vitoria, which had occupied the cover of the journal since its founding, was removed to mark the beginning of a 'second epoch'[45] in the mid-1960s. The new Spanish historiographical project was premised on a revision, as Aguilar Navarro, the director of the journal in its 'second epoch' (1964–1968), noted, of 'our attitude towards the classics.' This revision required Spanish international jurists to engage in an exercise of 'self-criticism' to examine the extent to which 'we might be prisoners of an inadequate assessment of what our classics were and this in function of a discussion not yet closed on our own past and origins as a nation, as a community with its own historical profile.'[46]

The outcome of these scholarly concerns with a new historical dimension of international law was the creation in REDI of a new section: Spanish Sources of International Law which wore the subtitle 'Notes for the History of Spanish Internationalist Thought.' This historical project, which was without precedents in the field, had the explicit purpose of 'offering from different perspectives a vision of what have been the ideas and realities of international law in Spain'.[47] It did so by reclaiming the study of the works of the pre-Civil War generation of international lawyers 'who had embarked on the enormous task of giving to Spain new intellectual schemes, opening modern roads of study and teaching as a necessary response to an obliged revision of falsely classic attitudes and inoperative traditional lures.'[48]

---

44 Id.

45 Reference to a 'segunda epoca' was expressly included in the cover of the journal. This reference replaced the figure of Francisco de Vitoria which has presided over it since its foundation in 1948.

46 Aguilar Navarro, 'Tareas de la doctrina' 1964, 503.

47 See Julio González Campos, Roberto Mesa y Manuel Medina Ortega, 'Notas para la historia del pensamiento internacionalista español: Aniceto Sela y Sampil, 1863–1935', Revista Española de Derecho Internacional XVIII (1964) 561–583, 561.

48 Aguilar Navarro, 'Tareas de la doctrina' 1964, 502.

However, only two very detailed and bibliographically rich research essays were to see the light in REDI[49] in the mid-1960s. The project 'Notes for the History of Spanish Internationalist Thought,' offering from 'different perspectives a vision of what the ideas and the realities of international law have been'[50] was followed in parallel in Revista de Derecho Español y Americano in 1966 by a work on the scientific contribution of another of the first doctrinal cultivators of international law in Spain.[51] However, the attention of Spanish international lawyers to the history of international law before the Spanish Civil War turned out to be dramatically ephemeral.[52] Less than four years after REDI had inaugurated a new epoch, Luis García Arias, a leading member of the post-civil war Spanish school of natural law,[53] reverted what he defined as the 'unimportant editorial coup'[54] of 1964, thus bringing the journal back to the philosophical line of continuity lost in 1963.[55] With the return of REDI to its previous structure, the mention of the 'second epoch' was eliminated, the project 'Notes for the History of Spanish Internationalist Thought' vanished from

49 The first one was a doctrinal bibliographical profile of one of the fathers of the internationalist thought in Spain, see Julio González Campos/ Roberto Mesa/ Enrique Pecourt, 'Notas para la historia del pensamiento internacionalista español: Aniceto Sela Sampil (1863–1935)', *Revista Española de Derecho Internacional* XVII (1964), 561–583. One year later, in 1965, R. Mesa consecrated a detailed study consecrated to the colonial Spanish thought in the 19th century, see Roberto Mesa (con la colaboración de Julio González Campos y Enrique Pecourt), 'Notas para la historia del pensamiento internacionalista español: Algunos problemas coloniales del siglo XIX', Revista Española de Derecho Internacional XVIII (1965), 380–414.

50 Ibid., 561.

51 Antonio Marín López, 'Notas para la historia del pensamiento internacionalista español: Manuel Torres Campos, 1850–1918', *Revista de Derecho Español y Americano* 12 (1966), 125–154. The historiographical concerns of the Spanish internationalists would anticipate in a couple of years the publication of the one of the major turning points in the study of the history of Spain in the 19th and early 20th centuries, the 1966's classic, Raymond Carr, *Spain, 1808–1936* (Oxford: Oxford University Press 1966).

52 For a more detailed account, see Ignacio de la Rasilla, 'Beyond the Spanish Classics—The Ephemeral Awakening of the History of International Law in Pre-Democratic Spain', Monde(s), Histoires, Relations 7 (2015), 137–157.

53 See representatively Luis García Arias, *Estudios de historia y doctrina del derecho internacional* (Madrid: Instituto de Estudios Políticos, 1964)

54 Luis García Arias, 'Fichero de Derecho Internacional Público de la REDI', *Anuario hispano-luso-americano de derecho internacional* 3 (1967) 257.

55 Antonio Remiro Brotons, 'El discreto encanto—y desencanto—de la Revista Española de Derecho Internacional (1948–1978)', *Estudios de Derecho Internacional. Libro-homenaje al Prof. A. Miaja de la Muela* Vol. I (Madrid: Ed. Tecnos 1979), 123–140, 132–135.

its pages, and the effigy of Francisco de Vitoria again returned to symbolically occupy the cover of the official journal on international law in Spain.

Having disappeared from the pages of REDI, the historiographical reconstructive project began 'a long parenthesis.' Only a study on the theory of international relations of J. Ortega y Gassett[56] was published in Anuario Español de Derecho Internacional in the early Transition to democracy. The project was also continued by a pioneering contribution from the perspective of international relations by Celestino del Arenal who provided a precious 'study of the historical-genetic development of international relations in Spain since the mid-nineteenth century.'[57] Although not eo nomine, this contribution, and others by the same author[58] were articulated with direct reference to 'the line of contributions made in recent times oriented to doing the groundwork which might allow for a better understanding of Spanish internationalist thought in the nineteenth and twentieth centuries.'[59] A few other contributions, which appreciated the 'clamorous topicality'[60] of the issue during the 'Transition', addressed the field in modern terms from within Spanish international law academia and the field of international relations only, however, to discontinue the task too soon.

Despite the emancipatory role of earlier attempts to renovate the study of the history of international law in pre-democratic Spain, there is still a great shortage of works on the subject written by Spanish international law scholars.[61] Only occasional contributions to particular themes by Spanish

56 Manuel Medina, 'Notas para la historia del pensamiento internacional español: La teoría de las relaciones internacionales de Ortega y Gasset', Anuario de Derecho Internacional III (1976), 349–375.

57 Celestino del Arenal, *La teoría de las Relaciones Internacionales en España* (Madrid: Internacional Law Association, Sección Española, 1979), 8.

58 See e.g. Celestino del Arenal, 'La génesis de las relaciones internacionales como disciplina científica', *Revista de Estudios Internacionales* 4 (1981) 849–892, 858–60.

59 Celestino del Arenal, 'El estudio de las relaciones internacionales en la España del siglo XIX,' *Revista de Estudios Políticos* 16 3(1979), 7–45, 7.

60 In particular, see Remiro Brotons, 'El discreto encanto' 1979, 123.

61 The main contributions come from legal historians studying the history of Spanish law and the evolution of university curricula through the nineteenth century and twentieth centuries as well as historians, legal philosophers and historians of Spanish foreign policy and Spanish international relations. The latter have contributed, more substantially since the mid-1990s, to the study of interrelated 'internationalist' themes such as the League of Nations. See e.g. José Luis Neila, 'La política exterior de la españa republicana (1931–1936): excepcionalismo y normalidad historiográfica', Studia Historia Contemporanea 22 (2004), 47–83.

international law scholars appeared scattered throughout the 1980s, 1990s and the early twenty-first century. These include a continuation of the earlier tradition of bio-bibliographical essays in homage[62] to leading Spanish international law scholars. Other scattered works examine particular events related to the history of international law in Spain in the nineteenth and twentieth centuries such as the Olivenza dispute,[63] the Hague Peace Conferences,[64] and the Conference of Algeciras,[65] or include recent overviews of the history of human rights throughout the nineteenth and twentieth centuries in Spain.[66] Some historical works have also been written about relevant doctrinal figures like the Marquis de Olivart,[67] Rafael de Altamira,[68] and Miaja de la Muela.[69] Histories of international law, a genre scarcely cultivated by Spanish international lawyers, make no effort to refer to the doctrinal contribution of Spanish international law scholars or to historically contextualize the evolution of the study of international law in Spain during the nineteenth and twentieth centuries either.[70] Even A. Truyol y Serra, (1913–2003), the

62 These remain valuable sources, see e.g. Truyol y Serra, 'Don Antonio de Luna García (1901–1967)', in Estudios de Derecho Internacional Homenaje a D. Antonio de Luna (Madrid: Instituto Francisco de Vitoria, 1968). See, Manuel Diez de Velasco Vallejo 'El profesor Miaja de la Muela: Ensayo biográfico' in Libro homenaje al profesor A. Miaja de la Muela (Madrid, Tecnos, 1979), 18–29, 22–27.

63 See e.g. Carlos Fernandez Liesa, 'La cuestion de Olivenza a la luz del Derecho Internacional Publico', *Encontros, Revista luso-española de investigadores en Ciencias Humanas y Sociales* 4 (2004), 230–281.

64 See e.g. C. Jiménez Piernas, 'El papel de España en la Conferencia de La Haya de 1899', *Revista Española de Derecho Internacional* LI (1999), 775–782.

65 See e.g. Carlos Jiménez Piernas y Millán Requena Casanova, 'Spain's Part in the 1906 Algeciras Conference: Internationalisation of the Moroccan Question and the Interests of Spain', *Spanish Yearbook of International Law* XII (2008), 1–18.

66 See e.g. Carlos Fernandez Liesa, *El Derecho internacional de los derechos humanos en perspectiva histórica,* (Madrid: S.L. Civitas Ediciones 2013)

67 Antonio Blanc Altemir, *El marquès d'olivart i el dret international (1861–1928) societat internacional i aportació científica* (Lleida: Institut d'Estudis Ilerdencs, 2000).

68 Yolanda Gamarra, 'Rafael Altamira, un historiador del derecho en el tribunal permanente de justicia internacional (1921–1939)', Revista Internacional de Pensamiento Político 6 (2011), 287–300.

69 Natividad Fernández Sola, *El pensamiento internacionalista del Profesor Miaja de la Muela. Su contribución al Derecho internacional público y al Derecho europeo* (Zaragoza, Mira Editores, 1999), 227.

70 Juan Antonio Carrillo Salcedo. *El Derecho Internacional en perspectiva histórica* (Madrid: Editorial Tecnos, 1997).

most internationally regarded historian of international law in Spain,[71] did not dedicate more than a few lines to the cultivation of international law in Spain in the nineteenth century in his widely-read 'Histoire du Droit International Public.'[72]

Only in recent years, a timid renaissance of the history of international law in Spain among Spanish international law scholars has taken place. This has been fostered by the combined impact of the Spanish Historical Memory Act of 2007 (which triggered a new peak of scholarly interest in the legal-political evolution of the almost 40-year dictatorial regime of General Franco and in the Spanish Civil War)[73] and that of the 'turn to history' in international law.[74] Nevertheless, no comprehensive effort to study the Spanish history of international law in the nineteenth and twentieth centuries has been attempted in Spain (or elsewhere) and a staggering historical lacuna still remains.[75]

71 Truyol participated actively in the 1940s in the post-Civil War Vitorian revival with his academic works. He continued to support the role of Vitoria as the founder of the idea of Jus Gentium as universal order until the end of his long career, see e.g. Antonio Truyol y Serra, 'El Derecho de gentes como orden universal', in A. Mangas Martín (ed), *La Escuela de Salamanca y el Derecho internacional en América. Del pasado al futuro* (Salamanca: AEPDIRI 1993), 17–25.

72 Truyol notes about the progress of the study of international law during the nineteenth century: 'l'Espagne, ou le contact avec les classiques de son Siecle d'Or s'etait rompu, est reste' quelque peu en marge sous cet aspect. Elle s'est nourrie surtout des traductions des manuels et traits en cours en Europe'. Parmi les ouvrages du pays, on retiendra celui de Ramón de Dalmau, Marquis d'Olivart (1861–1928)'. Antonio Truyol y Serra, *Histoire du droit international public* (Paris: Editions Economica, 1995), 124.

73 See e.g. Paul Preston, *The Spanish Holocaust. Inquisition and Extermination in Twentieth Century* Spain (London: Harper Press, 2012).

74 See e.g. Ignacio de la Rasilla and Yolanda Gamarra (eds) *Historia del Pensamiento Iusinternacionalista Español del siglo XX*, (Cizur Menor: Thompson-Reuters Aranzadi, 2012) and Carlos Fernandez Liesa, *La Guerra Civil española y el orden jurídico internacional*, (Madrid: Thompson Reuters Aranzadi, 2014).

75 It is remarkable, nonetheless, that the Spanish Yearbook began in 2014 a 'new classic's corner' which so far includes a translation into English of an essay by Antonio Truyol Serra 'The Jus Gentium as Universal Order' 18 *Spanish Yearbook of International Law* (2013–2014) 1–9 and Oriol Casanovas y La Rosa, 'A Debate over International Economic Law: The Discussion between Adolfo Miaja de la Muela and Mariano Aguilar Navarro in 1971/72', *Spanish Yearbook of International Law* 19 (2015) 1–21.

## 3.

The history of the two 'renaissances' of Francisco de Vitoria, and what I shall call the Vitorian aftermath of the fascist mimesis of international law in Spain, are embedded in the larger history of the effects that the three great turning points in Spanish history in the nineteenth and the first half of the twentieth centuries had on the study of international law in Spain. Over the course of 120 years, two colonial wars and a deleterious civil strife accompanied the historical path of Spain from its former status in the early nineteenth century as 'the first empire in history on which the sun never set' to the beleaguered and diminished fascistized National-Catholicist state that emerged from the ashes of the Spanish Civil War in 1939. Each of these three wars had momentous effects on the course of the study of international law in Spain. They also became points of inflection in the history of international law and its study in the world at large.

It hardly needs stressing that any history of international law in Spain, because of its external implications, its multiple intellectual influences, and so the multitude of external stimuli that shaped its course, is an inherent part of both the European and global histories of international law in the nineteenth and first half of the twentieth centuries. Two of these Spanish wars, the Spanish-American War of 1898, and the Spanish Civil War justify the integration of historical excursuses on the evolution of international law studies in the United States and the United Kingdom. The excursus on the history of the United States is justified by the effect that the Spanish-American war had on the establishment of the American Society of International Law (ASIL) in 1906. It is also justified because of the role that the 'behind-the-scenes leader' of ASIL, the long-standing editor -in -chief of the American Journal of International Law, and later President of ASIL, played along with other members of the Association Francisco de Vitoria in the elevation of Francisco de Vitoria as the 'founder' of international law in the interwar period.

The inclusion of an excursus on the history of international law in the United Kingdom is, in its turn, justified by the role that British international lawyers and British legal advisers played in the legal justification of the international agreement on non-intervention that sealed the dismal fate of the Second Spanish Republic. Although throughout the corresponding chapter numerous references are also made to the works of French, American, Italian and other contributors to the debate on the Spanish Civil War, the focus on British International Lawyers is justified because, particularly since the late 1970s and early 1980s,[76] British foreign policy regarding the Spanish Civil War has been presented 'as cynical, callous and objectively pro-Franco.'[77] This is so because of its enabling of what E. Moradiellos called an 'asymmetrical structure of international support and inhibition'[78] favourable to the insurgents. Historical research in the archives of the British Foreign Office has amply demonstrated that the Non-Intervention Agreement and the establishment of a supervisory committee in London served the principal British diplomatic objectives in the conflict well as they entailed 'restriction of the war to Spain, restraining the intervention of her French ally, avoiding any alignment with the Soviet Union, and any confrontation with Italy and Germany over their support for the rebels.'[79] However, although the case for 'British Macchiavellism' regarding the Spanish Civil War dominates the perspective of contemporary historians, no specific analysis of how British international lawyers contributed to the justification of British foreign policy goals had been produced until now.

A final word is warranted on the hybrid historiographical methodology employed by the author in constructing the narrative contained in the book. In exploring the almost historiographically barren terra incognita of this period of the history of international law in Spain, the narrative unabashedly combines diplomatic history, intellectual history and international legal analysis with historiographical reflections, excerpts on the history of international organizations and a sociological approach to the evolution of the discipline in Spain. The latter is reflected in the inclusion of bio-academic excursus on certain figures who accompany the story throughout different chapters, and complemented by a certain penchant for 'social history'. Throughout the book reference is, indeed, often made to the evolution of illiteracy in Spain, to the struggle for extending the access to education to different social classes and to different university reforms as these impacted the study of international law in Spain in different periods. The narrative also builds on insights explored by the recent post-colonial historiography of international law (such as i.e. in the case of the 'standard of civilization') and pays special attention to how the Spanish relationship with its colonies led to different orientations towards international

76 Seminally on the basis of those archives, Jill Edwards, *The British Government and the Spanish Civil War, 1936–1939*, (London: MacMillan Press, 1979).

77 Tom Buchanan, 'Edge of Darkness: British 'Front-Line' Diplomacy in the Spanish Civil War, 1936–1937', *Contemporary European* History 12 (2003) 279–303, 279.

78 Enrique Moradiellos, 'The Allies and the Spanish Civil War' in Sebastian Balfour/ Paul Preston (eds) *Spain and the Great Powers in the Twentieth Century* (London: Routledge 1999), 96–126, 107.

79 Id.

law after the independence of the Latin-American Republics in the 1820s, and after the 1898 Spanish-American war with the subsequent Spanish policy of 'colonial substitution' in North-Africa. The relatively linear chronology pursued throughout the book is methodologically designed to produce a 'historiographical' backbone that might be fleshed out by future historical research for each of the different periods covered in the present volume.

The author has made an effort to produce a historically 'contextualized' narrative that places its *dramatis personae* in non-judgemental terms as 'men of their times'. The part of the history of international law in Spain the author has been able to unearth during the period covered in the book is, one must add, a 'history of white (and educated) and educated men'. However, scattered references will be found in its pages on the access of women to university education in Spain and to what, to the author's knowledge, is the first ever book published by a woman on international law. The conclusion of the book explains why, despite the survival of the Franco regime and the key role played by international lawyers supporting that regime in the broader international law profession over the following decades, it concludes in 1953 to mark the end of a historical cycle which began for the history of international law in Spain in 1770. Some remarks on the neglected study of periodization in the history of international law are complemented, in the conclusion, by a notice of the some of lessons that the history of international law in Spain over almost two hundred years may offer from a longue durée perspective.

## 4.

A detailed summary perspective of the contents of each chapter is offered to better allow the the reader to situate herself within the narrative of each chapter and to better place each chapter within the broader narrative of the book. The reader will also find a 'Historical Timeline' that highlights, for ease of reference, some of the key moments of the History of international law in Spain explored in the book.

Chapter One surveys the effects on the study of international law in Spain from the first of the great turning point in its modern history—the independence of the new Latin-American Republics—up to the first rediscovery of Francisco de Vitoria and the School of Salamanca in the late nineteenth century. The first chapter begins by examining the ephemeral rise and fall of the study of natural law and the law of peoples in Spain in the late eighteenth century. It goes on to examine the international elements of the liberal Constitution of Cadiz and to survey the independence of the American colonies before providing a brief overview of Spanish participation in the Congress of Vienna and focusing on the ephemeral restoration of the study of natural law and the law of peoples during the liberal triennium (1820–1823) in Spain. It then accompanies the troubled consolidation of liberalism in Spain from the early 1830s, relating the establishment of some of the very first chairs in international law in Europe in the early 1840s, and looking into the early development of Spanish international law scholarship and the parallel abandonment of the study of natural law in Spanish universities in the first half of the nineteenth century.

The second part of Chapter One follows the evolution of international law studies in Spanish universities with reference to the first doctoral dissertations in international law produced at the Central University of Madrid in the 1850s and 1860s. Furthermore, it contextualizes the founding of the Institut de Droit International (1873) against the background of the Spanish 'Revolutionary Sexenium' (1868–1874), the colonial debates over Cuba and the abolition of slavery in Spain. The chapter goes on to look at the Spanish academic production of international law during the Bourbon Restoration after 1874. In this context, it examines the double impact on the study of international law in Spain of the founding of the Institución de libre Enseñanza (Institution of Free Teaching) in 1876 and the University Reform of 1883, when seven universities—other than the Central University of Madrid—were allowed to establish chairs in public international law and private international law. The final part of the chapter reviews the first ever, albeit short-lived, specialized international law journal established in Spain in 1887–1888 and the rise in academic production that accompanied the arrival of the post-1883 professional generation of Spanish international law scholars. It also examines the parallel rediscovery of the School of Salamanca of the sixteenth and early seventeenth centuries in both Spain and Europe and reflects on the influence that this rediscovery had in laying the foundations for an early Western historiography of international law. Moreover, it highlights how the international revival of interest in Francisco de Vitoria and the School of Salamanca provided Spanish international law academia with a quasi-national identity and fostered an all-encompassing approach to the science of international law at the end of the nineteenth century.

Chapter Two surveys the parallel effects that the second turning point in Spanish history in the nineteenth and twentieth centuries—the Spanish-American War—had in the study of international law in both Spain and the United States. In the United States, the aftermath of the Spanish-American war saw a rise in the cultivation of international law, which was already nurtured by its study in the nineteenth century. The particularities of the U.S.' approach to international law were partly epitomized by the establishment of the case method at Harvard Law School. As the chapter goes on to show, this took place against the background of the development of classical legal thought in the United States and the development of international legal studies in the US. This reached its climax with the foundation of the American Society of International law in 1906 and the creation of its journal in 1907. The moralistic-legalistic generation of American international lawyers who created the ASIL nurtured the soil for Wilsonianism and the creation of the League of Nations. Meanwhile in Spain, in the wake of the fin-de-siècle crisis, modernizing tendencies in education and Europeanization, together with a change of foreign policy orientation toward North Africa, made Spanish international lawyers, at least partially, 'distance themselves from the speculative aspects to focus their attention on international questions with practical repercussions.'[80] The Conference of Algeciras of 1906, which followed the first Moroccan crisis, was the first international stage on which the new Spanish Africanist orientation was integrated into the Franco-British entente as a factor of equilibrium. The chapter also examines how educational and university reforms in Spain led to an intellectual and scientific opening towards European circles that benefited the second scientific generation of international law scholars. This generation worked in the heyday of positivism—an era of unbridled nationalism and imperialism in Europe-during the last stage of the 'age of armed peace.' In this period, a slow rise of non-European states up the ladder of the standard of civilization was taking place. This movement ran parallel to the evolution of previous small codification efforts into proto-universal international legislation-making processes carried out at multilateral conferences and to the development of proto-institutional integration efforts in functional sectors. Mirroring these developments, in the early 1900s the Marquis d'Olivart and James Brown Scott became the respective founders and editors of the first two international law journals that broke, as Koskenniemi noted referring to the AJIL, 'the pattern (if it was such)' of 'pointing to [a] national and regional allegiance' in their titles.[81] An overview of the contents of Revista de Derecho Internacional y de Politica Exterior (1905–1910/13) accompanies a survey of major events that interested Spanish international law scholars during these years, including The Hague Peace Conferences and, in particular, what was to be known as the 'Moroccan question'. This chapter also revisits the forgotten figure of James Brown Scott,

80 Jiménez Piernas / Requena Casanova, 'Spain's Part in the 1906 Algeciras Conference' 2008, 4.

81 Martti Koskenniemi, 'The Case for Comparative International Law' Finnish Yearbook of International Law 20 (2009), 1–8.

once portrayed by one of his ASIL colleagues as 'our mentor, our engineer, our constant supporter from the beginning.'[82] Paradoxically, perhaps, for a man who rushed to enlist in the Spanish-American War, J.B. Scott developed strong ties with the Hispanic/Spanish world during the late 1900s and 1910s. This was to be the beginning of a lasting relationship which made of James Brown Scott the greatest champion of Francisco de Vitoria as the founding father of international law in the interwar period.

Chapter Three contextualizes the second renaissance of Francisco de Vitoria and the School of Salamanca and the contribution to it of international law scholars in the interwar period. The chapter begins by surveying the fundamental transformation that the establishment of the League of Nations brought to the consciousness of interwar international law scholars by highlighting some of the most innovative features that the new organization incorporated into the management of international affairs in the interwar period. It goes on to examine the Spanish diplomatic engagement with the League of Nations following Spain's official neutrality in the First World War. It surveys Spain's foreign policy manoeuvres to obtain and then to retain a post as a permanent member of the League's Council. This was in accordance with General Primo de Rivera's instrumentalist and revisionist approach to the League. It then examines Spain's subsequent withdrawal from the League against the background provided by the impacts of the Moroccan question and the Disaster of Annual on Spanish domestic and foreign policy in the 1920s. The latter was the 'greatest defeat suffered by a European power in an African colonial conflict in the 20th century.'[83] The chapter then focuses on the novel features of the second generation of professional Spanish international law scholars under the impact of university reforms in Spain in the 1920s, and reviews Spanish internationalist production on the League of Nations and theoretical inquiries into the nature and characteristics of international society and other works. This includes a reference throughout the chapter to all the courses offered by Spanish legal scholars at The Hague Academy in the interwar period. The chapter goes on to review the postulates of the various doctrinal schools of international law during the interwar period which were inspired by the promise of a new international community legal order under the auspices of the League of Nations. Particular attention is paid to the revival of sociological and natural law doctrines and the role of constitutional analogies in theoretical constructions of

82 William I. Hull, quoted by Ralph Dingman Nurnberger, 'James Brown Scott: Peace Through Justice', (Phd Diss., Georgetown. University, 1975 (on file at Harvard Law Library) 63.

83 Pablo La Porte, 'Rien a` ajouter': The League of Nations and the Rif War (1921–1926)' European History Quarterly 41 (2011), 66–87, 71.

international law. Against this background, the chapter examines the founding of the Association Francisco de Vitoria in 1926 and the development of a revival of attention to works on the Spanish classics of international law in Spain and, in particular, to Francisco de Vitoria as the first author to have connected the ius gentium with the international community, 'which, in a certain manner, is a republic' and as such 'has the power to enact laws which are just and convenient to all, like those of the law of peoples.'[84] In this context, the works of Barcia Trelles on Francisco de Vitoria and Francisco Suarez and the work of James Brown Scott on the Spanish origins of international law are examined against the rise of Spanish Americanists' cultural insistence on Hispanidad amidst codification projects in Latin America and the extension of the internationalist associational movement in Spain in the early 1930s. This is followed by an analysis of how the arrival of the Second Spanish Republic fostered the alignment of the new Spanish constitution of 1931 with the principles of the League of Nations which became perceived as the 'equivalent at the international level of what the Republic represented at the domestic level.' There is, furthermore, an examination of the re-organization of the Spanish foreign policy apparatus in Geneva under the helm of Salvador de Madariaga against the convulsed backdrop of the early 1930s. Reference in this context is also made to the rise of Nazi Germany, and the cultivation in Germany of doctrines of an extremely nationalistic strand of natural international law, and to the turn to neutrality among minor and medium powers amidst the gradual crumbling of the system of collective security of the League.

Chapter Four focuses on the third great turning point in Spanish history in the nineteenth and first part of the twentieth centuries: The Spanish Civil War. The first part of this chapter examines the drawing up of the international non-intervention agreement and the establishment of the London Committee and their combined neutralizing effect on the League of Nations in the light of a series of factors underlying the British-led non-intervention agreement. This was the death knell of the system of collective security established by the League of Nations and became the revolving door to the Second World War for Europe.The second part reviews the core issues and different doctrinal positions present in the international legal debates triggered by the Spanish Civil War. It pays particular attention to the contributions by the first two British judges at the International Court of Justice, A. D. McNair (1946–1955) and H. Lauterpacht (1955–1960), to these debates. Their writings can be seen as respectively representative of the two

---

84 Vitoria, *Potestate Civili* 1528.

stages through which British international lawyers went in the international legal debates on the Spanish Civil War. Up to early 1938, British International lawyers adopted a characteristically apologetic approach to the policy of the British Government on the advice of the British Foreign Office. The second stage, from early 1938 to the end of the Spanish Civil War in March 1939, was informed by a 'practitioner's approach' to the analysis of the domestic cases brought before the British courts as a result of the hostilities. The chapter also includes an overview of the evolution of the academic study of international law in England since the First World War which helps situating British international lawyers in the context of the academic study of international law in England at that time. It also provides an analysis of the case for British 'benevolent neutrality to the Nationalists'[85] in the Spanish Civil War in the light of the basic coincidence between British foreign policy goals and the strategy of General Franco's insurgents. Chapter Four concludes by examining how after the outbreak of the Spanish Civil War in 1936, a time by which the reputation of the classic 'Spanish School of International Law' had reached its climax in international circles, the Association Francisco de Vitoria became an essential centre for legitimizers of General Franco's coup d'état against the Second Spanish Republic, It does this by chronicling, with particular attention to members of the Association Francisco de Vitoria, the different fates during the Spanish Civil War of the interwar Spanish international law scholars who actively supported Franco's coup d'état, including by becoming signatories of the 'Advisory Opinion on the Illegitimacy of the Acting Powers on the 18th of July 1936' relying on the doctrines of the School of Salamanca.

Chapter Five examines the effects of the Civil War on the study of international law in Spain through the periods of the 'Fascist mimesis' of international law in Spain and its Vitorian aftermath focusing, in particular, on the rise of cultivation of the Spanish classics. To allow for a better understanding of the evolution of Spanish the academic approach to international law, which went hand in glove with the design of Spanish foreign policy during this period, this chapter is divided into two main sections. After introducing the Spanish University Law of 1943, which established that the Spanish university 'shall be catholic' and would have as its 'supreme guidance Christian dogma and morals', while also stressing that 'this law, in all its precepts and articles, commands the faithful service of the university to the ideals of the Falange which inspire the State,'[86] chapter Five focuses on

85 Enrique Moradiellos, *Neutralidad benevola.* (Oviedo: Editorial Pentalfa, 1990).

86 Ley de 29 de julio de 1943 Sobre ordenación de la Universidad española Boletin Oficial del Estado 212 (31 de julio de 1943), 7406–7431, arts. 3 and 4. See further Chapter v.

the reception of Carl Schmitt's works by Spanish political and legal theorists with a marked internationalist orientation as illustrative of the mermaid's song of the imperial temptation of the Axis powers that characterized Spanish international law from 1939 to 1943–5. Although the intellectual reception of Carl Schmitt in Spain was primarily aimed at instrumentally nurturing the theoretical legitimization of the new authoritarian regime, it also mirrored the acute climax of intellectual fascistization of Spain's combative counter-revolutionary elite between 1939 and 1943–5. This period of fascist mimesis in Spanish international legal thought is, moreover, examined in the light of the influence of the book 'Reivindicaciones de España' and other similar works with neo-colonialist credentials penned by Spanish international lawyers during the period. Although this pro-fascist breed of thought was gradually submerged under the rise of a more traditional nationalist purist orientation in response to official guidelines issued by the government as the allied cause gained ground during the Second World War, this long triennium and its slow historically autarchic aftermath casted a long shadow over the evolution of international law in Spain for many more years to come.

The second part of Chapter Five focuses on the Spanish transition from autarchy to international realignment with the West that took place from 1943–45 to 1953. First, it examines how a climate of severe intellectual repression and organically nationalist-directed scientific work in Spain, and the nationalist reaffirmation of a culture grounded in Catholic conservatism and traditionalism, fostered the adoption of a marked thematic orientation towards natural law and the reinstatement of the Siglo de Oro's Salamanca School among Spanish international lawyers. This orientation equated well with the prevailing atmosphere of atavistic Spanish nationalist cultural forms drawn from the mythology of the reconquista, the counter-reformation and empire, as well as with the myth of the crusade against the 'anti-Spain' that had been used as a justification for the Civil War in the name of national reunification. Following the pattern initiated in the 1920s of Spanish neo-colonialist orientation vis-à-vis its former colonies, the fruitful intellectual revival of the Spanish Siglo de Oro was also related to more concrete Spanish foreign policy goals. These included the defence of Hispanidad and a renewal in the importance of a sound diplomatic policy towards South America during the period of Spanish autarky. Attention is, finally, also paid, at the end of the final Chapter, to the third characteristic axis of Spanish international law during the 1940s, which was frontal opposition to the Soviet foreign policy and Marxism. These goals were pursued using the framework provided by international relations and foreign policy along three main lines: a geopolitical approach, a realpolitik strategic perspective, and one specifically aimed at building up a contrario a Spanish national identity myth. These three strands of work epitomized the scientific approach adopted in this period by Spanish internationalist academia vis-à-vis the Soviet Union and Marxism on the international plane.

The invocation and manipulation of the Salamanca School helped to anchor the Franco regime's preferred strategic portrayal of Spain as the last bastion of traditional European Catholic values after the Second World War. It also contributed to reinforcing the external image of Spain as the only European country that had successfully resisted the spread of Russian imperialism and atheist Marxism. This facilitated the reintegration of Spain with the United States and the Vatican in the Western bloc in the early stages of the Cold War and, ultimately, enabled the political survival of the longest personal dictatorship in the history of the Western world in the Twentieth Century.

CHAPTER 1

# The Study of International Law in the Spanish Nineteenth Century

## The Academic Study of International Law—An Early Spanish Awakening

Spain and the Spanish-speaking world appear almost nowhere in the patchy historical narrative that retraces the establishment of the first professorships of international law in the Western world in the nineteenth century. This narrative gravitates around the view that the consciousness and teaching of international law as a discipline of its own in European universities was a development that largely took place in the third part of the nineteenth century.[1] Although a professorship in international law was established, as M. Koskenniemi notes, in Paris in 1829, and another one existed in Strasbourg until 1867,[2] 'only in 1889 was international law introduced at French universities as a compulsory subject with an examination.'[3] The first chair of international law in Britain was established in 1848 at King's College where it was occupied by T. Twiss until 1854.[4] A few years later, in 1859, Oxford established a chair in international law, the Chichelle Chair of International Law and Diplomacy. Soon afterwards the Whewell Chair[5] was founded in Cambridge in 1868.[6] In Holland, a law passed in 1876 provided for the teaching of international law in state universities at a time when 'no chair of

1 Martti Koskenniemi, *The Gentle Civilizer of Nations: The Rise and Fall of International Law, 1870–1960* 12 (Cambridge: Cambridge University Press, 2001).

2 Koskenniemi notes that an international law professorship was established in Paris in 1829 although 'the courses given by its holders had been more about diplomatic history than diplomatic law.' Id., 31.

3 Id.

4 Michael Lobban, 'English Approaches to International law in the Nineteenth Century', in Matthew Craven/ Malgosia Fitzmaurice/ Maria Vogiatzi (Eds) *Time, History and International Law* (Leiden: Martinus Nijjhoff Publishers, 2007), 65–90, 70.

5 Anne Orford, 'Scientific Reason and the Discipline of International Law' 25 EJIL 2 (2014) 369—385, 374 quoting from Marshall, 'Whewell Scholarships: Letter 871 to Courtney Stanhope Kenny, 29 April 1907' in John K. Whitaker (ed.) *The Correspondence of Alfred Marshall, Economist: Volume 3, Towards the Close, 1903–1924* (Cambridge: Cambridge University Press 1996) 155–156.

6 Koskenniemi, *The Gentle Civilizer* 2001, 33.

 | DOI 10.1163/9789004343238_003

international law still existed'.[7] In Belgium, the University of Brussels introduced the study of the subject in 1884,[8] while, as S.C. Neff notes, 'in Germany there was not a single academic chair wholly devoted to international law until 1912'.[9] An early professorship in the subject was established in what was to become the Italian unified state, 'at the University of Turin, with P.S. Mancini as its first holder in 1851'. In 1873, A. Pierantoni devoted a long work to retracing the history of international law in Italy while he held the Chair in Constitutional Law and International Law at Modena.[10] Later, as professor of international law at Rome, Mancini published a history of international law in the nineteenth century in 1876.[11] In the United States, the first courses in international law were taught at Yale by T. D. Woolsey in 1846,[12] although further instruction on the subject was held, as Neff recalls, 'at the newly founded university of Wisconsin, in 1852'.[13] Elsewhere in North America, as Neff also notes, 'McGill University in Montreal followed suit in 1856 and, the year after, international law was also taught in Canada at Laval University'.[14] During the American Civil War, Harvard Law School (in 1863) and, at the initiative of F. Lieber, Columbia Law School (in 1865) offered courses in international law. In 1891, 'the first full professorship of international law in the country',[15] the Hamilton Fish Professorship of International Law and Diplomacy, was set up at Columbia University, where it was occupied by J. B. Moore. At Harvard, where F. Snow had offered the first case method based course in international law back in 1886, the Bemis Chair in International Law was endowed in 1897 for a 'practical co-operator in the work of advancing knowledge and good will among nations and governments'.[16]

---

7 Id.

8 Id.

9 Stephen C. Neff, *Justice among Nations. A History of International Law* (Cambridge: Harvard University Press 2014), 304 highlighting that 'international law was slow in obtaining a place in university curricula—a process that still awaits adequate study'.

10 Augusto Pierantoni, *Storia degli studi del diritto internazionale in Italia* (Modena: Carlo Vinzenzi 1869).

11 See Liliana Obregon Tarazona, *Writing International Legal History: An Overview, Monde(s) Histoire, espaces, relations* 7 (2015), 95–112, 108.

12 Liliana Obregon Tarazona, *Construyendo la region Americana: andres bello y el Derecho internacional* in Yolanda Gamarra (ed) La idea de América en el pensamiento ius internacionalista del siglo XXI (Zaragoza: Instituto Fernando el Catolico 2010), 65–86.

13 Neff, Justice among Nations 2014, 304.

14 Id., 304.

15 Id., 304.

16 Originally ccupied by Edward Henry Strobel, see 'A Changed World: The Bemis Chair' Harvard Law School accessible at https://www.youtube.com/watch?v=Z-UOh6zdZxg

Whereas Spain and the Spanish-speaking world have rarely appeared in modern historical accounts of the emergence of the first professorships in international law in the Western world, the term international law ('Derecho internacional') became widely employed for the first time on the occasion of the independence of the Latin American republics in the 1820s. University teaching under the term coined by J. Bentham in 1789[17] was first mandated in Colombia in 1826, then in Venezuela in 1827, and in Chile in 1832.[18] In a decree of 8 November 1825, F. de Paula Santander ordered Colombian chair holders to teach the principles of legislation, pace Bentham, and public international law following E. de Vattel. In 1827, the Universidad Central of Bogotá established the first chairs in international law. Against the convulsive background of post-independence Latin-America, V. Azuero Plata became the chair holder for Principles of Universal Legislation and Ignacio de Herrera Vergara (1769–1840), a 'prócer' (national hero) of Latin-American independence, became the first ever holder of a chair of 'Derecho internacional' (International Law) in the world.

The loss of most of its overseas empire and Spain's subsequent internationally diminished position spurred the rapid adoption of the new terminology in the former metropolis. The first Spanish chairs in Derecho internacional ('international law') were established in Madrid in the early 1840s at the end of the first of the three civil wars[19] that ravaged the northern parts of the Spanish peninsula in the nineteenth century. The immediate twin causes of the early awakening of the academic study of international law in Spain in the 1840s were the Spanish realignment with the Concert of Europe in the wake of the first Anglo-French entente, and the gradual renewal of Spanish diplomatic ties with the new Latin American republics. This began in the mid-1830s during the definitive transition to liberal constitutional government in Spain. In the 1840s, the establishment of both private and public chairs of international law in Spain, and as we shall later see, the inclusion of the subject in national education plans, the reorganization of the diplomatic foreign service, and the gradual widespread inclusion of the term in academic works penned by Spanish authors illustrate the relatively fashionable character of international law in Spanish intellectual milieu by the middle of the nineteenth century. These academic developments

17 See Jeremy Bentham, *An Introduction to the Principles of Morals and Legislati*on (Oxford: Clarendon Pres 1907 reprint of 1823 edition, first printed privately 1780). For a commentary, see Mark Weston Janis, 'Jeremy Bentham and the Fashioning of International Law', *American Journal of International Law* 78 (1984) 405–418.

18 See Rogelio Perez Perdomo, Los *abogados en América Latina: una introducción histórica* (Bogota: Universidad Externado de Colombia, 2004), 74–80.

19 The Carlist wars took place in 1833–1840, 1846–1849 and 1872–1876.

also reflected a gradual shift in focus in the study of the international realm in Spain, where a slow transition towards a more methodologically and systematized juridification of the external realm accompanied, as elsewhere in Europe, the domestic evolution of the constitutional liberal state in the nineteenth century. The establishment of the first chairs of international law in Spain in the 1840s was, however, the culmination of a long and convulsive historical process that had started some decades earlier.[20]

## Enlightened Despotism and the Study of the Law of Peoples in Spain

In 1770, the teaching of public law, natural law and the law of peoples was established in Spain with a Royal Decree by King Carlos III (1756–1788), a popular proponent of 'enlightened absolutism' who, through a series of reforms, including of university studies,[21] attempted to modernize the Spanish nation.[22] The effective inclusion of the study of public law, natural law and the law of peoples in a Spanish curriculum took place for the first time in the Royal School of Studies of San Isidro (est. 1770) in 1772. Its first chair holder was Joaquín Marín y Mendoza (1727–1782), who published the first treatise on the history of international law, the Historia del Derecho Natural y de Gentes[23] (History of Natural Law and the Law of Peoples) in Madrid in 1776.

Despite its notable precursors in the School of Salamanca, cultivation of the law of peoples in Spain had suffered from the inclusion in the 17th and 18th century of most of the works of H. Grotius and those of other modern authors of natural law and the law of peoples, such as Puffendorf, Wolff and Barbeyrac, in the list of works prohibited by the Inquisition.[24] De Iure Belli ac Pacis had been

20 A detailed summary of the contents of Chapter 1 can be found in the 'Introduction'.

21 See e.g. Ricardo Robledo, 'La difusion del pensamiento moderno en la universidad de Salamanca a fines del siglo XVIII', *Historia Constitucional* 6 (2005), 427–450.

22 Antonio Álvarez de Morales, 'La difusión del derecho natural y de gentes europeo en la universidad española de los siglos XVIII y XIX', in *Doctores y escolares. II Congreso internacional de Historia de las universidades Hispánicas* (Valencia: Editorial Universidad de Vàlencia 1995), 49–60.

23 Joaquín Marín y Mendoza, *Historia del Derecho Natural y de Gentes* (Madrid: Impr. Manuel Martín, 1776).

24 Julian Viejo y Harrassarry, 'El contexto de recepción de Grocio a mediados del siglo XVII en la Monarquía Hispana', *Espacio, Tiempo y Forma* IV (1998) 265–280. See also Pablo Gutierrez Vega, 'Vattel Larva Detracta. Reflexiones sobre la recepcion del ius publicum

included almost immediately after its publication in 1625 in the 1632 Novus librorum proibitorum & expurgatorum Index as 'item eiusdem de tur. Belli ac pacis donec expurgentur' (waiting to be expurgated), where it became listed as 'prohibited' in 1732. After the 'Siglo de Oro', or the 'Golden Spanish Age' in Spanish arts and literature, from the mid-late seventeenth century onwards, Spain lived through a period of cultural, artistic and intellectual decadence. In parallel to the practical abandonment of the ideal of the 'universitas christiana' that had informed the spiritual telos of the 'monarchia universalis' of Charles I and Philip II, this period saw the devaluation and forgetting of the doctrines of the Spanish legal theologians of the School of Salamanca of the sixteenth and early seventeenth century. These included, as systematized by L. Pereña, the so-called 'creative generation', from Francisco de Vitoria to Domingo de Soto (1494–1560), the generation of 'cultural expansion', including Pedro de Sotomayor (1500–1564), Fernando Vázquez de Menchaca (1512–1569), probably the first author to have used the expression 'Natural Law' in his De vero iure naturali (circa 1560),[25] and Bartolome Medina (1560–1584), and, finally, the 'stage of doctrinal systematization', from Domingo de Báñez to the Jesuit Francisco Suárez (1584–1617).[26] The long shadow of the Catholic culture of distrust towards the Reformation's new rationalist natural law tradition with its protestant roots contributed to further distancing Spanish authors from the study of natural law and the law of peoples.[27]

Compared to its 16$^{th}$ century and early 17$^{th}$ century predecessors, the Spanish doctrine of the law of peoples in the 18$^{th}$ century presented, according to A. Herrero Rubio, 'features of surprising poverty and lack of originality'.[28] However, the very few works—mostly general works although with some monographic exceptions devoted to diplomatic law[29] and maritime law[30]—that existed in Spanish in the early-mid 18$^{th}$ century, accomplished a 'modest but

europaeum en la universidad preliberal española' in Manuel Angel Bermejo Castrillo, (ed) *Manuales y textos de la ensenanza en la universidad liberal* (Madrid: Ed. Dykinson, 2004)537–578, 545–546.

25 Antonio-Enrique Perez-Luno, 'Natural Law Theory in Spain and Portugal', *The Age of Human Rights Journal* 1 (2013), 1–24, 2.

26 Pereña, 'La tesis de la paz dinámica' 1981, 65.

27 Herrero Rubio, *Le droit des gens dans l'Espagne du XVIII siècle* 1952, 313–327.

28 Id., 314.

29 Ignacio Joseph de Ortega y Cotes. *Questiones del derecho publico en interpretación de los tratados de paces* (Madrid: Impr. Antonio Marín, 1747).

30 Antonio Santos de Oreyta, *Tratado de derecho publico universal*, (Amsterdam: 1758). See Garcia Arias 'Adiciones sobre la historia de la doctrina hispánica' 1949, 481–483.

indispensable mission in the history of internationalist ideas'.[31] They helped to popularize the study[32] of the laws of peoples and contributed to the reception of ius publicum europaeum in Spanish universities.

This revived Spanish-European intellectual dialogue in international matters was, nonetheless, tempered by convenient expurgations of heretical doctrines from foreign works throughout the 18th century, as happened to the earlier work of Perez de Prados, 'Compendio de los tres derechos: natural, de gentes y evangélico' (Compendium of the Three Laws: Natural Law, Law of Peoples and Evangelical Law) published in Seville in 1726. Included among Spanish 18th-century academic production are, as examined by Herrero Rubio,[33] the twelve volumes of the Coleccion de Tratados de Paz ('Collection of Peace Treaties') by J. A. de Abreu y Bertodano (1717–1775) published from 1740 to 1752. This was the first work of its genre published in Spain since Leibniz's Codex Iuris gentium diplomaticum (1693), which was completed by his Mantissa Codicis iuris diplomatici of 1700. De Abreu justified the publication of his collection of treaties 'of peace, confederation, warranty, neutrality, commerce etc.' by stating that they were 'the sovereign laws of princes and states, the foundations of public faith and of the security of peoples, the bedrock of all the other political and civil laws and of what is properly called the public law or law of peoples.'[34]

Other remarkable works penned by Spanish authors[35] during the 18th century[36] include the 'Questiones del derecho publico en interpretación de los tratados de paces'[37] (Questions of Public Law in the Interpretation of Peace Treaties) by J. I. de Ortega y Cotes, published in Madrid in 1747. Although the main part of Ortega's book is dedicated to the 'study of questions of maritime law and more specifically to prize law'[38] (...), it also devotes several chapters to different aspects of peace treaties, to reprisals and to the effects of prescription. Two volumes of Apparatus juris publia hispanici were written by P. J. Perez Valiente (1713–1789) as part of an ambitious project: Theatro universali regni et regii patrimonii hispanici. This, however, remained at the project

31 Herrero Rubio, *'Le droit des gens dans l'Espagne du XVIII siècle'* 1952, 314.
32 Garcia Arias 'Adiciones sobre la Historia de la doctrina hispánica' 1949, 466.
33 Herrero Rubio, *Le droit des gens dans l'Espagne* 1952, 313–327.
34 Joseph Antonio de Abreu y Bertodano, *Coleccion de Tratados de Paz*, 12 vols. (Madrid: Antonio Marin, 1840–1852), 729.
35 See in detail, Herrero Rubio, *Le droit des gens dans l'Espagne* 1952, 329– 393.
36 Garcia Arias 'Adiciones sobre la historia de la doctrina hispánica' 1949, 465–494.
37 Ortega y Cotes. *Questiones del derecho publico*, 1747.
38 Id.

stage. These two volumes, nonetheless, had a particular influence on the later Spanish cultivation of the law of peoples because they included references to the by then abandoned classic Spanish authors as well as to works by foreign authors such as Gentili, Grotius, Puffendorf and Bynkershoek.[39] Also remarkable, De Iure Naturale et Gentium positions explicatae, written by J. I. Torres y Florez in 1767, remained, however, unpublished. This was devoted to an exposition of the Iuris Naturalis Disciplina,[40] a topic that J. Marín y Mendoza took up systematically in academic fashion for the first time in Spanish in his 'Historia del Derecho Natural y de Gentes' in 1776. Despite its brevity, Marín y Mendoza's 'Historia del Derecho Natural y de Gentes' is considered the first attempt to produce a doctrinal history of the law of peoples in the Spanish language.

Joaquín Marín y Mendoza was a disciple of Gregorio Mayans (1699–1781), who, together with Benito J. Feijoo (1776–1764), the author of the eight volumes of the celebrated Teatro Crítico Universal (1726 to 1739), were key figures of the elitist 'first Spanish enlightenment'. G. Mayans proposed a 'model of enlightenment based on the cultural legacy of Spanish Humanism'.[41] This included an important component of 'critical history' and aimed, as Rus notes, at 'the revitalization of the culture and education of Spain following the patterns of Humanism and incorporating those cultural and scientific foreign innovations that were not incompatible with the Catholic orthodoxy'.[42] Marín y Mendoza's own work fits squarely within this mid-late Eighteen century 'enlightened' Spanish counter-intellectual paradigm in its attempt to adapt foreign intellectual trends to the principles of the Spanish Catholic tradition and monarchic rule.

By the time Marín approached the transposition of this intellectual programme to his history of natural law and the law of peoples, the historiography of natural law was already a firmly established genre in cultivated European circles. This historiography of natural law had underwent a surge in the late seventeenth century in the wake, as Rus notes, of the 'new manner of understanding natural law proposed by the rationalist or modern school'.[43] The novelty of rationalist iusnaturalism prompted 'the need to write the previous history of the discipline in order to demonstrate the originality

39 See in detail, Herrero Rubio, *Le droit des gens dans l'Espagne* 1952, 335–339.

40 See Joaquín Marín y Mendoza, *Historia del derecho natural y de gentes*, 1776. Introducción, edición y notas de Salvador Rus Rufino (Valencia: Ed. Diputación de Valencia, Insótitución Alfonso el Magnanimo, 1999), 43.

41 Id., Rus Rufino, Introducción 1999, 19.

42 Id., 20.

43 Id., 50.

of the method, the ideas and the justification on which the new form of understanding, teaching and researching natural law rested'.[44] Starting with J.F. Buddeus's 'Historia Iuris Naturalis' in 1695 and F. Ludovicus's 'Delineatio Historiae Juris Divini Naturalis et Positivi Universalis' in 1701, and continuing with Chr. Thomasius's Paulo 'Plenior Historia Iuris Naturalis' of 1719, a series of works had already been cumulatively produced. All of them were founded on an earlier controversy, which turned into an intellectual war, over the moral philosophy of T. of Aquinas and the Seconda Scholastica in the seventeenth and eighteen centuries. They also had in common that they situated H. Grotius as the initial 'restorer of natural jurisprudence'[45] in order to better postulate the existence of a single ius-naturalist tradition founded on the Grotian method of secularized rational deduction.[46] It is this tradition of rational ius-naturalism, which presented Grotius as the 'means chosen by God to restore the correct use of reason, darkened and shadowed until then',[47] that Marín y Mendoza attempted to safely tame within the parameters of the Spanish Catholic tradition, under the attentive eye of the Spanish Inquisition, in his 'Historia del Derecho Natural y de Gentes'.

Marín y Mendoza's critical approach to the rational ius-naturalist tradition was consonant with the Royal Decree that created his own chair, which stated that it was to be occupied by 'a master who teaches natural law and the law of peoples, demonstrating above all the necessary union between religion, morals, and politics'.[48] Marín put his book at the service of the divulgation of the classical Aristotelian-Thomist tradition of natural law. Accordingly, the targets of his critique became the 'rationalism, the contempt for authority and tradition, the voluntarism and the individualist utilitarianism'[49] of the rationalist ius-naturalism enshrined in the doctrines of its most important representatives—Grotius, Pufendorf, Thomasius, Heineccius, Wolff. In doing so, Marín y Mendoza became an early contributor to the 'renaissance' of was later to become known as the Spanish school of Ius Gentium. The roots of the subsequent revivals of the School of Salamanca lie with a scholarly mid-eighteenth-century generation of 'enlightened' Catholic authors who began to revive the theories of the Spanish Seconda scholastica defining 'natural law within the trilogy of eternal law, natural law, and civil law, stressing the

44 Id., 51.
45 Id., 66.
46 Id., 45– 67, 67.
47 Id., 72.
48 Id., 154.
49 Id., 81.

pre-eminence of divine reason, affirming the original coincidence between natural law and eternal law and by keeping its association with moral philosophy.'[50]

The educational reform of Carlos III in 1770 largely contributed to a renewed interest in the law of peoples by Spanish authors. Evidence of this Spanish re-engagement with the law of peoples was the book by José de Olmeda y León (1740–1805) published in 1771, 'Elementos de derecho público de la paz y de la guerra, ilustrados con noticias históricas, leyes y doctrinas del derecho español'[51] (Elements of Public Law of Peace and War, illustrated with Historical Notices, Laws and Doctrines of Spanish Law). De Olmeda y León's work is considered the first systematic treatise on the law of peoples by a Spanish author. However, it borrows, so extensively from E. de Vattel's 'Le droit des gens' (1758) that charges of plagiarism have often been made against it.[52] Since its publication, Vattel's 'Le droit des gens' was much circulated in translations and re-editions across Europe and the United States,[53] but it was prohibited in Spain by the Inquisition in June 1779.[54] Although a partial translation of Le droit des gens was made by Ortiz de la Peña in 1774 in Salamanca, it had remained unpublished.[55] Vattel's work did not appear translated as a published work into Spanish, as we shall later see, until 1820. In this context, Olmeda y León justified his own scarcely veiled appropriation of Vattel's work in his own book by pointing both to the lacuna that existed in this domain in Spanish, and, shielding himself behind the 'absolutist' dogma, to the healthy need to

50 Id., 83.

51 Jose de Olmeda y León, *Elementos de derecho público de la paz y de la guerra, ilustrados con noticias históricas, leyes y doctrinas del derecho español* (Madrid: Impr. Viuda de Manuel Hernandez 1771). This was later republished in 1891 by the Ramón Dalmau de Olivart as *El primer tratado sistemático español de Derecho de gentes: Reimpreso literalmente sobre la edición de 1771 por el Marqués de Olivart* (Barcelona: 1891).

52 Gutierrez Vega, 'Vattel Larva Detracta' 2004, 547–555.

53 Emmanuellle Jouannet, *Emmer de Vattel et l'émergence doctrinale du droit international classique* (Paris: Pedone 1998). On the early influence of Vattel in the United States, see e.g. Vincent Chetail, 'Vattel and the American Dream: An Inquiry into the Reception of the Law of Nations', in Vincent Chetail / Pierre Marie Dupuy (eds) *The Roots of International Law. Liber Amicorum Peter Haggenmacher*, (Leiden: Martinus Nijhoff 2013) 251–300.

54 Elisabetta Fiocchi Malaspina, 'La circulación de Le droit de gens de Vattel en los Países hispánicos', Coloquio de Historia Canario-Americana XX (2012), 1074–1080 accesible at http://coloquioscanariasamerica.casadecolon.com/index.php/CHCA/article/view/9234/8686

55 Emer de Vattel, *Derecho de Gentes o principio de la Ley natural* [...] traducido del francés a castellano por B. D. Josef Ortiz (biblioteca de Salamanca) (1774).

filter 'the works of foreign specialists that often expose doctrines against the Catholic religion and the sovereign'.[56]

The 1770 reform also spurred a wave of adaptation of foreign scientific works. These included 'Elementa juris naturae et gentium' by J. Gottlieb Heineccius,[57] which was used by its translator, Marín y Mendoza, as a textbook in the Royal School of Studies of San Isidro in, once again, adequately expurgated form. Mendoza justified the expurgation of Heineccius's work as a means of saving students from the risk of being 'perverted by the delicious charm of the thoughts'[58] of the rationalist ius-naturalist authors included in it. The late 18th-century scholarly attempts to (re)create in Spain an autochthonous Spanish natural law free of protestant influences led to the study of natural law and the law of peoples acquiring an almost intellectual fashionable character in the 1770s and 1780s. While in Madrid, José Ferrer Bardaxi replaced Marín y Mendoza in the chair of Royal Studies of San Isidro in 1882, several universities, including those at Valencia, Valladolid and Granada created chairs in Natural Law and the Law of Peoples (or chairs in Public Law or Universal Public Law, which were sometimes used as synonyms).[59] This was not the case, paradoxically, at the oldest Spanish University—the University of Salamanca, founded in 1228—despite eminent voices from the so-called 'Escuela Iluminista Salmantina' (Salamanca Illuminist School)[60] in favour of the establishment of a chair to facilitate 'the truly scientific knowledge of civil laws'.[61] In teaching the subject, some Spanish universities, however, replaced Heineccius's book with the more orthodox work by G. B. Almici, 'Institutiones iuris naturae et gentium secundum catholica principia' (1768).[62] The academic fashion of the study of natural law and the law of peoples was captured in a satirical work published in 1781, under a pseudonym, by J. Cadalso (1741–1782), one of the central figures in Spanish literature in the 18th century. The title of the book 'Los eruditos a la violeta' has become an ironic derogatory epithet which is still used in the Spanish language to refer to those who 'pretend to know very much while studying very little'. [63]

56 Olmeda y León, Elementos de derecho público 1771.

57 Johann Gottlieb J. G Heineccio, Elementa Iuris Naturae et Gentium Castigationibus ex Catholicorum Doctrinae et Iuris Historia aucta ab J. Marín et Mendoza (Madrid: 1776)

58 Rus Rufino, Introduccion 1999, 43.

59 Gutierrez Vega, 'Vattel Larva Detracta' 2004, 559–562.

60 Perez-Luno, 'Natural Law Theory in Spain' 2013, 4.

61 Robledo, 'La difusion del pensamiento moderno' 2005, 438.

62 Alvarez de Morales, 'La ensenanza del derecho natural' 2004, 368–369.

63 Jose Cadalso (bajo seudónimo de Joseph Vazquez) *Los eruditos a la violeta o curso completo de todas las ciencias dividido en siete lecciones para los siete dias de la semana con el suplemento de este compuesto por don Joseph Vazquez, quien lo publica en obsequio de los*

In 1794, however, mistrust of foreign intellectual trends led to a decree by Carlos IV that suppressed in all the universities the chairs of public law, natural law and the law of peoples authorized by Carlos III in 1770.[64] This legislative measure was justified by fear of revolutionary contagion from the association of the law of peoples with the 'pernicious effects' of modern natural law doctrines in the Spanish national intellectual mindset after the 1789 French Revolution:

> 'Some wise and jealous men, ecclesiastic and secular, have been and are of the opinion that the chairs of natural law and of peoples established in some universities, in the Estudios Reales de San Isidro and in the Seminar of the Noblemen are highly dangerous, and more so in the present circumstances. Even if their aims were judged useful at the time when they were created, experience has shown that they bring with them the almost unavoidable risk that youth, imbued with principles that are contrary to our constitutions, could draw pernicious consequences which can spread and produce an upheaval in the way of thinking of the nation'.[65]

The study of the law of peoples in late eighteenth century Spain, and throughout the first third of the nineteenth century shared the fate of the study of natural law. The perceived ideological threat that the continuation of its study at a time of a magnified, as Neff notes, 'association between natural law and radical reformism'[66] across Europe, was thought to be too great for the pillars of the Spanish absolutist monarchy and Catholic tradition. A certain Spanish bishop went even to celebrate the prohibition of natural law and the law of peoples with enthusiastic bigotry:

'The chairs of pestilence have been abolished! The studies where the young and the old alike were corrupted and made abominable!'[67] The revolutionary events that were taking place beyond the Pyrenees for some required, in fact,

---

*que pretenden saber mucho, estudiando poco* (Sevilla: 1781). See a commentary by Adolfo Miaja de la Muela, 'Una satira española contra los iusinternacionalistas del siglo XVIII: la lección cuarta de 'los eruditos a la violeta'', in *Colección de estudios en homenaje al profesor Camilo Barcia Trelles* (Santiago de Compostela: Ed. Universidad Compostelana 1945), 101–131.

64 Jose Antonio Tomas Ortíz de la Torre, 'L'établissement de l'enseignement officiel en Espagne du droit international' *Annuaire de l'association des auditeurs et anciens auditeurs de l'Académie de droit international* de La Haye 40 (1970), 122–132, 128.

65 Archivo Histórico Nacional, Consejos, 1794, 5420–5443.

66 Neff, Justice among Nations 2014, 206.

67 Robledo, 'La difusion del pensamiento moderno' 2005, 438.

no less than 'an assault on both private and public libraries in order to throw the Grotius, the Puffendors, the Philangieres and the many more men of little good judgement and prudence away from them.'[68]

Despite its prohibition, the study of natural law and the law of peoples survived, as an emblem of the reformist rational enlightenment in some Spanish universities,[69] camouflaged as the teaching of other subjects such as moral philosophy.[70] Yet neither the study of natural law or of the law of peoples benefitted, except during short-lived revolutionary junctures, from the repeated political pronouncements and cyclical political turmoil that, amidst a dynastic crisis, the Spanish War of Independence against Napoleonic rule, and the Wars of Independence of the Latin-American republics, would ravage Spain and its Empire for the next four decades.

## The Law of Peoples in Spain From the 1812 Constitution of Cadiz to the Aftermath of the Independence of the Latin-American Republics

Iconically immortalized by Francisco de Goya in 1808, the public Spanish revolt against Napoleonic rule stirred up political turmoil in the Latin American colonies. The deposition of the Spanish monarch by Napoleon's brother, Joseph I (1808–1813), initially triggered a 'loyalist' reaction in the American territories. However, the language of sovereign rights[71] employed in the 1776 US Declaration of Independence, which had elicited, as D. Armitage notes, 'a rapidly evolving argument in this early positivist period over the theory of recognition of states',[72] soon became apparent in the discourses of the Latin American rebel leaders. It was during the impasse between these two

68 Orates in the original, quoted in Jose Carlos Fernández Rozas/Paz Andrés Sáenz de Santa María, 'La aportación de la Facultad de Derecho de la Universidad de Oviedo al progreso del Derecho internacional', in Santos Coronas González (ed) *Historia de la Facultad de Derecho* (1608–2008) (Oviedo: Servicio de Publicaciones de la Universidad de Oviedo 2010) 495–570, 42.

69 For a detailed account, see Manuel Martínez Neira, '¿Una supresión ficticia? Notas sobre la enseñanza del Derecho en el reinado de Carlos IV', *Anuario de Historia del Derecho español* 68 (1998), 532–544.

70 Robledo, 'La difusion del pensamiento moderno' 2005, 438.

71 David Armitage, *Foundations of Modern International Thought*, (Cambridge: Cambridge University Press 2013), 225.

72 Id., 209.

phases—loyalism against a foreign invasion of the metropolis and colonial independentism—that the first Spanish Constitution was passed in 1812.

The political aims of 'La Pepa', as the Spanish Constitution became popularly known, were that of 'halting the independence of the American territories while serving to unite the Spanish people against Napoleon'.[73] The drafting of this first constitutional offspring of 'early Spanish liberalism'[74] provided the American representatives with their first occasion to join in a discussion about the future of the 300-year-old political Spanish imperial entity. Forty-five American representatives, ranging from loyalist defenders of Spanish absolutist monarchic rule to progressive liberals, joined the liberal nationalist anti-Napoleonic resistance in Cádiz in the early 1810s. This heterodox group did not argue in favour of the independence of the American colonies, but instead—as Breña notes—in favour of 'equality of the overseas provinces with respect to Spain' and 'the recognition of the differential specificity of the American territories' vis-à-vis the metropolis.[75]

Although the Cádiz Constitution lacked a formal bill of rights, maintained a Catholic confessional state in Spain, did not abolish slavery and did not enshrine the claims of the American representatives, it remained comparatively advanced for its age both in constitutional and international legal terms. The Spanish Constitution of 1812 enshrined the principles of constitutional monarchy and the separation of powers and incorporated implicit references to 'the principle of sovereignty and the notion of nation'.[76] Furthermore, it devoted several articles to the 'elements of the state as subjects of international law', in particular, to the constituent elements of 'territory' and 'population'.[77] It also included—as C. Fernandez Liesa noted—the 'first constitutional norms' that 'implied a limitation of the royal power in the name of a limited democratization of external power'.[78] However, it only remained in vigour for a brief

73 Carlos Fernandez Liesa, 'La Constitución de Cádiz de 1812 en perspectiva internacional', in M. Aznar Gómez/J. Cardona Llorens/J. Pueyo Losa/J.L. Rodríguez-Villasante/J.M. Sobrino Heredia/M. Pérez González (eds) *Estudios de Derecho internacional y de derecho europeo en Homenaje al Profesor Manuel Pérez González*, (Barcelona: Tirant Lo Blanc 2012), 585–596, 587.

74 See e.g. Maria Luisa Sanchez-Mejia, 'Tradición histórica e innovación política en el primer liberalismo español' *Revista de Estudios Politicos* 97 (1997), 277–289.

75 Roberto Breña, 'Un momento clave en la historia política moderna de la América hispana, Cadiz, 1812', in Josefina Zoraida Vázquez (ed), *El nacimiento de las naciones iberoamericanas—síntesis histórica* (Madrid: Ed. *Fundación Mapfre Tavera*, Academia Mexicana de la Historia 2002), 63–98, 58.

76 Fernandez Liesa, 'La Constitución de Cádiz de 1812' 2012, 573.

77 Id., 574.

78 Id., 576–578.

period—from 19 March 1812 to 4 May 1814. Once the French troops had been expelled from Spain, its demise was soon followed by the restored absolutist rule of King Fernando VII.

The new king, known as el Deseado ('the Desired') annulled the constitution and set Spanish forces to the task of reconquering the American colonies. During the following 'absolutist six-year period', Spain also re-established its foreign relations in the Concert of Europe. The principle of monarchic legitimacy enshrined at the Congress of Vienna fostered a new wave of concerted interventionism against liberal revolutionary threats within European states. Fernando VII tried to export the principles of the European 'restoration' back to Latin America. Fernando VII's aggressive policies in the American territories[79] led to a series of royalist counter-revolutionary successes. Meanwhile, although present at the Conference of Vienna, Spain would only sign the Treaty of Vienna Act, along with the Holy Alliance, in 1817.[80] Spain, which had a long tradition of *traite negrière*,[81] also signed the declaration relating to the Universal Abolition of the Slave Trade of 18 February 1815.

In this declaration, 'the Plenipotentiaries' proclaimed 'in the name of their Sovereignties, their wish of putting an end to a scourge, which has so long desolated Africa, degraded Europe, and afflicted humanity'.[82] However, the declaration was deprived of binding character and was accompanied by a caveat according to which 'the said Plenipotentiaries at the same time acknowledge that this general Declaration cannot prejudge the period that each participant Power may consider advisable for the definitive Abolition of the Slave Trade'.[83] Two years after the Battle of Waterloo, on 23 September 1817, the Anglo-Spanish anti-slave Treaty was signed. This was one of the three anti-slave trade treaties that Britain signed in 1817; the other two were signed with Portugal

79 These, as Esquirol notes, triggered 'the first appreciable application of the international legal concept of belligerency' Jorge L Esquirol, 'Latin America', in Bardo Fassbender / Anne Peters (eds) *Oxford Handbook of the History of International Law* (Oxford: Oxford University Press 2012), 553–577, 554.

80 The Spanish participation at Vienna left some controversial frontier delimitation issues with Portugal, such as the 'question of Olivenza' that occupied Spanish diplomats and Spanish international lawyers for some time to come. See Carlos Fernandez Liesa, 'La cuestion de Olivenza a la luz del Derecho Internacional Público', in *Encontros, Revista luso-española de investigadores en Ciencias Humanas y Sociales* 4 (2004), 230–281.

81 For an early reference, see Georges Scelle's own doctoral thesis, Georges Scelle, *La traite negrière aux Indes de Castille* (Paris: L. Larose & L. Tenin 1906).

82 Quoted in Jenny Martinez, *The Slave Trade and the Origins of International Human Rights Law* (Oxford: Oxford University Press 2012), 33.

83 Martinez, *The Slave Trade* 2012, 33.

and the Netherlands. Although the scope of each treaty was adapted to the particular situation of the signatories, the three treaties established what J. Martinez terms the 'world's first international courts directed at the protection of human rights'.[84] These courts, according to Martinez, 'contained robust enforcement mechanisms' (…) such as a provision for 'the mutual right of search and seizure of suspected slave vessels and the vessels' trial and condemnation before the courts of mixed commissions'.[85] However, despite its participation in international legal regimes and the passing of some domestic legislative initiatives and international treaties regarding the slave trade in 1835[86] and 1845,[87] Spain did not act much upon its international obligations in this area. The abolitionist cause had to wait in 'the Western country that took longer to suppress the slave trade and slavery',[88] to the third part of the nineteenth century for, as we shall later see, its major champion, the international law scholar, and member of the Institución de Libre Enseñanza, Rafael María de Labra.

After the suppressive decree by Carlos IV in the aftermath of the French Revolution, the study of natural law and the law of peoples was, as we have seen, formally discontinued in Spain. It was only briefly restored by a Decree of 2 September 1820 at the start of the liberal triennium (1820–1823). This had been triggered by a revolt by officers, led by R. de Riego, who rejected an order to travel to America to combat the Latin American insurrectional leaders. Instead, they proclaimed the reinstatement of the 1812 Constitution. In the Royal Studies of San Isidro, M. Lucas Garrido, who was assigned to the chair in natural law and the law of peoples, prepared a new edition of Heineccius as a textbook.[89] Other universities followed suit. At the University of Seville, the first chair in natural law and the law of peoples was occupied by D. Fernandez Muñoz.[90] The study of natural law and the law of peoples, along with that of principles of universal jurisdiction, was also included in the programme

---

84 Id., 36.

85 Id., 36.

86 *Tratado entre España y la Gran Bretaña para la abolición de la trata de esclavos*, signed in Madrid on 28 June 1835.

87 Ley de 2 Marzo de 1845, sobre imposición de penas a los que se dediquen a la trata. For a complete list of domestic legislation, see Roberto Mesa Garrido 'Notas para la historia del pensamiento internacionalista español: algunos problemas coloniales del siglo XIX', *Revista Española de Derecho Internacional* XVIII (1965) 365, 385–387.

88 Carlos Fernandez Liesa, *El derecho internacional de los derechos humanos en perspectiva histórica*, (Madrid, *Civitas Aranzadi*, Thompson Reuters 2013), 467.

89 Alvarez de Morales, 'La ensenanza del derecho natural' 2004, 375–376.

90 Gutierrez Vega, 'Vattel Larva Detracta' 2004, 563.

of studies at the short-lived Central University of Madrid, created in 1822 as an assembly of the various university studies—the University of Alcala, the Royal Studies of San Isidro and others—that existed in Madrid at the time. The liberal triennium also saw a new wave of translations of foreign works. These included the first Spanish translation of E. de Vattel's Le droit des gens in 1820,[91] and the first Spanish translation of Rayneval's Institutions du droit de la nature et des gens in 1820.[92] Principles of Morals and Legislation (1789) the book in which J. Bentham, who at the time was writing Three Tracts Relative to Spanish and Portuguese Affairs (1821), and Letters on the Proposed Penal Code (1822), coined the term 'international law' was also translated (following the French translation of the book prepared by E. Dumont in 1802) and commented on in Spanish by R. Salas in 1821.[93]

As Metternich, who quickly felt the risk of a contagion effect that the Spanish uprising might have in the Europe of the early Restoration,[94] had predicted, the revolutionary influence of the Spanish liberal uprising spread to Italy and Portugal. The Constitution of Cádiz, one of the most democratically advanced in the first third of the nineteenth century in Europe, was adopted in the Kingdom of the Two Sicilies, in Piedmont-Cerdeña and in Portugal. However, the newly restored system of balance of power, on the basis of which supporters of the Restoration in Vienna argued in favour of a 'right to a political balance of power'[95] to justify armed interventions in the internal affairs of other states, made the Spanish liberal revolution short-lived. The Spanish 'liberal triennium' came to an abrupt end with the foreign invasion of the so-called 'One Hundred Thousand Sons of Saint Louis' mandated by the Quadruple Alliance at the Congress of Verona (1922). This military intervention also halted the study of natural law and the law of peoples once again in Spain.

---

91 Emeric de Vattel, El Derecho de gentes, o principios de la Ley Natural aplicados a la conducta y a los negocios de las naciones y de los soberanos (Traducción de M. Pascual Fernandez) (Madrid: Imprenta de I. Sancha, 1820). Fiocchi Malaspina, 'La circulación de le droit de gens de Vattel' 2012.

92 Mathias-Joseph Gérard de Rayneval, *Instituciones de derecho natural y de gentes* (Traduccion de M. Antonio López) (Madrid: D. L B. Masson é hijo, 1821).

93 Jeremy Bentham, *Tratados de legislación civil y penal* (Traducción de Ramón Salas) (Madrid: Imprenta de Fermín Villalpando, 1822).

94 See e.g. Ramon Arnabat i Mata El impacto europeo y americano de la proclamación de la Constitución de Cádiz en 1820, *Revista de historia moderna y contemporánea* 24 (2012), 47–64.

95 See Leonard von Dresch, *Naturrecht*, (Tübingen: 1822) 112 quoted in Milos Vec, 'De-Juridifying 'Balance of Power'—A Principle in 19th Century International Legal Doctrine' in Nico Krisch et al. (eds) ESIL Conference Paper Series Conference Vol. 1 Paper 5 (2011), 1, 8.

The study of natural law and the law of peoples, now more clearly identified as an emblem of political liberalism than ever before, was not included in the new programme of university studies approved in 1824 at the onset of what Spanish liberal historiography has termed the 'ominous decade' (1823–1833) of the 'restoration' of the absolutist rule of Fernando VII. This immediately led to a renewal of attempts to recover the colonies under the auspices of the Holy Alliance. However, the internal divisions in the metropolis brought about by the liberal triennium had already bitterly divided the troops fighting in America between 'royalists' and 'constitutionalists', thus helping to revive the struggling independence movement. In 1923, this benefitted, furthermore, from the declaration of an anti-interventionist framework for European powers in the American territory through what was to be known as the 'Monroe doctrine'. The Monroe doctrine, an initiative by Great Britain, which was greatly interested in the demise of the Spanish Empire because of its own mercantilist imperialist ambitions, was initially intended to be a bilateral declaration by Great Britain and the United States. However, the United States, which shortly before had obtained Florida under the Onís-Adams Treaty with Spain of 1819 in exchange for recognizing what turned out to be a fleeting Spanish sovereignty over Texas, decided to make a unilateral declaration. On the occasion of President J. Monroe's 1823 Annual Message to Congress, it was asserted that 'as a principle in which the rights and interests of the United States are involved, that the American continents, by the free and independent condition which they have assumed and maintain, are henceforth not to be considered as subjects for future colonization by any European powers'.[96] The swansong of the Spanish Empire in American continental territories was confirmed by the battle of Ayacucho in 1824. The definitive independence of the new Latin American Republics was reaffirmed at the first of the American conferences, the Congress of Panama in 1826 where the first attempt at a regional confederation of the New Republics was made, under the auspices of S. Bolivar, with the Treaty of Perpetual Union, League, and Confederation.

Meanwhile in the Spanish Peninsula, approximately three hundred and thirty years after the first voyage of discovery by C. Columbus, long-forgotten the exploits of the conquistadores, the glories of Potosi and the dreams of El Dorado, international legal studies gradually came back to the fore amidst the last remnants of the Spanish Empire, now limited to Cuba, Puerto Rico and the Philippines. An important signpost for this renewed academic interest in

96 Message from President James Monroe at the commencement of the first session of the 18th Congress (The Monroe Doctrine), 12/2/1823, National Archives and Records Administration (1823)

international law during the early part of Maria Cristina's Regency (1833–1840) was the gradual alignment of Spain with the new international framework of the European concert. The signing of the Treaty of the Quadruple Alliance on April 22, 1834, which put Spain within the orbit of British-French entente, was determined by the non-recognition of the future Spanish Queen Isabel II by Prussia, Austria and the Holy See until 1848, and until 1856 in the case of Russia. This international Spanish realignment coincided with a parallel move to moderate liberal rule, which resulted from a dynastic struggle spurred by the pretentions to the Spanish crown of the ultra-conservative Carlos, brother of the late Fernando VII. The first of the Carlist wars (1833–1840), considered 'the largest counter-revolutionary movement in nineteenth century Europe',[97] induced Regent Maria Cristina, mother of the infant future Queen Isabel II, to adopt a centralizing Pretorian-style of liberalism. This strategic turn to liberalism was aimed at preventing possible foreign legitimist interventions by the Holy Alliance in support of the dynastic rights of Carlos, and of its profoundly religious and reactionary upholders of medieval territorial privileges ('fueros') in the Basque region.

This new moderate liberal climate, together with the economic interests of Spanish nationals in the former colonies, the need to restore trans-Atlantic naval trade and to protect the remaining Spanish territories in the Caribbean,[98] led also to the gradual recognition of the independence of the former American colonies. A law of 4 December 1836 marked the beginning of the normalization of diplomatic and commercial relationships between Spain and the new Republics.[99] The ratification of a treaty of peace, friendship, and commerce with Mexico on 14 November 1837 initiated the official Spanish practice of developing diplomatic ties with the new Republics which would extend throughout the nineteenth century.[100]

---

97 Christopher A. Bayly, *The Birth of the Modern World* (1790–1914) (Oxford: Blackwell, 2004), 141.

98 Juan B. Vilar, 'Aproximación a las relaciones internacionales de España (1834–1874)' *Historia Contemporánea* 34 (2007) 7–42.

99 See Juan Carlos Pereira Castañares, 'España y Latino-América, Un siglo de relaciones (1836–1936)' Mélanges de la Casa de Velazquez 97 (1992), 30.

100 Ecuador (1840), Chile (1844), Venezuela (1845), Bolivia (1847), Costa Rica and Nicaragua (1850), R. Dominicana (1855), Guatemala and R. Argentina (1863), Perú and El Salvador (1865), Paraguay and Uruguay (1870) Colombia (1881), Honduras (1894) and Panama (post-1900). See e.g. Jorge Castel, *El restablecimiento de relaciones entre España y las Repúblicas hispanoamericanas (1836–1894)*, separata de *Cuadernos de Historia de las Relaciones Internacionales y de Política Exterior* (1955).

Following the previous pattern of oscillation in Spain during the first third of the nineteenth century between liberal and absolutist regimes and subsequent restoration and abolition of international legal studies, a university reform decree officially restored the study of natural law and the law of peoples in Spain in 1837. This coincided with the liberal revolution of 1835–1837 and the re-proclamation in 1836 of the 1812 Constitution of Cádiz. However, the 1812 Constitution was soon replaced by a new Constitution in 1837, an emblem of the liberal ideology of the 'men of order' of the moderate party who were defenders of the shared sovereignty of the king and the nation, the Catholic religion and a strong central executive government.[101] In competitive political rotation with the 'progressive' wing of liberalism—the 'men of freedom'—the two wings of Spanish liberalism would gradually dismantle the pillars of the ancien regime in Spain between 1834 and 1868.[102] The subsequent troubled rise of Spanish liberalism brought in its wake, once again, a revival of international legal studies in Spain.

## The First Professorships in International Law in Spain

After the 1837 university reform decree, which had officially restored the study of natural law and the law of peoples, a 'provisional plan' established the subjects of 'Natural law and the Law of peoples', together with that of 'Principles of Universal Jurisdiction' in the first year of law studies in the Spanish curriculum. This period coincided, once again, with a series of translations of foreign works on natural law and the law of peoples and diplomatic relations. These included the first translation into Spanish, for use as a textbook, of Heinecius's work, by J. A. Ojea on the basis of the Latin edition by Garrido, under the title Elementos de Derecho natural y de gentes[103] in 1837. Another author, R. Campuzano produced a translation of G.F. von Martens' 'Tratado de diplomática, o estado de relaciones de las potencias de Europa entre sí, y con los demás pueblos

101 See e.g. Luis Garrido Muro, 'Esta estúpida nación' La nación moderada'. in Antonio Morales Moya/Juan Pablo Fusi/Andres de Blas (eds) *Historia de la nación y del nacionalismo español* (Madrid, Galaxia Gutenberg 2013) 277–292.

102 Raymond Carr, 'Liberalism and Reaction 1833–1931' in Raymond Carr (ed) *Spain: A History* (Oxford, Oxford University Press 2000), 205–242.

103 Johann Gottlieb Heineccio, *Elementos de derecho natural y de gentes* (1837) Corregido y reformado por el profesor Don Mariano Lucas Garrido, a los que se añadió los de filosofía moral del mismo autor y traducción al castellano por el bachiller en leyes D.J. A. Ojea, 2 tomos, (Madrid, imprenta de Fuentenebro 1837).

del globo' in 1835 and wrote a prologue to it.[104] Other translations included one by J. de Aces y Perez of F. B. De Felice's 'Lecciones de Derecho natural y de gentes', published in 1841.[105] Several works on consular practice and diplomatic guidance for the use of Spanish diplomats were also printed, such as 'Manual para los consules de España en paises extranjeros' (Manual for Spanish Consuls in Foreign Countries) in 1835 and the 'Tratado de jurisprudencia diplomatico-consular' (Treaty of Diplomatic-Consular Jurisprudence) by A. de Letamendi in 1843.[106]

However, the first work published in Spanish bearing the new title of Derecho internacional (International Law) was not to be published in Spain until the period of the progressive liberal military regency of General Espartero (1841–1843), the so-called 'Duke of Victory' of the first Carlist War (1833–1840). The early 1840s also saw the emergence of the first chairs in 'international law' (so termed) now definitively separated from the study of 'natural law' which disappeared from the programme of studies of Spanish law faculties. During the 1840s, a key driving force of the academic establishment of the term Derecho Internacional in Spanish came from the infant Latin American Republics.

The sovereign independence of the American territories in the 1810s and 1820s signalled the outset of a new stage in the history of international law.[107] For Andrés Bello (1781–1865), a prolific and influential scholar in the field in the first half of the nineteenth century in Latin America, 'the appropriation and production of law with a regional perspective were fundamental elements to the project of constructing a distinct and autonomous region.'[108] However, this appropriation, which was believed to help safeguard the incipient nation-building processes in the new republics, required the new Latin-American states to first be admitted into the 'family of nations'. Such recognition, which had been fought

104 Jorge Federico Martens, *Tratado de diplomática, o estado de relaciones de las potencias de Europa entre sí, y con los demás pueblos del globo* (prologo y traducción de Joaquín Rodrigo Campuzano) (Madrid: Imprenta Real 1835).

105 Fortunato Bartolomeo De Felice, *Lecciones de Derecho natural y de gentes* (Madrid: Impr. Nueva Bernardo Marín, 1841).

106 See Garcia Arias 'Adiciones sobre la historia de la doctrina hispánica' 1949, 510.

107 See e.g. Liliana Obregón Tarazona, 'The Colluding Worlds of the Lawyer, the Scholar and the Policymaker: A View of International Law from Latin America', *Wisconsin International* Law Journal 23 (2005) 145–xxx. See also Arnulf Becker Lorca, 'International Law in Latin America or Latin American International Law? Rise, Fall, and Retrieval of a Tradition of Legal Thinking and Political Imagination', *Harvard International Law* Journal 47 (2006) 283—305.

108 Obregón Tarazona, 'The Colluding Worlds' 2005, 148.

for on legal-strategic grounds by the newly independent republics since their creation, involved challenging the enhanced 'principle of legitimacy' enshrined in the Congress of Vienna. As it had happened in the case of their North American predecessors, the struggle for recognition of the newly independent countries was inspired by the natural rights tradition. This inspiration fostered a reinterpretation favourable, according to Becker, to 'a change in the international rules towards a conception of sovereignty based on a people's rights to self-determination'.[109]

The first chairs in international law originated in Latin-America where Bentham's works played a dominant role in the intellectual formation of Latin America's liberal political ideology. In this context, the first book on international law published in the American continent appeared in 1832. Written by Andres Bello (1781–1865), 'Principios de Derecho de Gentes'[110] defined the law of peoples, or international law, as 'the collection of laws and general rules of conduct that nations must observe among themselves for their safety and common wellbeing.'[111] Bello was convinced of the service that international law could provide to the cause of emancipation and national identity in America. In the prologue to his 'Principios de Derecho de Gentes', he expressly indicated his hope that his book could be of 'use to the youth of the new American states in the cultivation of a science that, if it could not previously be studied with impunity, is now of the highest importance for the defence and vindication of our national laws'.[112] In Bello's opinion, the foreign policy of the new nations should strategically use the arguments of international law because their survival could only be guaranteed by its legitimizing language.[113] Throughout its three editions in 1832, 1844, and 1864, Bello's work was impregnated with methodological eclecticism between natural law and positive law, although with a marked preference for the latter. The augmented second edition adopted in its title the modern terminology of 'Principios de Derecho Internacional.'[114]

Like Bello, other Latin-American authors of the nineteenth century, such as Carlos Calvo, Carlos Ferreira, Rafael Fernando Seijas, and José H. Ramírez,[115]

109 Arnulf Becker Lorca, *Mestizo International Law. A Global Intellectual History 1842–1933* (Cambridge: Cambridge University Press, 2015), 104.

110 Andrés Bello, *Principios de derecho de gentes* (Santiago de Chile: Impr. de la Opinión, 1832).

111 Id., 6.

112 Quoted in Obregón Tarazona, 'Construyendo la región americana' 2010.

113 Id.

114 Andrés Bello, *Principios de* derecho internacional (Madrid: Viuda de Calleja e hijos, 1844).

115 Horace B. Jacobini, *A Study of the Philosophy of International Law as Seen in Works of Latin American Writers* (The Hague: Martinus Nijhoff, 1954), 39–50.

gradually aligned themselves, despite never completely losing the naturalist elements in their works, with the nineteenth-century rise of the positivist approach to the laws and general rules of conduct that nations must observe among themselves. Other Latin-American authors, albeit fitting into the dominant eclectic frame of the times in Latin America, remained closer to naturalism. Among these authors were, according to Jacobini, G. Pérez Gomar, J. Silva Santisteban,[116] and—of direct interest to our chronicle—José María de Pando (1787–1840). Born in Lima in 1787 from an aristocratic Spanish family, de Pando, who became the Spanish ambassador to Rome in 1812 and to the Netherlands in 1815, was the Spanish Secretary of State in 1823 during the liberal triennium. De Pando later became, at several intervals between 1826–1834, Minister of Foreign Affairs of Peru, where he wrote his *Epístola to Prospero*, dedicated to Simón Bolívar, before returning to Madrid as Honorary Consul in the Spanish state in 1835. De Pando's 'Elementos del Derecho Internacional',[117] which opened to subscriptions in 1838, and was published posthumously in 1843, was the first book to bear in its title the term Derecho Internacional in the Spanish language. The release of his book was almost immediately followed by accusations of plagiarism[118] from A. Bello, who treated it as little more than a new edition of his own 'Principios' and, subsequently, initiated a long dispute over the matter.[119] Despite this quarrelsome episode, both authors' works contributed to the rise of the official academic status of the term 'international law' in the Spanish language.

In 1842, a great structural curricular transformation affecting international law took place in Spain.[120] The study of 'natural law and the law of peoples' began to be taught in the last course of juridical studies and was required to obtain the degree of Doctor of Laws. This meant that 'natural law and the law of peoples' moved from its position as a first-year law subject, where their study had served to lay the foundations of legal principles for university students, to the tenth course, where it was to be taught along with other new subjects such as 'General Principles of Legislation' and 'Universal Comparative Legislation

116 Id., 58–67.

117 3382 *Gaceta de Madrid*, Dec. 18, 1843, at 4.

118 Andrés Bello, *El Araucano*, Aug. 29, 1845.

119 Miguel Luis Amunátegui, Vida de don Andrés Bello (Santiago de Chile: Imprenta de P.G. Ramirez, 1882).

120 In 1842, Spain was ruled by the Regent General Espartero, who sent the Queen Regent and the Burkean-like conservatives of the moderate party into exile in one of the frequent military liberal-political 'pronunciamientos' that were to mark out the subsequent decades of Spanish politics.

and Codification'. The study of natural law and the law of peoples, now situated far above the compulsory law curriculum required to practice the legal profession in Spain, was replaced in the first year of law studies by a new subject called 'Prolegomena of Law'. The 1842 Ministerial Order that established the guidelines for the various subjects in the new curriculum also signalled a more practical orientation of the teaching materials dealing with the law of peoples by stressing that the 'chair holder will occupy himself with the law of peoples as a practical part of its application, providing a notice of the state of our international relations'.[121]

Only three years after this curriculum reform, and only two years after the publication of de Pando's book, the term international law entered the General Plan of Studies of 17 September 1845. This reformist plan, better known as the 'Pidal Plan', was passed in the early stages of the reign of Queen Isabel II, under the moderate 1845 Spanish Constitution, under which only 1% of the male population had the right to vote. The Pidal plan was aligned with the political programme of the moderate party and represented a leap forward in the process of centralization of Spanish university education. Following in the footsteps of the reforms of 1842, it made the study of 'international law' for the first time academically independent in Spain by separating its teaching from natural law. It also contributed to the independent study of international law by making it one of the subjects that were required to obtain the degree of Doctor in Laws as well as a compulsory year-long subject of study to obtain the degree of Doctor in Jurisprudence in the last year of law studies. By contrast, the long-standing companion of the law of peoples in the Spanish curriculum, the study of natural law, disappeared from the official programme of legal studies in Spanish faculties. It did not return to it, albeit now completed revamped as an introduction to legal studies, until the third part of the century.

The Pidal plan, which, as A.M. Alonso notes, 'served as a point of modernization for the teaching of law in Spain, and specifically for studies to obtain a doctoral degree, making the new doctoral thesis more attuned with the requirements of original research',[122] also established the first official chair in international law in Spain in 1845. This was initially assigned to a professor of philosophy at the University of Valladolid, L. Arrazola (1795–1873). However, Arrazola, a former Minister of Justice (1838 to 1840), who was, later, to briefly

121 Quoted by Alvarez de Morales, 'La enseñanza del derecho natural' 2004, 379

122 Aurora Miguel Alonso / Alberto Raya Rienda, *La colección de tesis doctorales de derecho de la universidad central, 1869–1883*, Cuadernos del Instituto Antonio de Nebrija 13 (2010), 55, 56.

serve as President of the Spanish Supreme Court (1851–1853), and as President of the Spanish Council of Ministers (Prime Minister) of Spain in 1864, left the first official chair of international law for the political world early on.[123] Following the provision of chairs mandated by the Pidal plan, which included 60 in Jurisprudence, 71 in Medicine, 59 in Philosophy, 20 in Theology, and 12 in Pharmacy,[124] P. Sabau y Larroya (1807–1879) replaced Arrazola as 'chair holder in international law' in Madrid one year later. Sabau, who left certain syllabi of his teaching in international law during these years was appointed chaired professor for doctoral studies in the discipline of 'Philosophy of Law: International Law' in 1852. The insertion of international law in the official legal curriculum also coincided with the first professionalizing reform of the Spanish Ministry of Foreign Affairs (Ministerio de Estado), ordered in a decree on 4 March 1844. This legislative reform was, according to L. E. Togores and J. L. Neila, 'the first legal provision to organize the diplomatic career in a stable and unitary manner'[125] in Spain. Contributing to provide the newly-established official academic study of international law in Spain with a practical purpose, this reform also marked the beginning of the 'government interest in the amelioration of the preparation and training of the future members of the Spanish foreign service'.[126]

Despite the importance of 1845 for the establishment of the independent study of international law in Spain, by 1845, there had already been, at least, three instances of academic teaching of international law in Madrid. The first of these emerged as a result of the establishment of international law as part of the curriculum at a short-lived Special School of Administration (1843 to 1845)[127] created by a decree of 29 December 1842 by Regent General Espartero. The teaching of international law was, on this occasion, divided into two courses that were charged to J. Posada Herrera (1814–1885) and E. Moreno López. These two men, therefore, became the first professors to 'officially' lecture on international law in Spain in the year 1843. In addition, Isaac Núñez de Arenas was made professor in charge of the first course at the Special School of Administration from 1844 to 1845. The second instance of the teaching of international law in Spain coincided with the establishment of the first 'private' chair in international law

123 See e.g. Manuel Martínez Neira, *La creación del cuerpo de catedráticos de universidad (1812–1857) Estudio histórico-jurídico* (Madrid: Editorial Dykinson 2013), 41.

124 'Los 222 catedráticos de la universidad española en 1846' Proyecto de filosofia en español available at http://www.filosofia.org/ave/001/a176.htm

125 Luis Eugenio Togores/ Jose Luis Neila, *La Escuela Diplomática: cincuenta años de servicio al Estado (1942–1992)* (Madrid: Ed. Escuela Diplomática 1993), 55.

126 Id.

127 La Gaceta de Madrid, Jan. 2, 1843, 2–3.

at the Madrid Athenaeum in 1844. This chair was originally awarded to a diplomat, José María Ruíz López. However, Ruiz's appointment to a diplomatic position in Constantinople in early 1845 left the position vacant for Facundo Goñi—a lawyer, politician, and diplomat who later served as Spanish Ambassador to the United States in the late 1960s. Published in 1848, Goñi's 'Tratado de las Relaciones Exteriores de España', gathered together his lessons as 'chair holder in international law' from 1845 to 1847 at the Madrid Athenaeum. These lessons were presented as a 'reasoned and complete exposition of all the treaties and interests that determine Spain's relations with each of the civilized nations inside and outside Europe.'[128] Goñi's book, which is considered the first in Spain to trespass on the traditional confines of diplomatic history, and its immediate precursor in the genealogy of international relations, the historiography of international treaties,[129] has been credited with the introduction of the term 'relaciones internacionales' ('international relations') to Spanish academia.[130] This term came, according to Del Arenal, in the wake of the development of international historical studies and 'replaced the term 'diplomatic history' much earlier than in other European states.'[131] Goñi, who authored an extensive scholarly opus,[132] was also an early proponent of the Spanish colonialist policy in North Africa. Anticipating, as we shall see, ulterior Spanish colonial adventures, Goñi argued that Africa 'should soon be invaded by European colonization'[133] in the name of the European civilization and that, moreover, this should also strive for European unity. Finally, in January 1845, that is after the Athenaeum of Madrid's private chairs in international law had been established, but some months before the Pidal plan was officially approved, the Academia Matritense de Jurisprudencia y Legislación followed suit by establishing the subject of international law in its curriculum and assigning its teaching to M. L. Matienzo.[134]

---

128 Facundo Goñi, *Tratado de las Relaciones Exteriores de España* (Madrid: Impr. Ramón Rodríguez de Rivera 1848).

129 Celestino del Arenal, 'La génesis de las relaciones internacionales como disciplina científica', *Revista de Estudios Internacionales* 4 (1981), 849–892, 858–60.

130 See e.g. Juan Carlos Pereira, 'De la Historia Diplomática a la Historia de las Relaciones Internacionales: algo más que el cambio de un término', *Revista de Historia Contemporánea* 7 (1992), 155–182.

131 Id., 169.

132 Facundo Goñi, 'De la filosofía de la historia y sus principales escuelas', *Revista española de ambos mundos* 5 (1854), 613–615.

133 Goñi, *Tratado de las Relaciones* 1848, 145.

134 The reconstruction of the 1840s has greatly from the historical materials assembled under the project *Filosofía en Español* by Gustavo Bueno Sánchez, available in Spanish at http://www.filosofia.org/ave/002/b038.htm.

The establishment of both private and public chairs, the inclusion of the subject in national education plans, the reorganization of the diplomatic foreign service, and the gradual widespread inclusion of the term in academic works penned by Spanish authors in the 1840s illustrate the relatively fashionable character of the term 'international law' in the Spanish intellectual milieu during the 1840s. These academic developments reflected a gradual shift in focus in the study of the international realm in Spain, where, like elsewhere in the European continent during the following decades, a slow transition towards a more methodologically and systematized juridification of policies oriented to the external realm accompanied the domestic evolution of the constitutional liberal state. A hallmark of this early development was the production in Spanish of works which were, at least, nominally ius-internationalist during the 1840s. Collections of diplomatic materials recompiling international agreements and documents on Spanish foreign relations, such as one published in 1843 covering the period 1700 to 1843 by A. del Cantillo,[135] jumped on the bandwagon of the new terminology and were announced under the label 'international law.' A further proof of this terminological transition was a work by E. de Ferrater (1812–1878), 'Código de Derecho internacional, o sea, Colección metódica de los tratados de paz, amistad y comercio entre España y las demás naciones',[136] published in 1846, where the expression 'o sea' (or 'that is') links the terms 'Code of International Law' and its synonym in the terminology of the time 'Methodical Collection of Peace and Commercial Treaties between Spain and Other Nations.'

This terminological galvanization evolved further with the publication by A. Riquelme (1801–1879)[137] of the two volumes of 'Elementos de Derecho Publico Internacional con explicación de todas las reglas que, según los tratados, estipulaciones, leyes vigentes y costumbres constituyen el Derecho internacional español' ('Elements of Public International Law with Explanation of All the Rules that, according to the Treaties, Stipulations, Laws in Vigour and Customs, made Spanish International Law') in 1849. The work by Riquelme, a career diplomat, who was then a chief of section in the Ministry of State

135 Alejandro del Cantillo, *Tratados, convenios y declaraciones de paz, 1700–1840* (Madrid: 1843).

136 Esteban de Ferrater, *Código de derecho internacional, o sea, Colección metódica de los tratados de paz, amistad y comercio entre España y las demás naciones tomo primero* (Barcelona, Impr. Ramón Martín Indar, 1846).

137 Antonio Riquelme, *Elementos de derecho público internacional* (Madrid, Impr. Santiago Saunaque, 1849) see further Garcia Arias 'Adiciones sobre la historia de la doctrina hispánica' 1949, 498.

(foreign affairs) was divided into sections dealing with international law in times of peace and war, international maritime law, private international law, criminal jurisdiction and the law of diplomatic agents. It also included an appendix on the international law of Spain (Apéndice al Derecho Internacional de España) covering the texts of the treaties and laws cited in the first volume ranging from 1607 to 1846. In his 'Elementos de Derecho Publico Internacional', Riquelme defines international law as the 'the ensemble of rules that determine the relationships between civilized nations under positive, consuetudinary and natural law',[138] referring often to the practice of the main European powers. In turn, it classifies these rules as 'political law', which is subdivided into general and maritime law, and 'jurisdictional law', which is subdivided into civil and penal law. The structure and character of Riquelme's opus is symptomatic of the effort to order and systematize Spanish foreign affairs law under the new terminology of international law throughtout the so-called 'moderate decade' (1844–1854) of the reign of Queen Isabel II.

The academic rise of the study of international law continued to benefit during this period from a series of centralizing university education reforms centred around the Pidal plan of 1845. As a coda to these developments, the term 'international law' was included for the first time in the Dictionary of the Royal Spanish Academy in 1852. There, it appeared succinctly defined as '[t]he [l]aw that refers to the franchises or immunities that are reciprocally established'.[139] However, the more lasting university reform affecting international law had to wait to the 'progressive biennium'. The so-called progressive biennium (1854–1856) was the consequence of yet another political 'pronunciamiento' led by progressive generals and democratic forces whose claim for universal suffrage was recognized, despite it never entering into force, in the 1856 Constitution. Although university reform was passed under the title 'Project for Law of Public Instruction' in 1855, many of the university plans from the previous decades ended up flowing into the Moyano Law in 1857—the ground plan for the liberal construction of the Spanish university system which was to remain in vigour for the next 100 years.

The main novelties for legal education that the Moyano Law introduced were the division of the law schools into three sections: laws, canons, and administration. A whole heading in the new law section was devoted to the inclusion of selected textbooks published by the government every three years. Against the background of this modernizing academic movement, doctoral

138 Id., 2.

139 Diccionario de la Real Academia Española (Madrid: Real Academia Española, 1852).

studies in international law expanded at the Central University of Madrid. Throughout the 1850s, a considerable number of doctoral dissertations on international law topics were produced.[140] These dissertations coincided with the establishment of chairs for doctoral studies in the subject of 'Philosophy of Law: International Public and Private Law' in 1852, in the subject of 'The History of the Political, Diplomatic and Commercial Relations of Spain with the Other Powers', and in the subject of 'General International Law and Particular [Law] of Spain', both in 1857. Whereas some of these doctoral dissertations had a practical orientation, such as that presented in 1850 by J.M. Pérez-Caballero y de Posada, 'Discurso sobre el derecho de intervención'[141] (Discourse on the Right to Intervention), most of the topics covered by these early doctoral theses range from doctrinal-philosophical themes—such as one written by C. Martin de Herrera (1855), 'Discurso sobre el verdadero fin del Derecho internacional' (Discourse on the True Purpose of International Law),[142] to methodological ones, such as one written by R. Poo y Real, (1858), 'Necesidad imprescindible de adoptar un método único en el estudio del Derecho internacional' (On the Impervious Necessity of Adopting a Single Method in the Study of International Law).[143] Other doctoral dissertations, nonetheless, focused on the influence of the evolution of civilization in international law, such as that by A. Riva Espiga bearing the title 'Ha influido la civilizacion moderna sobre el Derecho Internacional?' (Has Modern Civilization influenced International Law?) (1853),[144] or that by M. Lasala y Villanova, 'Sobre la influencia de la civilización en el derecho internacional' (On the Influence of Civilization on International Law) in 1855.[145] However, the bulk of these early doctoral theses adopted a historical angle—such as those by de E. de Llauder and de Bransi 'Rápida sobre el

140 See Ignacio Forcada Barona, 'La influencia de la religión católica en la doctrina internacionalista española del período de entreguerras (1918–1939)' in Yolanda Gamarra/ Ignacio De la Rasilla, (eds.) *Historia del pensamiento internacionalista español del siglo XX*, (Cizur Menor: Thompson Reuters Aranzadi 2012), 212–285, 250.

141 José María Pérez-Caballero y de Posada (1850) *Discurso sobre el derecho de intervención*, (Madrid: Universidad Central, 1850).

142 C. Martin de Herrera, *Discurso sobre el verdadero fin del Derecho internacional* (Madrid: Impr. de J. Compañel, 1855).

143 R. Poo y Real, *Necesidad imprescindible de adoptar un método único en el estudio del Derecho internacional* (Madrid: Impr. de D. Eusebio Aguado 1858).

144 Angel Riva Espiga, *La civilización moderna ha influido en el derecho internacional?* (Madrid: Universidad Central 1853).

145 Mateo Lasala y Villanova, *Sobre la influencia de la civilización en el derecho internacional* (Madrid: Universidad Central 1855).

Derecho internacional antiguo y moderno',[146] (Overview of Modern and Ancient International Law, 1855) and A. Esteve y Vila 'Desarrollo histórico-científico del Derecho internacional' (The Scientific-Historical Development of International Law, 1855).[147] On occasions, these historical analyses were focused on the study of works by 16th Century Spanish authors, such as that by D. Álvarez de los Corrales y Melgarejo, 'Breves consideraciones sobre las doctrinas de los escritores españoles de derecho internacional del siglo XVI'[148] (Brief Considerations on the doctrines of the Spanish Writers of International Law of the 16th Century, 1859).

As shown by these first doctoral theses, Spanish authors soon adapted the contents of their writings to the rising academiic prestige of the term 'international law' in the Spanish language. They did so, however, without in any way shying away from ius-naturalist considerations or historical-political extensions, including sketches of the nature of the international relations in which Spanish foreign strategic interests were the key focus of attention. In 1856, E. Alonso y Pesquera continued along the path trodden by Goñi's 1848 Treatise on Spanish Foreign Relations with his 'Historia de las Relaciones Internacionales de España' (History of International Relations of Spain).[149] Eustaquio Toledano's 'History of treaties, agreements and declarations of commerce between Spain and the other Great Powers'[150] of 1858 followed in the footsteps of an earlier Spanish history of treaties and diplomatic documents by Alejandro del Cantillo from 1843. Various works on international legal matters were also published in the first professional law journal published in the Spanish language, *Revista General de Legislación y Jurisprudencia* (RGLJ), which began publication in Madrid in 1853. The term 'international law' appeared for the first time in Spanish in the title of a journal article published in this journal in 1854. The author of 'Derecho Internacional: Cuestión de Mr. Soulé'[151]

146 E. De Llauder y De Bransí, *Rápida ojeada sobre el Derecho internacional antiguo y moderno* (Madrid: Imprenta de Tejado 1855).

147 A. Esteve y Vila, *Desarrollo histórico-científico del Derecho internacional* (Madrid, Impr. de José Ducazcal 1855).

148 Diego Álvarez de los Corrales y Melgarejo, *Breves consideraciones sobre las doctrinas de los escritores españoles de derecho internacional del siglo XVI* (Madrid: Universidad Central, 1855).

149 Eusebio Alonso y Pesquera *Historia de las relaciones internacionales de España* (Madrid: Impr. de José M. Ducazca 1856).

150 Eustaquio Toledano, *Historia de los tratados, convenios y declaraciones de comercio entre España y las demás potencias*. (Madrid: Est. Tip. de J. Casas y Díaz 1858).

151 Carlos Duverdy, 'Derecho Internacional: Cuestión de Mr. Soulé', *Revista general de legislación y jurisprudencia* 2 (1854), 132–138.

(International Law: The Question of Mr. Soulé') was C. Duverdy. However, only two more articles, one again by C. Duverdy on the duties of neutrals[152] in 1854 and 'On the organization, progress and current state of human society'[153] in 1855 by P. Sabau Larroya and two short book reviews[154] on international law appeared in the pages of RGLJ in the rest of the decade.

This gradual extension of Spanish international studies under the banner of international law absorbed, according to del Arenal, the independent study of international relations in Spain. Despite the comparatively early emergence of the term in Goñi's work, these studies became entombed between the development of diplomatic history and the modern prestige gained by the label 'international law'. This all-encompassing tendency in Spain to give an important place to historical studies in the study of international law would, as we shall see, be further fostered by the gradual revival of the works of the Spanish Seconda Scholastica of the 16th and early 17th centuries from the 1860s onwards.

The rise in international prestige of the work by the Dominican friar and Prima Professor of Sacred Theology at the University of Salamanca, Francisco de Vitoria (1483–1547) have been developing in the wake of the emerging field of studies on the history of international law. In 1848, Von Kaltenborn published 'Die Vorlaüfer des Hugo Grotius auf dem Gebiete des ius naturale et gentium' (The precursors of Hugo Grotius in the field of natural law and the law of peoples).[155] However, as Koskenniemi notes, 'Kaltenborn disparaged the contribution of Catholicism to international law, and saw his own work as an effort to make the protestant heritage better known.'[156] The same anti-Catholic spirit infused the eighteen volumes of F. Laurent's 'Histoire du Droit des gens et des relations internationales', which he began in 1851. It was not, according to P. Haggenmacher, 'until 1860 that one witness[ed] the slow emergence in

152 Carlos Duverdy, 'Derecho Internacional. Derecho de los neutrales. Contrabando de guerra. Decreto de 24 de febrero de 1854. Corsarios neutrales'. *Revista general de legislación y jurisprudencia* 3 (1855), 686–97.

153 Pedro Sabau, *De la organización, progreso y estado actual de la sociedad humana Revista general de legislación y jurisprudencia* 3 (6) (1855), 62–85.

154 José Reus, 'Recensión de Mr.Laurent, Historia del derecho de gentes y de las relaciones internacionales, París 1857', *Revista general de legislación y jurisprudencia* 5 (1857) 128. José Reus, 'Recension de Teodoro Ortolan, Reglas internacionales et diplomatie de la mer, París, 1856', *Revista general de legislación y jurisprudencia* 5 (1857) 407–408.

155 Carl Baron Kaltenborn, Die Vorläufer des Hugo Grotius auf dem Gebiete des jus naturae et gentium sowie der Politik im Reformationszeitalter (Leipzig: Verlag von Gustav Mayer 1848).

156 Martti Koskenniemi, 'History of International Law Histories', in Bardo Fassbender / Anne Peters (eds) *Oxford Handbook of the History of International Law* (Oxford: Oxford University Press 2012), 943–971, 954.

the prestige of Vitoria in the internationalist milieu in search of the childhood of the discipline.'[157] In 1862, F. E. Cauchy concluded that Spain 'ha[d] served as the cradle of the science of the law of nations',[158] but it was not until the 'discovery in 1864 of De Jure Praedae that the decisive influence of Spanish scholars, and especially of Vitoria, on the thought of the Dutch jurist-consult became evident.'[159] Until then, Vitoria had been understood 'during the first part of the nineteenth century, ... for most, as a simple name that some evoked without having a true knowledge of his thought',[160] and following the prestige he had gained in the seventeenth and eighteen centuries from the various series of Iuris Naturalis Disciplina, H. Grotius was known as 'the founder of the discipline and, in principle, its only founder'.[161] Throughout the 1860s, the figure of Francisco de Vitoria gained more international ground in the framework of what P. Haggenmacher has described as the 'tournament of the putative founders of international law'.[162] The religious and philo-political contest for the historical paternity of the discipline between Catholics and Protestants, which has captured the imagination of scholars of international law ever since, was bound, as we shall later see, to have a profound intellectual influence on the cultivation of international law by Spanish scholars for many decades to come.

The gradual international revival of interest in the works of the sixteenth century Dominican Friar and Prima Professor of Sacred Theology at the University of Salamanca, and the so-called Spanish school of ius gentium over which his figure presides, coincided with a series of foreign prestige-seeking military interventions by Spain in Latin America in the early 1860s. These interventions were facilitated by a more favourable international environment and a positive domestic economic situation built on the economic reforms and legislative action addressing various economic sectors during the 'progressive biennium'.[163] The new period, which lasted from 1858 to 1865 under the rule of the Liberal Union—a new blend of moderate and progressive liberals—saw several Spanish foreign interventions under a Spanish new policy of international prestige.

---

157 Id.

158 Eugène Cauchy, *Le droit maritime international consideré dans ses origines et dans ses rapports avec le progrès de la civilisation* (Paris: Ed. Guillaumin 1862) 33.

159 Peter Haggenmacher, 'La place de Francisco de Vitoria parmi les fondateurs du droit international', in Antonio Truyol et al. (eds). *Actualité de la pensée juridique de Francisco de Vitoria* (Bruxelles: Bruylant 1988) 27–36, 31.

160 Id., 29.

161 Id.

162 Id.

163 Carr, 'Liberalism and Reaction' 2000, 214.

These foreign military interventions included a brief Spanish collaboration with France and Great Britain in a Mexican expedition of 1861–1862 against B. Juarez's government, a military conflict with Peru and Chile from 1863 to 1866, and the brief reincorporation at the request of the Dominican Parliament in 1861 of the Dominican Republic as a territory of the Spanish Antilles from 1861 to 1865. Other interventions of the governments of the Liberal Union included a Franco-Spanish expedition to Cochinchina in 1857–1862. Jumping on the bandwagon of mid-century imperialism, Spain also led a policy of affirmation in African territory in the War of the North of Africa (1859–1860), which consolidated Spanish positions in North Morocco, and conducted expeditions to the Gulf of Guinea to occupy territories granted by Portugal in the Treaties of de Saint Ildefonso (1777) and El Pardo (1778) as sources of slaves.

This period of renewed interventionism favoured the establishment of a series of new chairs in international law for doctoral studies at the Central University of Madrid on 'Historia de las relaciones políticas, diplomáticas y comerciales de España con las demás naciones' in 1866, 'Derecho internacional, público y privado' also in 1866, and 'Derecho internacional' and 'Historia y examen crítico de los principales tratados de España con otras potencias' in 1868. The development of the study of international law in Spanish universities during this period remained, nonetheless, marked by a period of conservatism and neo-Catholicism in the political milieu. The impact of this conservative political mood on the teaching in Spanish universities is exemplified by an order from the Minister of Public Development of 27th October 1964. This categorically reminded all university chair holders of the prohibition on addressing, either in their chairs or in the public arena, any attack on 'the doctrines of incontestable title which are considered the pillars on which our society rests', such as the Catholic Religion and the hereditary monarchical model.[164] Symptomatic of the conservative character of Spanish production in international law during this decade was a book by P. Lopez Sanchez (1840–1906), 'Elementos de Derecho internacional público, precedidos de una introducción a su estudio bajo los aspectos de su desarrollo histórico o positivo y de su teoría', published in 1866.[165] Lopez Sanchez, professor of Law at the Universities of Salamanca and Madrid, was deeply influenced by the Catholic positions of Taparelli d'Azeglio, whose work was translated into Spanish as 'El Ensayo Teorico

164 *Colección legislativa de España*, Tomo XCII (Madrid: Imprenta del Ministerio de Gracia y Justicia 1864), 589–595.

165 Pedro López-Sánchez, *Elementos de Derecho internacional público precedidos de una introducción a su estudio bajo los aspectos de su desarrollo histórico o positivo y de su teoría*, (Madrid: Impr. de la Revista de Legislación 1866).

del Derecho Natural' (Theoretical Essay on Natural Law) by J. M. Orti y Lara in 1866–68. In his study of the historical-political development of international law and international relations, Lopez Sanchez tried to shed light on what he saw as the international community's state of crisis, which, in his view, resulted from class struggle and socialism.[166] The strong Catholic influence on Lopez Sanchez was balanced by the methodological influence of the 18 volumes of F. Laurent's 'Histoire du Droit des gens et des relations internationales'. The writing of Francois Laurent (1810–1887), a Belgian liberal protestant, had the additional purpose of chastening the role of the Catholic Church.[167] Although Lopez Sanchez's historical work, in which he devotes particular attention to the doctrines of the main authors of the School of Salamanca, is a Catholic and Spanish nationalist counterpoint to Laurent's approach,[168] he relied very much on Laurent's method[169] for his understanding that 'for every science the study of history is useful and all sciences must know their own history.'[170]

López Sánchez explained the title of this work in the following manner:

> '[I]t is our purpose with this title to manifest, with scientific grounding, that it is not from mere curiosity, but it is a superior reason of method that obliges us that before the study of the science of international law, we expose the history of the various relationships between the peoples, preceded by the significance that in every science the study of law has'.[171]

### Revolution in Spain and 'Conscience Juridique du Monde Civilisé'

The so-called 'Glorious Revolution' of 1868 overthrew Queen Isabel II from the throne she occupied since 1833 and initiated the so-called 'democratic' or 'revolutionary sexenium' (1868–1874) in Spain. This 'was precipitated by the high economic costs and the weakening of parliamentary institutions deriving from the Spanish foreign adventures in pursuit of an international policy of prestige and the Spanish larger international trade interests during the prosperous period of 1856–1866. These causes were in addition to the effects of

166 Del Arenal, 'El estudio de las relaciones internacionales en la España del siglo XIX' 1979.
167 Obregon, 'Writing International Legal History' 2015, 105.
168 Garcia Arias 'Adiciones sobre la historia de la doctrina hispánica' 1949, 499.
169 Del Arenal, 'El estudio de las relaciones internacionales en la España del siglo XIX' 1979, 30.
170 López-Sánchez, *Elementos de Derecho internacional público* 1866, 35.
171 Id., 1.

the international financial crisis of 1866, an internal agrarian crisis and the deterioration and corruption of the moderate political regime. Supported by revolutionary assemblies ('juntas') of democrats and republicans, the new progressive liberal military 'pronunciamiento' initiated a six-year period marked by instability and crisis, including the first Cuban, or Yara War (1868–78) and the third Carlist War (1872–1876).

The 'revolutionary sexenium' (1868–1874) also saw a succession of governments and political regimes, such as a democratic constitutional monarchy under a new foreign dynasty (1871–1873), and a federal Republic (1873–1874) in Spain. As a corollary of the '1868 revolution', the first ever Spanish parliament elected by male universal suffrage drafted the first democratic Spanish constitution in 1869. This established a parliamentary democracy based on the principles of separation of powers and national sovereignty under a new monarch, Amadeo I of Savoy, who was elected by parliamentary vote. Accompanied by bicameralism and decentralization measures, the Constitution of 1969 enshrined the most extensive bill of rights and freedoms—supplemented by a numerus apertus caveat—until that time in Spain. This included direct popular suffrage—for males aged over 25—freedom of the press, freedom of association, freedom of thought, trial by jury, religious freedom, freedom of teaching and various other political and social liberties.[172] As a further sign of the progressive character of the period, a new legislation also enabled the eradication of slavery in Spanish overseas colonies in the wake of a campaign for colonial reform fuelled by a guerrilla War in Cuba.

The outbreak in Cuba of the Ten Years' War (1868–1878) was caused by a secessionist movement led by Cuban criollos (Creoles) reacting against the paralysis of social and political reforms resulting from the inapplicability in Cuba (until 1881) of any of the several liberal constitutions passed since 1834 in Spain. The island had, instead, been ruled by special legislation—always at the mercy of the so-called 'Law of Omnimode Faculties' of 1825, which gave the General Captain of Cuba supreme control over the island.[173] Rafael María de Labra (1840–1918), the most representative scholar of colonialism in Spain during this period was President of the Spanish Abolitionist Society (est. in 1865) from 1869 to 1887. Labra had won the first chair in 'The History of Colonization' in Central University of Madrid in 1870, but never occupied it because of his election to the Spanish Parliament in 1871. There, he became

172 See Jose Antonio Souto Paz, 'Las libertades públicas en la Constitución de 1869', *Revista de Derecho Político* 55–56 (2002), 107–158.

173 Luis Miguel Garcia Mora, 'El Ateneo de Madrid y el problema colonial en las vísperas de la guerra de independencia cubana', *Revista de Indias* LVI (1996), 429–449.

a champion, through multiple discourses and publications,[174] of 'autonomism' in the colonial order. Labra defended political and civil rights in equal measure for Spaniards and Antilleans alike, and the parliamentary representation of Cuba and Puerto Rico in the Spanish Congress, while, nonetheless, taking care to preserve the integrity of the Spanish territories.[175] Labra's membership of the Spanish Congress played a large part in the criticism of the Preparatory law for the abolition of slavery of 1870, or Moret Law—also known as the 'Law of the Free Wombs', which declared free slaves born after the revolution of 1868 and those over 60 by 1868.[176] Labra contributed to preparing the passage, at the onset of the First Spanish Republic in 1873, of the more inclusive Law of 22 March 1873 on the abolishment of slavery which included a provision that financially compensated slave owners affected in their 'legitimate rights' by the legislative measure but, nonetheless, tied the former slave (or liberto) to his owner for another five years under a labour contract.[177]

The new democratic-liberal progressive period of 1868–1874 in the bumpy political evolution of Spain in the nineteenth century coincided with the dawn of the European associational movement in favour of the scientific conception and codification of international law in Europe and the Americas. Codification of international law had been called for earlier by J. Bentham, the coiner himself of the terms 'to codify' and 'codification'[178] who wrote back in the mid-1820s that 'few things are more wanting than a code of international law.'[179] By the late 1860s, the spirit in favour of the codification and progressive development of international was ripe and it inspired the foundation of the first professional journal of international law, La Révue de droit international et de

174 See, among many others, Rafael Maria de Labra, *Sobre historia internacional contemporánea* (Madrid: 1870), Rafael Maria de Labra, *La colonizacion en la Historia* (Madrid: Editorial San Martín, 1877) or, already in 1916, Rafael Maria de Labra, *La política colonial y la revolución española de 1868* (Madrid: Tipografia Sindicato de Publicidad, 1916). A list of the several dozens of publications by Labra can be found in Roberto Mesa (con la colaboración de Julio González Campos y Enrique Pecourt), 'Notas para la historia del pensamiento internacionalista español: Algunos problemas coloniales del siglo XIX', Revista Española de Derecho Internacional XVIII (1965), 380–414.

175 See e.g. Maria Dolores Domingo Acebrón, 'Rafael Maria de Labra ante la cuestion de Cuba, 1898', *Anuario de Estudios Americanos* LV (1998), 153–164.

176 Ley de 4 de julio de 1870, de emancipación de los esclavos de España.

177 Ley de marzo de 1873 de la presidencia del poder ejecutivo, aboliendo para siempre la esclavitud en la isla de Puerto Rico.

178 Ernest Nys, 'The Codification of International Law', The American Journal of International Law 5 (1911), 871–900, 872.

179 Quoted in Armitage, *Foundations of Modern International Thought* 2013, 185.

la législation comparée (est. 1869). This mirrored in its title an internationalist and legal comparative interactivity of purpose as liberal reforms were becoming further consolidated in Western Europe and the Americas.

The Révue was an early offspring of l'esprit d'internationalité that accompanied the establishment in the same year of the Societé de législation comparée. This was favoured by the increasing consciousness among members of the professionally emerging discipline that they constituted 'a transnational professional community'[180] that was united by the belief that a common scientific and technical vernacular to promote the development of international law could foster progress and tame the propensity to inter-state conflict. The same hope to contribute to the progress of international law was expressly behind the establishment in 1868 of the Whewell chair and scholarships in international law. Just a few years before, in 1864 the codifying humanitarian spirit had, in its turn, inspired, after the publication of 'A souvenir of Solferino' by H. Dunant in 1862, the creation of the International Committee of the Red Cross and an agreement on the first 'Geneva Convention concerning the Amelioration of the Condition of the Wounded and Sick in Armed Forces in the Field'. Moreover, the move to codification was fostered by the fact that the mid-to-late nineteenth century had seen the rise of positivism with its symbolic extrapolation of an empirical method to the international legal science.[181] The positivist tendency was gradually realized in a system of sources of international law—international treaties, international customs, general principles, and the doctrines of the most prominent ius-publicists. The transposition of 'positive philosophy', which had been presented by A. Comte in the 1830s as 'the third and culminating stage of the collective human mind',[182] into 'a philosophy of international law', was put at the service of the enterprise of international legal codification. This was aided by the rise of the 'scientific' method across the social sciences in the nineteenth century. The 'scientific legal method'[183] jumped on the bandwagon of the development that the natural sciences had been experiencing throughout the nineteenth century in the period of the industrial revolution and breakthroughs in physics, biology, medicine, and zoology, as well as of the development of new applied technical sciences in transport and communications.

---

180 Neff, *Justice among Nations* 2014, 300.

181 See generally Monica Garcia-Salmones, *The Project of Positivism in International Law* (Oxford: Oxford University Press, 2013).

182 Neff, *Justice among Nations* 2014, 222.

183 Lassa Oppenheim, 'The Science of International Law: Its Task and Method', *American Journal of International Law* 2 (1908) 313, 333.

This across-the-board prestige of the new 'science' decisively contributed to the rise of positivism in international law by importing burnished categorical modes of thought to bear scientifically against the influential 'Austinian challenge' which had influentially presented international law as merely 'positive international morality' since early in the nineteenth century.[184] Classificatory schemes were, indeed, designed to be set against the disorder of international relations to identify the actual behaviour of sovereign states and the actual laws that they created through their conduct in an attempt to explain 'how international law could be created without a sovereign but without taking recourse to natural law'.[185] In the wake of the spread of international codification and the refinement of a doctrine of international legal sources, 'this scientific methodology' would then favour 'a movement toward abstraction—a propensity to rely upon a formulation of categories and their systematic exposition as a means of preserving order and arriving at the correct solution to any particular problem.'[186] The scientific approach was increasingly seen as a precondition for the manageable progressive development of international law as a field that was increasingly oriented towards the design of the most 'scientific' methodology possible for the practical international norm-identification said to emanate from the will of sovereign states—in other words, the recognised members of the family of (Western) nations. In 1873, the Institut de Droit International was founded in Ghent. The members of the Institut set a programme of working on the formulation of the general principles of the new science as a mirror of the 'conscience juridique du monde civilisé'.[187] In 1873, along with the creation of the 'first professional international society',[188] and mirroring the great hopes put on the codifying spirit of the times, the 'Association for the Reform and Codification of the Law of Nations' (later known, since 1897, as the International Law Association) was also born in Brussels.

---

184 John Austin, *Province of Jurisprudence Determined: The First Part of a Series of Lectures on Jurisprudence, or, The Philosophy of Law'* (London: John Murray, 1832).

185 Stephen Neff, 'Jurisprudential Polyphony: The Three Variations on the Positivist Theme in the 19th century', in Pierre Marie Dupuy / Vincent Chetail (eds) *The Roots of International Law* (Leiden: Martinus Nijhoff 2014), 301–34, 303.

186 Antony Anghie, 'Finding the Peripheries. Sovereignty and Colonialism in Nineteenth Century International Law', *Harvard International Law Journal* 40 (1999), 1–80, 21.

187 'Statuts de l'Institut de droit international' accesible at http://justitiaetpace.org/status.php?lang=fr. See also Vid Koskenniemi, *The Gentle Civilizer of Nations* 2001.

188 Alphonse Rivier, 'Notice historique sur l'Institut de droit international, sa fondation et sa première session', *Institut de Droit International. Annuaire* 1 (1877).

By then, in Spain the short parliamentary monarchy which had elected Amadeo I (1871–1873), who abdicated after an agitated reign during which he witnessed three general elections and six changes of government, was giving way to a fleeting first Spanish Republic (1873–1874). The collapse of this republic, which had only been recognized by the U.S. and Switzerland, and during which the 1873 Constitution[189] established a federal system, which crumbled after the rise of a violent 'cantonalist' movement in the East and South of Spain, brought about yet another military pronunciamiento in Spain. This dissolved the Cortes to restore order—and eventually monarchy in the form of the son of the overthrown Queen Isabel II. This marked the beginning of Bourbon Restoration also known as the 'Restoration', which, as R. Carr notes, was the 'most stable political structure erected by Spanish liberalism during the nineteenth century'[190] for the next 50 years of Spain's political history (1874–1923).

During the agitated domestic political period of the revolutionary sexennium, no Spanish national participated in the foundation of the Association for the Reform and Codification of the Law of Nations, and only one Spanish national directly participated in the foundation of the Institut de Droit International. This was Nicasio de Landa y Alvarez de Carvallo (1830–1891),[191] a doctor of Medicine and general inspector of the Red Cross in Spain, who had written in 1867 a volume on 'El derecho de la Guerra conforme à la moral'[192] that will know different augmented editions over the next decades. However, several members of the first scientific generation of Spanish international lawyers, such as Rafael Maria de Labra (1840–1918), Jose Dalmau, the Marquis de Olivart (1861–1928), Aniceto Sela y Sampil (1863–1935) and Manuel Torres Campos (1850–1918), were to join and participate in the activities and works of the two bodies during the early stages of the Restoration period.

## The First 'Professional Generation' in Spain

The Restoration system (1874–1923) was based on a peaceful rotation (turno pacifico) between the conservative and liberal parties. Anchored in the 1876 constitution, the Restoration used an 'efficient replacement of the mechanisms

189 The 1873 Constitution never came into force.

190 Carr, *España, 1808–1936,* 1970, 336.

191 Annuaire de l'Institut de Droit International, I (1877), 161.

192 Nicasio de Landa y Alvarez de Carvallo, *El derecho de la Guerra conforme à la moral* (Pamplona: Imprenta de Joaquín Lorda, 1867).

of military rebellion'[193] glued together by a system of local and provincial 'institutionalized electoral corruption'[194] that was to be known as 'caciquismo' (from 'cacique' or local boss) at a time when the illiteracy rate in Spain was still close to 70%.[195] The political stability brought about by the Bourbon Restoration in the person of the King Alphonse XII fostered the Peace of el Zanjon of 1878[196] by which Cuba was provided with political representation in the Spanish congress and a provincial and municipal legislation as part of a project of colonial reform. This was, however, to be only partially and inconclusively applied in the next decades. The measures that followed the Peace of Zanjon included the manumission of all slaves who had supported the Spanish cause but it did not include substantial reforms of Cuba's economic regime which by that time was increasingly dependent on trade relations with the United States. This matter was to loom large in the latter emancipatory upheaval in Cuba from 1895 to the Spanish-American War of 1898. Throughout the War of Yara, the relations between Spain and the U.S. had been strained. While the U.S. questioned the Spanish sovereignty over Cuba, the reconstruction of the South after the American Civil War conditioned the effectiveness of the U.S. support to the rebel forces in a conflict that caused an estimated 200.000 deaths and a great havoc to property on the island.

Since 1877, a new diplomatic relationship between Spain and the United States, based on the establishment of a commission of war reparations for losses suffered by U.S. citizens, a network of beneficial commercial agreements and the rise of the volume of U.S. foreign investment, fostered an ever-increasing economic dependence of the island upon the United States. This went to account for more than 80% of the Cuban exports in the next decades. However, Spain's unwillingness to comply with its obligations regarding the lowering of protectionist tariffs in Cuba and Puerto was combined with a Spanish more diplomatically pro-active policy in Latin-American affairs. This included Spain's offering of good offices in armed conflicts and arbitrations to resolve conflictive border delimitations between the Latin American republics in the late 1870s and 1880s. The gradual deterioration of the bilateral relationship on the diplomatic plane was further compounded by the Spanish

193 Carr, 'Liberalism and Reaction' 2000, 223.

194 Id. 344.

195 Alfredo Liebana Collado, La educación en España en el primer tercio del siglo XX: la situación del analfabetismo y la escolarización (Madrid: Universidad de Mayores de Experiencia Recíproca, 2009), 5.

196 See e.g. Volker Mollin, 'La singular historiografía de la guerra de los 10 años en Cuba (1868–1978)' EHSEA 15 (1997), 205–269.

efforts to counteract the rise of the leadership of the U.S. in the first Pan-American conferences. The non-inclusion of Spain as an 'American power' in these conferences was judged a 'threat to the cultural community of Spain and Hispano-America' and added fuel to a policy of cultural competition in defense of 'Hispano-Americanism' that went to affect the commemoration of the Fourth Centenary of the Discovery of America in 1892.[197] This competition for cultural and economic spheres of influence, as we shall see in following chapters, was to continue throughout the Spanish-American War of 1898 and well into the twentieth century.

The political stability brought about by the Bourbon Restoration also benefitted the growing hegemony of international law in Spanish academia. This culminated in the definitive academic professionalization of international law with the creation of chairs in public and private international law in all Spanish universities in 1883. This development fostered a greater academic production—including of translations of foreign authors as well as monographs, and general treatises written by the newly chaired-professors—and a consequent more marked opening of Spanish international law scholars to communication with foreign authors and trends in international legal thought across Europe. The Restoration was also the period when the early glimpses of Francisco de Vitoria in the 1860s would find a further echo among Spanish international law scholars.

Early in the Restoration period, progressive causes—including an awareness of American problems and colonialism—had found a home in a new academic institution. The Institución de Libre Enseñanza (Free Institution of Teaching—ILE) was founded in 1876 against the background of the political quarrel between religious constraints on the freedom of teaching known as the 'second university question'[198] and the related abandonment of their university chairs by a generation of progressive thinkers. Headed by Francisco Giner de los Ríos,[199] the Free Institution of Teaching (ILE) channelled an adapted Krause-positivist orientation that became known as 'institutionism'.[200]

197 Mariano Esteban De Vega/Francisco de Luis/Antonio Morales Moya (ed) *Jirones de hispanidad: España, Cuba, Puerto Rico y Filipinas en la perspectiva de dos siglos* (Salamanca: ediciones de la Universidad de Salamanca 2004).

198 See e.g. Vicente Cacho Viú, La institución libre de enseñanza, orígenes y etapa universitaria, 1860–1881 (Madrid: Sociedad Estatal de conmemoraciones culturales 2010).

199 See e.g. Francisco Giner de los Ríos, *Ensayos* (Madrid: Alianza Editorial 1969).

200 The most representative work of early Spanish Krausism was Christian Friedrich Krause, *El ideal de la humanidad para la vida* (con introducción y comentarios de Julian Sanz del Río) (Alicante: Biblioteca Virtual Miguel de Cervantes, 1999) (1 ed. 1860).

The pedagogical creed of the Institución de Libre Enseñanza greatly and positively influenced the development of international legal studies in Spain from the late nineteenth century until the Spanish Civil War:

> 'The professor has no other criterion than his own conscience; study, no other method than that which is dictated by reason; truth, no other system than that born out of nature; thought, no other school than free research; scientific life, in sum, no other guide, no other principle than an inquiry alien to any spirit of exclusivism, to any narrow sense of sect'.[201]

The founders of ILE included international law scholars such as Giner de los Rios, who, despite being more of a political and reformist thinker and philosopher, occupied a chair in international law in Madrid from 1867. Another noted 'institutionist' was the champion of the anti-slavery movement, R. Maria de Labra, who along with several others, made ILE a pole for internationalist progressive thinking over the years.

The admiration for the progressive spirit of international law embodied by the United States coloured the first conference on international law given at the Free Institution of Teaching on 1 April 1877 by Labra himself. In his conference, entitled 'Representation and Influence of the United States of America in International Law',[202] Labra decried the abandonment of international legal studies in Spain, criticized Spain's parochialism, and chastised Spain's tendency 'to remain anchored in things, institutions, meanings and ideas that are completely out of touch with the world'.[203] Labra wrote as an apologist of international law and highlighted its most important features in the nineteenth century: its contributions to progress and civilization which Labra understood to mean freedom both on the domestic plane and the religious plane.[204] In his conference, Labra tried to depict this concept through a sweetened image of the United States and by quoting, among others, Kent, Lawrence, Lieber, Wheaton, and Story—the U.S.'s main ius-internacionalists. Labra credited them with various contributions to international legal institutions in the United States, such as 'reform of the colonial regime, the principle of non-intervention, the freedom of the seas, the extension of the circle of nations,

201 Francisco Giner de los Rios, 'Memoria de 1877', Boletín de la Institución Libre de Enseñanza I (1877), 21.

202 Rafael María de Labra, *El derecho internacional y los Estados Unidos de América* (Madrid: Impr. A. J. Alaria: 1877).

203 Id., 6.

204 Id., 9.

the development of international law, the specification of the duties of neutral states, and the effectiveness of unwritten international law.'[205] Labra also presented an idealist, anglophile representation of the British colonial model[206] which for him embodied a plausible framework for a Commonwealth of Hispanic Nations that could be transposed to a more autonomous Cuba, Puerto Rico and the Philippines. Labra also defended the Monroe Doctrine[207] against those who criticized it for being a veiled form of U.S.' colonialism. He implicitly excused U.S.' foreign interventions and appeased fears of North-American expansionism in Cuba.[208] For Labra, the United States was 'the country par excellence of the nineteenth century',[209] nothing less than 'a true source of despair for reactionary people and the shame of pessimists.'[210] In the next decades, Labra continued fighting as elected representative of various Cuban and Puerto Rican districts in the Spanish Congress for colonial reform and—through subsequent legislative efforts in 1880—against the patronato (parrainage), a new institution of serfdom for former slaves in Cuba which was not abolished until 1886,[211] as well as against the contractual application of serf-like conditions (akin to neo-slavery) to Chinese workers in Cuba.[212]

The attention of Spanish international law scholars to developments across the Atlantic to foster the development of international law in Spain also extended to Latin America. Labra himself did not hesitate to affirm in 1877 that 'if the scientific world possesses works of international law written in Spain, this is exclusively due to our Latin American friends.'[213] Amongst this Latin American internationalist production was the work of Carlos Calvo, a key representative of what Obregón defines as 'a Creole legal consciousness of the region's elite by which they often assumed themselves to be part of the metropolitan centre (as descendants of Europeans) while at the same time challenging the centre with notions of their own regional uniqueness (as natives of America).'[214]

205 Id., 37.
206 Id., 13.
207 Id., 28.
208 Id., 23.
209 Id., 9.
210 Id., 38.
211 Real Decreto de 7 de octubre de 1886, dando fin a la relación existente entre patronos y patrocinados.
212 Real Decreto de 11 de mayo de 1872, prorrogando por tres anos el permiso para introducir en la isla de Cuba trabajadores chinos.
213 Rafael María de Labra, *El Derecho internacional y los Estados Unidos* 1877, 12.
214 Obregón, 'Between Civilization and Barbarism. Creole Interventions in International Law', *Third World Quarterly* 27 (2006) 815–832, 817.

Pradier-Fodére, who published Traité de droit international public européen et américain[215] in 1885, mirrored the example set by Calvo in his book Derecho Internacional teórico y práctico de Europa y América[216] in 1868. On some occasions, Latin-American authors focused on the Latin American political project and confederative ideal, with works such as R. F. Seijas' El Derecho Internacional Hispano-Americano Público y Privado, written in 1884. Like other works of the period, this work assembled a melting-pot of acts with ius-internationalist significance from Seijas's homeland of Venezuela and gathered all of Latin America international legal practice together to act as a consultative guide or source for dealing with European and other nations.[217] These efforts, which Becker dubs the 'particularist universalism'[218] of Latin-American authors, found a successor in A. Alvarez, the precursor of what he termed a 'new international law', who theorized and promoted the recognition of Latin American international law in the early twentieth century.[219]

The extension of the Western consciousness of international law to the American continent was also greatly favoured, as will be seen in more detail in Chapter Two, by the work of U.S. international law scholars during the nineteenth century. The first history of international law by a U.S. author, H. Wheaton, was written in French in 1841[220] and was translated into Spanish as Historia de los Progresos del Derecho de Gentes, en Europa y en América, Desde la Paz de Westfalia Hasta Nuestros Dias in 1861 by C. Calvo in an edition that was widely circulated. Calvo went on to publish a sixteen-volume collection[221] of 'treaties,

215 Paul Pradier-Fodére, Traité *de droit international public européen et* américain (Paris:Pedone, 1885).

216 Carlos Calvo, *Derecho Internacional teórico y práctico de Europa y América* (Paris, D'Amyot, 1868).

217 Jacobini, *A Study of the Philosophy of International Law* 1954, 39.

218 Arnulf Becker Lorca, 'Universal International Law: Nineteenth-Century Histories of Imposition and Appropiation', *Harvard International Law Journal* 51 (2010), 475–552, 478.

219 Alejandro Alvarez, *Le droit international américain: Son Fondement, sa Nature d'apres L'Histoire Diplomatique des Etats du Nouveau Monde et leur Vie Politique et Economique* (Paris: Pedone 1910).

220 Henry Wheaton, *Histoire du progress du droit des gens en Europe, depuis la paix de westphalie jusqu'au congress de Vienne: avec un precis historique du droit des gens europeens avant la paix de Westphalie* (Leipzig: F.A. Brockaus 1865).

221 Carlos Calvo, *Colección completa de los tratados, convenciones, capitulaciones, armisticios y otros actos diplomáticos de todos los estados de la América Latina desde el año 1493 hasta nuestros días precedidos de una memoria sobre el estado actual de América, de cuadros estadísticas, de un diccionario diplomático y de una noticia histórica sobre cada uno de los tratados más importantes* (Paris: A. Durand 1862).

statistics and other documents from the legitimation of the Spanish conquest to contemporary independent statehood'[222] in both French and Spanish between 1862 and 1869 in order, as Obregon notes, to 'demonstrate that there was a long standing tradition of international law in the region that would give the new nations equal standing before Europe'.[223] In the third quarter of the nineteenth century,[224] at a time of expanding European imperialism, the development of this post-independence Western integrationist effort by semi-peripheral authors was, however, aimed at reinforcing their embedding in an 'understanding distinctively Western of civilization and its attributes'.[225] This strategic defensive appropriation served as a guarantee against European neo-colonialist interventions (and, later, U.S. imperialist impulses in Latin America), which, as we shall see in Chapter Two, continued under the cloak of the standard of civilization throughout the first decades of the twentieth century.

During the early period of the Bourbon Restoration, another small milestone in the history of international law was the publication in Spain of the only book on international law written by a woman in the nineteenth century. Concepción del Arenal (1820–1893), an influential criminal law expert, sociologist and precursor of feminism, published Ensayo sobre el derecho de gentes (Essay on the Law of Peoples) in Madrid in 1879. Del Arenal had attended the law school in Madrid in the 1840s as an auditor disguised as a man many years before a Royal Order of June 1888 authorized women's attendance at the university as private students, although it took until 1910 for Spanish women to be able to attend universities as official students. Del Arenal's book, the first written by a woman on international law, remains one of the most remarkable efforts to popularize international law in Spanish in the nineteenth century. Its spirit is captured in del Arenal's phrase, 'only when the people understand certain truths may these [truths] become facts.'[226] Del Arenal's work also represents a declaration of faith in the 'progress' of international law:

---

222 Obregon Tarazona, Writing International Legal History 2005, 106.

223 Id., 106

224 Years later, the development of works by Latin American (and United States) authors throughout the late-nineteenth century, helped to convince Carl Schmitt, in his study on the dissolution of Ius Publicum Europaeum, that early in the second half of the nineteenth century Europe and America 'were confounded in the image of a Western European civilization.Carl Schmitt, The Nomos of the Earth in the International Law of the Jus Publicum Europaeum (translated by G. L. Ulmen) (Candor, NY: Telos Press Publishing, 2006).

225 Obregon Tarazona, Writing International Legal History 2005, 106.

226 Concepción del Arenal, *Ensayo sobre el derecho de gentes* (Madrid: Sucesores de Rivadeneyra, 1879), 68–69.

> 'The law of peoples was not and cannot be coactions, but harmony: it exists to the extent that high-minded feelings, exact ideas, well-understood interests concur with it; not by virtue of its armed force, which more often than not serves to trample on it. The facts that remain without being analysed are often thrown like mountains to bury intelligence and hope under their mole, and because something has not been yet, it is concluded that it will never be; but history is a master, not a tyrant; its law is not fatality, and its lessons teach that the progress of law, slow in other epochs, is fast in ours, and it will be more and more so, because when reason has been able to untie the knots that chained it, it falls upon mankind as weights do with an accelerated movement; we should trust its triumph'.[227]

Four years after the publication of del Arenal's work, the study of international law received a definitive boost with a Royal Order of September 2, 1883. This extended the compulsory establishment of courses in public international law and private international law to seven Spanish universities: Barcelona, Oviedo, Santiago de Compostela, Seville, Valencia, Valladolid and Zaragoza. These were in addition to the Central University of Madrid, which kept, nonetheless, the exclusive privilege of programming doctoral studies.

The post-1883 group of scholars who one may term, following Koskenniemi's study of other European traditions,[228] the first 'professional' generation of Spanish international law scholars, produced a considerable number of general works and treatises on international law, as well as translations of foreign works and monographs on particular subjects. In a clear sign of the incipient social role of international legal studies following the spread of its teaching in Spanish universities,[229] the late 1880s also saw the launch of Spain's first specialized international law journal. In 1887, along with a group of notable editors, A. García Montero founded the Revista de Derecho Internacional, Legislación y Jurisprudencia Comparadas, which was published briefly from 1887 to 1888. The editorial of its first issue highlighted:

---

227 Id.

228 Koskenniemi, *The Gentle Civilizer of Nations* 2001,

229 In 1884, the term 'international law', which have been included for the first time in the Dictionary of the Royal Spanish Academy in 1848, where it appeared succinctly defined as '[t]he [l]aw that refers to the franchises or immunities that are reciprocally established', benefited from a positivist caveat with the addition: '(…) and have treaties as foundation'.

> ... the convenience and need which are clear to anyone who has focused his attention on the greatest developments known in recent times in relations among peoples, which are increasing in the same proportion as the interest and the importance of international law and of everything that helps the knowledge of progress and the legal movement taking place in every state.[230]

García Montero and his group of editorial collaborators divided the first volume into various sections. The first of these sections was a 'Doctrinal Section,' which aimed to 'contain articles on private or public international law and comparative legislation.' The inaugural issue included, indeed, a work by P. Fiore on the 'International Effect of the Sentences of the Courts'[231] and another by the future Spanish judge at the Permanent Court of Justice, R. Altamira,[232] entitled 'The Communal Organization of all States.'[233] Altamira examined the field of collective property and found that 'studies of comparative legislation and legal customs can give the most beneficial results'[234] and casted light on the controversial series of disentailments of church property and communal lands—a key component of the dismantling of the economic property structure of the ancient regime brought about by successive liberal governments, beginning with the 'desamortizacion' (confiscation) of the properties of the Church in the 1830s by Mendiazabal during the nineteenth century. The second section, entitled 'International Political Chronicle,' announced that it would give an account of 'great topical questions of the present, or that could emerge in the future, among the diverse states.'[235] The third section, entitled 'Legislative Chronicle', included '[i]nternational treaties and ratified or sanctioned legal dispositions from different states, especially Spanish, Portuguese and American nations, that could affect this area in future years.'[236] The first issue of this section contained, among other things, the texts of an 1887 treaty between Spain and the Eastern Republic of Uruguay on the extradition of

230 Alejo García Montero. Editorial, *Revista de Derecho Internacional, Legislación y Jurisprudencia Comparadas* 1 (1887) 1.

231 Id., 2–26.

232 Yolanda Gamarra, 'Rafael Altamira Crevea. The International Judge as Gentle Civilizer', *Journal of the History of International Law* 14 (2012) 1.

233 Rafael Altamira, 'La Organización comunal de todos los Estados', *Revista de derecho internacional, legislación y jurisprudencia comparadas* 27 (1887), 39.

234 Id.

235 *Revista de Derecho Internacional, Legislación y Jurisprudencia Comparadas* 1 (1887), 1.

236 Id., at 1.

criminals, the text of the law for the protection of subMaríne cables, and the convention on literary protection signed in Colombia in 1885. The fourth section of the journal was a repertory of international case law, including notice 'of commercial case law that could have this (international) character or interest foreign people'.[237] The editors chose to report on decisions such as the one that spoke of the legal capacity of American married women to take part in judicial proceedings before Spanish courts, or another one which related to injuries to foreign princes. They also reported a series of excerpts from foreign decisions with an international element from courts in France, Belgium, Germany, England, Denmark, Egypt, the United States, Italy, and the Netherlands. The fifth section, 'Review of the Professional Press,' aimed to give 'account, with greater or lesser extension, depending on their importance for the object of our interest, of the most notable works that become published in our discipline.'[238] The journal's contents rounded out with a miscellany of news, bibliographies, and bibliographical announcements.

Like many other Spanish scholars of this period, A. García Montero, the founder of this first, albeit ephemeral, scientific Spanish publication on international law in Spanish, produced an extensive output of translations of foreign works—a practice which topped up the meagre stipendium of Spanish university professors at the time. One of the most characteristic features of the 1880s was, indeed, the proliferation of translations of works on international law supplemented with extensive original annotations and appendices by Spanish authors. Among these works were four volumes by F. Martens, translated by J. Fernandez Prida and published as Tratado de Derecho Internacional.[239] Garcia Montero himself translated P. Fiore's Tratado de Derecho Internacional Público, which he augmented with notes and an Appendix on the Treaties of Spain and the Rest of Nations,[240] in 1894–1895, along with other works by Fiore, who was one of the authors that, as Garcia Arias noted, had by means of his translated books a 'large influence' in Spanish quarters at the turn of the century.[241] Other relevant

237 Id., at 2.

238 Id., at 2.

239 See, e.g., De Martens, Jorge Federico. Tratado de Derecho internacional. Prólogo y notas de J. Fernández Prida, 4 vols. (Madrid: 1882).

240 See, e.g., Pasquale Fiore, Tratado de Derecho Internacional público vertido al castellano (de la tercera edición italiana) y aumentada con notas y un apéndice con los tratados entre España y las demás naciones por Alejo García Moreno (Madrid: Centro Editorial de Góngora, 1894).

241 See Garcia Arias 'Adiciones sobre la historia de la doctrina hispánica' 1949, 507.

translations of this period, as indicated by L. Garcia Arias, include Derecho Internacional Publico Moderno by A.G. Heffter in 1875, J. G. Bluntschli's Derecho Público Universal in two volumes in 1880, Principios de Derecho Internacional by J. Lorimer in 1888 and Derecho Internacional Publico Moderno by R. L. Neuman in 1893.[242]

The 1883 reform and the influence of work by international associations also led to the development of works and treatises on particular topics, such as the law of the sea and diplomatic and consular law. I. de Negrin published the second edition of its Tratado elemental de Derecho internacional maritimo (Elementary Treaty of Maritime Law) in 1883 with 50 appendixes and in 1884 published as Manual de las leyes de la guerra continental a Spanish version of the Manuel des droits de la Guerre from the Institut de Droit International.[243] The series of works for the use of consular and diplomatic agents continued in the last two decades of the nineteenth century with the publication by M. Maluquer y Salvador of Anuario Diplomatico Consular (1880) and Tratado de Derecho Consular (1899) and particular works for Spanish consuls and diplomats, such as the Guia practica del diplomatico español (Practical Guide for the Spanish Diplomat) by A. de Castro in 1886 and the Derecho Consular de España by Toda y Guell in 1889.[244] Several of the works produced during the last quarter of the 19th century included examinations of the laws of war, such as the new augmented editions of N. de Landa's El derecho de la Guerra conforme a la moral (3rd ed. 1877), Gil Maestre's Compendio de Derecho Internacional de la Guerra (1895) and a book by Jalon Campelo, Derechos de los beligerantes sobre las personas y propiedad enemigas (Rights of Belligerents over Foreign People and Property), of 1897.[245]

These translations and guidance works for the use of the navy, the diplomatic corps, and the army accompanied the parallel development of a national production of general treatises on international law in the 1880s and 1890s. Among these are such works as Elementos de derecho internacional público[246] written in 1891—although it underwent successive editions in 1904 and 1912—by M. Torres Campos (1850–1918),[247] one of the most prolific authors of the first generation of Spanish international law scholars who

242 Garcia Arias, 'Adiciones sobre la historia de la doctrina hispánica' 1949, 508.

243 Id., 509.

244 Id., 510.

245 Id., 516.

246 Manuel Torres Campos, *Elementos de Derecho Internacional Público* (Madrid: F. Fé, 1890).

247 Garcia Arias, 'Adiciones sobre la historia de la doctrina hispánica' 1949, 500.

was a chair holder at the university of Granada from 1886, and a member from 1885 of the Institut de Droit International. Other general works were written by L. Gestoso Acosta, who published Resumen de derecho internacional público in 1893 and Curso elemental de derecho internacional público and Historia de los tratados[248] (Elementary Course in International Law and History of Treaties) in 1897, in which the author considers natural law a source of international law 'insofar as it determines the nature and aims of the society of states, the conditions and capacity these should reunite to be counted among the members of that society and the fundamental or absolute rights that integrate the legal capacity'.[249] Other relevant treatises were Derecho Internacional Público by R. Sánchez Covisa, written in 1896,[250] and inspired by the lectures of R. Conde y Luque (1835–1921), chair holder in international law at Central University of Madrid,[251] and Derecho Internacional Publico published in 1890 with a second edition in 1905 by the chair holder of the University of Barcelona, J. de Dios Trias y Giro (1859–1914). Following the provision of chairs throughout Spain by the legislative reform of 1883 and the mushrooming of general works and treatises by the new chair holders, the study of private international law also benefited from general works such as Derecho Internacional Privado by Joaquin Fernández Prida (1865–1942) published in 1896 at a time when Fernandez Prida was a chair holder at the university of Valladolid, after having served in Seville (1886) and Santiago de Compostela (1893).

Despite being a 'non-professional' academic, one of the authors who contributed most remarkably to this post-1883 bibliographical development of general works on international law in Spanish in the last decade of the 19th century, and who was to become one of the greatest animators of the study of international law in Spain (and, as we shall see later, the world at large) in the following decades, was Ramón Dalmau, the Marquis de Olivart (1861–1928). The Marquis de Olivart, who was an occasional professor of international law at the University of Madrid, a well-travelled activist, and erudite liberal conservative scholar, stands as a paradigmatic prototype of the international law scholar in the late nineteenth century.

---

248 Luis Gestoso Acosta, *Resumen de Derecho Internacional Público* (Madrid: Imprenta Domenech, 1893); Luis Gestoso Acosta, *Curso Elemental de Derecho Internacional Público e Historia de los Tratados* (Madrid: Imprenta Domenech, 1897).

249 Id., quoted in Garcia Arias, 'Adiciones sobre la historia de la doctrina hispánica' 1949, 499.

250 Remigio Sánchez *Covisa, Derecho Internacional Público* (Madrid: 1896).

251 Garcia Arias, 'Adiciones sobre la historia de la doctrina hispánica' 1949, 500.

Dalmau was initially oriented to the study of the civil and Roman law tradition, to which he consecrated his doctoral thesis in 1884. His work on the concept of 'possession'[252] received a eulogy from Jhering[253] and enabled him to enter the Spanish Royal Academy of Moral and Political Sciences in 1885. However, his initial interest in private law soon gave way to a bibliographical passion for international law, to which Dalmau devoted almost his entire attention and writings for four decades. He was, indeed, among the first to offer a general treatment of the field in Spanish with his work Tratado de Derecho Internacional Público y Privado[254] (Treatise on Public and Private International Law), published in 1886. Highly representative of his many other works is his Tratado y Notas sobre Derecho Internacional Público[255] (Treatise and Notes on Public International Law), published in three volumes in 1887, which went through several editions until it became Tratado de Derecho International Publico in four volumes in 1903–1904. The systematic ordering in this textbook influenced a generation of Spanish manuals in the field and filled a lacuna in the Spanish discipline.

Dalmau's re-editions of Tratado showed constant dedication to the evolution of the discipline during the 40 years of contributions underpinned by natural law to the study of international law. Indeed, for the Marquis of Olivart, international law was 'the knowledge of the natural law of the society of states based on the rule of law and its recognition by those states in positive law.'[256] When 'understood subjectively,' international law became 'that part of public law that determines the relationships among states; that is why it can be called the external public law.'[257] The different editions of his treatise allow us to follow some of the doctrinal developments that the discipline went through before the end of the nineteenth century. Thus, in the first edition of his treatise, Dalmau expressly limited the application of international law to European and Christian

252 Ramón Dalmau de Olivart, *La posesión: apuntes y fragmentos de una nueva teoría posesoria. noción en el derecho abstracto. etimología, carácter jurídico, base de su protección* (Barcelona: J. Jepus, 1884).

253 Letter from Jhering to Ramón Dalmau de Olivart (November 28, 1884) quoted in Antonio Blanc Altemir, *El Marquès d'Olivart i el dret international* (1861–1928): *Societat internacional i aportació científica* (Lleida: Institut d'Estudis Ilerdencs 2000).

254 Ramón Dalmau de Olivart, *Manual de derecho internacional público y privado: extractado y traducido de las obras de Calvo, Bar, Neumann etc., con extensas notas y un bosquejo del derecho internacional privado español.* Tomo I (Madrid: Fernando Fe, 1886).

255 Ramón Dalmau de Olivart, *Tratado y notas de derecho internacional público* (Madrid: Manuel Murillo, 1887).

256 Dalmau de Olivart, de Olivart, *Manual de derecho internacional* 1886, 95.

257 Id., 71–72.

subjects; indeed, for the Marquis, 'with those peoples who do not belong to the European and Christian legal community, it is merely possible to apply natural law … besides, this is the universal international law by definition.'[258] However, Dalmau abandoned the absolute Eurocentricity of his conception of international law in the Appendix covering the 1887 to 1899 period in the third edition of his treatise. Instead, he replaced it with Lorimer's tripartite scheme of civilized, barbarous, and savage peoples, with the former being, in Dalmau's words, equivalent to 'plain humanity.'[259] In the 1899 edition, Dalmau began to integrate certain states like Turkey and Japan into the 'international legal community' of 'civilized humanity,' which he thought required 'complete legal recognition.'[260] In Olivart's view, states like China, Siam, and Morocco represented 'barbarous humanity', for which the 'observance of natural law … stated in treaties' was sufficient. [261] As for the third category of peoples, they had to confine themselves within the 'strict application of the principles of natural law.'

In the appendix to the third edition of his Treatise, the Marquis also echoed the spirit of the period at the time of the First Hague Convention by devoting attention to the area of 'Perpetual Peace: Disarmament and the International Tribunal.'[262] Olivart remained sceptical about the ultimate eradication of war and peaceful settlement of disputes because in his view, 'war is not … the law of force; on the contrary, it represents the force of law, its guarantee, and its ultimate defence.'[263] His viewpoint on war remained unchanged even after he considered the plans for a European state proposed by Lorimer and Blüntschli, and despite being a strong supporter of international arbitration.[264] This acknowledgment led Dalmau to reflect that 'perpetual peace is a state of affairs that the peoples can never attain. However, they (the peoples) must steer towards it indefinitely.'[265] Olivart also offered some insights on the didactic approaches of the time to international law, which he considered were limited to general works, collections of treaties, monographs, and diaries.[266] Despite his

258 Id., at 72.

259 Dalmau de Olivart, *Tratado y notas de derecho internacional público* (Madrid: Manuel Murillo, 1899), 379.

260 Id., at 349.

261 Id., at 350.

262 Id., at 350.

263 *Id.,* at 351.

264 Blanc Altemir, *El Marquès d'Olivart i el dret international* 2000, 128.

265 Dalmau de Olivart, Tratado y notas de derecho internacional público 1899, 71–72.

266 *Id.* at 89.

familiarity with North-American authors such as Wheaton, who he listed, as Blanc Altemir highlighted, among his favourites in the U.S., along with Dana and Kent,[267] no trace of the case-method approach to international law, which, as we shall see in the second chapter, was gaining momentum in the U.S. by then, can be found in Dalmau's analysis of didactic approaches to the study of international law.

The contribution by Olivart, who joined the Institut de Droit International as an Associate Member in 1888, eventually becoming its Vice President, also extended, among other works in this decade, to titles such as Del Aspecto Internacional de la Cuestion Romana (1895) (On the International Aspect of the Roman Question) and a study on El reconocimiento de la beligerancia y sus efectos inmediatos (1895) (The Recognition of Belligerence and its Immediate Effects) and the development of the field of Spanish foreign affairs through his recompilation, following in the footsteps of Cantillo's early referred seminal work on Spanish diplomatic history in 1843, of 13 volumes entitled Spanish Collection of Treaties, Agreements and Documents from 1814 to 1902, published between 1890 and 1902.[268] Olivart also made an enduring contribution to the bibliographical development of international law with his Catalogue of a Library of International Law and Auxiliary Sciences, which was first published in 1899.

Olivart's role to fostering the study of international law in Spain extended, as we shall see in Chapter Two, throughout the first decade of the twentieth century, when he founded and directed Revista Española de Derecho Internacional y Politica Exterior in 1905, the first journal on international law published in the Western world in the twentieth century, and also the first that, although implicitly, broke the pattern of 'not pointing to any national and regional allegiance' in its title,[269] after the publication of Kokusaihô Zasshi (Journal of International Law) from 1902 to 1912 in Japan.[270]

---

267 Blanc Altemir, *El Marquès d'Olivart i el dret international* 2000, 127.

268 Ramón Dalmau de Olivart, *Colección de tratados, convenios y documentos internacionales concluidos o ratificados por nuestros gobiernos con los estados extranjeros desde el reinado de doña Isabel II hasta nuestros días* (Madrid: Fernando Fé, 1902).

269 Attributing it to the *American Journal of Interntional Law*, Koskenniemi, 'The Case for Comparative International Law', *Finnish Yearbook of International Law* (2009) 1.

270 Onuma Yasuaki, 'Japanese International Law in the Interwar Period—Perspectives on the Teaching and Research of International Law in the Prewar Japan' 29 *The Japanese Annual of International Law* (1986) 26–47 at 37.

## The First 'Renaissance' of Francisco Vitoria

The extension of academic chairs in both public and private international law to seven universities outside Madrid and, in its wake, the emergence of the first generation of 'professional' Spanish international legal scholars led, as we have seen, to an array of new translations, specialized works in particular areas, and general treatises and textbooks on international law in the Spanish language in the last quarter of the nineteenth century.

The works that the first professional Spanish international lawyers produced in this period were generally characterized by a combination of socio-historical perspectives and positive law from an ius-naturalist perspective. The rise in prestige of Francisco de Vitoria in European circles in the mid-1870s shall consolidate this tendency among Spanish international law scholars. For Haggenmacher, 'it is at the moment of the famous original 1874 lesson given by Thomas E. Holland in Oxford on Alberico Gentili where one can retrace what we could call the battle of the founders of the law of peoples.'[271] It would, however, be Ernest Nys, whom Koskenniemi calls 'the first historian of the profession',[272] who became, through his intellectual influence, the leading voice, following in the footsteps of Lorimer whose work he had earlier translated,[273] in the Vitorian cause during this period.

In effect, as Koskenniemi notes, in 1883, the year of Grotius's tricentenary, Nys highlighted that 'there could be nothing that [could] be compared in the history of law to the short pages that compose the double dissertation of De Indis by Francisco de Vitoria.'[274] Koskenniemi also retrospectively contextualizes the first renaissance of Vitoria in an age in which 'the early

---

271 Haggenmacher, La place de Francisco de Vitoria 1988, 27–29.

272 Koskenniemi, A History of International Law Histories 2013.

273 Schmitt, The Nomos of the Earth, 2006 117 highlighting that James Lorimer considered Vitoria, Soto and Suarez as the founders of international law in James Lorimer, *Institutes of International Law. A Treatise of the Jural Relations of Separate Political Communities*, (1883–84)

274 Ernest Nys, 'Review of S. de Freitas: Justification de la domination portugaise en Asie', *Revue de droit international et de législation comparé* 15 (1883) 198. See also Ernest Nys, 'Les publicistes espagnols du XVI siècle et les droits des indiens', 21 *Révue de droit international et de législation comparée* 21 (1889) 532. Ernest Nys, 'Le droit des gens et les anciens jurisconsultes espagnols, (1914) extract re-published in G. van Hecke (Ed) *L'Espagne et la formation du droit des gens moderne* (1988), 57, 66–82. See also Ernest Nys, 'Introduction', in *Francisco de Vitoria, De Indis et de Iure Belli Relectiones, Classics of International Law* (Washington: Carnegie Institution, 1917). See further Chapter Three on the influence of Nys in the formative years of the Camilo Barcia Trelles.

international lawyers were liberals who supported the turn to formal empire in order to protect the natives from the greed of colonial companies and ensure the orderly progress of the civilizing mission.'[275] Whereas for Koskenniemi, the move from informal imperialism to formal empire that characterized this epoch was, nonetheless, grounded on what he terms a 'rigorous critique of the Spanish Empire', he also highlights that emergent liberal ius-internationalists clustering around the Institut de Droit International saw the tradition of the Seconda Scolastica of the University of Salamanca as something they 'could associate themselves with.'[276]

This European Vitorian revival in the field of international law, which was aided by E. Nys, and works such as those by Rivier, who in 1888 examined the law of peoples before the publication of Grotius's Iure Belli Ac Pacis,[277] can be further framed, according to Kunz, by the consolidation at a legal-philosophical level of the neo-Kantian reaction against sociological positivism. Indeed, the Catholic tradition of international law benefited from Leo XIII's encyclical Aeterni Patris of 1879, which encouraged neo-Thomist philosophy, and natural law, which was developing in the Hispanic world, in American Catholic faculties, and in the great European faculties of law, such as those in Paris, Milan, Leuven, and Freiburg.[278]

This gradual recovery of Francisco de Vitoria and the School of Salamanca had, moreover, an influential allure in a reconstructive historiographical narrative which served to provide with solid foundations to a Eurocentric conception of international law. In the classical Western European genealogy, the modern origins of international law continue to be conventionally retraced back to either 1625, with the publication of Grotius's De Iure Belli ac Pacis, or to 1648, with the Peace of Westphalia. The year 1648, in particular, has traditionally been reconstructed as the etiological (i.e. the mythical origin) birth date of the modern European state system within a partially secularized post-imperial sovereignty-based ius publicum europaeum. The late nineteenth century saw the consolidation of this retrospective celebratory reference to the Peace of Westphalia as the mythical birth date of the modern system of European states, or the European cradle of the legal equality of independent

---

275 Martti Koskenniemi, 'Empire and International Law: The Real Spanish Contribution', *University of Toronto Law Journal* 61 (2011). 1–36, 3.

276 Id., 4.

277 Alphonse Rivier, *Note sur la litterature du droit des gens avant la publication du J. B. ac P.* (Brussels: Bruylant 1888).

278 Joseph Stunz, 'Natural Law Thinking in the Modern Science of International Law', *American Journal of International Law* 55 (1961) 951–958. 953.

states and the principle of equal sovereignty of European states in both their internal and external facets. It is at this time, that Westphalia, thus, became firmly established as the symbol for an intellectual transition from a world view dominated by natural law towards an emerging voluntary law with the language of law and legality anchoring the balance of power in interstate relations. It also retrospectively crystallized as a symbol of the transition from empire to autonomous territorially delimited sovereign orders in a European political order which was by then inaugurating a new 'ius publicum europaeum'. The crystallization of the myth of Westphalia, also understood as the retrospectively-constructed stepping stone between theocracy and a secularist cuius regio eius religio informed by 'la raison d'Etat', consolidated the view of a European sovereignty-based international society. It is against the background of the historically-situated apex of the positivist method tied to the nation state and the gradual spread of the spirit of international codification in the Western world, that the history of international law consolidated a retrospective idealised projection of an ius gentium europaeum premised upon a general recognition of the principles of territorial sovereignty and the classical attributes of state sovereignty in the European past.

The rediscovery of Vitoria and the Spanish classics helped to provide with even deeper sources to a revamped orthodox historiography of international law which delves firmly into the Eurocentric and state-centric roots of international law. The historiographical paradigm of a Western Christian European foundational matrix provided, moreover, a solid anchor for the extension of international law through different waves of colonization as the age of formal empire unfolded towards Africa, the Middle East, and South Asia. This European imperial expansion, which fostered the gradual transition from jus publicum europaeum to a jus publicum universale, was permeated, as we shall see in more detail in the second chapter, by the development of the standard of civilization[279] in the name of 'la mission civilisatrice' or 'sacred trust of civilization' in the last third of the century.

This historiographical paradigm was further reinforced by its coincidence with a greater nationalist demarcation of the internal boundaries between European nation states in the mid-to-late nineteenth century. At the dawn of a historical period where the professional study of both history and law at the national level and of international law and the history of international law[280]

279 See Georg Schwarzenberger, 'The Standard of Civilization in International Law', *Current Legal Problems* (1995) 212. See also Gerrit W Gong, *The Standard of Civilization and the international Society* (Oxford: Clarendon Press 1984).

280 Koskenniemi, *The Gentle Civilizer of Nations* 2001.

emerged tangled with methodological nationalism,[281] this historiography became then almost exclusively focused on the reconstruction of a Western European and Christian foundational matrix for an early modern law of nations. As far as the dynamics of history-making in international law are concerned, both the need to provide solid historical foundations for the expanding European state-centric international order and the project of reconstructing European national histories in a unitary spirit help to account for the stress on the early modern period and classic 'founding fathers' of international law revolving around the Westphalian period and its immediate pre-foundational stage in the 16th century. This Western Eurocentric and state-centric dominant genealogy of the history of international law allied itself with positivism and the project of codification of international law either in totus or, gradually, by parcelling together different areas of state practice, identifying 'the countries of Western Europe together with their overseas offshoots in the Western hemisphere'[282] as the 'group of states [that] had been responsible for agreeing on the corpus of rules known as international law'.[283]

For Spanish international law scholars, however, the new retrieval and revival of Francisco de Vitoria and the School of Salamanca meant more than just a convenient prologue to a firmly established Western Eurocentric historiography of international law that indirectly generated exclusionary dynamics across the world in the age of imperialism. In 1884, Torres Campos wrote '[i]nternational law (which was initiated by our ancient writers Vitoria, Soto, Suárez and Ayala, who anticipated the authors of European treatises) is today in almost complete oblivion. It is the legal branch that has been least studied.'[284] The Vitorian revival influenced differently a semi-peripheral Western power like Spain, which was comparatively free of much of the practical deliberation in which other European powers were engaged regarding the form that liberal imperialism could take in that age. Although the Berlin Conference of 1885 had recognised the territories of the Gulf of Guinea as a Spanish Protectorate along with another area in north-western Africa facing the Canary Islands, by then, the Spain of Restoration, which had subscribed

281 For a critique of methodological nationalism 'as a key, if not the key feature of the history of the social sciences at large', see Daniel Chernilo, 'The critique of methodological nationalism: Theory and History', *Thesis Eleven* 106 (2011), 98–117.

282 Neff, *Justice Among Nations* 2014, 251.

283 Id.

284 Manuel Torres Campos, *Nociones de bibliografía y literatura jurídica de España* (Madrid: Impr. Ancha de San Bernardo 1884), 135.

to a self-preserving foreign 'policy of seclusion' to avoid being entangled in European alliances, was irremissibly advancing toward the Spanish-American War of 1898 and the definitive loss of its overseas colonies in America and South-East Asia at the hands of the new American Empire. Indeed, the first renaissance of the Salamanca School served somewhat as a compensatory refuge for what Del Arenal terms the 'little scientific relevance that, in general, Spanish international legal thought had until the end of the nineteenth century.'[285]

The unearthing of the Salamanca School in this particular period thus began to provide Spanish international legal scholarship with quasi-national intellectual identity traits. It also contributed to the emergence of a nationalist trend of Spanish intellectual thought with Catholicism at its indelible core. Indeed, the growing European historiographical focus on the role of Francisco de Vitoria in the genesis of the law of peoples found an echo in the intellectually eclectic Spain of 'tertulias' and the political-philosophical debates in Athenea and literary-philosophical gazettes. It is possible to broadly characterize this intellectual environment with reference to four broad intellectual camps. First, there were the traditionalist-integrist and Catholic ultramontano believers in the infallibility of the Pope and neo-Thomists, such as A. Pidal y Mon. Alongside this group was Catholic thinkers, such as Gumersindo Valverde and M. Menéndez Pelayo, who insisted that a new Spanish renaissance would only be possible if it were in keeping with Spain's Catholic roots. On the liberal wing, there were Krausists, influenced by Hegelian idealism through Sanz del Rio. After the failure of the Revolutionary Sexenium (1868–1974), this influence diverged into several orientations, including the Krausist-positivism of Institucionismo of the Free Institution of Teaching after 1876. Finally, the 'first school of Madrid'[286] included early neo-Kantians scholars like J. del Perojo (1850–1908), who became the founder of Revista Contemporánea in 1875 and was the first translator of Kant's Theory of Pure Reason in 1883, and M. de Revilla. The school fitted within the modernist and Europeanist trends that highlighted the weight of religious intolerance and political despotism on Spanish progress. The late nineteenth-century Spanish contributions to the rediscovery of the School of Salamanca benefited in particular from

285 Del Arenal, 'El estudio de las relaciones internacionales en la España del siglo XIX' 1979, 19.

286 Fernando Hérmida de Blas, 'La primera escuela de Madrid', Lecciones del Curso 'Cincuenta años de Ortega y Gasset (1955–2005)', (Madrid: Asociación de Hispanismo Filosófico, Biblioteca Virtual, 2005), 1–33.

the work of the Dominican order in Spain, as well as secular authors.[287] This scholastic revival took place in parallel with the evolution of the process of codification in Spain (the Commercial Code, 1885, and the Civil Code, 1889) during the apogee of the influence of German legal science and the historical school in Spanish legal academia. The works by Eduardo de Hinojosa y Naveros (1852–1919) are of special interest in this framework.

Considered the father of modern Spanish legal historiography,[288] E. Hinojosa Naveros was the brother of J. de Hinojosa Naveros (1854–1896), who occupied the chair—established in 1868 and 1880—of doctoral studies on the 'History and Critical Study of the Main Treaties of Spain with other Powers' in La Habana (1884) and then at the Central University of Madrid (1885). Hinojosa's inaugural speech to the Royal Academy of History in 1889 took the Dominican friar Francisco de Vitoria as its subject matter. Two main elements can be highlighted in Hinosoja's discourse 'On the influence the Spanish philosophers and theologians of earlier centuries had on the public law of their motherland and, singularly, on penal law.'[289] First, it is apparent that Hinojosa wanted to highlight the methodological renovation that was owed to Vitoria by the neo-Thomist genealogy of Spanish Catholic traditionalist thought. There is an insistence on the importance of Vitoria in the genesis of the modern law of peoples vis-à-vis the works of foreign authors[290] such as Grotius and Gentili. Hinojosa was adamant in highlighting the fact that it was unfair to conclude that the constitution of international law as an autonomous science dated back to the works of Gentili and Grotius. For Hinojosa, neither of them can be understood without Vitoria, Suárez, and Ayala, in the same manner that the Spanish contributions cannot be understood without the enormous task carried out in earlier centuries by scholastic theologians, particularly Saint Thomas, and by the canonists and civilists under the influence of Roman law.[291]

---

287 Other authors who began to approach the study of the jurists and theologians of the 16th and early 17th century in Spain during the late 19th century and early 20th century include Álvarez de los Corrales, Bravo Murillo, Pérez de Gomar, López Sánchez, Marqués de Villa-urrutia, Ceferino González, Conde y Luque, Hinojosa, Menéndez y Pelayo, Abad y Cavia, Fernández Prida and Alonso Getino. See, further, Chapter Two.

288 See i.e. Eduardo de Hinojosa y Naveros, *Historia general del derecho español.* Tomo I. (Madrid Tip. de los Huérfanos, 1887).

289 Eduardo de Hinojosa y Naveros, 'De la influencia que tuvieron en el Derecho público de su patria, y singularmente en el derecho penal, los filósofos y teólogos españoles anteriores a nuestro siglo' (Madrid: Tipografía de los Huérfanos, 1890).

290 Id., 195–196. Hinojosa mentions Mackintosh, Pradier Foderé, Holland, De Giorgi, Gierke, Holtzendorg and a series of contemporary German scholars.

291 Id., 193.

Hinojosa advanced, moreover, a future research agenda, which he considered a 'complement to the present Memoria'[292] with the aim of examining the influence that Spanish philosophers and theologians had on the public law of their motherland, This agenda would be 'circumscribed to expose to study the influence that they had in the scientific development of political law and European international law through the reception of their doctrines in the works of foreign authors, especially those by Gentili, Grotius and Conring.'[293] According to Hinojosa, the 'study of this influence is bound to constitute one of the most interesting chapters in the history of Spanish science; but this work does not yet exist.'[294] Hinojosa also criticized foreign authors such as Lorimer, highlighting the fact that 'Suarez's concept of international law, which was qualified as grandiose by Heffter, is none other than a development of that formulated by Vitoria.'[295] 'This is an affiliation,' wrote Hinojosa, 'that no one has, to my knowledge, stopped to pay attention to until now because the text by Vitoria alluded to is not in the Relectiones De Indis, consulted by the authors of international law, but in the De Potestate Civili.'[296] Hinojosa stressed Vitoria's preeminent role as an essential part of the merits of De legibus et Deo legislatore by Suarez, the 'Eximius Doctor' for Catholics, whom their Protestant adversaries called Papa Metaphysicorum et Anchora Papistaruni.

The second aspect worth noting is how Hinojosa's work is fully conscious of the parallelisms between the 'question of the title that authorized the Spanish Kings to conquer the world'[297] and the immediate thematic interest of the topic for international lawyers in the age of European imperialism in the nineteenth century, a 'question that has also worried international law authors of our time and age without them achieving until now a definitive and uniform solution'.[298] Hinojosa pointed to this when he noted:

> 'When thinking whether the civilized peoples can use force to oblige savage peoples to open their borders and their ports to foreign relations, while some resolve the question negatively, founding their views on the assertion that between civilized peoples and barbarian ones, there is no link to community, and there cannot be mutual duties and rights, others,

292 Id., 193.
293 Id., 194.
294 Id., 193.
295 Id., 193.
296 Id., 193.
297 Id., 187.
298 Id., 188.

> such as our theologians, resolved it in a contrary sense, recommending no recourse to violence if it were not motivated by the conduct of the savages'.[299]

M. Menéndez Pelayo (1856–1912), who was the greatest exponent of the 'nationalist school' in Spanish historiography and had already written about Vitoria in the 1870s, answered Hinojosa's 1899 speech to the Academy of Moral and Political Sciences.[300] By the turn of the nineteenth century, the influence of the interpretation of this erudite polygraph, leader of the 'purist' strand of Spanish thought and science within the 'nationalist school' of the historiography of ideas was already widely extended through influential and voluminous works including the famous La ciencia española (1876),[301] and Historia de los heterodoxos españoles (1880–1882).[302] In his response to Hinojosa's discourse, Menéndez Pelayo highlighted Vitoria's role as an emblem of a purist Spanish tradition built upon Catholicism and praised 'Spain, the evangelizer of half of the world; Spain, the hammer of heretics, the light of Trento, the sword of the Pope; Spain, the cradle of Saint Ignacio. Such is our greatness and our glory: we do not have any other.' Three decades later, in the early 1930s, as we shall later see, the works of Menendez Pelayo became interpreted in a radically polarized ideological manner by far-right wing Catholic intellectuals fighting the socially revolutionary reforms of the Second Republic. In the aftermath of the Spanish Civil War, and the first decades of the Franco period, the works of Menendez Pelayo, by then according to R. Carr a 'lay saint of the Spanish Phalanx',[303] became, as it would also happen in the case

299 Id., 188 referring, among others, to Charles Salomon, *De l'occupation des territoires sans maitre* (Paris: A. Giard 1889) which examines the theories of Vitoria on the topic through a close and exact analysis of *Relectiones de Indis*.

300 Marcelino Menéndez Pelayo, *Discurso leído ante la Academia de la Historia* (1879), in Menéndez Pelayo, Marcelino. Edición Nacional de las Obras Completas de Marcelino Menéndez Pelayo, 65 Vols. (Madrid: Consejo Superior de Investigaciones Cientificas, 1940–1959).

301 Marcelino Menendez Pelayo, *La ciencia española* (1876). (1880–1882), in Menéndez Pelayo, Marcelino. Edición Nacional de las Obras Completas de Marcelino Menéndez Pelayo, 65 Vols. (Madrid: Consejo Superior de Investigaciones Cientificas, 1940–1959).

302 Marcelino Menendez Pelayo, *Historia de los heterodoxos españoles* (1880–1882), in Menéndez Pelayo, Marcelino. Edición Nacional de las Obras Completas de Marcelino Menéndez Pelayo, 65 Vols. (Madrid: Consejo Superior de Investigaciones Cientificas, 1940–1959).

303 Carr, *España, 1808–1936,* 1970, 343 noting Years later, during the Spanish Civil War and the Franco period, some would describe Menéndez Pelayo as 'lay saint of the Spanish Phalanx.'

of Francisco de Vitoria, an intellectual cornerstone of 'national Catholicism, fostering a national edition of 65 volumes of his complete works and hundreds of works of academic commentary.[304]

In the late nineteenth century, however, after the academic development of international law as an emblem of liberalism accompanied the gradual establishment of the liberal state in Spain throughout the troubled nineteenth century, the first renaissance of the Salamanca School, forgotten in Spain during the mid-seventeenth and eighteenth century, further spurred a conception of international law as a holistic science of international relations in Spain. The encyclopedic perspective of the field that Spain, mostly orphaned of external ambitions during an epoch marked by a defensive foreign policy of seclusion is epitomized by natural law authors, such as Gestoso Acosta.[305] This author attempted to integrate the philosophy of international law, 'the investigation into the existence, foundations and ends of international society',[306] together with the history of international law and the politics of international law, all wrapped up with a natural law caveat against the background of the progressive codification fostered by the emergence of international associations, international conferences and international conventions in the 1890s. Ultimately, this initial riveting of an all-encompassing science of international law, prone to universalist abstract speculations, which Spanish authors understood as a socio-historical structure, was the legacy of the misery and greatness of the first School of Salamanca's revival in the late nineteenth century for the study of international law in Spain. The long shadow cast by the re-awakening of interest in the works of Francisco de Vitoria and the School of Salamanca extended, however, both in Spain and across international legal circles elsewhere, far beyond the turn of the nineteenth century.

---

304 See e.g. Edición Nacional de las Obras Completas de Menéndez Pelayo, 65 Vols. (Madrid: Consejo Superior de Investigaciones Cientificas, 1940–1959).

305 Luis Gestoso Acosta, *Curso elemental de Derecho internacional público e Historia de los tratados* (Madrid: 1897).

306 Id., 185.

CHAPTER 2

# A Point of Inflection for International Law in Spain and the United States

## The Spanish-American War—A Point of Inflection for International Law

The progress of international law in the United States in the 1900s owes much to the outcome of the 1898 Spanish-American War. Since the mid-nineteenth century, the United States had also been developing the outlines of an informal empire through an extended network of 'unequal treaties.'[1] Continental expansion from the Thirteen Colonies[2] in the wake of the doctrine of 'manifest destiny' had been previously legally privileged by the Marshall Court[3] at the expense of the Native American nations.[4] In its quest for overseas expansion, the United States had, furthermore, annexed several groups of islands in the Pacific Ocean in the 1890s, including Hawaii in 1898. The daybreak of the new American Empire also bore witness to the rise of elite corporate law firms. These soon became central agents in the transnational emanation of an 'American mode of production of law'.[5] Movement between private international legal counselling for clients, such as the

1 See e.g. Francis Bowes Sayre, 'The Passing of Extraterritoriality in Siam' American Journal of International Law 21 (1927) 70–80 (providing an example of the repetition of substantially the same fiscal provisions of an Anglo-Siamese Treaty of 1855 containing no time limit and only modified with the consent of both parties in the respective treaties of Siam with the United States (1856), France (1856), Denmark (1858) Portugal (1859), Netherlands (1860) Germany (1862) Sweden (1868) Norway (1868) Belgium (1868), Italy (1868), Austro-Hungary (1869) and Spain (1870).

2 See David Kennedy, 'International Law and the Nineteenth Century: History of an Illusion', *Quinnipiac Law Review* 17 (1997) 99–136, 106.

3 James Thuo Gathii, *War, Commerce and International Law* (Oxford: Oxford University Press, 2010) 39.

4 See as introduction, Ken Coates, 'North American Indigenous Peoples' Encounters', in Bardo Fassbender/ Anne Peters, *The Oxford Handbook of the History of International Law* (Oxford: Oxford University Press 2012), 787–810.

5 Or 'Cravathism' see, interestingly, David Trubek/ Yves Delazay/ Ruth Buchanan/ John R. Davis, Global Restructuring and the Law: Studies of the Internationalization of Legal Fields and the Creation of Transnational Arenas, *Case Western Reserve Law Review* 44 (1993–1995), 407, 423.

 | DOI 10.1163/9789004343238_004

United Fruit Company, and 'public service' in the foreign policy establishment grew into a salient feature of the management of the outer realm. At the turn of the 20th century, as the United States was transitioning from a semi-peripheral Western country to an imperial power with overseas territories, a new breed of American leaders took the reins of the foreign policy establishment.[6]

American commercial universalism required a new enthusiasm for international law[7] and from this strategic realization, as Boyle notes, a 'large-scale co-optation of the skills of American international lawyers [...] by all branches of the American government'[8] ensued. This thriving internationalist *fin de siècle* mindset aligned itself with a boost from the 'scientific' development of international law in the last third of the nineteenth century in the United States. On the diplomatic plane, the soil had been nurtured by the successful American experience with international arbitration since the Jay Treaty of 1794, which was corroborated by the fruitful outcome of the 1868 United States-Mexican Mixed Claims Commission and the Treaty of Washington of 1871.[9] Culminating in The Hague Peace Conference of 1899, international private and associational codifying efforts had been carried out since the 1870s. Meanwhile, the intellectual tradition of the peace movement in the United States throughout the second part of the nineteenth century coincided with the growing professionalization of American law schools in the wake of the 'Harvard method'. Against this background, the Spanish-American war in 1898 paved the way for the establishment of the American Society of International Law (ASIL) in 1906. The stellar group of founders of the ASIL included the, by then, U.S. Secretary of State, E. Root, and three U.S. Supreme Court Justices. These were accompanied by two former U.S. Secretaries of State and a future U.S. President, W.H. Taft, who, after having served as the first Governor-General of the Philippines,[10] was the U.S. Secretary of War. The judicial

6 See e.g. a modern classic such a Eric Hobsbawn, *The Age of Empire, 1875–1914* (London: Abacus 1989) 69 noting that 'at the turn of the century, the USA followed international fashion by making a brief drive for a colonial empire of its own'.

7 See i.e. Benjamin Allen Coates, *Legalist Empire. International Law and American Foreign Relations in the Early Twentieth Century* (Oxford: Oxford University Press, 2016). See also Marti Koskenniemi, 'Book review of Mark Janis: The American Tradition in International Law', 100 *American Journal of International Law* (2006), 266–270.

8 Francis Anthony Boyle *Foundations of World Order Foundations of World Order, The Legalist Approach to* International Relations (1898–1922) (Durham N.C.: Duke University Press, 1999), 17.

9 Treaty of Washington, May 8, 1871, 12 Bevans 170, 143 Consol. Treaty Ser. 145

10 See Anghie, *Imperialism* 2014, 279–286.

and political aftermaths of the Spanish-American war meant a definitive leap forward towards a new American overseas' Empire and a new era of military interventionism. For the American foreign policy elite, international law had definitively become a '*question d'État*'.

In Spain, by contrast, the loss of Puerto Rico and Cuba in the Caribbean, and of the Philippines and Guam in the Pacific Ocean, would trigger a national identity crisis. What was to be known as the 'Desastre ('Disaster') of 1898' contributed to further undermining the legitimacy of the Bourbon Restoration system. Founded on the principles of liberal doctrinariarism contained in the Constitution of 1876, the Restoration system had managed to provide the highly asymmetrical industrializing Spanish society with a much-coveted political stability since 1874. In 1890, a new electoral system based on universal suffrage for men of more than 25 years, and with full use of their civil rights, had replaced the electoral scheme of restrictive suffrage based on property and level of instruction, which barely entitled 5% of the population to vote. However, this 1890 electoral reform remained functionally and politically hijacked by the rigged rotation of political parties. In practice, the turno pacífico ('peaceful rotation') was limited, as S. Balfour notes, to 'the two monarchist—conservative and liberal—main political factions imperfectly representing the landowning and financial oligarchies whose power rested on patronage and electoral fraud administered by local bosses or 'caciques'.'[11]

After the 'desastre del 98', an extended perception that the causes of the Spanish military humiliation of 1898 lay with Spanish educational backwardness and international isolation prompted a widespread intellectual debate on the 'Spanish problem', to which 'the solution'—as José Ortega y Gasset famously remarked—was 'Europe.'[12] This post-conflict awareness fostered the rise of different political, economic and cultural variants of Spanish 'Regenerationism'.[13] Politically, 'regenerationism', generally understood

---

11 Sebastian Balfour, 'Spain and the Great Powers in the Aftermath of the Disaster of 1898', in Sebastian Balfour / Paul Preston (Eds) *Spain and the Great Powers in the Twentieth Century* (London: Routledge 1999), 13–31, 20.

12 The bibliography on Ortega y Gasset and Spain is enormous, see e.g. Juan P. Fusi, 'Ortega y España', in Antonio Morales Moya et al. (eds) *Historia de la nación y del nacionalismo español* (Barcelona: Galaxia Gutenberg. Circulo de Lectores 2013), 638–650.

13 The bibliography on Spanish regenerationism is extremely extensive see e.g. Andres de Blas Guerrero, 'Regeneracionismo español y cuestion nacional', in Antonio Morales Moya et al. (eds) *Historia de la nacion y del nacionalismo español* (Barcelona: Galaxia Gutenberg. Circulo de Lectores, 2013), 638–650.

as a 'generalized conscience of Spanish ills and proposals for solutions',[14] had been initially proposed by its main intellectual champion, Joaquin Costa (1846–1911), as a democratic reformist agenda for the 'live forces' of society to overtake what Costa himself termed 'caciquismo', or rigged government, by local bosses and members of the economic elite. However, the slow rise of workers' parties in Spain[15] made the reformist agenda of regenerationism a powerful bourgeois-socio-liberal alternative to radical socio-political movements. Conservative leaders would see in the Spanish regeneracionist movement a recipe for a 'revolution from above' against the threats posed by anarchism and anarcho-syndicalism in the big landowner agrarian areas of the South and industrial Catalonia. A re-orientation in Spanish foreign policy, and by extension, in the Spanish engagement with international law, followed in its wake in the early 1900s.

Culturally, the main influence of the regenerationist movement was the ruthless postulation of education as the bedrock of Spanish modernization. This widespread campaign led to important education and university reforms in the first decade of the 1900s. Indeed, education reforms were badly needed. Having barely decreased from 70% in 1860,[16] illiteracy in Spain remained at a staggering 64% at the turn of the twentieth century. The post-1898 regenerationist modernist tendencies, the introduction of reforms at all levels of the educational spectrum, including university education, and the scientific opening of the Spanish elite to Europeanization would, furthermore, greatly benefit the development of international legal studies in Spain in the first third of the 20th century. At the onset of what, in the image of the Spanish *Siglo de Oro* of the 16th century, is occasionally termed 'la Edad de Plata; (the 'Silver age') of Spanish culture' (1898–1936), another factor was also to decisively contribute to the gradual abandonment of abstract speculation among Spanish international law scholars. After the foreign policy adventures of the final years of the Kingdom of Isabel II, the leaders of the Restoration system opted for a foreign policy of seclusion ('política de recogimiento') aimed at avoiding entanglements in the shifting and complex chessboard of imperial politics. Spurred by the loss of the last remnants of the overseas colonies, the

14 See e.g. Javier Varela, 'Crisis de la conciencia nacional en torno al 98', in A. Morales Moya et al (eds) *Historia de la nacion y del nacionalismo* español (Barcelona: Galaxia Gutenberg, Circulo de Lectores 2013), 543–562.

15 The Spanish Worker's Socialist Party (PSOE) was founded in 1879, but it only won its first seat in Parliament in 1910.

16 Liebana Collado La educación en España en el primer tercio del siglo XX 2009, 5.

Spanish foreign policy elite came, nevertheless, to rethink its defensive strategy of cautious retreat from the 'global process of colonial redistribution in an era of expansionism.'[17] A political consensus thus emerged on the necessity to turn the helm of Spanish foreign policy and jump on the last available bandwagon of the scramble for Africa.

The Berlin Conference in 1885 had recognised the territories of the Gulf of Guinea as a Spanish Protectorate along with another area in northwest Africa facing the Canary Islands. These were added to a coastal strip of northern Morocco (known as Sidi Ifni) that had been under Spanish control since 1860 and to some cities and former penitentiaries facing the south coast of Spain[18] that had been under Spanish control since the 16th century. Building on these enclaves, the post-1898 wave of Spanish colonialism towards North Africa promised to compensate for lost commercial and industrial interests in America, and to provide Spain with some degree of international prestige after the recent swift and humiliating defeat at the hands of the new U.S.' empire. This strategy remained, nevertheless, more a reflection of post-1898 Spanish insecurity than a proof of Spanish assertiveness on the international plane. The Spanish foreign-policy elite was indeed aware that the risks of international isolation included the possibility that a Spanish territorial disintegration of uncertain limits might ensue.[19] Spain, as a semi-peripheral, yet strategically well-positioned player in the Mediterranean, joined the great chessboard of imperial policies towards Africa by profiting from their recent refashioning in Fashoda in 1898. The ensuing redirection of French colonial interests towards North Africa provided Spain with a narrow yet geo-strategically beneficial framework for its colonial expansion in the western Mediterranean. This new colonial policy of substitution, which aimed, as Balfour highlights, to 'ensure the defence of the Peninsula and her islands (notably the Canary Islands) in the new volatile context of competitive imperialism,'[20]crystallized in Spain joining the British-French Entente Cordiale of 1904. The 'Morocco question' added, as we shall see, a practical edge to the revitalization of international law studies in Spain in the early twentieth century.[21]

17 Balfour, 'Spain and the Great Powers' 1999, 13.

18 Ceuta and Melilla, the Rock of Vélez de la Gomera, the Rock of Alhucemas and the Chafarinas Islands under Spanish possession since the end of the 15th century.

19 Jose Luis Neila, *España y el Mediterraneo en el siglo XX. De los acuerdos de Cartagena al proceso de Barcelona.* (Madrid: Silex 2011), 114.

20 Balfour, 'Spain and the Great Powers' 1999, 19.

21 A detailed summary of the contents of Chapter 2 can be found in the 'Introduction'.

## The Legacy of the Nineteenth-Century in the U.S.' International Legal Academia

At the turn of the twentieth century, the literature on international law was on the rise in the United States where it already acquired a long-standing pedigree.[22] This nineteenth century academic revolution can be retraced back to the publication of Henry Wheaton's Elements of International Law in 1836, the first book in the English language to wear in its title the neologism coined by Jeremy Bentham.[23] Wheaton went on to publish the first treatise on the history of international law by a North American author [24] in French in 1841. A year later, he republished it in English with a different title to underlie the inclusion of the United States in the history of international law.[25]

As it had happened in Latin America, the university teaching of international law emerged and extended comparatively earlier in the United States than in the British Empire, its former metropolis. At Yale in 1846, Theodore D. Woolsey taught some of the first courses in international law in the United States. In 1860 Woolsey went on to publish the earliest textbook on international law by a North American author[26] under the title of Introduction to the Study of International Law.[27] Although, as Neff notes, one could find instruction in international law 'at the newly founded university of Wisconsin, in 1852',[28] it was during the American Civil War (1861–1865), that Harvard Law School (in 1863) and Columbia Law School (in 1865) began to offer courses on international law under the magisterium of Francis Lieber. Althoug the American Civil War marked a turning point in the study of international law in the United States, the influential drive of the tradition of the American Christian peace movement for the establishment of mechanisms for the peaceful settlement of international disputes dates from the antebellum period. In line with the enlightened idealism of Abbée de

22 See further John M. Raymond and Barbara J. Frischholz, 'Lawyers who Established International Law in the United States, 1776–1914' The American Journal of International Law 76 (1982), 802–829, 827.

23 Henry Wheaton, Elements of International Law with a Sketch of the History of the Science (London: B. Fellowes, Ludgate Street 1836).

24 Henry Wheaton, Histoire du progrès du droit des gens en Europe, 1841.

25 Henry Wheaton, 'History of the Law of Nations in Europe and America from the Earliest Times to the Treaty of Washington' (New York: Gould Banks 1842).

26 Raymond/ Frischholz, 'Lawyers who Established International Law in the United States' 1982, 818.

27 Theodor D. Woolsey *Introduction to the Study of International Law* (1860).

28 Neff, Justice Among Nations 2014, 304.

Saint-Pierre, J.J. Rousseau, and Immanuel Kant, Benthamite ideals appeared ingrained, as Weston Janis has explained, in the 'pacifist' religious imagination in the works and pamphlets of a series of early supporters of the international court movement in the United States.[29] The U.S. Christian peace movement, which was rooted in the pacifist testimony of the Quakers[30] and other peace churches, was heralded by pacifists such as N. Worcester, the author of 'A Solemn Review of the Custom of War' in 1814, and W. Ladd, who wrote 'Essay on a Congress of Nations' in 1840. As Weston explains, Ladd himself became the President of the American Peace Society after the consolidation of the various peace societies throughout the country. Other peace activists and 'religious utopians who flourished between 1815 and 1860 in America'[31] include the figures of D.L. Dodge and E. Burritt.

The application of the utilitarian method to international law was paramount in the writings of authors such as F. Lieber. Spurred by the American Civil War, Lieber's efforts to codify the rules of law in armed conflict had binding effects on the U.S. Army,[32] and influenced domestic army manuals in several Western states, including Spain. After the American Civil War, Bentham's work continued to exert a great influence on the late-nineteenth-century penchant for the codification of what, in line with the positivist spirit of the times, was by then beginning to be known as the 'science of international law'.[33] In 1872, D. Dudley Field, an earlier champion of the codification of international law, published the 702 articles of his Draft Outlines of an International Code,[34] thus

29 See Marc Weston Janis, *Jeremy Bentham and the Fashioning of 'International Law,* 78 *American Journal of International Law* (1984) 405, 405. See also Marc Weston Janis, *The Quest for an Ethical International Law,* 109 *West Virginia Law Review* (2006–2007) 571.

30 In 1947 the Religious Society of Friends (Quakers) was, as a worldwide religious group, awarded the Nobel Peace Prize.

31 On the roots of peace movement in the United States, Marc Weston Janis, The American Tradition of International Law, Great Expectations, 1789—1914, (Oxford: Oxford University Press 2004), 72–91.

32 U.S. Adjutant-General's Office, General Order No 100: instructions for the government of armies of the United States in the field. prepared by Francis Lieber lld, and revised by a board of officers (1863)

33 See Marc Weston Janis, *America and the Law of Nations 1776–1939,* (Oxford: Oxford University Press 2010) 72 highlighting that 'the international courts of today are the offspring of nineteenth-century American utopians, religious enthusiasts by and large untrained in the law'.

34 David Dudley Field, *Draft Outlines of an International Code* (1872). That is soon after Johann Gaspar Bluntschli had published his influential code in 1868. See Johann Gaspar Bluntschli, *Das Moderne Volkerrecht* (1868) For a commentary, see Marc Weston Janis, The American Tradition of International Law 2010, 118–122.

joining parallel efforts privately made by European scholars like J. G. Bluntschli in 1868. American scholars readily joined the international codification project which took an early international professional associational turn in the 1870s. Working within the *Institut de droit international* and the International Law Association, North-American authors continued to contribute to and to influence subsequent early codification efforts of international norms.

Whereas Christian pacifist doctrine, and Benthamite ideals of 'common and equal utility of all nations' had inspired the emergence of the international codification project, these were soon to be complemented by the influence on international law of the very understanding of 'law as a science'. This began to go global in the mid-late nineteenth century,[35] by the time C. C. Langdell (1816–1926) was appointed as the first Dean of Harvard Law School (1870–1895). At the time, 'professional' legal education in the United States was still emerging in the footsteps of a tradition of university law lectures—from the first ones held in 1779 at The College of William and Mary to those taught by I. Parker as the holder of the inaugural Royall Professorship at Harvard. It was the slave owner's family money of the Royall family from which the 'first collegiate school of law'[36] in the U.S. developed uninterruptedly from 1817.[37] In 1829, Joseph Story (1779–1845), who served as Justice at the US' Supreme Court since 1811, laid the foundations of Harvard Law library. After his appointment as the 'Dane professor of Law', Story sold his own private legal collection to Harvard for a low price.[38] This added some hundred volumes to the 587 titles that the Law School library counted in the first 'unofficial' library catalogue that two students had prepared back in 1826.[39] The reputation of Story's Commentaries on the Constitution of the United States (1833), and its offering 'systematic legal instruction' at a time of a rapidly evolving spread of legal materials in the expanding North American Republic, helped Harvard Law School to become the first 'national' law school[40] in the United States by the mid 1840s. At the time, legal training in the United States was still dominated by a tradition of law office education, a legacy of the British legal system. This law

35 See, magisterially, Duncan Kennedy, 'Three Globalizations of Law and Legal Thought', in David Trubek/Alvaro Santos (Eds), *The New Law and Economic Development: A Critical Appraisal* (Cambridge: Cambridge University Press, 2006), 19.

36 Charles Warren, *History of the Harvard Law School and of Early Conditions in America* (1908) 371.

37 Id., 47.

38 Id., 89–90.

39 *The Centennial Story of the Harvard Law School, 1817–1917*, (1918) 88–89.

40 Id., 47–48.

apprenticeship training lay behind the popularity of the 'Everyman His Own Lawyer' type of book.[41] However, as Fisher recalls, the pragmatism of apprenticeship education, in which 'from the outset, practising law took precedence over theorizing about it'[42] had, however, already been somewhat tamed by a complementary process of self-education grounded on 'the treatise tradition, which did so much to shape law-office education, [and] also greatly influenced the substance and methods of instruction in early law schools'.[43]

When, in 1870, C. C. Langdell was appointed as the first Dean of Harvard Law School, law studies were still 'intended to supplement apprenticeship not to replace it.'[44] The need to address the 'perceived failure of the apprenticeship system to teach law as a system of interrelated principles', found a perfect ally in the pragmatic drive to '[extract] principles from an ever-expanding body of decisions' that accompanied the new scientific understanding of law that was to characterize American 'Classical Legal Thought'.[45] The development of Langdell's case method approach to legal instruction, which is still viewed as 'the central event in the history of American legal education'[46] was, furthermore, premised on the idea that the library was to become 'what the laboratory is to the chemist or the physicist and what the museum is to the naturalist'.[47] Under Langdell's impulse, the new focus on the library as the 'laboratory for the study of law' became a key component of 'the establishment and dissemination of the Harvard Model'.[48] This new orthodoxy in the study of anything but 'pure law' coincided with the establishment at Harvard Law School of what was to become the standard first-year curriculum for American law schools: contracts, property, tort, criminal law and civil procedure. The practical mindedness and non-theory-oriented nature of 'American legal thought and education during the formative period'[49] connected well with the Law School movement of the 1870s and 1880s. The success of the case method approach, spread by a circle of strictly-disciplined acolytes, converted other law schools during the 1880s and 1890s. When the American Bar Association (ABA) was founded in 1878,

41 See Fisher, *'Legal Theory and Legal Education'* 2008, 38.

42 Id., 37.

43 Id., 44.

44 Id., 50.

45 See Duncan Kennedy, *The Rise & Fall of Classical Legal Thought: With a New Preface by the Author, 'Thirty Years* Later' (Washington: Beard Books 2006).

46 Fisher, Legal Theory and Legal Education 2008, 38.

47 Id.

48 Id.

49 Fisher, Legal Theory and Legal Education 2008, 42.

one of its first subgroups was the Committee on Legal Education and Admission to the Bar.[50] By 1887, Harvard Law Review's first editorial was brazenly flagging as one of its primary goals 'to give, if possible, to all who are interested in the subject of legal education, some idea of what is done under the Harvard system of instruction'.[51] By the turn of the century, the case method formed a symbiotic relationship with the professionalization of law schools, which in 1900 became unionized in the Association of American Law Schools (AALS) under the presidency of J. Bradley Thayer, a Harvard Law School professor.

The success of Langdell's method of instruction, with the law library as its foundation stone, owed much, as we have seen, 'to the congruence of his ideas with the version of legal science prevailing in the late nineteenth century'.[52] The case-method approach was a development in American legal education inextricably connected to a conception of the study of law as a scientific endeavour. This scientific conception projected itself as a mental framework inducing principles from facts and deducing principles to rule the facts in which the aspiration was that the 'common law will work itself pure' in a gapless system that could thus achieve a deeper harmony between morals and the law. The new 'scientific' approach, which helped to manage the reins of the social and economic transformations through which U.S. society was traversing at the time,[53] was the child of the rise of positivism in law. This mid-late nineteenth-century orthodoxy, as D. Kennedy notes, of 'confidence in deduction as the central tool for legal reasoning and the ambition to unify the law by linking rules to a small set of central concepts or organizing principles'[54] as a mode of legal thought made possible 'a late nineteenth-century consensus of Classical Legal Thought'.[55]

---

50 Id., 49.

51 'Editorial', Harvard Law Review I (1887), 35.

52 Fisher, Legal Theory and Legal Education 2008, 43.

53 Duncan Kennedy has remarked that the scientific method acted as a social de-politicization factor, favoring a 'conception of law that appeared to transcend the old conflicting schools and to ally the profession with science against philosophical speculation and the crudities of democratic politics'. Kennedy, *The Rise and Fall of Classical Legal Thought* 1975, 15. For a socio-historical background, see further Eric R. Wolf, *Europe and the People Without History*, (Oakland: University of California Press 1982), 366.

54 David Kennedy, 'Lon L. Fuller', in David Kennedy and William W. Fisher III (eds) *The Canon of American Legal Thought* (Princeton: Princenton University Press, 2006), 209.

55 David Kennedy/ William Fisher III, Introduction, in David Kennedy and William W. Fisher III (eds) *The Canon of American Legal Thought* (Princeton: Princeton University Press 2006), 209.

Classical Legal Thought was in itself a product of the codification spirit which sprang from the eighteenth-century Germanic codifications of the modern period—a tendency that would later be crowned by the individual rational universalist pretensions of the French Civil Code of 1804. In several European states, the Civil Code acted as a catalyst for the development of national codifications. In others, such as the future Germany, however, the nationalistic rejection of it on liberation from the Napoleonic Empire was coloured by a powerful romantic zeitgeist leading to the opposition by the Savigny historical school of jurisprudence to a universalist codification. Although, according to the Savigny School, codification could per definitionem not capture the particularities of the *Volkgeist,* this, however, did not prevent the evolution of the highly conceptual jurisprudence of the Pandectists and their belief, as Glyn Watkin notes, that 'legal principles of general application were as discoverable as the laws of nature disclosed by science'.[56] The U.S. version of classical legal thought (CLT) flourished in a 'context of legal reception'[57] (or emulative importation—what modern legal comparativists call the diffusion of 'legal transplants by prestige')[58]—of foreign legal thought.

This phenomenon corresponded well with the position of the United States on the semi-periphery of the nineteenth-century world system. Indeed, as D. Kennedy has highlighted, the 'German model spread not just to France, but across Europe (both Western and Eastern), and across the channel, and to the United States and Latin America'.[59] The unique American original feature in this context was the extension 'to public law'[60] of this 'mode of legal consciousness that globalized between 1850 and 1914'.[61] The American reception of German Pandectism was favoured by Austin's founding of the English analytical school of jurisprudence.[62] However, the scientism of Classical Legal Thought, with its legal principles induced from an array of legal materials developed over centuries through judicial decisions with the premise of their internal coherence, was

56 Thomas Glyn Watkin, *A Historical Introduction to Modern Civil Law* (Aldershot: Ashgate 1999), 141.

57 Kennedy, 'Three Globalizations of Law' 2006, 24.

58 See Alan Watson, *Legal Transplants: An Approach to Comparative* Law (Athens: The University of Georgia Press 1974).

59 Kennedy, 'Three Globalizations of Law' 2006, 28.

60 Id., 25.

61 Id., 25.

62 Duncan Kennedy, 'Savigny's Family/Patrimony Distinction and its Place in the Global Genealogy of Classical Legal Thought', *American Journal of Comparative Law* 58 (2010) 811–842, 837.

thought to be betrayed by a system of instruction like a textbook which was not fitted to teaching the science but only its results. Instead, Langdell's scientific justification within the legalist paradigm of Classical Legal Thought for the case-method approach relied on the idea that 'law, considered as a science, consists of certain principles or doctrines; to have such mastery of these as to be able to apply them with constant facility and certainty to the ever-tangled skein of human affairs is what constitutes a true lawyer'.[63] This perspective took on a more professionally pragmatic formulation with James Barr Ames, the second Dean of Harvard Law School (1895–1910), who 'contended that the purpose of the case method was not to teach students the content of legal principles' (...) but 'to train them to think like lawyers'.[64] The practitioner's orientation in legal teaching was soon to find a natural ally in an emerging elite network of law firms serving corporate interests. When the United States definitively crossed the threshold of overseas imperialism, law firms were even more prone to extend their incipient global networks in close association with what was soon to become known as the foreign policy establishment.

In the 1870s and 1880s, coinciding with the establishment of the *Institut de droit international* and the International Law Association, the international legal field in the United States was, as its jurisprudential domestic counterpart, also being influenced by the development of the positivist method, an emerging progressive codification development, and the quest for clarification of the sources of the international legal order. In response to this scientific impulse, a new attention to national state practice, with attention to the US practice, had been initiated by John Cadwalader,[65] who produced a one-volume Digest of Published Opinions of the Attorneys-General, and of the Leading Decisions of the Federal Courts, with reference to International Law, Treaties and Kindred Subjects in 1877. This was followed by the three volumes of the Digest of International Law of the United States which by F. Wharton began publishing in 1886.[66]

The new conception of law as a science with a practical orientation also influenced the slow transformation of the study of international law as a university discipline in the United States with the first chairs being formally

---

63 Fisher, Legal Theory and Legal Education 2008, 60.

64 Fisher, *Legal Theory and Legal Education* 2008, 60.

65 John Lambert Cadwalader, Digest of the Published Opinions of the Attorneys General, and of the Leading Decisions of the Federal Courts with Reference to International Law, Treaties and Kindred Subjects (Washington: Government printing office, 1877).

66 Francis Wharton, A Digest of the International Law of the United States Taken from Documents Issued by Presidents and Secretaries of State, and from Decisions of Federal Courts and Opinions of Attorneys-General (3 volumes) (1886).

established in Columbia in 1891 and Harvard in 1897. The spread of a growing preference for the 'case method' as a method of legal instruction in the wake of its establishment at Harvard Law School under Langdell extended to new didactic methods for the study of international law. In 1886–1887, Freeman Snow offered the first case-method-based course in international law at Harvard Law School and, in 1893, he went to publish the first casebook on international law published in the U.S.[67] With this book, Snow attempted to fill the gap of what he perceived to be the only drawback of the case method as a system of instruction in international law vis-à-vis traditional lectures and textbooks. This, according to Snow, was the 'difficulty of finding the necessary materials in a convenient form'.[68] Inspired by the same perspective, Basset Moore's six volumes on International Arbitrations (1898)[69] are equally representative of the escalating attention in the United States to international legal practice by the time of the Spanish-American war. In the immediate post-1898 period of American imperial thrust, the detailed scientific positivistic attention to state practice inaugurated by Wharton's efforts[70] was continued in the eight volumes of the new American Digest of International Law edited in 1906 by John Bassett Moore.[71] Basset Moore was influenced by the parallel development of interest in international law practice in Europe. This is epitomized by the publication in London in 1899, with 4 editions until 1904, by W.E. Darby of 'International Arbitration'.[72] This was the outcome of a resolution adopted by the International Law Association in 1895 in view of the project for the establishment of a permanent court of arbitration by W.E. Darby, secretary of the Peace Society. The purpose of Darby's work was to present materials on "the literary, political, and diplomatic work done in connection with international

67 Id.

68 Freeman Snow, *Cases and Opinions on Internation*al Law with Notes and Syllabus, (Boston: The Boston book company, 1893), III.

69 John Basset Moore, *History and Digest of the International Arbitrations to which the United States has been a Party* (Washington: Government Print Office 1898).

70 Marc Weston Janis, 'The American Tradition of International Law' 2010, 124.

71 John Bassett Moore (ed) *A Digest of International Law as Embodied in Diplomatic Discussions, Treaties and Other International Agreements, International Awards, The Decisions of Municipal Courts And The Writings Of Jurists, And Especially In Documents Published And Unpublished, Issued By Presidents And Secretaries Of State Of The United States, The Opinions Of The Attorney's General And The Decisions Of The Courts, Federal And State* (Washington, D.C.: Govt. Printing Office 1906).

72 William Evans Darby, *International arbitration. International Tribunals. A collection of the various schemes which have been propounded; and of instances in the nineteenth century* (London: Peace Society, 1899).

arbitration during the past 300 years".[73] In France in 1905, De La Pradelle and Politis began "publishing a collection of arbitral opinions—the first series of international law case reports".[74] Other treatises on International Law by American authors included works such as the one that had been published by George Grafton Wilson and George Fox Tucker[75] in 1901 were to be republished with various additions and in re-editions over the following decades. These treatise-type works were complemented by a series of early specialized works on topics of direct interest to the realm of foreign policy management, like one on the treaty-making power of the United States by Charles Henry Butler in 1892.[76] Among Snow's students at Harvard Law School was James Brown Scott, whose own collection of international law cases published in 1902 would be one of dominant works in the field throughout North-America, knowing several editions, in the next decades.[77] James Brown Scott also became the animating spirit behind the foundation of the American Society of International Law in 1906. A development that was greatly influenced, as we shall now see, by the aftermath of the Spanish-American War of 1898.

### The Insular Cases. The Standard of Civilization and Universal Particularism

The political and judicial phases of the aftermath of the Spanish-American war took place at a time when the vaunted anti-colonialist and anti-imperialist moral fabric of the American identity was at stake. American leaders customarily boasted of the seminally principled anti-imperialist character of the American Declaration of Independence of 1776 in a nation which still prided itself on having become self-constituted through a successful anti-colonial struggle.

The ensuing political Gordian knot was cut by the U.S. Senate's ratification by a narrow margin of the 1899 Peace Treaty of Paris and by the fact that the 1900 presidential elections went on to confirm the popular support

---

73 Darby *International Arbitration*, 1899.

74 A De la Pradelle, N. Politis, Recueil des arbitrages internationaux, vol. I, Les editions internationales, Paris, 1905.

75 George Grafton Wilson & George Fox Tucker, *International Law* (1901).

76 Charles H. Butler, *The Treaty-Making Power of the United States* (1902).

77 James Brown Scott, *Cases on International Law: Selected from Decisions of English and American* Courts (St. Paul: West Publishing Company, 1906). It was dedicated to the memory of Freeman Snow because the book had begun as 'a revision of the late Dr. Snow's (1893) Cases and Opinions on International Law.'

for the Republican government of President McKinley with a greater margin than in 1896. However, if the rise of popular nationalism triggered by the successful outcome of the war had swiftly solved the political dilemma, the solution to the legal dilemma required a technical answer to the question of the 'right to acquire territory and the status of the territory once acquired'.[78]

This was an old question that had often preoccupied the Supreme Court throughout the course of the U.S.'s continental expansion in the nineteenth century. However, the overseas nature of the new possessions in the Caribbean and the Pacific Ocean, and the different cultural, linguistic and racial characteristics of their inhabitants—who, this time, could not be simply swept away—gave a new twist to the old question. It was for the Fuller Court,[79] on the occasion of what came to be known as the Insular Cases,[80] to decide, as the popularized version of the juridical dilemma read, whether the 'constitution should (or should not) follow the flag'.

Lurking beneath the popularized version of the legal dilemma lay the much narrower technical question of whether the Congress could impose a tariff on the commerce between the mainland and the former Spanish colonial islands. The matter was intrinsically connected with the Supreme Court's development of a constitutional doctrine to respond to the continental aggrandizement of the U.S. territory during the nineteenth century. Given the silence of the Constitution on the matter, debates had traditionally revolved around the 'congressional interpretation of the power of Congress with respect to territories'.[81] A series of cases, such as those dealing with the

78 James Edward Kerr, *The Insular Cases. The Role of the Judiciary in American Expansionism* (Port Washington, N.Y.: Kennikat Press 1982), 15.

79 An examination of the insular cases from the perspective of those sitting on the U.S. Supreme Court bench can be found at Willlard L. King, *Melville Weston Fuller, Chief Justice of the United States 1888–1910* (New York: The MacMillan Company 1950), 262–277.

80 *The Insular Cases* is a denomination by which is primarily understood the series of cases submitted to the Court in 1900 and judged in early 1901. Other cases that are generally included in this category dealing with the status of the newly acquired overseas possessions were submitted between 1903 and 1905 and another dozen cases decided over a 20-year period would further test the 1901 rulings. Perhaps the two most significant cases argued were those of DeLima v. Bidwell and Downes V. Bidwell. Cases: De Lima v. Bidwell, (1901) Goetze v. United States, (1901) Armstrong v. United States, (1901) Downes v. Bidwell, (1901) Huus v. New York & Porto Rico S.S. Co., (1901) Dooley v. United States, (1901) Fourteen Diamond Rings v. United States, (1901) Hawaii v. Mankichi, (1903) Kepner v. United States, (1904) Dorr v. United States,(1904) Rasmussen v. United States, (1905) Dowdell v. United States, (1911) Ocampo v. United States, (1914) Balzac v. Puerto Rico, (1922).

81 Kerr, *The Insular Cases* 1982, 5.

annexation by the treaty of Louisiana (1803) and Florida (1819), and the annexation by joint resolution of Texas in 1845, had resulted in an amalgam of determined and undetermined issues concerning territoriality in the case law of the Supreme Court. In 1901, they arose again in a new light. More importantly, the Insular Cases offered the Court its first opportunity to examine fundamental questions regarding the Constitution's 'geographic scope'. While there had until then been 'little need to explore the outer boundaries of the Constitution's geographic reach'[82] for the Supreme Court, the decision by Congress to discontinue its previous practice of extending constitutional rights to the new territories by statute for the first time confronted it with the question of 'whether the Constitution, by its own force, applies in any territory that is not a state'.[83]

Opposite ideological and political positions became embedded in the technical legal perspectives that were crafted to find a solution to the juridical dilemma. The balance finally struck between opposite perspective put in place a new and lasting set of legal arrangements regarding the status of the new overseas possessions and their relationship to the United States. The 'doctrine of territorial incorporation' inaugurated by the Insular Cases differentiated between the application of the Constitution to incorporated territories destined for statehood—where it applied in full—and to unincorporated territories—where it only applied in part.[84] At the turn of the twentieth century, the issue of the Constitution's extraterritorial application fitted, as Kerr notes, within the 'rationalization of colonialism as being a first step' (along what was, nonetheless, going to prove to be a very long road) 'towards self-government'.[85] This approach, which gained, as we shall later see, the seal of approval of the League of Nations for the whole of the mandates system, also allowed a transposition of the legal-colonial scaffolding of the British Empire's model of 'parliamentary imperial sovereignty'[86] to the Philippines. It left the legal status

82 Id.

83 Id.

84 By this token, the Insular cases became a link in the chain of what would in time become a 'functional approach' to 'the selective application of constitutional limitations to the U.S. government outside its sovereign territory'. The Supreme Court referred to the Insular Cases in the recent Guantanamo case: Boumediene v Bush 128 S. Ct. 2229 (2008) See Gerald Neuman, 'The Extraterritorial Constitution After Boumediene v. Bush', *Southern California Law Review* 82 (2009) 259.

85 Kerr, *The Insular Cases* 1982, 112.

86 The Philippine only became a fully independent state in 1946. See A. V. Dicey, *Introduction to the Study of the Law of the Constitution* (1915), 101. See his analysis of the Colonial Laws Validity Act of 1865.

of Guam and Puerto Rico as that of 'an unincorporated territory of the United States.'[87]

During the early 1900s, the new American imperial drive was realized through the gradual enforcement of an 'open door policy' in the Far East and by means of active participation in the Caribbean and Latin America affairs under the cloak of a revamped 'Monroe doctrine'. The latter, which had initially aimed at limiting Europe's intervention in the U.S.'s Latin American backyard at the time of the restoration of Fernando VII's absolutist rule in Spain, was completed by the self-proclaimed right of the United States, enshrined in the Roosevelt Corollary to the Monroe doctrine in 1904, to intervene in Latin America in cases of 'flagrant and chronic wrongdoing by a Latin American Nation'.

Once 'the traditional U.S. idea that colonialism was inconsistent with U.S. legal and moral values'[88] was left aside with the legal imprimatur of the U.S. Supreme Court in the insular cases, a new generation was now ready to emerge around the American Society of International Law. This generation entered a world characterized by the heyday of positivism, in which semi-peripheral countries such as Japan, Turkey and—following in their footsteps but still constituting, a semi-civilized category– China, Persia, Siam, Korea, and Abyssinia were still perceived to be climbing up the ladder of the 'standard of civilization'.[89]

Barely a couple of decades before in 1883, Japan and Turkey had been classified as belonging to 'barbarous humanity' in the influential classification penned by the Scottish J. Lorimer.[90] According to Lorimer, 'humanity is divided into three zones or concentric zones: civilized humanity, barbarous humanity, and savage humanity.'[91] The first sphere included Europe and its colonies

---

87 This status remains up to the present day. 'Unincorporated territory' is a legal term of art in United States law denoting an area controlled by the government of the U.S. 'where fundamental rights apply as a matter of law, but other constitutional rights are not available'. See, e.g. U.S. Insular Areas Application of the U.S. Constitution, United States General Accounting Office, Report to the Chairman, Committee on Resources, House of Representatives, (1997), 24.

88 Yves Dezalay / Bryant G. Garth, *Law, Lawyers and Empire*, in Michael Grossberg / Christopher L. Tomlins (eds), *Cambridge History of Law in America. The Twentieth Century and After (1920–)* (Cambridge: Cambridge University Press 2011) 718, 724.

89 Gong, *The Standard of Civilization and the international Society* 1984, 70.

90 See i.e. Martti Koskenniemi, 'Race, Hierarchy and International Law: Lorimer's Legal Science' *European Journal of International Law* 27 (2016) 415–429.

91 James Lorimer, *The Institutes of the Law of Nations: a Treatise of the Jural Relations of Separate Political Communities*. (Edinburgh & London: William Blackwood & Sons, 1883).

(or former colonies) in America—including the United States and the Latin American Republics; the second sphere was composed of Turkey, Persia, China, Siam and Japan; and the remaining one comprised the rest of humanity. This crude tripartite classification mirrors the influx of the apogee of the doctrine of the 'standard of civilization' at the height of the imperial age. The 'standard of civilization' worked as a yardstick for granting access to the 'family of nations', understood, according to Oppenheim, as those able to 'understand and carry out the command of the rules of international law.'[92]

The rise of the 'standard of civilization' throughout the nineteenth century was both consonant with a law, as Schwarzenberger notes, 'congenial to the needs of industrial pioneer and the capitalist investor'[93] and with a fully-fledged absolute external sovereignty of the European nations, some of which, such as Germany and Italy, had just culminated their nineteenth-century processes of national unification. The relationship between Christianity and international law had by then already known a long process of secularization—which marked the transition from 'classical ius-naturalism' to 'rationalist ius-naturalism' in the seventeenth and eighteenth centuries. Whereas the upswing of the 'standard of civilization' coincided with a stage of positivist undermining of rationalist ius-naturalism, the deepening of the secularization of international law that the scientism of positivism in the mid-late nineteenth century might seem to indicate should, nonetheless, be seen in relative terms.

On the one hand, the Western Christian origins watermark of international law was put at the service of European nation-building processes and was intellectually hammered by the first historians of international law. On the other hand, a religiously underpinned moral and cultural sense of superiority also accompanied the graduated expansion of international law's 'mission civilisatrice', or civilizing mission, vis-à-vis other religions, regions, and cultures. In the period of transition from the informal empire to the formal empire which Koskenniemi referred to as one in which 'the early international lawyers were liberals who supported the turn to formal empire to protect the natives from the greed of colonial companies and ensure the orderly progress of the civilizing mission,'[94] the 'standard of civilization' practically helped

92 Lassa Oppenheim, *International Law* (London, New York: Longmans, Green, and co. 1905) 16 quoted in Becker Lorca, *Mestizo International Law* 2015, 35.

93 Schwarzenberger, 'The Standard of Civilization in International Law' 1955, 220.

94 Koskenniemi, 'Empire and International Law' 2011.

to deny 'sovereign legal equality'—either partially or completely—to non-European peoples.

The 'standard of civilization' was provided with internal and external facets. Externally, it acted as the benchmark for membership in the enjoyment of the attributes that derive from the acquisition of legal personality by sovereign states as the main subjects of an international legal order commanded to rule over an expanding international society. The application of the standard of civilization responded to a criterion of respect for the rules of 'European' international law and 'civilized behaviour'—criteria which, it hardly needs stressing, always came second to the interests of the territorially expanding Western imperial powers.[95] With its complementary internal facet, a lesser or greater conformity with the standard of civilization depended, in practice, on a greater or lesser degree of adaptation by the 'other' to institutions designed to guarantee the protection of life and property, as well as the preservation of Western interests in non-Western societies.

Elihu Root (1845–1937), President of the Carnegie Endowment until 1925 and previously U.S. Secretary of War (1899–1904) and U.S. Secretary of State (1904–1909) under Republican presidencies, wrote unambiguously in the American Journal of International Law in 1910 that all countries were obliged to foreign citizens by 'an established standard of civilization' and that the latter was 'a standard of justice, very simple, very fundamental, and of such general acceptance by all civilized countries as to form a part of the international law of the world.'[96] Some have considered this extra-territorial 'internal facet' of the standard of civilization to be revealing of how 'general concepts of human rights began to take root in international legal thought in this period'—the early 1900s—'in a more or less explicit way'.[97] In practice, however, the effective application of the standard of civilization, with the correlated correction of the principle of sovereign equality among members of the Concert of Europe, and its withholding, or a graduated concession of recognition of international legal personality to external members, was adapted to the many variable techniques of colonization used by the imperial powers during the mid-late nineteenth century.

---

95 Arnulf Becker Lorca, 'Universal International Law: Nineteenth-Century Histories of Imposition and Appropriation', *Harvard International Law Journal* 51, (2010) 475–552, 499.

96 Neff, *Justice among Nations* 2014, 273 quoting Elihu Root, 'The Basis of Protection to Citizens Residing Abroad', *American Journal of International Law* 4 (1910) 517–528, 521.

97 Neff, *Justice among Nations* 2014, 273

The standard of civilization can be seen lurking beneath the assimilation, after conquest or cession, of territories, which became controlled by a colonial scheme in which the legal relationships were characterized as issues pertaining to the domestic sphere of the metropolis. On other occasions, the standard of civilization appears to underlie fictions of dependent sovereignty in conformity to which non-Western territories and peoples maintained their sovereignty over their domestic affairs while the metropolis managed their international relations. Other than through its application to the different types of protectorates and colonial formulae, the standard of civilization reappears as a conceptual axis of reference after the celebration of unequal treaties (including the exigencies of 'hinterland', special port treaties, the founding of mixed tribunals and consular jurisdiction) among the European powers and states in the semi-periphery with a far lesser degree of industrial development and military muscle. These systems of capitulation[98] were employed as catalysts of reforms oriented to fostering a degree of economic and legal harmonization that provided a series of extraterritorial jurisdictional rights to Western powers for the safeguard of the commercial interests of Western companies.

However, the economic and legal harmonization channelled through the standard of civilization by international law mainly took place on the planes of the relationship between the foreign national and the non-Western state, the non-Western state and the market, the non-Western state and the non-Western state, and the non-Western state and the international society.[99] At this stage of the evolution of international law, the projection of the standard of civilization did not (per se) affect the specific form of government of the non-Western state or its relationship with its own nationals.[100]

Although for influential authors like L. Oppenheim, writing in 1905, it was still clear that new members of the 'family of nations' are 'not born into that

98 David P. Fidler, 'The Return of the Standard of Civilization', *Chicago Journal of International Law* 2 (2001) 137–157, 143.

99 Gong, *The Standard of Civilization and the international Society* 1984, 14–15.

100 Indeed, what post-colonial critical scholarship has critically interpreted as the new 'standard of civilization' based on what they term the external imposition democratic forms of government, respect for human rights and open-markets channeled by the norms of international law had to wait to find its ultimate expression to the last decade of the twentieth century. However, it is on the basis of this historical narrative, that Anghie suggests that 'international law is fundamentally animated by the civilizing mission that is an inherent aspect of imperial expansion which, from time immemorial, has presented itself as improving the lives of conquered peoples'. Antony Anghie, 'On Critique and the Other', in Anne Orford (ed.), *International Law and Its Others* (Cambridge: Cambridge University Press 2009), 389–400, 384.

international community' but 'admitted into it through recognition,'[101] by the early twentieth century the standard of civilization was already being partially eroded. This erosion can be attributed to the fact that the late-nineteenth century witnessed the gradual strategic appropriation of 'Westphalian civilization'[102] by semi-peripheral international lawyers whose positions, in the representation of their respective states, became more audible in the first multilateral conferences held at The Hague in 1899 and 1907. This appropriation had begun in the wake of the independence of the Latin American Republics. It continued, as we saw in Chapter One, throughout the nineteenth century as North and Latin American international lawyers embraced the study of international law as part of their nation-building processes. According to Becker Lorca, this cultivation contributed to the formation of a 'distinctive semi-peripheral legal consciousness' of 'Western international legal thought', which was to play a major role, in the 'transformation of the doctrinal structure of international law'.[103]

As previously non-Westernised states joined the wave of appropriation, they contributed throughout the first third of the twentieth century against the background, as we shall see in Chapter 3, provided by the League of Nations to the gradual universalization of international law. The 'particularist universalism'[104] of international law reflects the different doctrinal mutations of international law as the outcomes of the diplomatic, practical and intellectual engagement of semi-peripheral diplomatic elites. This engagement was, in itself, a mirror of the relative power of semi-peripheral states and, therefore, of a perceived need to perfect the retailoring of norms, rules, and doctrines to serve their own 'national interests' by trying to limit the dominance of Western powers through the language of international law.[105]

In the Latin American case, as Obregon Tarazona highlights, the appropriation of the civilizing discourse, and of 'its distinctive understanding of civilization and its attributes, were associated with attempts to articulate

101 Lassa Oppenheim, *International Law* 1905, 16.

102 Fidler, 'The Return of the Standard of Civilization' 2001, 138.

103 Lorca Becker, *Mestizo International Law* 2015, 44.

104 See e.g. Becker Lorca, 'Universal International Law' (2010). See also Gustavo Gozzi 'The Particularistic Universalism of International Law in the Nineteenth Century' *Harvard International Law Journal—online* 52 (2010) 73–86 and Umut Ozsu, 'Agency, Universality, and the Politics of International Legal *History' Harvard International Law Journal—online* 52 (2010), 58–72.

105 Lorca Becker, *Mestizo International Law* 2015, 45.

specific Latin American conceptions of international law'[106] such as in the case of A. Alvarez.[107] The process of engagement and appropriation of international law by other previously non-Europeanized territories was not carried out in terms of a self-reinforcing re-integration into a common Euro-American Western civilization, but in more distinct terms, as a way to gradually overcome a more clearly defined, and racially underpinned, graduated standard of civilization.[108]

The mid-late nineteenth century standard of civilization, which established the 'legal-political categories of colonial domination and imperialism,'[109] was also echoed in Spanish publications. In the 1900 edition of 'Tratado Elemental de Derecho Internacional Público' by the Marquis de Olivart, the tripartite classification adopted a form undergirded in its Spanish reception by natural law caveats:

1. Civilized humanity—Complete legal recognition—All cultivated states from Europe, America, and Africa, Turkey, Japan. Full validity and observance of international law.
2. Barbarous humanity—Partial recognition—No civilized nations of Asia and Africa, China, Persia, Morocco etc. Observance of natural law and positive law in reciprocal terms and in accordance with which is explicitly stated in the treaties.
3. Bare humanity—No recognition. Savage peoples of Africa and Asia. Strict application of the principles of natural law.[110]

---

106 Obregon Tarazona, 'Completing Civilization: Creole Consciousness and International Law in Nineteenth-Century Latin America' in Anne Orford (ed.), *International Law and Its Others* (Cambridge: Cambridge University Press 2008), 247–264, 248.

107 Both phenomena contributed, nonetheless, to the 'New International Law' preconized by Alejandro Alvarez which in the interwar years became a precursor of similar positions to those later adopted by the panoply of predominantly African and Asian states that emerged during the decolonization period in the 1950s and 1960s, Alejandro Alvarez, Le droit international américain (1910).

108 Alejandro Alvarez, 'The New International Law', *Transactions of The Grotius Society* 15 (1929), 35–51.

109 Antonio Remiro Brotons, *Civilizados, barbaros y salvajes en el nuevo orden internacional* (Madrid: McGraw-Hill 1996), 136.

110 Ramón Dalmau de Olivart, *Tratado elemental de Derecho Internacional Público. Segunda edición con un apendice del autor sobre el estado de la ciencia* (Madrid: Impr. Los hijos de R. Álvarez, 1900).

## Education and Spanish International Lawyers—The 'Institutionist' Creed

After the Spanish-American War of 1898, Spanish philosophers and thinkers busied themselves with the 'Spanish problem' making it evolve into a deeply psychologically-rooted national cultural and ideological phenomenon. This Novecento-like preoccupation contributed to a renewed interest in international law at a time when education reforms were underway, a gradual modernization of the universities was slowly taking place, and Europeanization began to mean a greater engagement with the intellectual and cultural trends dominant in the continent. This reformist era went hand in hand, as we shall see, with a movement towards the study of 'international questions with practical repercussions'[111] which in the wake of a new Spanish colonial policy.

At the turn of the century, an important driver of the Spanish engagement with modern international legal studies were works by several scholars affiliated to the Institución Libre de Enseñanza, also known as the 'institutionists'. One of them, Aniceto Sela y Sampil (1863–1935), was the holder of one of the 458 chairs that existed in what R. Macías Picavea in a regenerationist critical vein had called 'esa cosa muerta por dentro' ('that thing dead inside') when referring to the Spanish university.[112] Following the Royal Decree of 2 September 1883, which, as seen in Chapter 1, broke the exclusivity of the Central University of Madrid by establishing chairs in 'Public International Law' and 'Private International Law' in seven other Spanish universities, Sela was appointed catedrático of public and private international law at the University of Valencia in 1888. In 1891, he became a professor of international law at the University of Oviedo.

In Oviedo, Sela y Sampil joined the so-called 'Group of Oviedo', often considered the 'epicenter of Spanish legal Krausism'.[113] Two other distinguished international legal scholars of the first Spanish professional generation, Joaquín Fernández Prida (1865–1942), and Rafael Altamira Crevea (1866–1951), a remarkable historian who went, as we shall see in Chapter Three, to serve as the Spanish judge at the Permanent Court of International Justice from its

111 Fernández Rozas/Andrés Sáenz de Santa María, 'La aportación de la Facultad de Derecho de la Universidad de Oviedo' 2010, 518.

112 Ricardo Macias Picavea, *El problema nacional Hechos, causas y remedios* (Madrid: Biblioteca Nueva 1899).

113 Fernández Rozas/ Andrés Sáenz de Santa María, 'La aportación de la Facultad de Derecho de la Universidad de Oviedo' 2010, 519.

inception in 1921, were also members of the 'Group of Oviedo'. Krausism was by then a highly influential cultural and pedagogical secular movement. It had arisen in Spain in the second half of the nineteenth century and owed its name to an obscure German thinker, K. Ch. F. Krause—a follower of Hegelian idealism whose thought had been interpreted and adapted to the Spanish milieu in the form of a public moral engagement with social reformism through education by Julián Sanz del Río (1814–1869).

The movement's most representative intellectual figure in Spain was Francisco Giner de los Ríos (1839–1915) who had been appointed to the chair of philosophy of law and international law in the programme of doctoral studies at the Central University in 1867. Together with several other catedráticos, such as Gumersindo de Azcarate and Nicolas Salmeron, Giner de los Ríos was expelled from the Central University for his defence of the principle of academic freedom and his refusal to adapt his university teachings to official dogmas. These concerned religion, politics (where no explanation should have the effect of 'putting in question the person of the king or the monarchical constitutional regime') and morals as mandated by a restrictive Ministerial decree—known as the Orovio decree—of 1875. This group, which received the solidarity of progressive scholars and politicians such as Rafael Maria de Labra, co-founded, as we saw in the first chapter, the Institución Libre de Enseñanza (ILE) in 1876 at the dawn of the Bourbon Restoration.[114]

From 1898, under the impulse of Sela y Sampil and other committed 'institutionists',[115] the University of Oviedo pioneered the provision of university extension courses in Spain. University extension became one of the main emblems of the regenerationist movement, and understandably so. At the turn of the century, in the Spanish population of 18.6 million there were only around 16,000 students registered at the ten existing Spanish universities. Fewer than two thousand university degrees were awarded in 1900—more than half of them in law. The only university authorized to award doctoral titles was the Central University of Madrid—a centralist privilege it had kept since the Plan Pidal centralized and standardised doctoral studies in 1845. It granted barely two hundred of them in 1900. With a Spanish illiteracy rate at 64%,[116] access by women to university education was, moreover, almost negligible. Whereas a Royal Order of June 1888 had allowed women's attendance at university only

114 The bibliography on both Krausism and the ILE is extremely extensive, see, introductorily, Elías Díaz, *La filosofía social del krausismo español*, (Madrid: Edicusa 1973).

115 Such as Rafael de Altamira who later became the first Director General of Primary Education in Spain.

116 Liebana Collado, La educación en España en el primer tercio del siglo XX 2009, 5.

as private students, only in 1910 a decree by the Council of Ministers authorised their enrolment as official students.[117] The influence of the regenerationist creed, which posited education as the instrument to renew Spanish social and political structures, led to important educational and university reforms in the first decade of the 1900s. These included the creation of the Ministry of Public Instruction and Arts in 1900 and the upgrading of teachers to the position of public civil servants in 1901.

As part of his engagement with education methods and university reform, in the Official Bulletin of the Institución Libre de Enseñanza (ILE) in 1902, Sela published a chronicle about the didactic methods employed in teaching Public International Law and Private International Law at the University of Oviedo:[118]

'In public international law, I have predominantly attempted to assist the development of the intelligence and the skills of students by often transforming the classroom in a true exercise of thought and by relating the special topic of this teaching to natural law, political law, geography and history [...] The subject matter allows, as very few others do, the implementation of this procedure. The indeterminacy and vagueness of the positive law of peoples, its undoubted delay compared to other legal branches, the need to overcome through vigorous efforts of the mind the sadness and pessimism of the present state of international politics [...] There is no code to be chained to, obliging us to follow the exegetic procedure, no writer whose authority cannot be discussed or rules consecrated by use that do not admit modification: nothing which interferes with the free flight of intelligence'.[119]

117 Only 8 women received university doctorates between 1878, when Dolores Aleu and Martina Castells obtained a doctoral degree in Medicine, and 1910. In 1922 a Spanish woman gained the first university degree in law; still another six years had to pass for the first doctorate in laws to be awarded in Spain to Carmen Cuesta in 1928. With the only exception of *Ensayo sobre el Derecho de gentes* written in 1876 by Concepción del Arenal (1820–1893) who had attended as an auditor disguised as man in the mid-1840s the law school of Madrid, international legal studies in Spain—with the only relative exception of the period of the Second Spanish Republic (1931–1936)—mirrored this profound gender gap until the last quarter of the 20th century.

118 Julio González Campos/ Roberto Mesa Garrido/ Enrique Pecourt García, 'Notas para la historia del pensamiento internacionalista español: Aniceto Sela y Sampil (1863–1935)', *Revista Española de Derecho Internacional* XVII, (1964), 561–583.

119 Aniceto Sela y Sampil, 'Los procedimientos de enseñanza en la Facultad de Derecho internacional de la Universidad de Oviedo: Derecho in internacional Público y Derecho Internacional Privado', *Boletín Oficial de la Institución Libre de Enseñanza XXVI* (1902), 223–234, 223.

Sela went on to explain a classic weekly programme at the turn of the twentieth century:

'[...] On Wednesdays, we study contemporary history and especially the history of international relations in an elementary manner as obliged by the scarce preparation of the students; with maps in sight, tracing general frameworks which are later on filled in by selected readings from good historians [...] On Fridays, we focus on positivist developments in international law [...] this year, we have devoted the first part of the course to the study of the first Hague conference of 1899 [...] the Brussels declaration of 1874, the Saint Petersburg conference of 1868, the Treaty of Geneva of 1868, the Paris Declaration of 16th April 1856, the instructions for the campaign service of the army of the United States'.[120]

Sela's *avant-la-lettre* attention to the didactic methods employed in an international law classroom at the turn of the twentieth century reflects the practical influence of ILE in fostering an emerging Europeanizing and reformist thought in the scientific and cultural life of Spain. One of the major outcomes of this cultural and scientific reformist trend was the establishment of the Junta de Ampliación de Estudios e investigación científica (Board of Extension of Studies and Scientific Research, known as the JAE) in 1907. Under the presidency of S. Ramon y Cajal (1852–1934), a histologist who had won the first Spanish Nobel Prize for Medicine, the JAE aimed to nurture a more engaged integration of Spanish scientists and scholars in European intellectual and scientific research trends. The JAE integrated it within the structure of the recently-created Ministry of Public Instruction and Arts, building on a previous provision for scholarships that in 1901[121] and 1903[122] allowed the best students and professors to complete their studies in foreign countries.

The JAE was one of the several similar institutional enterprises established in European countries oriented towards fostering the internationalization of

120 Id., 225.

121 Real decreto relativo a la concesión de pensiones para ampliar sus estudios en el extranjero a los alumnos que hayan dado mayores pruebas de capacidad y aprovechamiento, de 18 de julio de 1901. Gaceta de Madrid del sábado 20 de julio de 1901, ano CCXL, n 201, tomo III, 295–296 quoted in Carlos Espaliu Berdud, La junta de ampliación de estudios e investigaciones científicas y el derecho internacional in Yolanda Gamarra/Ignacio de la Rasilla (eds) *Historia del pensamiento internacionalista español del siglo XX* (Cizur Menor: Thomson Reuters Aranzadi 2012), 153–184, 159.

122 Real decreto referente a la concesión de subvenciones al profesorado, y pensiones a los alumnos y a los obreros alumnos de todos los centros de enseñanza oficial dependientes del ministerio de Instrucción publica, para ampliación de estudios en el extranjero, de 8 de mayo de 1903. Vease Gaceta de Madrid del 9 de mayo de 1903, n 129, 501–502 quoted in Espaliu, 'La junta de ampliación de estudios' 2012, 159.

science as a remedy for the scientific, cultural and educational stagnation that ensued from a lack of exchanges and contacts. Similar national research institutions included, as Espaliu Berdud notes, the Caises de Recherches Scientifiques in France in 1903; the Kaiser-Willhelm-Gesellschaft, established in Germany in 1911, and the Comitato Nazionale Scientifico Tecnico per lo Sviluppo e l'Incremento dell'Industria italiana established in Italy in 1916.[123]

In Spain, the legislative provision that established JAE was very much inspired by the Krausism of the Institution of Free Teaching (1876–1936) and the work of Giner de los Rios for its guiding principles.[124] It highlighted the need to foster the Europeanization of Spanish universities and science because 'a people that isolate itself will come to a halt and disintegrate; that is why all civilized countries are part of a movement of international scientific relations'.[125] JAE developed a series of research promotion activities, including the founding of research centres in different disciplines and the establishment in Madrid in 1910 of the famous Residencia de Estudiantes,[126] where some of the most illustrious figures of the so-called Age of Silver of Spanish culture, such as Federico García Lorca, Salvador Dali and Luis Buñuel, went to study. Between 1907 and 1938, the JAE awarded 3604 scholarships to extend studies in foreign countries, around 111 for the extension of studies in Spain, and some 747 certificates of equivalence of foreign research stays.[127] It is estimated that around 10% (circa 212) of the scholarships benefitted legal scholars. Among these, one finds the names of key figures in Spanish politics in the first half of the century such as the President of the Second Republic, Manuel Azaña, and Jimenez de Asua, President of the Commission of the Cortes which drafted the 1931 Spanish Constitution and became the Spanish representative at the League of Nations.

The JAE also supported the formative years of some of the most prominent and influential members of the second and third 'professional' generations of international law scholars,[128] and of other legal scholars who shaped

123 Espaliu, 'La junta de ampliación de estudios' 2012, 160.

124 Francisco Giner de los Rios, *Escritos sobre la Universidad española* (Madrid: S.L.U. Espasa Libros 1990).

125 Vid gaceta de Madrid del martes 15 de enero de 1907, ano CCXLVI, n 15, tomo 1, p. 165 quoted in Espaliu, 'La junta de ampliación de estudios' 2012, 159.

126 See bibliographical reference Espaliu, 'La junta de ampliación de estudios' 2012, 162.

127 New detailed digitalized archives can be found at Residencia de Estudiantes, Archivo de la JAE (accessible at http://www.residencia.csic.es/100digital/jae/index.htm).

128 The database indicates 19 scholarships were specifically granted for research in international law for details on grant-holders including particular reports and documentation, see: http://archivojae.edaddeplata.org/jae_app/ (accessed 20 September 2016).

the discipline of international law in Spain during the interwar period. As we shall encounter in Chapters Three, Four, and Five these included Camilo Barcia Trelles, to whom Carl Schmitt attributed the honour of providing 'the strongest breakthrough for the world at large'[129] regarding Francisco de Vitoria; José Yanguas Messia, who, among many other positions such as Minister of Foreign Affairs in the mid-20s, served as the first—and so far the only—Spanish President of the Institut de Droit International; Fernando Maria Castiella, who was to become the longest-serving Spanish Minister of Foreign Affairs in the twentieth century; Adolfo Miaja de la Muela, the youngest 'catedrático' in international law in the history of the twentieth-century Spain, and Antonio de Luna, one of the co-founders of Revista Española de Derecho Internacional and the first Spanish member of the International Law Commission. All of these, and others, many of whom developed their careers in the Spanish Foreign Service, benefited from research stays in international law in foreign countries. Along with them, other relevant figures in the history of international law in Spain in the first part of the twentieth century also benefitted from the opportunities granted by JAE. These included inter alia Rafael Altamira, Spanish judge at the Permanent Court of International Justice (1919–1940), or Quintiliano Saldaña, a Spanish pioneer of international criminal justice in his course on 'La Justice Pénale Internationale' at The Hague Academy in 1925.

The academic production of general treatises on international law in Spanish before the First World War followed in the footsteps of successive and augmented editions of works produced in the 1890s by the first chair-holders in international law of the first professional generation. These included augmented re-editions of the general treatises by Fernandez Prida, Gestoso Acosta in 1907–1908, Trias y Giro (1905) and the Marquis of Olivart (1903–1904). A more clearly-defined colonial policy orientation and extended interest in Spanish foreign policy also fostered a series of research monographs during the first decade of the twentieth century. These included works of the history of Spanish international relations during the nineteenth century, such as those by Jeronimo Becker Gonzalez, who wrote 'España y Marruecos: sus relaciones diplomaticas durante el siglo XIX' (1903), 'España -Inglaterra: sus relaciones politicas desde las paces de Utrecht (1907) and Relaciones Diplomaticas entre España y la Santa Sede durante el siglo XIX' (1909). To the area of diplomatic history, one should add publications in specialized areas such as consular and

129 Carl Schmitt, *The Nomos of the Earth* 2003, 124.

diplomatic relations[130] and, in particular, the law of the sea.[131] Following in the footsteps of earlier works that had emerged, as we saw in Chapter One, in the wake of the Paris 'Declaration on Respecting Maritime Law in Times of War' of 1856, and more recent late-nineteenth-century works, such as 'Tratado de gentes y maritimo internacional' by M. Mozo of 1898, new books appeared that paid a more detailed attention to Spanish practice regarding the law of the sea. These included works such as the 'Derecho maritimo internacional español' published by Carlos Nunez de Prado in 1913,[132] monographs on specific issues such as territorial waters[133] by M. Rodriguez in 1905, neutrality in maritime war[134] by G. Maura Gamazo in 1910, and the so-called right of shipwreck, in 1911, by J. Fernández Novoa.[135]

New international areas, such as aerial space in international law,[136] and the study of the development of peaceful means of dispute,[137] which was the object of the First Hague Convention, were added to the attention given to codifying developments in the laws of war at The Hague Conferences. The Hague Conventions were mirrored in two editions (1906 and 1910) of 'Manual de Derecho internacional para uso de Jefes y Oficiales del Ejército y Armada' (Textbook on international law for use by army and navy chiefs and officers)[138] by Manuel Conrotte. A further pole for the development of Spanish production in international law in the first decade of the twentieth century was, as we shall see in more detail below, the foundation of Revista Española

130 Miguel Allue Salvador, La condicion juridica de los consules (Zaragoza: Mariano Salas, 1909).

131 See Garcia Arias, 'Adiciones sobre la historia de la doctrina hispánica' 1949, 517.

132 See Garcia Arias, 'Adiciones sobre la historia de la doctrina hispánica' 1949, 509.

133 Manuel Rodriguez, Mares territoriales (Cadiz: Impr. Rodríguez de Silva 1905).

134 Gabriel Maura Gamazo, *La neutralidad en la guerra marítima* (Madrid: 1910).

135 José Fernández Novoa, *Del llamado derecho de naufragio y su abolición por la cvilizacion contemporánea* (Madrid: RDIPE, 1911).

136 Antonio de Calatayud, *La condición jurídica del espacio aéreo ante el derecho internacional* (Valencia: Est. tip. hijos de F. Vives Mora, 1913).

137 Gonzalo Fernandez de Cordoba, *La solución jurídica de los conflictos internacionales* (Madrid: Imprenta de La revista de legislación, 1903).

138 Manuel Conrotte, *Manual de Derecho internacional para uso de Jefes y Oficiales del Ejército y Armada* (Madrid: Imprenta del Patronato de Huérfanos de Administración Militar, 1906) (2nd ed, rev, 1910). Conrotte gained international reputation with his book, Manuel Conrotte, *La Intervencion de España en la Independencia de Los Estados Unidos,* (Madrid: Libreria general de Victoriano Suarez, 1920) Reviewed by R. Manning The American Journal of International Law 15 (1921), 308–309.

de Derecho Internacional y Politica Exterior by the Marquis de Olivart in 1905.

The development experienced by the study of international law—and international relations and Spanish foreign policy more generally—in the 1900s in Spain was consonant with the modernizing and regenerationist idearium. This greater cultivation was also related to a Spanish strategic 'logic of appropriation' of international law. This, as we have seen, adopted, first a defensive, and then an offensive reformist orientation among the former colonies and other semi-peripheral states during the nineteenth and early twentieth centuries. At a time when the language of international law was becoming a more sophisticated instrument 'civilized nations' had to master as part of their foreign-policy toolkits, its use appeared increasingly important for Spain to play a more active role in international alliances while safeguarding its interests as a semi-peripheral state on the international chessboard. The Spanish *fin-de-siècle* crisis had led to a gradual re-orientation of Spanish international lawyers from the all-encompassing science of international law of the late part of the century to gradually distancing 'themselves from the speculative aspects to focus their attention on international questions with practical repercussions'.[139]

This new Spanish instrumentalist drive was consonant with the prevalent view in Europe at the time of the climax of positivist international legal theories. Since the late nineteenth century, the rise of the 'scientific' method[140] had both supported the European nation-state building project and had facilitated, as we have seen, with its accompanying 'standard of civilization' premised in the ius publicum europaeum, new European colonial enterprises. Indeed, by 1905, in the last stage of the European 'long nineteenth century',[141]

139 Fernández Rozas/Andrés Sáenz de Santa María, 'La aportación de la Facultad de Derecho de la Universidad de Oviedo', 2010, 518

140 Lassa Oppenheim, 'The Science of International Law: Its Task and Method', *American Journal of International Law* 2 (1908), 313, 333. Writing in the second volume of the American Journal of International Law, Oppenheim stressed that 'The positive method is that applied by the science of law in general, and it demands that whatever the aims and ends of a worker and researcher may be, he must start from the existing recognized rules of international law as they are to be found in the customary practice of the states or in law-making conventions.'

141 See Eric Hobsbawm's conspicous trilogy *The Age of Revolution, 1789–1848* (London: Weidenfeld & Nicolson, World Publishing Company, 1962). *The Age of Capital, 1848–1875* (London: Hachette, 1975) and *The Age of Empire 1874–1914* (London: Abacus, 1987).

almost two-thirds of extra-European territories were dominated—and more or less ruled—by colonial regimes.[142] At the height of this 'imperial age', there was little theoretical dispute regarding the 'absolutist' theoretical justification of the state's freedom to bind itself externally (or not) to international legal obligations. Although a series of theoretical schools—filtering the ideological trends of the times—attempted to temper the excesses of positivism, the mid-late nineteenth century had seen the partial disbandment of natural law doctrines in international law. In this European scenario of competing imperial powers with overseas empires and burgeoning nationalist passions, international legal theorists saw international law in markedly Western-centred and voluntarist-dualist terms.

The theoretical imprint of the early twentieth century was dominated by perspectives which considered international law either as the 'state's external law', or as a 'law of coordination' presided over by E. Kaufman's principle of 'nur, der, der kann, darf auch',[143] or as a product, in Jellinek's description, of the state's 'self-commitment or self-limitation'[144] or else, as conceptualized by Heinrich Triepel, as a common will resulting from normative agreements (Vereinbarung)[145] in which the domestic and international legal orders remained separated as two distinctly different legal systems.[146] Despite the dominance of dualist approaches on the international legal theoretical front, this period, anticipating theoretical trends that would consolidate in the interwar period, also witnessed the emergence of some positivist monist theories of international law which, nonetheless, accorded normative supremacy to municipal law over international law. The theoretical plane also witnessed experimentation with the refashioning of dualist theories, prominent among which was Dionisio Anzilotti's normative approach[147] which fixed pacta sunt servanda as an a priori assumption to surpass strict voluntarism.

142 Douglas M. Johnston, *The Historical Foundations of World Order. The Tower and the Arena*, (Leiden: Martinus Nijjhoff, 2008), 549.

143 'Only the one who can, may also' Erich Kaufmann, *Das wesen des völkerrechts und die clausula rebus sic stantibus* (Berlin: J. C. B. Mohr, 1911), 151.

144 See Koskenniemi, *The Gentle Civilizer of Nations* 2001, 198.

145 Heinrich Triepel, *Völkerrecht und landesrecht* (Leipzig: Verlag, 1899).

146 Heinrich Triepel, 'Les rapports entre le droit interne et le droit international', Collected Courses of The Hague Academy of International Law 14 (1923), 227–332.

147 Giorgio Gaja, 'Positivism and Dualism in Dionisio Anzilotti', 3 European Journal of International Law, 1992, 123.

### Revista de Derecho Internacional y Política Exterior

Mirroring the spirit of the times in international law in the early twentieth century and a more internationally assertive orientation of Spain on the international plane, the Marquis de Olivart founded his Revista de Derecho Internacional y Política Exterior (RDIPE) in 1905.

RDIPE followed in the footsteps, as we saw in Chapter 1, of the short-lived publication of Revista de Derecho Internacional, Legislación y Jurisprudencia comparadas in 1887–88, after which periodical publications on international law had disappeared from Spain. RDIPE was announced in 1905 as the 'first and only journal' published in Spain that was 'exclusively devoted to the study of international law in its two variants, public and private, and to—as for what in both is relevant to—the study of comparative legislation and to the examination, divulgation and critique of the main questions of foreign policy'.[148] The first editorial, signed by Olivart, who had been a Conservative Party Member of Parliament in 1896 and 1899, and by the journal's editor-in-chief, E. Garcia Herreros, assistant professor at the Central University of Madrid, placed the journal squarely within the conservative intellectual wing of the post-1898 regenerationist movement. Flagging a lack of knowledge of foreign affairs as responsible for the Spanish decadence which triggered the loss of the last colonies, the editors wondered whether 'a more exact knowledge of the terms in which the Spanish action was developing, of the trends in foreign policy, of the moral and material force of our adversaries, of our own weakness, and of the fatal gravitation of the events propitiated by ourselves more than a century ago could not have avoided the catastrophe of seven years ago?.'[149] Although supportive of the goal of 'Europeanizing' Spain, the editors, nonetheless, stressed that this task should begin with 'Europeanising what represents us before Europe, giving it prestige and dignity and the respect that it possesses everywhere'.[150] Nowhere is the role of international law as part of the enterprise of national regeneration in the outer realm clearer than in the identification of the aim of the publication as allowing 'those who know to teach and those who ignore it to learn in the areas of the law of peoples and in its use in support of national interests'.[151]

The branding of Olivart's journal anticipated two novel features of the early twentieth century's generation of international journals. The first of

148 *Revista de Derecho Internacional y Política Exterior*, back cover of first volume (1905).

149 *Revista de Derecho Internacional y Política Exterior*, Editorial, 3.

150 Id. 3.

151 Id., 1.

them was a now only tangential interest in comparative legislation, which appeared explicitly subordinated 'to what in it may be relevant to the study of public and private international law' and did not, indeed, feature prominently in its pages. This abandonment of the comparative element marked a gradual departure from the early faith in the comparative-internationalist interactivity of purpose that had inspired the emerging professional discipline since the first international legal journal, La Révue de droit international et de la législation comparee was established in 1869 by G. Rolin-Jaequemyns. The second novel feature was an emerging instrumentalist nationalist bias, which was early on represented by Olivart's title and his decision to devote part of his journal to 'the examination, divulgation and critique of the main questions of (Spanish) foreign policy'.[152] This double—specializing and instrumentalist nationalist—orientation would find a parallel overseas, as we will see, with the publication of the first issue of the American Journal of International Law in 1907.

Revista de Derecho Internacional y Politica Exterior (RDIPE) was published in six volumes dated between 1905 and 1910, with the last volume being released in 1913 to cover around 1876 pages of text. Each volume provided an annual index classified by reference to the journal's sections: Public International Law, Private International Law, Foreign policy of Spain, Foreign policy of other countries and bibliographical notes. Although most of the texts are in Spanish, the journal also contained several works in French and Italian. Indeed, it prided itself on its list of international collaborators from several European and American universities, including members of the Institut de Droit International, which D'Olivart had joined in 1888. This list of collaborators represented a Who's Who of international law at the time, containing the names of T.C.M. Asser, P. Fauchille, P. Fiore, E. Nys, T.E. Holland, W. Hrabar, W. Kaufmann, F. de Martens and A. La Pradelle among others.

Alongside its regular contents, over the years RDIPE also featured a series of supplements devoted to international treaties and international acts, such as a chronicle published on International and Foreign Policy between 1905 and 1906, a bilingual version in French[153] and Spanish[154] of the Act of the Hague Peace Conference of 1907, and the Declaration relative to Maritime Law signed in London in 1909.[155] With various reprises throughout its different volumes, the Revista also included references to the sessions of the Institut de

152 See Revista de Derecho Internacional y Politica Exterior, 1905.

153 Revista de Derecho Internacional y de Politica Exterior 4 (1908), 222–240.

154 Revista de Derecho Internacional y de Politica Exterior 4 (1908), 361–378.

155 Revista de Derecho Internacional y de Politica Exterior 4 (1908), 222–238.

droit international. Coverage of the scientific sessions held in Gant (1906),[156] Florence (1908) and Paris (1910)[157] was completed by a special symposium dedicated to the 1911 Madrid session of the Institut, the first celebrated in Spain since the Institut's founding in 1873. The symposium gathered speeches by the Spanish Minister of Foreign Affairs with, among other things, several congratulatory letters addressed to the proud host of the event.

Other documents appearing in RDIPE are more idiosyncratic and their inclusion seems to respond to the bibliographical whims of its director. Nowhere, perhaps, is this more apparent than in the reproduction of a series of obscure historical pamphlets on early-eighteenth-century Spanish military excursions in North Africa.[158] This took place at a time when Morocco had become the main focus of Spanish foreign policy in the aftermath of the 1906 Conference of Algecirasand, as we shall see later, one of the main sources of tension between European powers before the First World War. Several supplements were also devoted to one of Olivart's most obsessive pursuits: the publication of his bibliographical collection on International Law and Diplomacy.

Olivart's famous bibliographical collection of international law was involved in an episode that can be referred as illustrative of the influence of positivist theoretical trends on the perspective of the outer realm of Spanish international lawyers and the Spanish foreign elite, including Olivart himself, in the early 1900s. In 1898, the Marquis had offered his large bibliographical collection to the Spanish Ministry of State.[159] Difficult negotiations ensued, but Olivart insisted as a conditio sine qua non that the collection remains united, and that guarantees be given for its conservation, extension, and regular updating, with him occupying the position of curator. The Spanish Ministry's final acceptance of Dalmau's requirements took place in 1902 and a commission to organize the gradual extension and regular updating of the library, with Dalmau holding a consultative vote, was set up. Moreover, the Marquis was made legal advisor to the Spanish Ministry of Foreign Affairs, which agreed with his purpose of providing bibliographical materials to the Spanish Ministry so 'that when examining certain international questions, the absolute legal

156 Ramón Dalmau de Olivart, *La sesión de Gante del Instituto de Derecho internacional*, Revista de Derecho Internacional y de Politica Exterior 3 (1907), 142.

157 Revista de Derecho Internacional y de Politica Exterior 5 (1909–10) 138–144. Revista de Derecho Internacional y de Politica Exterior 6 (1909–10) 138–144.

158 Anónimo, 'Relacion del Sitio de Melilla' Revista de Derecho Internacional y de Politica Exterior 4 (1908) 293–315.

159 The Ministry of the State is the former denomination of the current Spanish Ministry of Foreign Affairs and Cooperation.

criterion concerning them may be established.'[160] However, this tribute to the late nineteenth-century rise in prestige of scientific positivism in international law and the juridification of foreign policy soon evaporated. Promises were not turned into deeds: the brand new bibliographical commission did not convene for two years; the library was left in a state of abandonment, and the Marquis' well-paid advisory position was suppressed and replaced with another post of lower rank at 10% of his previously negotiated salary. In view of this state of affairs, Dalmau requested that his collection, which was by then languishing in the attic of the Ministry of Foreign Affairs, be returned to him, and this was accorded in 1905. Some years later, Harvard Law School acquired, as we shall see, the Marquis de Olivart's collection of international law and diplomacy which 'formed the basis of what became, for many years, the standard bibliography of international legal literature.'[161]

RDIPE dedicated several works to both the present and history of Spanish foreign policy and Spanish international relations, with extensive references to international treaties and international law matters. Reflecting the post-1898 consensus on the need to develop clear guidelines for a new Spanish foreign policy, Luis Amado[162] devoted an article to the relation between foreign policy and public opinion in 1907/1908.

According to Amado:

'Spain, due to its strategic and geographical position, due to the value of its commerce, because of what it represents in Europe and in the eyes of Europe, due to its history, its present and its future, needs [...] a complete, adequate, energetic and fixed foreign policy'.[163]

In a state-centred positivist vein, Amado judges the 'respect due to the rights of others'[164] to be the only limit to the overriding single fundamental self-serving principle which should inspire the modern foreign policy of a state. Although convinced that 'without an educated and autonomous public opinion it is not possible to confront the tasks required by a well-oriented foreign policy,'[165] the work presents, nonetheless, a dim picture of the prospects of its salutary influence in Spain as in the author's view 'there is not in Spain

160 Blanc Altemir, *El marquès d'olivart i el dret international* 2000, 84–94.

161 Neff, *Justice Among Nations* 2014, 304.

162 Luis Amado, 'La Opinión española y la política exterior', *Revista de Derecho Internacional y Politica Exterior* 2 (1907), 61–71 and Luis Amado, 'La Opinión española y la política exterior (cont.)', *Revista de Derecho Internacional y Politica Exterior* 3 (1908), 62–70.

163 Id., 1908, 70.

164 Id., 1908, 62.

165 Id., 1908, 64.

a collective opinion, either homogenous or heterogeneous, as far as our inter-state tendencies and relations are concerned.'[166]

Other contributions on Spanish foreign policy covered a larger historical canvas. These included articles on Spain's alliances, such as one penned by Damián Isern,[167] and Mariano Marfil Garcia's long article, published in two parts, which adopted a historical perspective on the relationship between Spain and Great Britain from the Peace of Utrecht until the early twentieth century.[168] These can be found accompanied by works on more remote Spanish diplomatic history, such as a project for a treaty between Turkey and Spain in the Kingdom of Philip the Fifth by the army officer and historian M. Conrotte.[169] M. Conrotte (1862) was, as already mentioned, the author of Manual de Derecho internacional para uso de Jefes y Oficiales del Ejército y Armada[170] (Textbook of international law for use by army and navy officers) in 1906.

Particularly interesting among works on Spanish diplomatic history is the first journal article on the history of international law in Spain. Written by Manuel Torres Campos (1850–1918), chair-holder in international law at the University of Granada (1886), the article is devoted to providing a brief biographical portrait, with reference to their works on international law, of Esteban de Ferrater and Antonio Riquelme. These were authors, as seen in the first chapter, of some of the earliest compilations of international treaties which appeared in the 1840s wearing in their titles the denomination 'Derecho internacional'.[171] D'Olivart himself had been engaged since 1890 in completing the task—under an official commission from the Ministry of State—initiated by these authors, and had edited thirteen volumes entitled Spanish Collection of

166 Id., 1908, 64.

167 Damian Isern, 'Las alianzas de España' *Revista de Derecho Internacional y Politica Exterior* 1 (1905), 169.

168 Mariano Marfil Garcia, Relaciones entre España y la Gran Bretaña, desde las paces de Utrecht hasta nuestros días'. *Revista de Derecho Internacional y Politica Exterior* 2 (1906), 8. and Mariano Marfil Garcia, Relaciones entre España y la Gran Bretaña, desde las paces de Utrecht hasta nuestros días' *Revista de Derecho Internacional y Politica Exterior* 3 (1907) 100.

169 Manuel Conrotte, Un proyecto de Tratado entre Turquia y España en el reinado de Felipe V, *Revista de Derecho Internacional y Politica Exterior* 3 (1907), 223–267.

170 Manuel Conrotte *Manual de Derecho internacional para uso de Jefes* 1906.

171 See, as mentioned in Chapter One, Esteban de Ferrater *Código de Derecho internacional, o sea, Colección metódica* 1846, and Antonio Riquelme, *Elementos de Derecho Público Internacional con explicación de todas las reglas que, según los tratados, estipulaciones, leyes vigentes y costumbres constituyen el Derecho internacional español*, 1849.

Treaties, Agreements and Documents from the Reign of Isabel II to the present.[172] Under the auspices of the journal, in 1911 Olivart published the last volume on those treaties celebrated during the first years of the majority of Alphonse XIII.

The journal also dedicated attention to the Spanish 'classics' of international law, an area that would reach its apogee, as we shall see in Chapter III, IV and V, first, in the interwar period, when Olivart himself co-founded the Association Francisco de Vitoria in 1926, and even more acutely in Spain during the Spanish Civil War and its aftermath. In line with the development of works about the jurists and theologians of the sixteenth and early seventeenth centuries, RDIPE included a reproduction of the Seville edition of 1552 of the 'Controversy between Fray Bartolomé de las Casas and Ginés de Sepúlveda on the legitimacy of the Conquest of the Indies'.[173] Fidel Abad y Cavia devoted an article to Francisco de Vitoria and the modern principles of the laws of war.[174] In this, in line with the works of Menendez Pelayo in defence of a 'Spanish philosophy' understood as a 'true scientific tradition, as an organism that deserves the name of a national science by presenting through the ages a dominant and characteristic feature,'[175] Abad y Cavia anticipates the future ideological celebrations of the 'Spanish school of international law' during the apogee, as we shall later see, of 'national Catholicism' after the Spanish Civil War.

Building on the revival of 'neo-Scholasticism' and the importance that the works of Vitoria, De Soto and Suarez were regaining among foreign scholars[176] at a time of Catholic 'renewed militancy [that] was to strengthen the religious commitment of the Right'[177] in the 1910s, Abad y Cavia defines the *Relectio de iure belli* by Francisco de Vitoria as the 'initial cell, the germinating seed of today's gigantic tree of the science of international law on the law of

---

172 Ramón Dalmau de Olivart, *Colección de tratados, convenios y documentos internacionales concluidos o ratificados por nuestros gobiernos con los estados extranjeros desde el reinado de doña Isabel II hasta nuestros días* (Madrid: Fernando Fé, 1902).

173 Controversia entre Fray Bartolomé de las Casas y Ginés de Sepúlveda sobre la legitimidad de la Conquista de las Indias Revista de Derecho Internacional y Politica Exterior 3 (1908).

174 Fidel Abad y Cavia, 'El dominico español Sr. Francisco de Vitoria and los principios modernos sobre el derecho de la guerra', *Revista de Derecho Internacional y Politica Exterior* 4 (1909), 241–292.

175 Id., 290.

176 Barthelemy, Jean. François de Vitoria, in A. Pillet (ed.), Les fondateurs du droit international, leurs œuvres, leurs doctrines (Paris: V. Giard & E. Brière, 1904), 1–36.

177 Carr, 'Liberalism and Reaction' 2000, 233.

war'.[178] Francisco de Vitoria is portrayed as one the glories of 'our century of Catholicism', one of 'the many geniuses thrown by the omnipotent hand of God onto the soil of Spain to compensate it for the rivers of blood spilt for the faith in the Crusade of more than seven centuries against Islam'.[179] Abad y Cavia ends up by encouraging Spaniards to 'accept the total possession of this extensive legacy that our ancestors left us and that we [Spaniards] have looked down on like the rags of a beggar, while they were the patrimony of a prince'.[180]

## International Codification—The Hague Conferences

Contributions to the RDIPE also mirrored the classic themes of the period such as international functional institutional integration, the codification of different areas of international law, in particular, the codification of the laws of armed conflict, and the development of methods of dispute settlement. Writing for the journal in 1907, M. Leroy evoked a future 'societé des nations,' understood as a moral federation of states which he considered was currently emerging from the mid-late nineteenth-century development of scientific and functional international associations.[181] Among Spaniards, the legal historian Rafael de Ureña (1852—1930) wrote on the historical evolution of the principle of intervention[182] up to the Drago Doctrine. Olivart himself wrote on the origin and development of the Drago Doctrine and its partial acceptance by the second peace conference.[183] T. E. Holland had already focused on the duties of neutrals in maritime war (in the light of recent events)[184] which was to be the object of a convention during the Second Hague Conference. RDIPE was

178 Id., 289

179 Id., 242.

180 Id., 292.

181 Maxime Leroy, La Societe des Nations, Revista de Derecho Internacional y Politica Exterior 3 (1907) 197 Maxime Leroy, 'La Societe des Nations', Revista de Derecho Internacional y Politica Exterior 4 (1908) Maxime Leroy, La Societe des Nations, Revista de Derecho Internacional y Politica Exterior Tome 5 (1909–10), Maxime Leroy, La Societe des Nations, Revista de Derecho Internacional y Politica Exterior 6 (1909–10), 89–93

182 Rafael üreña y Sanz, 'Nuevas orientaciones del principio de intervención, Revista de Derecho Internacional y Politica Exterior' 5–6 (1909–1910), 1–70.

183 Ramón Dalmau de Olivart, 'Origen y desarrollo de la doctrina de Drago y su aceptación parcial por la segunda Conferencia de la Paz', *Revista de Derecho Internacional y Politica Exterior* 3 (1907) 232.

184 T.E. Holland, Les devoirs des neutres dans la guerre maritime et les evenements recents, Revista de Derecho Internacional y Politica Exterior 2 (1906) 97—118.

particularly attentive to the process of international codification carried out at The Hague, as is shown by the publication of a bilingual version in French[185] and Spanish[186] of the Act of The Hague Peace Conference of 1907,[187] and also of the Declaration relative to Maritime Law signed in London in 1909,[188] which, despite never coming into force, complemented the work produced on some of the thorniest issues treated at the Second Hague Conference.

The Hague Conferences of 1899 and 1907 crowned a series of codifying efforts made by private scholars during the nineteenth century in the form of general codes of international law—Bluntschli (1868), Fiore (1890), Dudley Field (1891)—or codes in specific areas—such as the 157 articles of the Lieber Code (1863), which was to influence the legislation of several countries, including Spain. The new professional associations of international law scholars played a vehicular role in fostering the spirit of international codification. The Institut de droit international, founded in 1873, set among its paramount goals to favour the development of international law 'en donnant son concours à toute tentative sérieuse de codification graduelle et progressive du droit international.'[189] The International Law Association, also born in 1873, was initially named the 'Association for the Reform and Codification of International Law'. With the Institut acting as 'an organ of the legal conscience-consciousness of the civilized world', small-scale codification efforts—of unofficial yet referential character—extended to various areas[190] of traditional diplomatic practice, communication routes and the laws of war.

Works in the latter field included a manual on the law of land warfare (1880) that built on codifying efforts and humanitarian initiatives that included the 1856 Declaration of Paris Respecting Maritime Law, the Geneva Convention of 1864, which sprung from H. Dunant's effort in writing his 'Souvenir de Solferino', the 1868 St. Petersburg Declaration, and as the most immediate precedent the Brussels Declaration of 1874 on the laws of war. Also known as the Oxford

185 *Revista de Derecho Internacional y Politica Exterior* 4 (1908) 222–240.

186 *Revista de Derecho Internacional y Politica Exterior* 4 (1908) 361–378.

187 See Carlos Jiménez Piernas / E. Crespo Navarro, 'La organización de la paz y la limitación del uso de la fuerza en pleno apogeo del imperialismo: las Conferencias de Paz de La Haya', in Gregorio Peces Barba / E. Fernández García / R. de Asís Roig, (Eds), *Historia de los Derechos Fundamentales* (Madrid: Dyckinson, 2005) and Carlos Jiménez Piernas, 'El papel de España en la Conferencia de La Haya de 1899', Revista Española de Derecho Internacional LI (1999), 775–782.

188 Declaracion relativa al Derecho Maritimo. Firmada en Londres 26 de febrero de 1909 *Revista de Derecho Internacional y Politica Exterior* 4 (1908), 222–238.

189 Neff, *Justice Among Nations* 2014, 321–323.

190 Id., 323.

Manual of 1880, the rules contained were proposed 'as a basis for national legislation' at a time when—as R. Kolb notes—'international law was often perceived as a sort of annex of constitutional law applying to external relations' and 'short and generic international texts' were designed to be subsequently 'spelled out in the municipal laws of the various states'.[191] Spain was one of the states that joined the 'intense process of national legislation on military issues'[192] which was by then underway. A Spanish Reglamento para el Servicio de Campaña, an army manual, reflected these influences in 1882, while also presenting 'public opinion' as 'the principal authority, the most impartial and respectable judge, the organ and regulator' [...] which 'condemns irregular acts, creates usages and customs, [and] gives sovereign and final judgements'.[193] The codifying efforts of the Institut also covered a manual on prize law (1882–1883) and went on to include, among other things, attention to civil wars, such as, for instance, in the 1900 resolution on Duties of Foreign Powers towards a Government which is Fighting an Insurrection.[194] The efforts of individual scholars and epistemological communities, along with the foundations of the International Committee of the Red Cross, laid in 1863, contributed to the gradual codification and development of certain sectors of international law and was a prelude to the institutionalization of the periodical convening of multilateral conferences for the purpose of drafting 'international legislation'.

This move took place against the evolving backdrop of a globalizing international society whose functional needs required new international conventions and institutions for managing 'progress' at the end of the nineteenth century. It was supported by initiatives by the international peace movement, such as those by the Bureau International de Paix, established in Berne in 1892, and the impulse given by transnational social-solidarity movements, such as the 'Second International'.[195] Moreover, the pacifism-internationalism duo, as

---

191 Robert Kolb, *Advanced Introduction to International Humanitarian Law* (Cheltelham: Edward Elgar 2014) 9.

192 Id.

193 Reglamento para el servicio de campana (art.826) (1982) reprinted in Estados Mayor del Ejercito, Manual de Derecho de Guerra (329–30) (M-O-23-1, 1986) Quoted in Theodore Meron, 'The Martens Clause, Principles of Humanity and Dictates of Public Conscience', 94 *American Journal of International Law*, 2000, 78–89, at 84–85.

194 This would years later become an object of contentious analysis in the context of the British-led international policy of non-intervention during the Spanish Civil War—see Chapter Four.

195 On pacificism and internationalism in this epoch see e.g. Marcel Merle, *Pacifisme et internationalisme* (París: Coüin 1966), 1066.

Lopez Cordon notes, filtered back into the domestic political reformist programmes of workers' movements and democratic parties across Europe.[196] Codifying efforts in the area of the humanitarianization of conflicts allied themselves with an increasing faith in public opinion, which benefitted from a far greater domestic and international exchange of ideas and news as a result of developments in the mass media, in the slowing down of the arms race, and in methods of peaceful dispute settlement, particularly in the light of cyclical peaks of international tension within Europe.

It was in 1898, during one of those periods of rising tension, when a proposal was made by Tsar Nicholas II to convene an international conference to study 'the most efficacious methods to assure for all nations the benefits of a real and lasting peace and to put, above all, an end to the present armaments'.[197] In 1901, the founder of the International Committee of the Red Cross, H. Dunant, and F. Plassy, the founder of the Société française pour l'arbitrage entre nations, jointly received the first Nobel Peace Prize. In 1903, the American steel magnate turned philanthropist and self-styled 'apostle of peace' Andrew Carnegie (1835–1919), donated a $ 1,5 million gift to begin making possible the building of the Peace Palace (which was to be inaugurated in 1913).[198] In 1904, the Institute of International Law became the first institution to receive the Nobel prize for its salutary influence on the outcomes of The Hague Peace Conference in 1899.

Although inspired by precedents and preparatory work which influenced the treaty codification of the laws of war on land and sea, the outcome of the peace conference fell short of meeting the high aspirations of the international peace movement in the areas of mandatory arbitration and disarmament. The Hague Conference of 1899 (18th May—29th July) stood out, nonetheless, for being the first international conference in which, as Neff states, 'the states of the world in general (were invited) to participate, en masse, in the drafting of

196 Including in Spain, with reference to the Partido Federal see Maria Victoria Lopez Cordon, 'España en las Conferencias de la Haya de 1899 y 1907' Revista de Esludios Internacionales 3 (1982) (1982), 703–756, 707.

197 Russian comunique 24th December 1898 quoted in Émile Bourgeois, Manuel historique de politique étrangère (Paris: Librairie classique Eugène Belin, 1898).

198 See Randall Lessafer, 'The Temple of Peace The Hague Peace Conferences, Andrew Carnegie and the Building of the Peace Palace' in Mededelingen van de Koninklijke Nederlandse Vereniging voor Internationaal Recht, Preadviezen, 140 (2013) 1–38 available as Tilburg Law School Legal Studies Research Paper Series No. 024/2013 accesible at http://papers.ssrn.com/sol3/papers.cfm?abstract_id=2350189

international legislation'[199]—although at the end of the day only twenty-six states attended it and only six of them were not European. The main developments took place in the area of the law of war. Building on the Brussels Conference of 1874 and the Manual on the Law of Land Warfare (1880), two conventions were passed, and the famous 'Martens Clause' with its appeal to 'the laws of humanity and the requirements of public conscience' was originally introduced as a residual protection in the Preamble of the Hague Convention (II, and later in 1907, Hague IV) with respect to the laws and customs of war on land.[200] Moreover, the Convention for the Peaceful Settlement of Disputes, which contemplated the creation of an (optional) Permanent Court of Arbitration—which was famously not permanent nor a court—and three accompanying Hague Declarations that banned certain types of armament were also agreed upon and entered into force in 1900.

The Spanish government, which was at the time involved in the immediate aftermath of the Spanish- American War of 1898 and the negotiation of the Treaty of Paris, confronted the Hague Conference, as Lopez Cordón, notes between the poles of the 'greatest scepticism in international cooperation [...] and the need to find a guarantee that could close the Spanish question'.[201] The Spanish delegation which represented Spain at The Hague came from an isolated and debilitated country, where peace movements were barely organized, and in which public opinion[202] shared a perceived sense of deep contradiction and distrust between the attempts to come up with general principles regarding mechanisms for the peaceful settlement of disputes and the abandonment and despoilment that Spanish rights had recently suffered at the hands of the American imperial thrust. Hastily and unprofessionally prepared, Spanish diplomatic representatives from the permanent delegations in Belgium and Holland headed by the Duke of Tetuan were sent to The Hague without having engaged in any lengthy substantial previous analyses and devoid of any particularly refined instructions other than that of non-accepting the proposal regarding the 'present military status quo as regards land or naval forces, as our recent misfortunes have

199 Neff, Justice Among Nations 2014, 324.

200 On the Martens Clause, there is an extremely large literature see e.g. Theodore Meron, 'The Martens Clause, Principles of Humanity and Dictates of Public Conscience', 94 American Journal of International Law XXX (2000) 78–89.

201 Lopez Cordon, 'España en las Conferencias de la Haya de 1899 y 1907' 1982, 714.

202 For an analysis of the coverage in the Spanish press and intellectual circles of the 1899 Hague Conference, ibid., 716–724.

reduced us to a state of inferiority quite out of proportion to our needs and our resources'.[203] Despite the lukewarm public support for the 1899 Hague Conference, and the peripheral role of Spanish delegates in its negotiations, Spain was nonetheless one of the only thirteen countries that subscribed to the Hague Conventions in their entirety[204] and that, furthermore, made good on its promises by signing general arbitration treaties with twenty countries between 1902 and 1907.[205] Manuel Torres Campos, a professor of international law at the University of Granada, who since 1885 was the first Spanish member of the Institut de Droit International, was the only international lawyer out of the four Spanish nationals who were designated to serve at the 'the world's first permanent arrangement for the judicial or arbitral settlement of disputes'.[206]

In 1907, from 15 June to 18 October and after protracted negotiations, the number of states attending the Second Hague Conference was forty-four, including seventeen Latin American states. The Conference helped to refine and improve many of the provisions of the Conventions of the First Hague Conference (e.g. Hague Convention II become Hague Convention IV) and to address other areas of warfare with the adoption of ten new conventions, including Hague Convention II on the limitation of the employment of force for the recovery of contract debts, which partially codified the Drago Doctrine, and a considerable extension (Conventions VI-XIII) concerning warfare at sea. Among the latter, there were initiatives on international adjudication, such as a failed project, despite signature by thirty countries of the Prize

203 As noted by Carlos Jimenez Piernas, the instructions or 'pro-memoria' entitled 'La conferencia de Desarme' was annexed (Palacio, 5th May 1899) to the order appointment of the Duke of Tetuan as President of the Spanish Delegation. This, as Jimenez Piernas, highlights 'was prepared by the Political Section of the Ministry of State with particular reference to the reports of the Ministers of War and Marine'. See further, Carlos Jimenez Piernas, 'The Role of Spain in The Hague Peace Conferences of 1899', in Fritz Kalshoven (ed) The Centennial of the First International Peace Conference, Reports and Conclusions, (The Hague: Kluwer Law International), 1–8, 5. See also, Carlos Jimenez Piernas, 'El papel de España en la conferencia de la Haya de 1899', Revista Española de Derecho Internacional LI (1999), 775–782, 780.

204 AMAE. Tratados y Negociaciones, núm. 558. S. XIX. Actas de ratificaciones y declaraciones de la Conferencia de La Haya y Caceta de Madrid de 22 de noviembre de 1900.

205 Francisco Cadiz Deleito, España y el Tribunal de La Haya: El Tribunal Permanente de Justicia Internacional y el Tribunal Internacional de Justicia (Madrid: Imprenta del Ministerio de Asuntos Exteriores, 1968) quoted in Lopez Cordón, 'España en las Conferencias de la Haya de 1899 y 1907' 1982, 716.

206 Neff, Justice Among Nations 2014, 331.

Court Convention (Hague XII), for the creation of an international court of prize.[207] Also unsuccessful was an attempt to establish a Court of Arbitral Justice—a precedent for the permanent court of international justice.[208] At the Peace Conference of The Hague, the states' inability to agree on the selection process for judges proved to be an insurmountable obstacle and some voices blamed Latin American jurists for the failure of the conference to create the Court.[209] However, although, as Becker has noted, the structure of 'classical international law' remained unchanged, the Hague Conferences contributed to accelerating the universalization of international law by making the voice of semi-peripheral states heard more clearly. In the regulation of the laws of war, the dominant paradigm also remained a classical one, focusing on the limitation of the means of warfare premised on the pivotal principle of military necessity.[210] The Second Hague Conference decided to reconvene eight years later in 1915. However, the outbreak of the First World War halted the plans to hold a third codification conference.[211]

Spain supported the facilitation of the participation of Latin American states which in 1899 had been limited to Mexico. The far greater participation by Spanish-speaking countries in the second Hague Conference gave Spain a much greater role as mediator. Moreover, The Hague Conference of 1907 took place in a far more favourable international context for Spain, which reflected its integration in the Franco-British Entente of 1904 and, as we shall see below, a promising horizon for the colonial ambitions of Spain in North Africa after the Conference of Algeciras in 1906 and the Cartagena Agreements of 1907. This far more participative and constructive attitude is reflected in the fact that Spain attended the conference after having examined at length with consultative bodies and the participation of several ministries clear guidelines regarding Spanish interests. The instructions sent by the government to the

207 International Court Prize.

208 Despite these failures, Central America saw the establishment in 1907 of The Central American Court of Justice to maintain peace and resolve disagreements among Central American states, which operated for 10 years in Costa Rica.

209 Becker Lorca, Mestizo International Law 2015.

210 And, thus, still far from the more detailed and complete codification of the post-1945 modern international humanitarian law 'that places at the centre of the new law the principle of humanity and the idea of protected persons, albeit always in tensional cohabitation with the classic paradigm'. See Robert Kolb, *Advanced Introduction to International Humanitarian Law* 2014, 6–7.

211 which eventually took place in 1930.

head of mission, Villa-Urrutia on the main themes of the conference included a general recommendation:

> 'The predominantly legal character of many of the themes that will be discussed during the conference shall allow all countries to expose their thoughts without an attitude finally being adopted to attribute to other motives, and in particular to the character of the relationships that can exist between those countries. However, there is no lack of problems—and very important ones—in respect of the proposals and the votes, either because of the character of the question or due to the antecedents and circumstances of political character. In those cases you should have always in mind the wish of the government of his Majesty to advance, without affecting our cordial relations with other countries, in close intelligence with the foreign offices of Paris, London, and Lisbon, and to make present the intimate links that tie us to the Hispanic-American republics'[212]

The Spanish mission once again did not include any Spanish international lawyer. This contrasted sharply with the even greater presence, when compared with 1899, of prominent international lawyers in other delegations as scientific delegates, including among others F. Martens, J.B. Scott, L. Renault, Asser, C. Hurst and M. Huber. Spain signed nine of the fourteen conventions and the final act. This left Spain 'as the country that together with China left more conventions unsupported and, as time went on, as one of the countries that took longer to be able to implement them'.[213]

## Colonial Policy of Substitution—The Moroccan Question

Along with the interest devoted to international codification in the wake of The Hague Conferences, RDIPE also paid great attention to the main focus of concern of Spanish foreign policy before the First World War. Mirroring the greater attention to Spanish foreign policy that characterized the works of international lawyers in the aftermath of the Desastre of 1898, the second issue of the RDIPE devoted a symposium to the Conference of Algeciras of 1906.

212 Quoted in Lopez Cordon, 'España en las Conferencias de la Haya de 1899 y 1907' 1982, 734. AMAE. Neg. 163. Él Ministro de Estado a don Wenceslao Ramírez de Villa-Urrutia (Madrid, 12 de junio de 1907). Punto VIII.

213 Id. 739. For a detailed analysis see 724–756.

Under the title 'The Algeciras Act and the Future of Spain in Morocco', the second volume of RDIPE featured contributions by T. Barclay, J. Gutiérrez Sobral, R. M. de Labra, L. de Montluc, L. Strisower and the Marquis de Olivart.[214] The exchange in the journal's pages focuses on the new possibilities brought about by the outcome of the conference for Spain in North Africa.

Delegates from thirteen states, including Morocco and the United States, met at the initiative of Kaiser Wilhelm II of Germany in the coastal city of Algeciras to discuss the de facto de-internationalization of Morocco between 16 January and 7 April 1906. The North African substitutive orientation of Spanish foreign policy had initially been facilitated by Spain's assigned role as an equilibrating factor of England and France's contest for the Western Mediterranean.[215] However, the role of Spain in this context was, perceived, as, Nino highlights, as one of 'a passive factor, a piece, the importance of which derived almost exclusively from its geographical position'.[216] The Declaration between the United Kingdom and France Respecting Egypt and Morocco of 8 April 1904 was part of a pragmatic settlement of the potentially conflictive puzzle of Franco-British colonial rivalry that underlined the Entente Cordiale of 1904. It recognized, as J. Piernas and Requena note, 'the French pre-eminence in Morocco in return for a solid British hold on Egypt, as well as British sponsorship of the Spanish presence in Western Morocco to keep France away from its main imperial sea route'.[217] The Franco-British Declaration was accompanied by a Franco-Spanish Declaration of 3 October 1904, and also on the same date by the signature of a secret Franco-Spanish Convention which ascribed a sphere of influence for Spain in North Morocco.[218] The German discomfort with the 1904 Anglo-French scramble for North Africa made the first Moroccan crisis a very present danger in the minds of its contemporaries. The Conference of Algeciras was, in this context, formally 'called in order to introduce reforms

214 See Rafael M. de Labra, 'Marruecos y la Conferencia de Algeciras', *Revista de Derecho Internacional y de Politica Exterior* 2 (1906), 274–321.

215 See Susana Sueiro Seona, 'La política exterior de España en los años 20: una política mediterránea con proyección africana', in Javier Tussell/ Juan Aviles/ Rosa Pardo (eds) *La política exterior de España en el siglo XX*, (Madrid: Ed. Biblioteca Nueva 2000), 135–157.

216 Antonio Nino, 'Politica de alianzas y compromisos coloniales para la regeneracion internacional de España', in Javier Tussell/Juan Aviles/Rosa Pardo (eds) *La Politica Exterior de España en el siglo XX* (Madrid, Biblioteca Nueva, 2000), 77.

217 Carlos Jiménez Piernas/ Millán Requena Casanova, 'Spain's Part in the 1906 Algeciras Conference: Internationalisation of the Moroccan Question and the Interests of Spain', *Spanish Yearbook of International Law* XII (2008) 1–18, 4.

218 This was, however, not to be made public until 1912. Id., 5.

based on three principles: the Sultan's sovereignty, Morocco's territorial integrity and economic equality among the participating powers'.[219] The final Algeciras settlement 'created a de facto Franco-Spanish protectorate under vague international control, which put an end to the Sultan's sovereignty and in the medium term paved the way for occupation of Morocco by France and Spain and the sharing out of its resources among the European powers.'[220]

This is the background against which the RDIPE featured the interestingly countervailing perspectives of a man of action, the future Counter Admiral, J. Gutierrez Sobral, who had navigated and often visited the African continent, and the perspective of the international law scholar, Rafael Maria de Labra (1840–1918). This was, as we saw in Chapter One, a champion of the antislavery movement, a long-standing reformist and an outspoken critic of the ills of Spanish colonization in Cuba and Puerto Rico.

Gutierrez Sobral's essay is a cry against the conformism of the strategic-political dimension of the Spanish penetration of North Africa.[221] Gutierrez Sobral emphasised the technical progress and the commercial advantages brought about by the colonial enterprise since the Berlin Conference and decried the state of abandonment of the Spanish possessions in the Guinea Gulf. Instead, he champions their commercial exploitation through further investment assured by military control, because it was only—he argued—through 'economic action, by recourse to the mercantile elements of trade and exploitation that the land is really conquered.'[222] A proactive Spanish colonialist, Gutierrez Sobral also stressed the need to reinforce commercial penetration as the main driver of the Spanish colonial policy towards North Africa and criticizes the main focus on solely 'political action in Morocco in order to satisfy a badly understood desire for influence in the international concert.'[223] This strategic conformist policy only made Spain, according to Gutierrez Sobral, 'a blind tool of more pragmatic peoples'[224] because today's 'dominance does not spring up from political sovereignty' but from what he called 'commercial sovereignty'.[225]

219 Id., 8.

220 Id., 8.

221 José Gutiérrez Sobral, 'Conferencia de Algeciras y España', *Revista de Derecho Internacional y Politica Exterior* 2 (1906), 268–273.

222 Id., 272.

223 Id., 271–272.

224 Id., 272.

225 Id., 273.

The aggressive commercial exploitative vision of Gutierrez Sobral finds in Labra's long essay on Spanish foreign policy in Africa[226] a counterpoint based on the idea of the role of international law as a civilizing mission. Indeed, Labra considered the Conference of Algeciras 'a new and plausible sign of progress of contemporary public law'.[227] In other words, as a step in the right direction within a historical progressive trend that 'rectifying the ancient concept of the nation and national sovereignty, puts the fundamental rights, the elements of civilization, the primary and inexcusable factors of every society, under the safeguard of international concerts in a manner that fosters that nations, no matter how great their force, cannot evade their international relations (in the same way that individuals cannot subtract themselves from their social milieu and their legal relationships)'.[228] This perspective derived from Labra's teleological conception of the international law of the time as being engaged in 'the resolute work of rectifying international isolation in order to achieve the guarantees of the civilized world for the fundamental principles of modern civilization'.[229] For Labra, this civilizing mission[230] was based on the 'incontestable right that the cultivated peoples possess to provide backward and irregular peoples, who fundamentally deny the first principles of civilization, with those conditions in the virtue of which they can be admitted to the enjoyment of international relations.'[231] The civilizing mission could, however, only be a basis for intervention, according to Labra, 'when this intervention is the outcome of the concert of nations that propose to guarantee the fundamental principles of civilization in everyone's interest in the intervened nations.'[232] Against this background, Labra examined, in particular, the legal obligations assumed by the 'Spanish legal entity'[233] at the conference of Algeciras.[234]

Adopting a legalistic perspective, he highlighted the legal significance of the diverse negotiations between the various powers and the legal relevance of unilateral acts of states as a source of legal obligations.[235] He also decried the legality of secret treaties in the conduct of a well-ordered Spanish legal foreign

226 Rafael Maria de Labra, 'Marruecos y la Conferencia de Algeciras' 1906, 274–321.
227 Id., 286.
228 Id., 291.
229 Id., 291.
230 Id., 291.
231 Id., 298.
232 Id., 291.
233 Id., 302.
234 Id., 305.
235 Id., 296 et al.

policy and proposed a reform of the 1876 Spanish Constitution (which authorized secret treaties as long as they did not contradict public treaties) in order to advance a progressive legalistic perspective on the role of the thread of earlier Spanish treaties on Morocco (e.g. the Treaty of Madrid of 1880, the treaty of Madrid of 1861, and the treaty of Tetuan of 1860) embodying 'conquests of the universal law' in favour of the freedom of conscience, the freedom of religious belief, the right to property etc. in North-Africa.[236] The most important of these antecedents was, according to Labra, the 1880 Treaty of Madrid, as this sanctioned the 'internationalisation' of the economic order—and was, therefore, the legal basis for the self-appointment of the Kaiser as 'the defender of the Sultan's sovereignty and of the need for peaceful penetration of Morocco—largely economic in nature—by all the European nations'.[237]

The Conference of Algeciras consolidated the re-orientation of Spain's foreign policy and initiated a long-standing, albeit always subaltern, Spanish competition with France in North Africa. This, which extended over a period of three decades, knew, as we shall see in Chapter Three, diverse avatars and fluctuations. In 1907, the signature of the Agreements of Cartagena signalled a tripartite Spanish-Franco-British agreement which was oriented to maintaining the status quo. The Cartagena agreements provided Spain with a long-sought guarantee of territorial integrity and fostered a more dynamic engagement with the Moroccan project. This gradually began to be coloured—albeit not without domestic political opposition—with the attributes of a 'national mission' by military and commercial Africanist elements close to the Spanish Crown. The parallel further penetration of France and Spain in its disparate zones of influence—the Spanish one, as it was pointed out to Lord Curzon, being 'a rugged area peopled by natives who are the most turbulent and difficult to control in Morocco'[238]—initiated a pattern of domestic crisis triggered by events in Morocco such as the one surrounding the conscription system during the 'Tragic Week of Barcelona' that followed the defeat suffered by Spanish troops in the 'Desastre' of Barranco del Lobo in 1909.

In line with the topicality of Spanish foreign policy in North Africa, the Moroccan question continued to attract the attention of the RDIPE until its last issue published in 1913. On some occasions, the reflections penned by Spanish authors on North African colonial policy in the pages of RDIPE have an

236 Id., 305.

237 Jiménez Piernas/ Requena Casanova, 'Spain's Part in the 1906 Algeciras' 2008, 3.

238 PRO FO 371/4525 Clark Kerr to Lord Curzon, 30 March 1920. Quoted in Pablo La Porte, 'Civil Military Relations in the Spanish Protectorate in Morocco: The Road to the Spanish Civil War', 210.

enlightened culturally-elevated character that sets them apart, as in the case of the work by A. Huici Miranda (1880–1973).[239] As a humanist 'vox clamans in deserto', Huici decried the lack of official support of Arab studies in Spain and postulated the urgent development of scientific studies of Moroccan and Arab culture. According to Huici, the goal that would be served by these studies would be twofold. First, their development was essential to Spanish medieval history, about which, according to Huici, Spanish historiography remained at the bare chronicle level—a level from which it would not rise 'until the scholarly critique cannot use Arab sources, as only they will allow it to comprehend the framework of life in the peninsula during the Reconquista'.[240] However, if Spain aspired to go beyond a stage when 'the extremely brilliant poetry of our Arab-Andalusian philosophy, theology, and the mystic and literary narrative of all the institutions of the Andalusian-Moroccan and Arab tradition are—and will remain so for a long time—res nullius in Spain,'[241] it should also go beyond classical Arabism to engage in scientific studies and prepare a scientific mission to learn more about modern Morocco. Only this scientific cultural mindset would allow, according to Huici, the resolution of a number of conflicts and misunderstandings which might have already been resolved with a far greater knowledge of the language, of the local traditions, of the social polis, and the political and legal regimes under Islamic law.[242]

However, not all the approaches to North Africa in the pages of RDIPE were as intellectually enlightened as that of Huici, or that of Fernando Rodriguez Roa,[243] who presented the design of a colonial policy for Spain built on the three pillars of the educational, political and economic dimensions. The Marquis de Olivart himself went on to support, somewhat incongruously in the light of other contributions to his own journal, a crude realpolitik strategic and self-protective design for the bedrock of Spain's engagement in Morocco. Commenting on what de Olivart terms the dislocation of Spanish policy in Morocco, he noted that Spanish public opinion should be persuaded that:

> 'what interests us in Morocco is the soil and not the buildings, and therefore the economic mining and agricultural value of the territory is

---

239 Ambrosio Huici Miranda, 'Los estudios árabes y el africanismo español' Revista de Derecho Internacional y Politica Exterior 5 (1910), 94–106.

240 Id., 96.

241 Id., 105.

242 Id., 106.

243 Fernando Rodriguez Roa, 'España en el Rif' Revista de Derecho Internacional y Politica Exterior 5 (1909–1910), 70–93.

> absolutely indifferent and accessory; if this exists, so much the better; if it is non-existent, for us it should be all the same, because what is important is that, whatever wasteland or vegetable patch, it is not fortified by someone else and especially not by France.'[244]

The Spanish penetration of Morocco became consolidated with the partition of Morocco after the Agadir Crisis of 1911, which was once again a result of the German imperial competition with France and Britain in Africa. Once Germany had eventually bargained its earlier position as defender of the sovereignty of the Sultan and of the territorial independence of Morocco for territorial concessions in west-central Africa, 'the 'Spanish sphere of influence' in Morocco became the 'Spanish Protectorate' ceded by France under a Franco-Spanish Convention of 27 November 1912'.[245]

From 1912 onwards, the diplomatic-commercial and peaceful orientation of the Spanish penetration in Morocco was replaced by a more clear-cut military occupation of the spoils of the Moroccan territory left to it by France[246] and by recurrent fighting against the bellicose tribes or cabilas that served as the basis for the administrative-territorial organization of the Spanish protectorate. This strategy, as we shall see in Chapter 3, was bound to greatly influence Spain's neutrality in the First World War, and both foreign and domestic events in Spain during the interwar period. Ultimately, through the deeds of the man who was to become in 1926 the youngest general in Europe in the North African campaigns, the Africanista General Franco, it will also tragically influence the Spanish Civil War and its aftermath.

## The Founding of the American Society of International Law

In 1913, the Marquis de Olivart's journal Revista de Derecho Internacional y Política Exterior was interrupted. The First World War halted the plans of James Brown Scott to grant a new lease of life to Olivart's journal under the auspices of the American Society of International Law and the Carnegie Endowment for International Peace.[247] James Brown Scott (1866–1943) was

244 Ramón Dalmau de Olivart, 'De la Dislocacion de la política exterior española en Marruecos' Revista de Derecho Internacional y Politica Exterior 5 (2009–2010), 107–137, 137.

245 Jiménez Piernas/ Requena Casanova, 'Spain's Part in the 1906 Algeciras' 2008, 3.

246 Neila, España y el Mediterraneo en el siglo XX 2011, 123.

247 See announcement in the introduction to the last two volumes of Revista de Derecho Internacional y Politica Exterior (covering 1909 and 1910) published in September 1913.

almost a ubiquitous figure in both American international legal academia and the American 'foreign policy establishment' during the first third of the twentieth century. Praise, bordering on eulogy, is a recurrent trait in almost any portrayal that his contemporaries offered to J.B. Scott, who was also nominated six times for the Nobel Peace Prize which Elihu Root, for him Brown Scott worked, received in 1912. Brown Scott became the recipient of seventeen honorary degrees, including one from Salamanca University, where Francisco de Vitoria had been Prima Professor of Sacred Theology four centuries earlier.

J. Brown Scott began his career, after obtaining his B.A in 1890, and his MA. in 1891 from Harvard University, by holding a three-year-long Parker Fellowship to study international law in Berlin, Paris, and Heidelberg, where he obtained his doctor utriusque juris. While at Harvard, Scott studied international law with Freeman Snow, and it is on the basis of Snow's seminal Cases and Opinions on International Law (1893) that, in 1902, he published (and re-published in 1906) what 'for 25 years would be the dominant work in the field throughout North America'.[248] After his study visit to Europe, Scott went back to California to take the first steps in a fruitful and extremely institutionally activist career. In California, he practised law, and in 1896 founded the Los Angeles Law School (later, the Law School of the University of Southern California) to become, soon afterward, the Dean of the College of Law at the University of Illinois (1898–1903). His flourishing academic career continued with his appointment as professor at Columbia Law School in 1903.[249] His arrival on the East Coast was the turning point of a multi-faceted career, the first milestone of which was the foundation of the American Society of International Law.

The ASIL was born against the background of a U.S. expansionist-imperial drive which had traversed the nineteenth century and that, having reached the limits of the 'manifest destiny' of continental expansion, largely at the expense of the Native American nations, further extended its quest for overseas expansion with the legal imprimatur of the U.S. Supreme Court. The immediate commercial and imperialist drive of the United States in the aftermath of the Spanish-American War was accompanied by several concomitant factors, all of which contributed to the foundation of ASIL. These included, first, the worldwide boost and rise in prestige of international arbitration during the nineteenth century, and, second, the parallel rise, as we have seen, of the international codifying spirit supported by the weight of an idealist tradition in

248 Id., 41–42.

249 This was soon followed by his position at George Washington University (1906–1911), the John Hopkins University (1909–1916) and Georgetown University (from 1920 until his retirement as professor emeritus).

the U.S. of a number of international lawyers who belonged to the American peace movement, long-standing campaigners for mechanisms of peaceful international dispute settlement which was ultimately expressed in The Hague Peace Conferences of 1899 and 1907.

The success of the history of the field of international arbitration during the nineteenth century and, in particular, its role as a preferred means of international dispute settlement for the United States, played a decisive role in the foundation of ASIL. The U.S. Jay Treaty in 1794 (536 awards between 1799 and 1804) had early been identified by J. Basset Moore 'as the turning point in international arbitration fortunes'. Furthermore, a series of cases decided by the 1868 United States-Mexican Mixed Claims Commission and the successful outcome of the 1871 Treaty of Washington[250] to arbitrate the Alabama claims, together with dozens of subsequent new cases submitted to arbitration in the following decades, established the reputation of international arbitration among the U.S. legal elite.

By 1899, as we have seen, the rise in prestige of international arbitration had seen its first institutional outcome in the form of the Permanent Court of Arbitration (which, famously, was never permanent nor was it a Court) which materialized at the 1899 Peace Conference at The Hague and for which Andrew Carnegie—one of the ASIL's founding members—had already in 1903 agreed to build the Peace Palace, the future site of the Permanent Court of International Justice in The Hague. In practice, the very foundation of the American Society of International Law stemmed from the Lake Mohonk Conferences, which had been held annually since 1895 on the topic of international arbitration as a dispute settlement mechanism between governments. The Report of the Eleventh Annual Meeting of the Lake Mohonk Conference on International Arbitration[251] (1905) contained the Kirchwey Resolution, which was approved by the Business Committee[252] to establish the American Society of International Law and the launching of the first periodical in English devoted to the interests of international law in the United States. A committee of seven to research the project further was then established under the leadership of James B. Scott with the support of a stellar group of elite officials and academics who were critical of the 'unscientific' character of the peace movement.

250 Treaty of Washington, May 8, 1871, 12 Bevans 170, 143 Consol. Treaty Ser. 145.

251 See, e.g. Kirgis, 'The American Society of International Law's First Century' 2006.

252 See further 'History of the Organization of the American Society of International Law' *Proceedings of the American Society of International Law at Its Annual Meeting* 1 (1907–1917), 23–39.

The founding of the American Society of International Law, which for Raymond and Frischholz was the 'single factor [that] has contributed more to the study, the open discussion, the understanding, and the development of international law in the United States' coincided, as we have seen, with the heyday of positivism in international law. The Kirchwey Resolution, which had itself stressed the 'scientific character of international law that should serve as the focus for the peace movement,'[253] meant an enduring de-politicization of the peace movement in exchange for international scientific legal ideas. Moreover, the scientific approach was increasingly seen as a precondition for the manageable progressive development of international law. As Lassa Oppenheim, who had replaced John Westlake as the holder of the Whewell Chair of International law at Cambridge in 1908, and was the author of the most influential treatise in the English language of the early 20th century,[254] wrote, celebrating the progressive spirit of positivism in 1908 in the recent American Journal of International Law (AJIL), 'for the knowledge of realities enables the construction of realizable truths, in contradistinction to hopeless dreams'.[255]

A second driving force behind the foundation of ASIL was the U.S. domestic culture of the legalistic rule reflected in the vaunted emblem of 'government by laws and not by men'. Indeed, according to, to the classic theorist of British constitutionalism, A.V. Dicey, writing in the early 1910s, 'the main reason why the U.S. has carried out the federal system with unequalled success is that the people of the Union are more thoroughly imbued with legal ideas than any other existing nation'.[256] This culture of legalistic rule, captured in the conspicuous non sub homine sed sub deo et lege spirit, and the related predominant role that lawyers played in the U.S. domestic realm and in shaping public opinion and ideas on national policy, was to invariably be transposed onto the framework of international affairs through a new generation of 'lawyers qua lawyers'. The projection of the creed that America was a government of laws, not of men[257] became a blank check for a generation of lawyers who became the new elite intelligentsia entrusted with governing the international realm. The result of balancing the anti-colonial spirit of the Declaration of Independence with the domestic cultural legalist approach was that the American imperial project soon found itself wrapped in a legalist approach to international relations that would, one would argue, culminate in the Wilsonian readiness to promote

253 Id.

254 Oppenheim, International Law 1905–1906.

255 Lassa Oppenheim, 'The Science of International Law' 1908, 355.

256 A.V. Dicey, *Introduction to the Study of the Law of the Constitution* (1915).

257 Boyle, *Foundations of World Order* 1999, 17.

international law and the development of international organizations at the end of the First World War.

Another feature of American culture that influenced the emergence of the legalist approach to international relations among the elite intelligentsia at the turn of the twentieth century was confidence in the positive role of public opinion. According to another external observer of the U.S. in this epoch, J. Bryce, Reius Professor at Oxford and highly influential British Ambassador to the U.S. (1907–1913), echoing a liberal disposition also prevalent in the UK at the time which stressed the positive effects of an informed democratic public opinion in fostering progress in public policy and law,[258] in 'no country is public opinion so powerful as in the United States'.[259] 'Towering over presidents and state legislatures, over conventions, and the vast machinery of party, public opinion stands out, in the United States, as the great source of power, the master of servants who tremble before it'.[260]

This almost colossal quality that Bryce attributes to public opinion in the U.S. finds an echo in the first ever article published in the American Journal of International Law. Under the title 'The Need of Popular Understanding of International Law', the first President of ASIL, and by then also the 38th U.S. Secretary of State, Elihu Root wrote:

> The increase of popular control over national conduct, which marks the political development of our time, makes it constantly more important that the great body of the people in each country should have a just conception of their international rights and duties. [...]. Of course, it is not to be expected that the whole body of any people will study international law, but a sufficient number can readily become sufficiently familiar with it to lead and form public opinion in every community in our country upon all important international questions as they arise.[261]

This liberal belief in the beneficial effects that an informed public opinion could have on the conduct of foreign policy led, moreover, to an

258 See, representatively, A. V. Dicey *Lectures on the Relation between Law and Public Opinion in England during the Nineteenth Century* (1905).

259 Bryce, James. The american Commonwealth (London: Macmillan and Company, 1889), 909.

260 Id., 923.

261 Elihu Root, 'The Need of Popular Understanding of International Law', *American Journal of International Law* 1 (1907), 1–3.

avant-la-lettre academic campaign, as we shall see, in the first years of ASIL in favour of bolstering the teaching and study of international law in U.S. law schools.

All these background drivers informed the so-called 'moralistic legalistic' label, which F.A. Boyle attributed as a defining feature of US international lawyers of this generation.[262] This pre-Wilsonian generation of U.S. international lawyers was set to attain the following concrete objectives, which 'were pursued in a roughly contemporaneous manner because of their highly interdependent and mutually supportive nature':[263]

> '1) The creation of a general system for the obligatory arbitration of disputes between states; 2) the establishment of an international court of justice; 3) the codification of important areas of customary international law into positive treaty law; 4) arms reduction, but only after the relaxation of international relations by means of these and other legalist techniques and institutions; 5) the institutionalization of the practice of convoking periodic peace conferences for all states in the recognized international community.'[264]

However, the aspirational equation of peace and justice with scientific international law embodied by the legal-universalist high-mindedness of the new organization was soon to be combined with a strict 'Americanness' in the works of the organization. The founders of ASIL were, as we have seen, the intellectual inheritors of a nineteenth-century peripheral idealistic tradition. They were also the elite members of a rising semi-peripheral Western nation that, after having extended and consolidated its own domestic frontiers through continental expansion during the nineteenth century, had just experienced its own transition into an imperial power with overseas territories.

Indicative of how important international law was perceived to be by the foreign policy elite in the U.S. at the beginning of the 20th century is that the ASIL sprang up, indeed, from the heart of the American political 'establishment' of the day and age. The founding group of the constituent assembly of the Society took place in New York City on January 12, 1906 and included the incumbent U.S. Secretary of State as the first president of ASIL (a post that E. Root would hold for 18 years). It also comprised three Supreme Court Justices (including

262 See Boyle, *Foundations of World Order* 1999, 22.

263 Id., 23.

264 Id., 22.

Chief Justice Melville Fuller) as vice-presidents of the new society, two former U.S. Secretaries of State, a large-scale philanthropist (Andrew Carnegie—who funded the construction of the Peace Palace), and even the future U.S. President (1909–1913) and then Supreme Court Chief Justice (1921–1930) W. Howard Taft. Taft, who was by then Secretary of War and had previously gained experience in the colonial rule as the first Governor General of the Philippines between 1901 and 1904[265] would, in 1915, preside over a League to Promote Peace which dedicated itself to promote a 'League of Nations'.[266]

The rise of a foreign policy generation of 'lawyers qua lawyers,' who reached the apex of their influence in shaping U.S. foreign policy during the progressive era (1890s-1920s) is shown by the programme of the first annual meeting of the Society on April 19 and 20 1907 that included a reception by the President of the United States of the members of the Society at the White House. In 1907, the first issue of the American Journal of International Law (AJIL), which was the first periodical 'devoted exclusively or indeed generally to the exposition and development of international law' to be published in the English language, was published. The AJIL contributions were to stimulate the production of international legal literature and to re-channel the previously dispersed international legal publications from other law reviews.

Not surprisingly, its foreign-policy instrumentalist and nationalist bias was, from the onset, conveyed by the organization's 'particular interest in what came to be called the Foreign Relations Law of the U.S. and in international law issues of particular interest for the U.S.'[267] This interconnection is apparent in the often-portrayed 'behind the scenes leader,'[268] James Brown Scott, who other than being the first Editor-in-Chief of the American Journal of International Law between 1907 and 1924, and a constant contributor to its pages, developed an intense agenda of diplomatic activities until the First World War. A protégé of E. Root, among his posts, James Brown Scott, served as solicitor-general of the U.S. State Department between 1906 and 1911 during a period when the U.S. internationally extended its interests and activities by joining a number of international institutions,[269] and by participating in the drafting

265 Id.

266 William G. Ross, 'Constitutional Issues Involving the Controversy Over American Membership in the League of Nations, 1918–1920', *American Journal of Legal History* 53 (2013), 1–88, 3.

267 Representative of this tendency, Charles Cheney Hyde, International Law Chiefly as Interpreted and Applied by the United States (1922).

268 Nurnberger, James Brown Scott: Peace through Justice 1975, 8.

269 Such as the International Institute of Agriculture in 1906.

of many international conventions.[270] J. Brown Scott also served as a U.S. technical delegate to most of the major international conferences of the time, including the Second Hague Peace Conference of 1907, under a detailed set of guidelines set up by E. Root to foster the 'creation of a permanent international court as the country's single most important objective'.[271] After the conference, Brown Scott went on to publish his book 'The Hague Conferences of 1899 and 1907', where he builds on the domestic judiciary analogy,[272] and traces parallelisms between the Roman court system of justice, the development of the U.S. federal judiciary system, and the progress of permanent bodies of international dispute settlement on the international stage.

Working for the ASIL, and serving as the first general editor of the AJIL until 1924, James Brown Scott was also a powerful engine behind the establishment of international law in American Law Schools in consonance with the foundational goals of the ASIL. The goal of reaching out to the lay person to plant the seeds for the dissemination in the popular conscience of the need to abide by international legal principles in the ordered management of the state's foreign relations was one of the rhetorical factors that led to an early campaigning in favour of the bolstering of the teaching and study of international law. This educational drive was consistent with Brown Scott's creed that the path to peace was a 'process of education, not a process of treaty making and treaty breaking [...] winning over one generation, winning over another generation, until justice shall be the great interest of the world'.[273] Despite his

270 Ranging from the International Red Cross to telecommunications, from the acquisition of military bases to the establishment of rules and procedures for the extradition of criminals' and the suppression of the white slave traffic.

271 Martti Koskenniemi, 'The Ideology of International Adjudication and the 1907 Hague Conference', in Yves Daudet (Ed) *Topicality of the 1907 Hague Conference, the Second Peace Conference/ Actualité de la Conférence de La Haye de 1907, Deuxième Conférence de la paix* (Leiden/Boston: Brill, 2008), 137.

272 As explained by Paolo Amorosa the references to the framework provided by the US Constitution as a model for the progress of international law continued in diverse forms to influence Scott's international legal though and writings such as e.g. in James Brown Scott 'The United States: A Study in International Organization (Oxford: Oxford University Press, 1920) and Gaillard Hunt / James Brown (ed) *The Debates in the Federal Convention of 1787 which Framed the Constitution of the United States of America reported by James Madison* (Oxford: Oxford University Press, 1920) see further, Paolo Amorosa, 'James Brown Scott's International Adjudication between Tradition and Progress in the United States', *Journal of the History of International Law* 17 (2015), 15–46.

273 James Brown Scott, 'International Organization: Executive and Administrative', *Proceedings of the American Society of International Law* 11 (1917), 91–107.

extensive campaigning, and his activist role in the internationalisation of legal education both domestically and, as will be seen below, also internationally, international law in American law schools—by 1907 only ten law schools offered to teach on the subject—remained relatively marginal.[274]

This status quo was not affected by the holding of the First Conference of Teachers of International Law (1914), the first of the seven Conferences of Teachers of International Law and Related Subjects organised by the ASIL until 1941. These 'earnestly requests all law schools which now offer no instruction in international law to add to their curriculum a thorough course in that subject'. Nor it was dramatically affected by other calls that 'urged the American Bar Association to take action toward the inclusion of international law among law school subjects and those required for admission to the bar'.[275] Nonetheless, the prestige of international law began to be apparent in the bibliographical acquisitions of international law materials by American law schools.

The 1911 December issue of The Green Bag, An Entertainment Magazine for Lawyers, a journal established in Boston in 1889,[276] the section devoted to the 'Analysis of Leading Events of the Legal World'[277] reported the purchase in October 1911 by Harvard University of the 'library that has long been regarded as the most complete collection of works relating to international law and diplomacy'.[278] The 1912 May issue of The Green Bag went on to give the news of the fabulous contents of the Marquis de Olivart's collection

274 Charles Noble Gregory, 'The Study of International Law in Law Schools', *American Law School Review* 2 (1907) 41, 45.

275 See Proceedings First Conference of Teachers of International Law, Proceedings of the American Association of Professors of International Law (1914) noting 'Resolved, That, in recognition of the growing importance of a knowledge of international law to all persons who plan to devote themselves to the administration of justice, and who, through their professional occupation, may contribute largely to the formation of public opinion and who often will be vested with the highest offices in the State and nation, this Conference earnestly requests all law schools which now offer no instruction in international law to add to their curriculum a thorough course in that subject' Held in 1925, the Second Conference of Teachers of International Law reported that a study of 110 law school catalogues showed 65 carrying no course in international law, and 45 offering some kind of a course'. This report added that 'a contemporaneous survey of the 61 schools then members of the Association of American Law Schools gave 31 as offering the subject and 30 not teaching it'. The second conference of teachers of international law and related subjects held in Washington, 23–25 April 1925 19 American Journal of International Law (1925).

276 See cover-front, *The Green Bag, An Entertaining Magazine for Lawyers* (1889).

277 *The Green Bag,* (Arthur W. Spencer, Ed. 1911) XXIII, 665.

278 id.

under the heading 'The Acquisition of the Olivart Collection by Harvard Law School'.[279] According to The Green Bag's account, the Spanish bibliographical treasure Harvard University had acquired comprised nearly '60,000 volumes', and 'upward of 15,000 titles' including '1,550 volumes in Latin, some of them dating back to the 15th century'.[280] The Olivart Collection came just in time for it to be included in the list of more than five hundred libraries of the United States of America and Canada that The Law Library Journal published in 1912. There, the 150,000 volumes of Harvard Law School represented triple the contents of the second best university library in North America. The closest to it in terms of volumes was a library of one of the American Bar Associations that held 96,000 books. Not even the Library of the U.S. Congress and of U.S. the Supreme Court, with 145,000 volumes, could dispute Harvard Law School's reputation, which remained irrefutable ever since, of possessing the largest academic law library in the world.[281] The acquisition by Harvard University of the Marquis de Olivart's collection, which, as noted by S. Neff, 'formed the basis of what became, for many years, the standard bibliography of international legal literature',[282] was, furthermore, to make Harvard Law School to 'become a major center of international law scholarship'[283] in subsequent decades.

Scott combined his institutional efforts to bolstering the teaching of international law in the first half of the twentieth century with the spread of a particular type of international legal education. He, who had been educated at Harvard when the new Socratic case method was in its prime, also became the first General Editor of the American Casebook Series in 1906 (until 1915). He wrote in the preface to the first volume of the collection, which he had promoted, a strong argument in favour of the Harvard method.[284] In 1914, the United States Bureau of Education published a report declaring the triumph of the Harvard method: 'today the case method forms the principal, if not the exclusive, method of teaching in nearly all of the stronger law schools of the country'.[285] A staunch defender of international law as part of American domestic

279 XXIV *The Green Bag* (1912) 233.

280 Id,

281 The Centennial Story of the Harvard Law School, 1817–1917, (1918) 109–110, 86–122.

282 Neff, Justice Among Nations 2014, 304.

283 Id., 305.

284 William Ephraim Mikell, *Cases on Criminal Law Selected from Decisions of English and American Courts* (1908).

285 United States Bureau of Education, prepared by the American Bar Association's Committee on Legal Education in 1914, quoted in William R. Vance, *Preface* to the American Case Book Series (1922).

law, in the author's preface he stressed that the idea underlying his Cases on International Law was 'that international law formed a part of the common law of England and that, as such, it passed to the United States with that law of which it formed a part'. Scott's preference for the case approach found a corollary in 1910 when he also became the first President of the American Society for the Judicial Settlement of International Disputes. Brown Scott's profession of faith in the method continued unaltered throughout the years. In his updated 1922 Cases on International Law released in the framework of the American Casebook series, he argued for the greater availability of foreign material, by noting that:

'It is devoutly to be wished that members of the profession in foreign countries [...] produce collections of cases, not only for the benefit of the profession to which they belong, but also for the purpose of instruction in the law schools, universities, and other seats of learning in their respective states'.[286]

## James Brown Scott—The Omnipresent 'Amigo Americano'

James Brown Scott's career,[287] the 'behind the scenes leader'[288] of the American Society of International Law, developed through the main interconnected poles of his work as an activist academic in favour of international law, which he considered to be a 'common ground of contact between nations' as well as a vehicle 'of social and intellectual cooperation',[289] and as a diplomat and legal adviser. It was, however, in occupying the position from 1911 to 1940 of Director of the International Law Division of the Carnegie Endowment for

286 James Brown Scott, *Cases on International Law* (St.Paul: West Publishing Company, 1926), XVII.

287 Recent works that touch upon the figure of James Brown Scott include inter alia: Hatsue Shinohara, US *International Lawyers in the Interwar Years. A Forgotten* Crusade (Cambridge: Cambridge University Press, 2012) Christopher R. Rossi, *Broken Chain of Being: James Brown Scott and the Origins of Modern International Law* (Boston: Kluwer Law International, 1998), Anne Orford, 'The past as law or history? The relevance of imperialism for modern international law' in Emmanuelle Jouannet, Hélène Ruiz-Fabri and Mark Toufayan (eds), Tiers Monde: Bilan et Perspectives (Paris: Société de Législation Comparée, 2017). Paolo Amorosa, 'James Brown Scott's International Adjudication between Tradition and Progress in the United States' Journal of the History of International Law 17 (2015) 15–46.

288 Dingman Nurnberger, James Brown Scott: Peace through Justice 1975, 8.

289 James Brown Scott, 'American Institute of International Law', University of Pennsylvania Law Review 61 (1913), 580–587.

International Peace, founded 'to hasten the abolition of international war, the foulest blot upon our civilization', that he would more directly develop academic ties with the Hispanic world.

The extensive variety of activities he developed in this post included the foundation on the note day of 12 October 1912 of the American Institute of International Law (AIIL),[290] of which he remained president until his death in 1943, a date which also effectively signalled, after a brief interim period, with A. S. de Bustamante as president, the end of the Institute's activities. James Brown Scott co-founded AIIL with A. Alvarez, who at the time, as Obregon notes, was potentiating 'the institutionalization of his regionalist Latin-American perspective.'[291] 'He understood that it was necessary to include, rather than antagonize, the USA to avoid furthering the separation between the region's hegemony and the Latin American states'.[292] The codifying project of international law in the American continent had roots going back, as we saw in Chapter One, to the American Congress of Panama of 1826 and the Bolivarian project for a post-independent united America. In 1899, the first Pan-American conference held in Washington created the Pan-American Union. This regional international organization fostered through different Pan-American conferences and the establishment of a Committee of Jurists in 1906, a discussion of the codification of international law in America and of a particular breed of 'American international law'. This paved 'the long road' to the convention on the rights and duties of states signed in Montevideo in 1933.[293]

From 1912, the AIIL became the centrepiece of a network of national associations of international law representing twenty-one American republics. Each of the affiliated associations was conceived as 'a centre for the study and investigation of questions of international law and the principles of justice by which they should be settled, each disseminating just principles of international law and creating within each country a public opinion on their behalf'.[294] Management of numerous logistical aspects and a good deal of diplomatic manoeuvres, as well as the need to placate the Eurocentrism of the

290 The record of the establishment of the Institute and of its activities may be found in numerous articles in the *American Journal of International Law*, vols. 6–22, and particularly in the Special Supplements for 1926 and 1928.

291 Obregón, 'Between Civilisation and Barbarism' 2016, 825.

292 Id.

293 On the long road to Montevideo, see e.g. Becker Lorca, Mestizo International Law 2015, 327–352.

294 James Brown Scott, 'The American Institute of International Law', Advocate of Peace 78 (1916), 8–10.

profession, was, however, needed for the Institute to begin to function at its inaugural meeting held in Washington in 1915. Indeed, Brown Scott had to appease the raised eyebrows of some members of the Institute of International Law when he, and Alejandro Alvarez, who had just published his Droit international américain,[295] presented their project to them.

Scott did not hesitate in using his diplomatic skills to inform the Institut that 'there may be no mistake as to our purpose, which is to contribute, to the full extent of our abilities, to the development and the dissemination of a system of international law, as it has been created by the weight and wisdom of European publicists.'[296] However, no more than four years after Scott's earlier solemn plea, he was proposing to the new AIIL to study whether the principles of the US Declaration of Independence might be applicable to each American state in order to allow them to begin to develop an American international law 'based on an American conception of the state and the American conception of the government thereof'. As a follow-up to the first AIIL conference, the Declaration of the Rights and Duties of Nations was presented as being 'based exclusively upon decisions of the Supreme Court of the United States', and premised on the assessment that 'the principles of the Declaration are, as far as the United States is concerned, the law of the land'. Scott went even further to conclude, after stressing that 'these principles obtain in each of the American republics' law', that 'the Declaration is, in reality, a statement of the fundamental principles of international law, as they are understood in the New World'.[297]

Elihu Root would echo Scott's works on the occasion of the adoption of The Declaration of the Rights and Duties of Nations by the American Institute of International Law in 1916:

'This institution has been established not as a competitor of the Institut de Droit International, which selects its members from among all the civilized countries, and not with the idea that there is such a thing as American international law to be distinguished from general international law, but with the idea that there may be special American views upon international questions; that the circumstances of the American republics may make it desirable for them to insist upon and press forward the development of particular principles in the law; that there are varieties of opinion upon such subjects which it may be useful to subject to common discussion and comparison of views;

295 Alvarez, *Le Droit International Americain*, 1910.

296 George Finch, Unpublished Biography of James Brown Scott, unnumbered chapter, George A. Finch, Adventures in Internationalism: A Biography of James Brown Scott (William E. Butler (ed.)) (Pennsylvania: The Law Book Exchange, 2012).

297 Id., XVI.

that the promotion of the habit of thinking broadly and internationally and not narrowly or locally, and a knowledge in each country of the points of view and habits of thought of each other country, will make all the American states more useful members of the family of nations, more considerate, more tolerant of differences of opinion, and more conscious of the international duties which are correlative to international rights.'[298]

This Declaration, which included an avant-la-lettre section on the 'International Rights of the Individual', was both the basis and provided substantial content to the Convention on Rights and Duties of States concluded, as we shall later see, at the Seventh Pan-American Conference in Montevideo in 1933.[299]

Brown Scott's contribution to the shaping of the international legal 'conscience of the Americas' was also channelled by his bolstering of international legal studies in Spanish. This included the publication of a Spanish translation of the American Journal of International Law for ten years (from January 1912 to 1922). By the tenth year of the translated issues of the AJIL, there were already two periodicals published in Latin America, namely the Revista Mexicana de Derecho Internacional (from 1919) and the Revista Argentina de Derecho Internacional (from 1920). The Spanish translation of AJIL was subsequently replaced by the Revista de Derecho Internacional, which was published under the aegis of the American Institute of International Law and directed by Antonio S. de Bustamante in La Habana. Scott hoped that the Revista de Derecho Internacional could 'find favour in the sight of Spanish-American publicists, serving as a convenient means of communication and interpreting the enlightened views of the Spanish-speaking world to the world at large'.[300] Once again, the credit for the lion's share of pan-Americanism goes to the AJIL's Editor-in-Chief, who was also one of the architects of the 'good neighbour' policy of the U.S. Department of State during this period. The members of the association met at irregular intervals until the mid-1940s and collaborated through draft projects on the works of the International Commission of American Jurists for the Codification of International Law.

However, it was Scott's role as Editor-in-Chief of the collection of Classics of International Law from 1906 until 1940 that led him to develop strong ties with Spain. He proposed The Classics of International Law to the Carnegie

298 Elihu Root, 'The Declaration of the Rights and Duties of Nations Adopted by the American Institute of International Law', *Proceedings of the American Society of International Law at Its Annual Meeting* 10 (1916) 1–11.

299 Becker Lorca, Mestizo International Law 2015.

300 James Brown Scott, 'The Revista de Derecho Internacional', American Journal of Iinternational Law 16 (1922), 437–438.

Institute in Washington in 1906, which began to publish it in 1911 with Scott as both the General Editor and as the occasional author of some of the introductions and prefaces of the collection. From 1917 onwards, it was published under the auspices of the Carnegie Endowment for International Peace, reaching its 22nd and final volume in 1950. Amongst the classics from Spain were re-editions of works by Baltasar Ayala (2nd Volume with a Preface by J.B. Scott in 1912), Francisco de Vitoria (7th Volume in an edition by Ernest Nys in 1917), and Francisco Suarez (20th Volume published in 1944 with a posthumous introduction by J.B. Scott). The Classics of International Law marked the beginning of a lasting relationship between James Brown Scott and the Dominican friar and Prima Professor of Sacred Theology at the University of Salamanca, Francisco de Vitoria (1483–1547).

According to Scott,

'From justice nations must derive their rules of law. And this is so, although they may affect to consider themselves the source instead of the agent whereby the principles of justice, expressed and made visible in rules of law, enter the minds and the thoughts of men before they pervade the practice of nations'.[301]

This perspective brought him close, as we shall see in Chapter Three, to the 'Spanish Classics' that Brown Scott did himself much to reconstruct as an inspiration for the 'new international law' of the interwar period.

In his General Editor's Preface to the first volume of The Classics of International Law in 1911, Brown Scott wrote:

'It is hoped the series will enable readers as well as specialists to trace international law from its faint and unconscious beginnings to its present ample proportions and to forecast, with some degree of certainty, its future development into that law which Mirabeau tells us one day will rule the world.'[302]

The aftermath of the First World War would provide the international community with the first great litmus test of this ambition.

301 Brown Scott, *Cases on International Law*, 1926, XVII.

302 James Brown Scott, 'Preface', 'Preface', in Thomas Erskine Holland (ed.), The Classics of International Law, Richard Zouche, *Iuris et iudicii fecialis, sive, iuris inter gentes, et quaestionum de eodem explication* (Washington: Division of International Law, Carnegie Endowment for International Peace, 1911).

CHAPTER 3

# The Silver Age of International Law in Spain

## 'The Strongest Breakthrough for the World at Large'

The renaissance of Francisco de Vitoria and the Spanish legal theologians of the 16th century Salamanca School in the interwar period owes much to the personal contribution of two international law scholars. The most famous of these was James Brown Scott who, according to M. O. Hudson, had 'fathered and fostered the development of international law during its greatest period of history'.[1] The other, far more obscure international law scholar, was Camilo Barcia Trelles (1888–1977). From the mid-late 1920s, Barcia Trelles, a professor of international law at Valladolid University since 1920, became the author to whom Carl Schmitt attributed the role of bringing about 'the strongest breakthrough for the world at large'[2] regarding the seminal contribution of Francisco de Vitoria to international law in the 16th century and the contemporary relevance of the intellectual legacy of the Salamanca School in the new international legal order of the interwar period.

Barcia was invited three times to contribute to the courses at The Hague Academy of International Law on what was to become known as the 'Spanish School of Ius Gentium'. He lectured at The Hague Academy on Francisco de Vitoria and the Modern School of International Law[3] in 1927, on Francisco Suarez and the Spanish Theologians of the Sixteenth Century[4] in 1933, and on Fernando Vazquez de Menchaca and the 16th century Spanish School of International Law[5] in 1939 respectively. In 1928, within the framework of

1 See Manley O. Hudson, *Portrait of Dr. James Brown Scott, Harvard Alumni Bulletin* XXIII (1931) 419.

2 Schmitt, *The nomos of the Earth* 2003, 124.

3 Camilo Barcia Trelles, ' Barcia Trelles, Camilo. Francisco de Vitoria et l'ecole moderne du droit international', Collected courses of The Hague Academy of International Law 17 (1928), 109–342.

4 Camilo Barcia Trelles, 'Francisco suarez (1548–1617): les théologiens espagnols du xvie siècle et l'école moderne du droit international', Collected courses of the Hague Academy of International Law 43 (1933), 385–554.

5 Camilo Barcia Trelles, 'Fernando Vázquez de Menchaca. L'école espagnole du droit international du xvie siécle', Collected courses of the Hague Academy of International Law 67 (1939), 430–534.

 | DOI 10.1163/9789004343238_005

the Section of Americanist Studies, over which he presided at Valladolid University, Barcia also published in Spanish 'Francisco de Vitoria, fundador del Derecho international moderno' (Francisco de Vitoria, Founder of Modern International Law)[6] and a prologue to James Brown Scott's 'El origen español del Derecho internacional moderno' (The Spanish Origins of Modern International Law).[7] This was an earlier version of Brown Scott's 'The Spanish Origins of International Law. Francisco de Vitoria and his Law of Nations',[8] Brown Scott's own influential contribution to Vitorian debates in the interwar period. With this book, Brown Scott, who at the time was the President of the American Society of International Law (1929–1939), established, as we shall later see, the global reputation of Francisco de Vitoria as the founder of the law of nations[9] 'far beyond the scholarly disciplines of history and international law'.[10]

Barcia Trelles' inquiries and re-readings of the School of Salamanca in the light of interwar developments was paralleled by an intense interest in U.S. foreign policy and its effects on incipient projects for Latin-American regional integration ranging from analyses of American foreign policy in the aftermath of the First World War[11] to the study of regional and continental trends in the Americas, pan-Americanism and Ibero-Americanism. In 1925, he authored 'El imperialismo del petroleo y la paz mundial' (World Peace and Oil Imperialism). In this book, he examined 'the influence of U.S. oil companies in pushing forward an imperialist trend, overwhelming, scarcely scrupulous, which puts the activity of American foreign policy at the service of interested views, even when the latter may lead to involvement in the sphere of independent sovereignties.' This line of research gained him a fellowship from the Carnegie Endowment for International Peace and a tour of academic conferences across North American universities in 1928–29. While in residence, under the patronage of the Carnegie Endowment for International Peace, he conducted research for the second of the courses he

6 Francisco de Vitoria, 'Fundador del Derecho internacional moderno' (Valladolid: talleres tipográficos Cuesta, 1928).

7 James Brown Scott, 'El origen español del Derecho internacional moderno' (Valladolid: talleres tipográficos Cuesta, 1928).

8 James Brown Scott, *The Spanish Origin of International Law. Francisco de Vitoria and his Law of Nations* (New York: Oxford University Press, 1934).

9 James Brown Scott, *El origen español del Derecho* 1928.

10 Schmitt, *The Nomos of the Earth* 2003, 119.

11 Camilo Barcia Trelles, *La política exterior norteamericana de la postguerra*, (Valladolid: talleres tipográficos Cuesta, 1925).

was invited to offer at The Hague Academy in 1930: 'The Monroe Doctrine in its Historical Development, particularly as far as Inter-American Relations are Concerned'.[12] In his course, Barcia retraced the antecedents of the Monroe Doctrine back to Francisco de Vitoria's writings on 'a new world and a new law' and subsequent doctrines. Examining its historical evolution in great detail, Barcia paid particular attention to the debated inclusion of the Monroe Doctrine in Article 21 of the Covenant of the League of Nations[13] as an example of 'regional understandings [...] securing the maintenance of peace' and its influence on regionalist discussions in the Americas in the 1920s. Barcia's research stay in the United States also informed his related books on 'La Constitución Norte-Americana y la Sociedad de Naciones' (The North American Constitution and the League of Nations)[14] and 'La Doctrina Monroe y el problema de la cooperacion internacional' ('The Monroe Doctrine and the Problem of International Cooperation'),[15] published in 1930 and 1931.

Barcia's critical and analytical works on Americanist themes in the mid-1920s and his studies on the School of Salamanca were published at a time of both cultural and, to a far lesser degree, economic competition between Spain and the United States in Latin America. As we saw in Chapter 1, this competition for spheres of influence can be retraced to the troubled attempts to generate stable diplomatic relations around the Spanish possessions of Cuba and Puerto Rico between Spain and the United States since the War of Yara in the late 1860s and 1870s. Since the Spanish-American war of 1898, as the U.S. transitioned into an imperial power with overseas territories, the U.S.' assertion of hegemony in the region had steadily increased. In 1903, the U.S. took control of the Panama Canal with the Hay-Bunau-Varilla Treaty. Soon thereafter, in 1904, Theodore Roosevelt announced his 'Big Stick' corollary to the Monroe Doctrine, proclaiming the right to act as a regional 'police power' and allowing U.S. military forces to intervene as a last resort to ensure that

---

12 Camilo Barcia Trelles, 'La doctrine de monroe dans son développement historique particulièrement en ce qui concerne les relations interamericaines', Collected Courses of the Hague Academy of International Law 32 (1930), 391–603.

13 Article 21 Covenant of the League of Nations, 'Nothing in this Covenant shall be deemed to affect the validity of international engagements, such as treaties of arbitration or regional understandings like the Monroe doctrine, for securing the maintenance of peace'.

14 Camilo Barcia Trelles, 'La Constitución Americana y la Sociedad de Naciones', (Valladolid: talleres tipográficos Cuesta, 1930).

15 Camilo Barcia Trelles, 'La Doctrina Monroe y el problema de la cooperación internacional' (Madrid: Ed. Mundo Latino, 1931).

other American nations fulfilled their obligations to international creditors, and to restore internal stability to nations in the region. The new doctrine would be used in a dozen interventions by the United States in Central America and the Caribbean in the 1900s and 1910s.

The U.S.' new foreign interventionism added fuel to the flames of the appeal of the linguistic and cultural unity of the Hispanic world. Since the 1898, the Spain's transatlantic foreign policy, which had been mainly addressed to the linguistic, cultural and 'spiritual' terrain, benefited from new literary Latin-American trends emerged in the search for a Latin-American identity free from what became known as the 'Nordmania'. Inspired, among other works, by the essays on 'Hispanic-Americanism' by M. de Unamuno, who identified the Spanish language, 'the blood of my spirit', with the true motherland of all those who employ it, the new 'Hispanist' cultural movement was marked by an influential essay Ariel penned by the Uruguayan J. E. Rodo, sponsor of a literary Americanism[16] which reinforced ties with Spanish literary circles. Rodo's work became a sort of "American gospel' that preached a type of idealism—the 'Arielism'—as a Latin model against the aggressive and expansionist U.S model.'[17] Adding to the momentum of this literary cultural movement, the modernist Nicaraguan poet Ruben Dario also challenged the U.S. President in his 'To Roosevelt': 'You are the United States, you are the future invader of the naive America that has Indian blood, who still prays to Jesus Christ and still speaks Spanish'. In 1905, Darío also famously invoked the 'inclitas razas ubérrimas, sangre de Hispania fecunda' ('distinguished fructiferous races, blood of prolific Hispania') to reclaim the Hispanic legacy and to call for a renovation of Pan-Hispanic transnational ties based on the Spanish language and the Latin race. In 1914, under the auspices of the Ibero-American Union, the date of 12 October began to be celebrated as the day of 'Hispanidad' and the 'day of the (Hispanic) race'.

Against the background of U.S. interventionism, this rise in political and cultural leverage of the notions of Hispano-Americanism, Ibero-Americanism, and 'Hispanidad' coincided with a move by Latin-American nations, as we saw, in chapter Two, on the occasion of The Hague Conference of 1907, to participate more actively in the international juridical sphere. The more

16 Florencia Bonfiglio, 'Los principios hispanoamericanos: la crítica de José Enrique Rodó y la literatura peninsular', in Raquel Macciuci (ed) Huellas de la Constitución de Cádiz; Diálogos transatlánticos (La Plata: Mercado Editorial, 2011).

17 Fernando Ainsa, 'El centenario de Ariel: una lectura para el 2000', Cuadernos Americanos-Nueva Epoca 85 (2001), 18–35.

assertive role of Latin-American countries on the international legal arena included the reclamation of recognition of equality with European nations, the pronouncement of doctrines of non-intervention such as the Drago Doctrine,[18] and the postulation of the recognition of a regional corpus of international law and Latin-American particularities[19] amidst projects for the regional codification of international law.[20] This tendency was reinforced in the international political sphere in the wake of the establishment of the League of Nations, which further stimulated internationalist debates on the cohabitation of universalism and regional particularism. The establishment of League furnished, moreover, Spanish foreign policy with the opportunity to countervail Spain's own semi-peripheral status in Europe by becoming a strategic bridge between Europe and a group of Latin-American nations which were no longer disparagingly perceived as 'stand[ing] on the margin of international life'.[21]

The first rediscovery of the School of Salamanca among international law scholars took place in the late 19th century at a time when the new academically organized profession was looking to set up a genealogy of the origins of the science of international law and to justify a new strand of 'civilizing' European formal imperialism. The second and definitive renaissance of Francisco de Vitoria, and the ensuing consolidation of the international reputation of the 'Spanish classics of international law' as the 'founders of international law', materialised in the mid-1920s and early 1930s. It did so against the background of projects for international codification in the Americas and the renewal of cultural and linguistic ties under the cloak of 'Hispanidad' between Spanish and Latin-American nations. This propitious diplomatic backdrop coincided, furthermore, with an intellectual re-alignment and updating of the doctrines of Francisco de Vitoria and the Spanish classics of the Seconda Scholastica at a time when the European international legal academia across Europe was looking for a natural law-based ancillary stone of the 'international community' to further legitimize the appeal of the League of Nations and the binding force of international law.[22]

---

18 Building on the Calvo doctrine, see earlier Carlos Calvo, International Law of Europe and America in Theory and Practice (1868).

19 Alejandro Alvarez, 'Latin-America and International Law', *American Journal of International Law* 3 (1909), 269–353.

20 See Esquirol, 'Latin America', 2012.

21 See e.g. Percy Alvin Martin, 'Latin America and the League of Nations', *The American Political Science Review*, 20 (1926), 14–30, 14.

22 A detailed summary of the contents of Chapter 3 can be found in the 'Introduction'.

## The League—A Fundamental Transformation

The year of the founding of the League of Nations can often be found depicted as a symbolic turning point in the standard periodization of the history of international law,[23] on a par with the aetiological quality of Westphalia in the discipline. The routine characterization of the interwar years as the 'foundational period of contemporary international law'[24] owes much to the pivotal role played by the establishment of the League of Nations and its role as a transmission belt from a pre-institutional to a proto-institutionalised world order.[25] The 'move to institutions'[26] in the aftermath of the First World War, itself a classic 'stereotypical context-breaking event'in the history of international law,[27] embodied the first attempt at a transposition with universalist pretensions and permanent character of the institutions of the domestic constitutional liberal model to the supra-national sphere. This transition fostered theoretical reflection and the emergence of a series of new schools of thought in international law inspired by an 'anti-sovereignist ethos'.[28] It also engendered the development of new functional areas that, in the image of the domestic branches of law, nurtured the soil for new branches of international law such as international administrative law, international criminal law, international refugee law and for the forerunners of international human rights law.

The interwar generation of international law scholars lived through a major structural transformation in the history of international 'legal consciousness',[29] a period when, as D. Kennedy has noted, the field [of international law] became professionalized and its basic concepts and structures were set in place.[30] The institutional and intellectual structural transformation brought about by the League of Nations and the geopolitical implications of the post-war settlement were also deeply felt by Spanish international law scholars. The early

23 The classic example is Wilhem Grewe, *The Epochs of international law.* translated and revised by Michael Byers (Berlin: De Gruyter 2000).

24 Andreas paulus, 'The International Legal System as a Constitution', Jeffrey L. Dunoff/ Joel P. Trachtman (eds) *Ruling the World? Constitutionalism, International Law, and Global Governance* (Cambridge: Cambridge University Press 2009) 109, 112.

25 Kennedy 'The Move to Institutions', 1987, 841.

26 Id.

27 Koskenniemi, 'Vitoria and US' 2014.

28 Martti Koskenniemi, *From Apology to Utopia. The Structure of the International Legal Argument* (Cambridge: Cambridge University Press 2006).

29 Kennedy, The Rise and Fall 1975/2006.

30 Kennedy, The Move to Institutions 1987, 846.

interwar period coincided, moreover, with the confluence of the first and a second, more Europeanized, professional generation of international law professors in Spain. This confluence contributed to reinforcing the integration of interwar Spanish international lawyers in the works of the European doctrine.

The great intellectually diversifying boost that the founding of the League gave to international law as a juridical discipline was also accompanied by a parallel transition from the dominance of diplomatic history and state-centred international law towards a sociological approach to the study of international society that heralded the coming into being of a new science of international relations. Indeed, what Del Arenal describes as the growing 'affirmation of the hegemonism of international law as the science of international society'[31] in late-nineteenth century Spain had facilitated, as we saw in earlier chapters, the scientific autonomy of international law in Spanish universities. The establishment of the League, insofar as it allowed the teleological 'scientification' of international law to become institutionalized, fostered the development of legalistic trends aiming to further crystallize, around the notions of bindingness and enforceability, the scientific cycle of legalistic internationalism of codification and mechanisms of international dispute settlement surveyed in earlier chapters. However, the League also opened a new cycle in this evolution by fostering the gradual emergence of a parallel scientific paradigm that attempted to transcend, in a revamped international sphere, the exclusivism of the solipsistic state-centric conception underlying classical international law so as to extend its scientific gaze towards, as Del Arenal notes, 'emerging social, political and economic realities that were impacting with even greater strength international relations and international law itself.'[32] The sociological turn in the study of international society, which was mirroring parallel scientific developments in economically and socially transforming domestic societies, inspired, as we shall see, new sociological conceptions within international law. This academic turn, transforming diplomatic history in new sociological and historical directions,[33] would also prepare the ground for the gradual birth of a new discipline able 'to occupy itself with international reality in all its dimensions'[34] in the aftermath of the Second World War.

The interest in the study of a semi-institutionalized international society further benefitted from the development and specialization of the administrative organization of the foreign offices of various states in their relations, albeit

31 Del Arenal, 'La génesis de las relaciones internacionales' 1981, 873.
32 Id., 874
33 Id.,
34 Id.,

not uniquely, with the new permanent international institutions. In Spain, the Spanish ministry of Foreign Affairs created a special section in 1920, the Spanish Office of the League of Nations, to formulate Spanish foreign policy regarding the League and to coordinate the activities of the various Spanish delegates. The political interest in the study of international relations was soon reflected in the setting up of new expert bodies, such as the Council on Foreign Relations in New York and the Royal Institute of International Affairs in London, both in 1919. Academic parallels can be found in the establishment of the first chairs in international relations at Aberystwyth and the London School of Economics in the early 1920s.[35] The functional and technical study of international relations were, furthermore, spurred by the role that the League Secretariat assumed in new fields of activity and technical areas involving 'economic and social duties through which it intervened in international health, economics, and communication'[36] beyond its original mandate concerning the field of peace and security. New specialized staff—steadily growing in numbers at the permanent secretariat of the League (i.e. from 411 members in 1924 to 685 in 1929)[37]—fostered international functional cooperation through numerous committees and commissions. This, which is often credited as one of the League's great successes,[38] lay the origins of international civil service careers 'based on the principles of internationalism, independence, and neutrality.'[39] In addition to paving the way for future specialized agencies and functional organs in a panoply of future international organizations, these developments also led to works on international administrative law and to an early theory of 'functionalism' in international organizations.[40] They fostered, furthermore, the new international 'professional consciousness' of what F.Megret calls 'international man', that is, 'a unique class of individuals dedicated to the international cause, whose naturally internationalist predispositions suggest that they

35 See Neila, 'La política exterior de la españa republicana' 2004, 47–83.

36 Stephen Legg, 'The Life of Individuals as well as of Nations': International Law and the League of Nations' Anti-Trafficking Governmentalities' *Leiden Journal of International Law* 25 (2012), 647–664, 648.

37 The League of Nations—Ten Years. Editorial research reports 1930 (Vol. I). (Washington, DC: CQ Press 1930).

38 Christian J.Tams, 'League of Nations' *Max Planck Encyclopedia of Public International Law* (2006), 11.

39 Id.

40 See in general, Jan Klabbers, 'Institutional Law', Oxford Bibliographies of International Law (accesible at http://www.oxfordbibliographies.com/view/document/obo-9780199796953/obo-9780199796953-0002.xml).

can be expected to rise above their national origins' and to 'whom worthy and even sacred tasks of international government could be entrusted.'[41] In 1927, the Institut d'hautes etudes internationales, founded in Geneva by W. Rappard and P. Mantoux, two high-ranking officials from the League's Secretariat, became the first specialized academic institution in continental Europe for 'the study'—as Salvador de Madariaga would have put it—'of world affairs from the world point of view'.[42]

However, the origins of the new interwar international order were inauspicious. The enthusiasm among the defeated powers for the new international organization was dampened by the twin births of the Covenant and the postwar settlement in the Treaty of Versailles with its 'return to a concept of just peace'[43] for, as Clemenceau put it, for 'the greatest crime against humanity and the freedom of peoples that had ever been committed by a nation that pretends to be civilized'.[44] James Brown Scott, who acted as an advisor to the US government at the negotiation and drafting of the Treaty of Versailles, and who was also a member of the Advisory Committee of Jurists, or 'Committee of Ten,' who drafted the Statute of the PCIJ, echoed a widespread perception at the launch of the League when he noted that 'the statesmen have [...] made a peace that renders another war inevitable.'[45] Moreover, minor and medium powers, including neutral states that had initially shared the Wilsonian fervour that swept across Europe at the end of the war, soon came to fear that the non-accession of the U.S. over constitutional questions about national sovereignty and the separation of powers[46] would result in a collapse of the U.S. 'leadership bridge', thus making the League an instrument of power politics for the winners of the First World War.

---

41 Frederic Megret, 'The Rise and Fall of International Man', in Prabhakar Singh/Benoît Maye (eds.) Critical International Law (Oxford: Oxford University Press 2014).

42 Salvador de Madariaga, *Theory and Practice of International Relations*, (Filadelfia: Swarthmore College. 1937 republished Literary Licensing, LLC 2013),94.

43 Randall Lesaffer, 'Peace Treaties and the Formation of International Law' in Bardo Fassbender / Anne Peters (eds) *Oxford Handbook of the History of International Law* (Oxford: Oxford University Press 2012), 71–94, 91.

44 President Clemencau, President of the Peace Conference wrote to the President of the German Delegation in 16th june 1919 quoted in Fernandez Liesa *El derecho internacional de los derechos humanos en perspectiva histórica* 2013, 111.

45 Ferdinand Foch 'This is not a peace. It is an armistice for 20 years'

46 See William G. Ross, 'Constitutional Issues Involving the Controversy Over American Membership in the League of Nations, 1918–1920' 53 American Journal of Legal History 1, 2013. 1–88.

Despite the final U.S. Senate's decision to 'break the heart of the world,'[47] by not signing the U.S. accession to the League, the seminal and unprecedented character of the new order ushered in by the Preamble of the Covenant,[48] which was subscribed to by the forty-two original members[49] of the organization, was apparent to the interwar generation of international law scholars. First and foremost, the control of the use of force in international relations[50] became pivotal to the development of a new form of communal 'legalistic internationalism' in the interwar period. Although the system of collective security established by the League's Covenant turned out to be short of effective sanctions,[51] it embodied the pacifist ideals contained in the generational project of 'building peace through law'. This project had inspired, as we saw in Chapter 2,[52] the early efforts of ASIL, along the axis of international dispute settlement mechanisms, the codification of international law, and efforts to educate public opinion, and had led to a growing rise in prominence of the peace movement during the period of 'la paix armée.' The Covenant contained a seminal system of international dispute settlement including 'three specific provisions against war' addressed to the conflicting parties to facilitate a 'cooling off' period and a collective sanctions regime in case any Member of the League resorted to war. The obligation undertaken by the state members 'to respect and preserve against external aggression the territorial integrity and existing political independence of all the League's Members'[53] was complemented by their recognition that 'the maintenance of peace requires the reduction of national armaments to the lowest point consistent with national safety and the enforcement by common action of international obligations.'[54] The design of a framework for cooperation among nations in areas of peace

47 President Wilson, in presenting the treaty to the Senate on July 10, 1919, asked: 'Dare we reject it and break the heart of the world?', quoted in Ross, 'Constitutional Issues Involving the Controversy' 2013, 3.

48 Robert Kolb (ed.), *Commentaire sur le Pacte de la Société des Nations* (Bruxelles: Bruylant 2015).

49 Tams, League of Nations 2006, 4–5.

50 International Law and International Events (1908–1960), 693.

51 See e.g. Stephen Wertheim, 'The League of Nations: a Retreat from International Law?', *Journal of Global History* 7 (2012), 210–232.

52 Frederic L. Kirgis, 'Elihu Root, James Brown Scott and the Early Years of the ASIL',. Lawyers as Statesmen: Twentieth-Century Attitudes Toward International Law. Are international institutions doing their Job? Proceedings of the Annual Meeting of the American Society of International Law 90 (1996), 139–143, 140.

53 Covenant of the League of Nations, Art. 10. See also Arts. 11,12, 13, 15 and 16.

54 Covenant of the League of Nations Art. 8.

and security, which extended to other technical areas, represented the culmination of the aspirations of the pre-war peace-movement projects, including stepping away 'from the sovereign right to wage war, long regarded as an essential attribute of statehood,'[55] and paying homage to earlier visionary constructions built on I. Kant's *foedus pacificum.*

Also in the image of the domestic state, the 'move' to an international organization in the political and other spheres was paralleled by the development of permanent international courts and a recognizable international judicial technique. The principle of peaceful resolution of international disputes by judicial means was paramount in the League's agenda. A hard-won battle for pre-war international lawyers, the most representative of their dreams realized was the establishment of a Permanent International Court of Justice open to non-state members. The new statute of the Court, as well as including a list of formal sources,[56] encompassed other novelties such as the possibility for organs of the League to request advisory opinions and the inclusion of an optional or compromissory clause under which states could issue declarations—forty-four had done so by 1930—accepting the compulsory jurisdiction of the League in matters arising between member states. The compulsory registration of treaties—also a long-sought measure to prevent the signing of secret treaties—and the leaning towards multilateralism and the engagement of public opinion with international questions were also watermarks of the 'New Diplomacy' with which the League tried to distance itself from the 'Old Diplomacy' that many signalled as the cause behind the horrors of the First World War. The institutionalization of the 'New Diplomacy' was fostered by 'the decision of the First Assembly in 1920 to meet annually', which was afterwards cited by the League authorities as 'the most momentous single act in the whole development of international intercourse.'[57] Moreover, the inclusion in Article 227 of the Versailles Treaty of a Special Tribunal to try the former Kaiser, which built on the codification efforts in the laws of war at The Hague Conferences, despite being ultimately ineffectual, paved the way for precursors of international criminal justice in the interwar period.[58]

---

55 Tams, League of Nations 2006, 4.

56 See Thomas Skouteris, 'The Force of a Doctrine', in Fleur Johns, R. Joyce & S. Pahuja (eds), *Events: The Force of International Law* (London: Routledge, 2011), 69–80.

57 The League of Nations—Ten Years. (1930). Editorial research reports 1930 (Vol. I) (Washington, DC: CQ Press 1930) (accesible at http://library.cqpress.com/cqresearcher/cqresrre1930010800)

58 See i.e. Mark Lewis, The Birth of the New Justice (Oxford: Oxford University Press, 2014).

The perception of international innovation and the opening of new horizons for international law as part of the new interwar *zeitgeist* was reinforced by a further modification of traditional notions of sovereignty. This was brought about by the enshrinement of a series of 'obligations of international concern' that were 'placed under the guarantee of the League of Nations'[59] regarding the treatment of minorities. The minority treaty system of the League addressed the need for the internationally administered protection of minorities after the exchange of populations brought about by the collapse of former empires and the challenges posed to multinational states by Wilson's championing of the principle of self-determination of peoples at a time of the creation of seven new states with thousands of miles of new frontiers in the aftermath of the First World War. The seminal character of the minority treaty system, which is evidenced by the sets of rights contained in the network of treaties, is often seen as a forerunner of international human rights law, and a prelude to a 'new era of relations between state and individuals'[60] belonging to racial, linguistic or religious minorities. The ideals of minority protection, however, betrayed a security concern regarding ethnic conflicts, the problem of cultural difference, the nationality principle and the risk of unilateral interference by kin states in the complex post-war re-drawn map of Europe.[61] As the Director of the Department of Minority Protection Affairs and Deputy Secretary-General of the League of Nations, Pablo de Azcarate (1933–1936) admitted, the main aim of the minority protection regime was 'to avoid the many interstate frictions and conflicts which had occurred in the past because of the frequent ill-treatment or oppression of national minorities.'[62]

The transformational impact of the League, aligning humanitarian purposes with the goal of bringing domestic stability,[63] was further compounded by the

59 The standard formula contained in the Treaty between the Principal Allied and Associated Powers and Poland (June 28, 1919) became a blue-print for other international treaties.

60 Peter Hilpold 'The League of Nations and the Protection of Minorities—Rediscovering a Great Experiment', Max Planck Yearbook of United Nations Law 17 (2013), 87–124.

61 Antony Anghie, 'Nationalism, Development and the Postcolonial State: The Legacies of the League of Nations' *Texas International Law Journal* (2006) 447–463, 450 pointing, in a post-colonial vein, to the use of the apparently benign term 'civilisation' as yet another example 'vocabulary of international law, far from being neutral, or abstract, is mired in this history of subordination and extinguishing alien cultures.'

62 Pablo de Azcarate y Florez, *League of Nations and National Minorities: an Experiment* (Washington: Carnegie endowment for international peace, 1945), 14.

63 See eg. Carol Weisbrod, 'Minorities and Diversities: the "Remarkable Experiment" of the League of Nations' *Connecticut Journal of International Law* 8 (1992–1993), 359.

inclusion of an innovative 'mandate system'[64] championed by Wilson as an alternative to the annexation of the Ottoman territories and German colonies by the victorious powers. This led to fourteen mandated territories divided into four categories being established across the Middle East, Africa and the Pacific[65] under the supervision of the League's Mandates Commission, whose works, following the logic of the 'sacred trust of civilization' to prepare the mandated territories for self-government, constituted, 'the basis of a new code of international mandatory law and practice whose influence is felt throughout the whole domain of colonial administration.'[66] Another innovative milestone, which further contributed to the impression on its contemporaries of the seminal historical quality of the fundamental transformation brought about by the Treaty of Versailles and its protocols, was the creation of an International Labour Organization. Conceived as an institutionalized liberal response to the 1917 Revolution, the ILO, which evolved into being 'regarded as the League's self-governing agency for the prosecution of problems falling within the industrial field',[67] was provided in its organizational structure with a General Conference, a Governing Body and a secretariat in the form of an International Labour Office with several hundred officials serving dozens of international labour conventions.

## The Spanish Policy of Prestige and Revisionism at the League and the Second 'Professional Generation' of Spanish International Law Scholars

The position of Spain at the outbreak of the war in 1914 had been conditioned by Spain's strategic interests in North Africa within the British-French orbit of influence and its under-developed military and economic capacity. As we saw in Chapter Two, the Cartagena Agreement of 1907 had confirmed the role of Spain as a buffer state in the balance between British and French

64 On the mandate system and how this 'exerted considerable power in the formation and transformation of non-european nations and states during the interwar period', see e.g. the series of contributions to the symposium Fleur Johns, Thomas Skouteris / Wouter Werner (eds) 'The League of Nations and the Construction of the Periphery'. *Leiden Journal of International Law* 24 (2011), 797.

65 Susan Pedersen *The Guardians: The League of Nations and the Crisis of Empire* (Oxford: Oxford University Press 2015).

66 The League of Nations—Ten Years, 1930.

67 Id.

interests in North Africa for both commercial and security purposes. Since 1907, the parallel penetration of France and Spain in their disparate zones of influence—the Spanish one, as noted by Lord Curzon, 'a rugged area peopled by natives who are the most turbulent and difficult to control in Morocco'[68]—initiated a pattern of Morocco-triggered domestic political crisis in the peninsula that would culminate with the outbreak of the Spanish Civil War.

Already in the late 1900s, inegalitarian conscription systems of new recruits for Moroccan campaigns had led to the 'Tragic Week of Barcelona', when anti-war protests were bloodily repressed after the military defeat known as the 'Disaster of Barranco del Lobo' in 1909. There was renewed fighting to conquer and pacify Spain's territorial possessions against the numerous and diverse tribes, or 'cabilas', as the Spanish army, now reinforced with the recruitment of native troops (the so-called Regulares), moved towards the interior following the establishment of the Spanish Protectorate in 1912 and the ensuing colonial administration. Spain's marginal position in the bloc system was further assured by its under-developed military capacity being hostage to Moroccan affairs. Out of its 140,000 soldiers, around 76,000 were deployed in Morocco by 1914. Together with its under-developed economic capacity, this gave its potencial war effort minimal value. As the First World war lingered on, the role of Spain, dependent, especially since 1915, on France and Britain out of strategic and economic necessity as a benevolent pro-entente neutral, intensified on the economic front. However, German efforts to exploit the Spanish Germanophile army rivalry with France in Morocco to turn, as in the case of the Ottoman Empire, 'Arab countries into allies',[69] overall forced Spain to keep its strict neutrality. Despite occasional ambivalence, Spain remained officially committed to neutrality throughout the First World War,[70] a neutrality that the future President of the Second Republic, Azaña, defined in 1917 as 'a forced neutrality, imposed by our own lack of defences'.[71] The Spanish King Alphonse XIII, eager to participate in the diplomatic post-war settlement for the future peace, as Rafael Altamira, the future judge at the PCIJ, had recommended in his book 'La Guerra actual y la

68 Lord Curzon, quoted in La Porte, 'Civil Military Relations in the Spanish Protectorate' 2004, 210.

69 La Porte, 'Civil Military Relations in the Spanish Protectorate' 2014, 210.

70 For a recent detailed account, see Fernando García Sanz, *España en la Gran Guerra. Espías, diplomáticos y traficantes* (Barcelona: Galaxia Gutenberg/Círculo de Lectores 2014).

71 Manuel Azaña. 'Los motivos de la germanofilia'. (Madrid: Imprenta Helenica, 1917).

opinión española' (The Current War and Spanish Opinion) in 1915,[72] offered, nonetheless, his humanitarian services as a mediator in the later stages of the war.[73]

Throughout the conflict, Spanish public opinion, mirrored and stimulated by the press[74] and public intellectuals,[75] have been divided along ideological lines between Germanophiles, supported by the conservative classes,[76] and liberal and socialist supporters of the pro-British-French entente. However, by late 1918, the Spanish political establishment almost unanimously shared the Wilsonian euphoria that traversed Europe. In December 1918, the government appointed a High Commission of Experts to 'study, from the perspective of national interests and conveniences, the possible constitution of a League of Nations and the participation of Spain and its absolute sovereignty in it.'[77] Along with a number of other neutral states during the First World War, (such as Norway, Denmark, Holland, Sweden, and Switzerland), Spain was left out of the discussions on the project for the Covenant of the League of Nations. However, the groundwork prepared by the High Commission informed Spanish views at the informal 'conference of the neutrals' that took place in Paris in March 1919. During this conference, Spain exerted diplomatic pressure to be invited to join the League as a founder member. Although Spain achieved this goal together with twelve other neutral states,[78] the aspirations of the government were higher. They included to be the only neutral founder member to

72 Rafael Altamira, La Guerra actual y la opinión española (Barcelona: Araluce, 1915) (republ. Pamplona: Editorial Analecta, 2015).

73 Juan Pando, *Un Rey para la esperanza. La España humanitaria de Alfonso XIII en la Gran Guerra* (Madrid: Temas de Hoy 2002).

74 See e.g. Santos Juliá Diaz, 'La nueva generación: de neutrales a antigermanófilos pasando por aliadófilos', *Ayer* 91 (2013), 121–144. See also Matteo Tomasoni 'La Gran Guerra llega a España: la revista Los Aliados y la causa aliadófila. Propaganda y debate político en un país neutral' *Rubrica Contemporanea* 3 (2014), 71–88.

75 See e.g. David Jiménez Torres, 'What is an Intellectual? The Spanish Debate during the First World War' *Hispanic Research Journal* 15 (2014), 515–529.

76 See e.g. David Jiménez Torres, 'Journalists at the Front: Ramiro de Maeztu, Inglaterra en armas and Spanish Intellectuals during the First World War', *Bulletin of Spanish Studies* 90 (2013), 1291–1311.

77 Dictamen de la comisión creada por el real decreto de 9 de diciembre de 1918 para estudiar, desde el punto de vista de los intereses y las conveniencias nacionales, la eventual constitución de una sociedad de las naciones y la participación de España en la misma en su plena soberania (Madrid: Graficas Excelsior 1944), 44.

78 Annex 1 of the Covenant of the League of Nations.

take a seat as a 'non-permanent member' of the Council[79] until the scheduled elections by the Assembly could take place.[80]

The Spanish Parliament ratified the Covenant in August 1919 and Spain officially deposited its instrument of adhesion with the League of Nations in January 1920. It soon began organizing its diplomatic administrative apparatus in Geneva where it was represented by J. Quiñones de Leon until 1931. In parallel, in 1920 the Spanish Ministry of Foreign Affairs created a special section, the Spanish Office of the League of Nations, to formulate Spanish foreign policy regarding the League and to coordinate the activities of the various Spanish delegates. Fulfilling its aspirations, Spain was elected as a non-permanent member of the Council in recognition of its claimed special status as a European medium power, its reinforced post-war economy,[81] and because of its perceived moral and cultural influence over the Spanish-speaking community of Latin-American nations.

The strength of the Hispanic transatlantic link was apparent from the first session of the Assembly of the League of Nations, where it was requested that Spanish featured as one of the League's official languages in view of the fact that 'the fifteen nations of Spanish language represented here constitute all by themselves 36% of the countries belonging to this society.'[82] By then, the cultural notion of 'Hispanidad', which also included Portugal and Brazil under the Latin etymology of 'Hispania,' was already an influential phenomenon on the diplomatic plane. A narrative based on the historical, linguistic, racial, cultural and religious ties between the American continent and the 'Madre Patria' (Motherland) was portrayed as the foundation of a 'great family of nations and peoples' and a platform for the achievement of common international goals. This was apparent to representatives of the Latin-American republics by 1920. As the Panama's representative proclaimed in the assembly, 'Spain makes an effort to conquer our hearts and spirits through good deeds of peace, friendship, trade, the invocation of the common glories of our race and

79 Art. 4. in fine of the Covenant of the League of Nations.

80 See, e.g. Luis V. Perez Gil, 'El primer decenio de España en la sociedad de naciones (1919–1929)', *Anales de la Facultad de Derecho de La Laguna 15* (1998), 199–215.

81 José Luis García Delgado/Santiago Roldán/Juan Muñoz, *La consolidación del capitalismo en España, 1914–1920* (Madrid: Confederación Española de Cajas de Ahorros 1974).

82 Arístides de Agüero y Betancourt (Cuba), Actes de la première Assemblée, Société des Nations, Séances des Commissions, 1920, 181 quoted in Thomas Fischer, 'El español en el mundo: hispanoamericanismo en la Liga de las Naciones Iberoamericanas', Iberoamericana 13 (2013), 119–131, 120.

our language, through our spiritual and ethnic affinities, and with the ties of blood and thought.'[83]

Although Spanish, despite being 'the most widespread language among the members of the League of Nations' did not become an official language of the League,[84] the development of a transatlantic 'Hispanic' cultural policy constituted one of the vectors of Spanish foreign policy at the League. In 1921, reflecting the scientific and cultural Europeanizing substratum of previous reforms, the Office of Cultural Relations of Spain was established at the Ministry of Foreign Affairs. This followed a proposal by Américo Castro,[85] a noted representative of the intellectual reformist generation of 1914,[86] philologist, and modernizer of Spanish cultural historiography. The Office of Cultural Relations of Spain was established 'with provisional character' with the goal of 'diffusion of the Spanish language and the defense and expansion of Spanish culture abroad.'[87] It also became a strong basis for the formation of a Spanish/Latin-American alliance as a cultural and political bloc in Geneva. This, despite occasional disagreements, paralleled developments that were taking place in meetings and discussions within the framework of the Pan American Union. Founded in 1912, as we saw in Chapter Two, this international regional organization will foster discussions, with the contribution of Spanish 'Americanists' such as Barcia Trelles of the codification of international law in America, and of a particular breed of American international law, thus paving

83 Narciso Garay (Panama), Actes de la première Assemblée, Société des Nations, Séances plénières, 1920, p. 222 quoted in Fischer, *El español en el mundo* 2013, 120.

84 Id., Although the proposal led to the elimination of 'official languages' allowing the possibility for every delegate to use his mother tongue on the condition of organizing a service of translation in English and French, Peter Munch, Peter, 'L'assemblée des delégués', in Peter Munch (ed.) Les origines et l'œuvre de la Société des Nations (Copenhague: Gildendalske Boghanel-Nordisk Forlag 1924) 358–415, 366 quoted in Thomas fisher *El español en el mundo* 2013, 126.

85 Nota confidencial dirigida al ministro Manuel González Hontoria, 'Sobre el problema de la difusión de la Cultura Hispánica en el Extranjero' (AMAE, R. 1380/26) quoted in Niño Rodriguez, 'La europeización a través de la política científica y cultural en el primer tercio del siglo XX', CLXX (2001), 95–126, 117.

86 Id.

87 Lorenzo Delgado Gómez-Escalonilla, 'Un siglo de diplomacia cultural española: de la Junta para Ampliación de Estudios al Instituto Cervantes', Real Instituto Elcano, Documento de Trabajo 12 (2014), 11.

the long road, to the Convention on the Rights and Duties of States signed in Montevideo in 1933.[88]

The second generation of Spanish international law scholars, who like Barcia Trelles, took up university chairs at the beginning of the interwar period, was the offspring of the educational and university reforms introduced in Spain under the influence of 'regenerationism' in the 1900s. Twenty years had elapsed since the 'Disaster of 1898' and Spain was leaving the First World War undamaged, its international prestige and strategic importance in the new multilateral scenario relatively reinforced by its neutrality in the war, its diplomatic alliance with Latin-American nations and the fact that it was economically invigorated, possessing a more modernized industry and more diversified commerce. In parallel, the efforts to Europeanize Spanish culture and science had begun to bear fruit. Several members of the second generation of Spanish international law scholars had spent part of their formative years studying abroad thanks to the establishment of the Junta de Ampliación de Estudios e investigación científica (JAE—Board for Extension of Studies and Scientific Research) in 1907. Although illiteracy, as we shall see, remained a major problem and the Spanish university system still needed to traverse major reforms, an elite of Spanish interwar legal scholars shared a more cosmopolitan outlook. This went hand in glove with the new stage in international relations inaugurated by the League and the perceived transformational quality of the 'foundational period' of modern international law to bring about a noticeable intellectual contribution of Spanish international lawyers to interwar discussions on international law.

The formative years of Camilo Barcia Trelles (1888–1977), the 'Americanist' who breathed a new spirit into 'Vitorian' studies, epitomize the effect of the combination of the magisterium of members of the post-1883 reform first generation of Spanish international law scholars and the intellectual impact of the post-1898 efforts to Europeanize Spanish culture and science. Barcia Trelles had been exposed thanks to A. Sela y Sampil to the attention given to didactic methods inspired by the 'institucionistas' at the Law School of the University of Oviedo, a pole, as we saw in Chapter Two, for the spreading of Kraustist ideas in legal education. Barcia went on to study for his doctorate at the Central University of Madrid with J.M. Fernandez Prida

88 On the long road to Montevideo, Becker Lorca, Mestizo International Law 2015, 327–352. See also Yannick Wehrli, 'Latin America in the League of Nations: Bolívar's Dream Come True?', in Claude Auroi/Aline Helg (eds.) Latin America 1810–2010. Dreams and Legacies (London: Imperial College Press 2011) 67–81.

(1865–1942)[89] in 1909. Fernandez Prida was one of the most notable members of the 'first professional generation' of Spanish international law scholars. He had occupied the chairs of international law at the universities of Seville (1886), Santiago de Compostela (1893) and Valladolid (1893) and since 1898 he had held the chair of 'History and Critical Studies of the Most Important Treaties of Spain with Other Powers' at the Central University of Madrid. Author of an extensive opus specialising in private international law, Fernandez Prida, who was among the first Spanish members of the Institut de Droit International and the International Law Association, became directly involvement in Spanish politics as senator (1904–1918), Minister of Justice (1917), Minister of the Interior (1920), Minister of Naval Affairs (1921) and, eventually, as Minister of Foreign Affairs (1922). After his doctoral work with Fernandez Prida, Barcia Trelles was among the first international law students to benefit from JAE's research fellowships which had been established to end the Spanish 'intellectual segregation from Europe'.

From 1911 to 1913, Barcia went to study in Brussels with Ernest Nys whom Koskenniemi calls the 'first professional historian of international law.' Ernest Nys (1851–1920) was well acquainted with the Salamanca School. In the 1880s and 1890s, he had included the works of Grotius's predecessors[90] in the study of the origins of international institutions and spearheaded the role of the Salamanca School in connection with their 'humane' treatment of the Indians,[91] devoting works to the origins of international law,[92] the law of peoples and the ancient Spanish jurisconsults.[93] When Barcia went to Paris in the early 1910s, Nys was interested in the advancement of international codification—about the progress of which during the 19th century he produced a

89 See José María Puyol Montero, 'Joaquin Maria Fernandez Prida', Diccionario de catedráticos españoles de derecho (1847–1943) Universidad Carlos III de Madrid. Instituto Figuerola de Historia y Ciencias Sociales, 2011- accesible at http://www.uc3m.es/diccionariodecatedraticos.

90 Ernest Nys, *Le droit de la guerre et les précurseurs de Grotius* (Bruxelles et Leipzig: Muquardt, Merzbach et Falk, 1882)

91 Ernest Nys, *Les droits des indiens et les publicistes espagnols* (Bruxelles et Leipzig: Muquardt, Merzbach et Falk, 1890). Ernst Nys, 'Les publicistes espagnols du xvie siècle et les droits des indiens', *Revue de Droit International et de Legislation Comparee* 21 (1889) 532.

92 Ernest Nys, *Les origines du droit international* (Bruxelles: A. Castaigne, 1894)

93 Ernest Nys, *Le droit des gens et les anciens jurisconsultes espagnols* (Bruxelles: M. Weissenbruch, 1914).

history[94]—and in the historical development of a theory of sources of international law with a view to their use by peaceful international dispute settlement mechanisms, including by the projected permanent court of international justice.[95] Nys, in addition to using ample historical erudition to advocate the progress of international law, and being—in its own words—among those who are now 'striving their utmost to wage war against war',[96] continued to contribute works on Vitoria in the 1910s.[97] He also became the editor in 1917 of the volume dedicated to Francisco de Vitoria in the Classics of International Law series.[98]

After another research stay in Paris, once again supported by JAE, Barcia moved to Berlin (1913–1914) to study under von Liszt, Kaufmann, Triepel and von Martitz. During his time in Berlin, Barcia prepared works on 'The Law of Maritime Warfare and The Hague and London Conferences' in syntony with the doctrinal programme of the times in the area of codification of international law. He later moved to Switzerland (1916–1917), where he began to take an interest in the role of imperialism in both Latin America (writing 'The original significance of the Monroe Doctrine') and in Germany, to which he devoted his 'Essay on an Imperialism of Race. Pan-Germanism'. On his return from these cosmopolitan years of study abroad, Barcia Trelles was appointed chair-holder in Public and Private International Law at the University of Murcia in 1918, and in 1920 he moved to occupy the chair of Public and Private International Law at the University of Valladolid. There, he soon founded the 'Section of Americanist studies,' which became, as earlier mentioned, a major pole for both 'Americanist' themes and for the study and updating of the doctrines of the 'Spanish founders' of the law of nations in the interwar years.

Spanish international law scholars, such as Barcia and others, continued through the 20s and early 30s to travel extensively to academic and international law conferences. In some cases, they actively participated as international

94 Ernest Nys, 'The Codification of International Law', *American Journal of International Law* 5 (1911), 871–900, 872.

95 Ernest Nys, 'The Development and Formation of International Law', *American Journal of International Law* 6:2 (1912), 1–29. Ernest Nys, 'The Development and Formation of International Law', *American Journal of International Law* 6: 2 (1912), 279–315.

96 Id., 315.

97 Ernest Nys, 'Le droit des gens et les anciens jurisconsultes espagnols' (1914) extract reprinted in G. van Hecke (ed.) *L'Espagne et la formation du droit des gens moderne* (Leuven: Aedibus Peeters, 1988), 66–82, 57.

98 De Vitoria, Francisco. *De Indis et De iure belli relectiones* (Classics of International Law. Preface, by J.B. Scott. Introduction, by Ernest Nys) (Washington: The Carnegie Endowment, 1917).

legal servants and as Spanish representatives in the works of the League in both Europe and the Americas, and assumed parliamentary roles and government positions in the management of Spanish foreign policy. The influence of the new methodological and doctrinal perspectives developed through study abroad, and their familiarity with foreign languages was allied with an eagerness to actively participate in international debates. Their academic production also extended and diversified.

One of the major axes of Spanish doctrinal interest during the interwar years was the League of Nations, as well as theoretical inquiries into the nature and characteristics of international society.[99] Spanish scholars devoted a considerable number of works to the positive and theoretical organization of the international community. These, as García Arias highlights,[100] started to be published as early as the immediate aftermath of the First World War. Among these works are the double volume by Abelardo Merino and the Marquis de Olivart from 1919, 'Antecedentes historicos de la liga de las naciones' (Historical Antecedents of the League of Nations)[101] and 'Examen y juicio critico del proyecto aprobado por la conferencia de la paz en París el 28 de abril de 1919' (Examination and critical analysis of the project approved by the peace conference on the 28 of April 1919), the Marquis de Olivart's 'La Sociedad de Naciones' (The League of Nations)[102] and J. Yanguas Messia's 'España y la Sociedad de Naciones' (Spain and the League of Nations), all in 1919.[103] In this illustrative work of the Spanish internationalism of the early interwar period, Yanguas Messia, a key representative of the second generation of Spanish international law scholars, highlighted that the 'league of nations should aspire to define the new international law, to coordinate the rights and interests of states and to erect itself not just in judgement of all nations, but as the supreme juridical organ of mankind.'[104] Yanguas Messia points also to Francisco Suarez and Francisco de Vitoria as 'the true precursor apostles of Wilson in setting up the basis of an international community, and in saying that the normal and permanent

99 Del Arenal, 'El estudio de las relaciones internacionales en la España del siglo XIX' 1979, 50.

100 See Garcia Arias, 'Adiciones sobre la historia de la doctrina hispánica' 1949, 528.

101 Abelardo Merino, *Antecedentes historicos de la liga de las naciones* (Madrid: Real Sociedad Geografica 1919)

102 Ramón Dalmau de Olivart, *La Sociedad de Naciones* (Madrid: Imprenta Patronato de huerfanos de la intendencia e intervencion militares 1919).

103 Jose Yanguas Messia, *España y la Sociedad de Naciones* (Valladolid: 1919).

104 Id., 10.

basis of justice and peace should be sought in the moral unity of the human genre.'[105] On the other hand, coverage of the Permanent Court of International Justice was early on assured by Rafael Altamira Crevea, a member of the Advisory Committee of Jurists, or 'Committee of Ten,' which drafted the Statute of the PCIJ[106] and one of the three judges (with the A. Sanchez Bustamante and D. Anzilotti) who served throughout the full life cycle of the PCIJ. In 1921, he initiated a series of related publications with 'El proceso ideologico del Proyecto de Tribunal de Justicia Internacional' ('The Ideological Process of the Project for the International Court of Justice').

However, despite Spain having somewhat regained its international status, and the internationalism of its scholarly elite in the aftermath of the Great War, the vicissitudes of the European struggle had fostered 'ideological polarization and radical social and economic transformation'in Spain.[107] This Spanish domestic polarization reflected the beginning of a polarised ideological crisis affecting all of Europe in the interwar period between the poles of the Bolshevist Revolution and Civil War in Russia and the early rise of the wave of counter-revolutionary totalitarianism marked by the electoral victory of Mussolini in Italy in 1922. In 1923, the new 'pronunciamiento' that put an end to the Restoration cycle initiated in 1874, and brought about the dictatorship of General Miguel Primo de Rivera, 2nd Marquis of Estella and 22nd Count of Sobremonte (1923–1930), was a direct consequence of the chronic instability of Spanish politics and the international post-war economic crisis that affected neutral states, such as Spain, which had greatly benefited in commercial terms during the war. The pressures of a modernizing society were evident in the instability of the numerous ministerial cabinets between 1918 and 1923. Party fragmentation and a crisis of governability would eventually put an end to the stability of the half-century-long Restoration system of political alternation between liberal and conservative monarchical parties. However, the immediate factor that triggered the pronunciamiento of Primo de Rivera, a general who saw himself as the 'iron surgeon' of 'Regenerationism', was the avatars of Spanish foreign policy in western North Africa in the 1920s.

After the First World War, the Treaty of Versailles (1919) ratified the pre-war status quo, favoured by Great Britain, reached at the Conference of Algeciras

105 Id., 9.

106 Yolanda Gamarra, 'Rafael Altamira y Crevea (1866–1951). The International Judge as Gentle Civilizer', *Journal of the History of International Law* XIV (2012), 1–49, 28–37.

107 See Francisco Romero, 'Spain and the First World War', in Sebastian Balfour and Paul Preston (ed.) *Spain and the Great Powers in the Twentieth Century* (London: Routledge 1999), 32–52, 34.

in 1906. This, following agreements between Spain and Morocco,[108] had been confirmed, as we saw in Chapter Two, by the Treaty of Fez by which the French Protectorate over Morocco was established in 1912. In 1919, the definitive exclusion of Germany from the Moroccan scenario left France and Spain as protecting powers with no responsibility or jurisdiction whatsoever held by the League itself over the Moroccan question.[109] At a time when the underlying logic of imperial politics meant that effective colonial power determined the influence and ranking of Western powers,[110] Spain's foreign policy attempted to exploit its geostrategic position in the Mediterranean Sea, aiming to completely dominate 'the Spanish zone in an attempt to meet French military advances once again.'[111] Realistically described in 1919 by José Yanguas Messia (1890–1974), this quest for a Spanish hinterland was justified in the understanding that:

'Our role in the North of Morocco has been reduced to occupying, without the solace of an extensive hinterland (of an interior zone) the coastal fringe in order to guarantee with Spanish blood the freedom of commerce of all states in an unwelcoming country, and to act modestly as 'porters' in the Strait of Gibraltar, not for our own benefit but for the benefit of the great rival powers who, in choosing us for this mission, trusting our impotence could not provoke second thoughts, more than recognizing a right to us, were imposing upon us a truly international servitude.'[112]

The occupation of the Spanish Protectorate, which was halted militarily during the First World War, started again in 1919 leading to the beginning of a protracted military struggle with the leader of the Rif province's nationalist uprising. The consequences included yet another 'Desastre' 'the Disaster of Annual', which involved the massacre of thousands of Spanish soldiers in 1921, and meant that 'all territory conquered since 1909 ended up again in the rebels' hands.' After what is known as the 'greatest defeat suffered by a European power in an African colonial conflict in the 20th century,'[113] Mohammed ben Abd-el-Krim, militarily reinforced with the spoils of the defeated Spanish army, declared the 'Republic of the Rif', and this feat spread the rebellion to

108 Convention Between Spain and Morocco, *The American Journal of International Law* 6 (1912), 54–61.

109 La Porte 'Rien à ajouter' 2011, 68.

110 Neila, España y el Mediterraneo en el siglo XX, 2011.

111 Pablo La Porte, 'Civil Military Relations in the Spanish Protectorate in Morocco' 2004, 216.

112 Yanguas messia, *España y la Sociedad de Naciones* 1919, 19.

113 Id., 217.

other tribes. However, despite public pressure in journalistic commentary, and claims addressed by certain organizations and representatives of the self-appointed Rif government, 'the League of Nations not only declined to play a mediating role in the conflict, it also refused to even allow the matter to be brought up in its various discussion forums, such as the Council or the Assembly.'[114] The status quo was not affected by growing popular humanitarian concerns over the development of the conflict amidst allegations of use of chemical warfare[115] by Spain in fighting the Riffian tribes. As highlighted by La Porte, despite the power that the then Secretary General, E. Drummond, had in accordance with article 11, to bring before the Council an issue on his own initiative which he deemed of importance,[116] the answer from Paul Mantoux, head of the 'Political Section,' remained unchanged: '*La question est en dehors de la competence de la Société*.'[117]

It is against this background that the 'revisionist policy regarding the status quo in Western Mediterranean'[118] was made a priority by Primo de Rivera at the helm of a military directorate from 1923 to 1925. Although Primo de Rivera's policy was initially characterized as a 'policy of pseudo-defeatism'[119] oriented towards halting the drainage of economic and military resources, the extension of the rebellion to the French protectorate favoured French cooperation against the rebels. The opportunity was seized by Primo de Rivera who feared the consequences for his rule of allowing a new humiliation of the Spanish army. In 1925, the amphibious landing at Alhucemas Bay in 1925[120] became the 'greatest military and political-diplomatic success'[121] of his regime and the decisive blow that paved the road to the end of the Riffian war in 1927. Moreover, the victorious campaigns initiated in Alhucemas increased the prestige of the army, reinforcing the 'Africanism' and the feeling of military independence—from civil society and the rest of the army—of the special elite force in North Africa.[122] The fact that their members gained rank through 'war action merit', and not seniority, would accentuate the tense relationship with the

114 La Porte Rien 'Rien a` ajouter' 2011, 71.

115 Id., 74–83.

116 Id., 79.

117 Id., 76.

118 Neila, España y el Mediterraneo en el siglo XX, 2011, 154.

119 Id., 157

120 Jose E. Alvarez, 'Between Gallipoli and D-Day: Alhucemas, 1925', *The Journal of Military History* 63 (1999), 75–98, 83.

121 Neila, España y el Mediterraneo en el siglo XX, 2011, 159.

122 La Porte, 'Civil Military Relations in the Spanish Protectorate in Morocco', 2004, 216.

government of the Second Republic[123] since 1931. This historical background was, as we shall later see, deeply felt by generals, such as Jose Sanjurjo, the director of the Alhucemas' campaign,[124] who plotted a coup against the Second Republic in 1932, and the Africanist General Franco, who became the 'youngest general in Europe' because of his actions in the Alhucemas military campaigns and the subsequent 'dirty war' in Morocco.

Although the orientation of Spanish foreign policy did not alter substantially under Primo de Rivera, there was now a greater focus on creating deeper ties with Latin-American states, partly by acting as a bridge between Europe and Latin America in the League of Nations and fostering notions of Hispanidad with 'peoples of brother race.' The instrumental politicisation of the aspiration to sponsor a cultural and scientific modernizing of Spanish foreign policy to animate 'Hispanic vitality dispersed around the world'[125] was embodied with a better-defined character as a vehicle for 'cultural expansion and political propaganda,' in the rebaptised as the 'Board of Cultural Relations' under Primo de Rivera.[126] This included supporting initiatives such as the founding by the international lawyer and Minister of Foreign Affairs, Yanguas Messia, as we shall later see, of the 'Association Francisco de Vitoria' in 1926.

The new policy of prestige aimed for Spain to be considered a great European power. Primo de Rivera, who also assumed the Ministry of Foreign Affairs since 1927, wrote that the 'whole world recognizes the justice of giving entrance to Spain in the concert of the great world powers due to its glorious past, its progressive present and its exalted love of peace.'[127] However, Primo de Rivera's policy had to bow before the indirect consequences for Spain of the outcome of the Locarno Treaties, negotiated in 1925 and ratified in 1926, to guarantee Germany's Western borders. These seven agreements, in which the western European First World War allied powers and the new states of central and eastern Europe sought to secure the post-war territorial settlement and normalize relations with the defeated Germany, led to the incorporation of the Weimar Republic to the League in 1926. This posed a dire threat to the Spanish ambition 'to gain a position as a permanent member of the Council.'[128]

123 Id., 220.

124 Jose Sanjurjo died in a plane crash when he was to assume the leadership of the rebellion against the Spanish Republic initiated in the North of Morocco on the 17th of July 1936.

125 Delgado Gómez-Escalonilla, 'Un siglo de diplomacia cultural española' 2014, 10.

126 Id., 11.

127 A. M. A. E., Sec. Polít., Leg. R. 851 exp. 33, Tel. cifr. núm. 88 deI Ministro de Estado al Embajador de España en Washington, 2 de agosto de 1928.

128 Perez Gil, El primer decenio de España en la sociedad de naciones 2010, 208.

The reorganization of the Council with five permanent members (Great Britain, France, Japan, Italy and Germany) and nine non-permanent members for three years (only re-electable by a qualified majority of the Assembly) led to a serious diplomatic crisis between Spain and the League. Spain rejected the offer of a post as a semi-permanent member of the Council. Instead, it declared that, whereas it accepted the amendment of article 4 to allow for the reform of the Council—and the incorporation of Germany—it was also formally withdrawing from the League with effect from 11th September 1926.[129]

The gradual diplomatic distancing of Spain from the League coincided with a period of economic prosperity during which the League attempted to honour its pacifist commitments. The Commission's work prepared the ground for the codification of international law by launching the Geneva Protocol for the Peaceful Settlement of International Disputes in 1924 which was intended to fill the gaps in the Covenant. It focused on arbitration, security, and disarmament, creating an automatic system for the settlement of all disputes. In 1925, the Conference for the Supervision of International Trade in Arms and Ammunition and in Implements of War, also called the Arms Traffic Conference, was held in Geneva. Also from 1925 is the Protocol for the Prohibition of the Use in War of Asphyxiating, Poisonous or other Gases, and of Bacteriological Methods of Warfare. Even though the 1924 Geneva Protocol did not come into force after the suspension of a disarmament conference on which it depended,[130] it prepared the ground for the Conference for the Reduction and Limitation of Armaments of 1932–1934 and the Kellogg-Briand Pact. The Kellogg-Briand Pact, which originated as a bilateral agreement between France and the US, ended up being signed, first by the great powers, Germany, Great Britain, Italy, and Japan, in August 1928, and then by 60 countries, including non-members of the league such as the USSR. Widely seen as an American rapprochement to Europe, it 'did not remedy the systemic weaknesses of the League Covenant, as it did not provide for sanctions and was not integrated into the League's existing regime'.[131] However, it was regarded as an important step towards a general prohibition of the use of force because of the parties' promise to renounce war and to resolve all questions by peaceful means.

---

129 Following the conditions of two years' notice and the fulfillment of all its obligations, including those under the League Covenant in accordance with article 1.3.

130 Tams The League of Nations 2006.

131 Id.

Under the direction of Primo de Rivera, who had by then personally assumed the helm of the Ministry of Foreign Affairs, Spain, which was not a signatory of the Locarno Treaties, attempted to be included among the great powers invited to be the original signatories of the Briand-Kellogg Pact.[132] Eventually, Spain acceded to the Pact in Washington on 7 March 1929, after waiting for its ratification by the US senate because of fears, shared by Spain and the Latin-American republics, that this would become an opportunity for the US to make reservations that could contain another formulation of the Monroe Doctrine. Meanwhile, Spain's prestige-seeking policy, evidenced in its withdrawal from the League, was eventually resolved a day before the lapse for the effective withdrawal was about to expire. After a purely symbolic victory for Spain in a treaty signed in July 1928 regarding the city of Tangiers, which had been used by Primo as a bargaining chip in his diplomatic battle with the League, the Assembly re-elected Spain as non-permanent member of the Council and voted favourably on a resolution guaranteeing Spain that post for the next 6 years.[133]

However, the avatars of Primo de Rivera's foreign policy did not detract from the internationalist engagement of Spanish international law scholars with the League's themes. In the mid-late 20s, Spanish international lawyers produced more specifically oriented inquiries into the League of Nations and its activities. These included works on 'The positive and legal value of the League of Nations and its contribution to the problem of Peace'[134], and on 'The Treaty of Versailles and the Pact of 5 November 1918[135] penned by Carlos Rivera Garcia in 1927 and R. Aguilera de la Arena in 1930 respectively. Other works addressed the influence of the League of Nations in the development of Constitutional law[136] and on particular areas of development of the League of Nations such as naval disarmament,[137] international mandates[138] and, as in the

132 See in detail Ana María Tamayo Barbena, 'España ante el Pacto Briand-Kellogg', *Cuadernos de Historia Moderna y Contemporanea* 5 (1984), 187–231.

133 Perez Gil, El primer decenio de España en la sociedad de naciones 2010, 210–215.

134 Carlos Rivera Garcia, *La Sociedad de Naciones: su valor positivo y juridico y el problema de la paz* (Madrid: Ed. Reus, 1927).

135 Rafael Aguilera de la Arena, *El tratado de versalles y el pacto de 5 de noviembre de 1918 ante el derecho internacional contemporaneo* (Madrid: Imprenta y encuadernación de Julio Cosano, 1930).

136 Antonio Posada, *La sociedad de naciones y el derecho político* (Madrid: Editorial Caro Raggio, 1925).

137 Claudio Alvar-Gonzalez, *Desarme naval y sociedad de naciones* (Madrid: 1931).

138 Leopoldo Palacios Morini, Los *mandatos internacionales de la sociedad de naciones* (Madrid: Sobrinos de Sucesora de M. Minuesa de los Ríos, 1927).

work of A. Fabra Rivas, the International Labour Organization.[139] Coverage of the Permanent Court of International Justice continued to be assured by Judge Altamira who edited several volumes on the Court's sentences and advisory opinions, and other works such as 'La Sociedad de Naciones y el Tribunal de Justicia Internacional' (The League of Nations and the International Court of Justice) in 1931. A series of doctoral works on the League of Nations also accompanied the development of internationalist studies in Spanish law schools during the 1920s and 1930s.[140] Meanwhile, the founding of The Hague Academy of International Law under the patronage of the Carnegie Endowment in 1923[141] gave new opportunities to interwar Spanish international law scholars to truly join international legal debates and to reflectively contribute to the study of international law in various areas. Ten courses, among which four by C. Barcia Trelles, were delivered by five Spanish legal scholars at The Hague Academy between 1927 and 1939.

The first Spanish author to be invited during the dictatorship of Primo de Rivera to lecture at The Hague Academy was a criminal lawyer, Quintiliano Saldaña Garcia Rubio (1878–1938), professor of criminal anthropology and advanced criminal studies at the Central University of Madrid since 1911. Saldaña, who was one of the founders and vice-president of the Association Internationale de Droit Penale (AIDP) in 1924, and the author of a very extensive and pioneer work in criminal law and criminology informed by sociology and anthropology, delivered the first Hague course in the field of international criminal justice in 1925. One of the leading international proponents of legal pragmatism in European criminal law circles in the 1920s and early 1930s, he approached this field as a historical institution resulting from the convergence of three 'distinct processes': the 'evolution of facts', 'the evolution of ideas' and the 'evolution of institutions'.[142] For Saldaña, each of these evolutions resulted in a great contemporary transformation. On the factual plane, the evolution 'from international legal assistance to supra-national legal existence involved a transformation of international legal life as a whole', whereas the ideological evolution was in turn responsible for the on-going transformation 'from

139 Antonio Fabra Rivas, La organización internacional del trabajo (Madrid: Ed. Javier Morata Pedreño, 1925).

140 Catalogo de tesis doctorales de la universidad complutense de madrid, 1900–1987 (Madrid: Ades 1988).

141 See James Brown Scott, 'The Hague Academy of International Law', *American Journal of International Law*, 17 (1923), 746–751.

142 Quintiliano Saldaña, La Justice pénale internationale, Collected Courses of The Hague Academy of International Law 10 (1925), 223–396.

international law to international justice.'[143] Regarding the institutional plane, Saldaña emphasised the third great transformation: the 'passage from international arbitration to the permanent court of international justice'.

Saldaña completed his analysis of these three great transformations with an 'avant-project' for an International Criminal Code with 23 articles to be added as an appendix to all the criminal codes of the state members of the League of Nations. This code was divided into a preliminary section—where Saldaña makes explicit the scope of application of the code in relation to other laws and its temporal, territorial and personal scopes of application—a general part devoted to criminal infraction and its repression, and a special part consecrated to the individual infractions and their repression. The special part contains two headings. The first deals with crimes against the international community, or against its members or committed in their domains, and the second deals with crimes against directly protected individuals or nationals of the League of Nations.[144] The influence of Saldaña, who was one of the most cosmopolitan Spanish legal scholars of the interwar period, member of several European academies and international learned societies, visiting professor at many universities, and the Spanish representative at numerous international conferences,[145] can be suspected in the resolution approved by the League of Nations that qualified aggression as an international crime which was adopted at the initiative of the Spanish government in 1925.[146]

Invitations to deliver courses at The Hague Academy were also twice addressed to José Maria Trías de Bes (1891–1965) who, together with Camilo Barcia Trelles and Jose Yanguas Messia, is considered one of the members of conservative 'golden triumvirate' of interwar Spanish international lawyers. In 1916, Trías de Bes replaced his father, J. de Dios Trias y Giro (1859–1914), who had occupied the chair of international law at the University of Barcelona since 1886. A monarchical conservative who was, nonetheless, a very active member of the Spanish Parliament in the 1920s and 1930s as an activist for 'Catalanism', Trias de Bes became a member of the Institut de Droit International in

143 Id.

144 Id. avant-projet de code pénal international (le nouveau droit pénal international codifie), 387.

145 See further, Ignacio de la Rasilla del Moral, 'International Criminal Justice as Universal Social Defence, Quintiliano Saldaña (1878–1938)' in F. Megret and I. Talgrenn (eds), *The Dawn of a Discipline—International Criminal Justice and Its Early Exponents* (Cambridge: Cambridge University Press, 2018, forthcoming)

146 Manfred Lachs, 'The development and general trends of international law in our time' Collected Courses of The Hague Academy of International Law 169 (1980), 320.

1928. He developed his academic interests mainly in private international law and it was in this area that he was invited to deliver a course on the 'Conception du droit international privé d'après la doctrine et la pratique en Espagne' (Conception of Private International Law following the Doctrine and the Practice in Spain)[147] in 1930. In it, after an interesting survey of the historical evolution of private international law, he examined the traditional core aspects of the Spanish private international legal regime. Years later, during the Spanish Civil War when Trias de Bes was actively collaborating with the internationalist side of General Franco's cause in Salamanca,[148] he delivered another course on the 'Règles générales des conflits de lois' (General Rules of the Conflicts of Laws) at The Hague Academy of International Law in 1937.

Another Spanish author who was invited to lecture at The Hague Academy on two occasions during the interwar period was Jose Gascón y Marín (1875–1962). A professor of constitutional and administrative law at Seville University (1902), Zaragoza University (1907), and the Central University of Madrid (from 1916), he served as member of Parliament between 1916 and 1923 and became Minister of Public Instruction and Arts for a brief period in 1931 in the last monarchical government before the establishment of the Second Spanish Republic. In 1930, Gascón y Marín delivered a course on the transformation of administrative international law[149] in which he functionally extrapolated the study of the categories of domestic administrative law to the organs and functions of the League of Nations and the International Labour Organization in defence of the interests of international society and the common interests of peoples. In 1932, Gascón y Marín was again invited to The Hague to highlight the importance of 'the study of international society's administrative activity, the public services of a non-national nature, and of organs which had emerged to cater for the achievement of goals common to different states'[150] with a

147 Jose Maria Trias De Bes, *Conception du droit international privé d'après la doctrine et la pratique en Espagne* Collected Courses of The Hague Academy of International Law 31 (1930), 623–708.

148 A fact that he highlights in the Notice Bibliographique of his course: 'Privé de sa chaire à l'Université de Barcelone en juillet 1936, actuellement attaché à l'Université de Salamanque et Conseiller juridique au Ministère des Affaires étrangères'. Jose Maria Trias De Bes, 'Règles générales des conflits de lois', *Collected Courses of The Hague Academy of International Law* 62 (1937).

149 Jose Gascón y Marín, *Les transformations du droit administrative international, Collected Courses of The Hague Academy of International Law* 34 (1930), 1–74.

150 Jose Gascón y Marín, Les fonctionnaires internationaux, *Collected Courses of The Hague Academy of International Law* 41 (1932), 721–798, 725.

course on the so-far little studied category of international civil servants. Gascón y Marín was, in this sense, one of the precursors of the study of the public international functions and the international administrative status of international servants. However, the vaunted internationalism showed by these authors at The Hague, and of other Spaniards, who also taught at The Hague Academy in the early 1930s, did not prevent any of them, as we shall later see, from supporting the Franco's side against the democratic elected government of the Spanish Second Republic during the Spanish Civil War.

Spanish international lawyers, as well as contributing to the specialized areas mentioned, by showing, as Del Arenal noted, the 'absolute primacy of the legal perspective in the Spanish academic approach to international problems,'[151] continued during the interwar period to publish in traditional areas such as the law of treaties, international maritime law, and the laws of war. These included general treatises such as the three volumes with a prologue by James Brown Scott of 'Tratado de Derecho Internacional Publico' published under the patronage of the Carnegie Endowment in 1928–1930 by the diplomat and minister of Foreign Affairs in 1919–1920, and also between 1920 and 1921, Manuel Gonzalez-Hontoria.[152] Works on diplomatic history and, in particular works, on the foreign relations of Spain, such as the three volumes by Jeronimo Becker 'Historia de las Relaciones Internacionales de España en el siglo XIX' in 1924–1926,[153] set the basis for the development of international relations as a field of scientific study. Spanish scholars also mirrored developments in international codification by the League of Nations, such as the 1930 Codification Conference convened by the League at The Hague, charged with addressing questions of nationality, territorial waters and state responsibility for injury to aliens, as well as developments in international disarmament such as in the work published by Salvador de Madariaga in 1929. Moreover, after the foundation, as we shall later see, of the Association Francisco de Vitoria in 1926, Spanish international law scholars devoted much attention to the study and updating of the works of the legal theologians of the 16th century and the Spanish 'classics' of international law. This updating of the scholastic natural law orientation had a mutually reinforcing relationship with the doctrinal

151 Del Arenal, 'El estudio de las relaciones internacionales en la España del siglo XIX' 1979, 50.

152 Manuel Gonzalez-Hontoria, *Tratado de derecho internacional publico* (Madrid: Voluntad, 1928–1930).

153 Jeronimo Becker Gonzalez, *Historia de las relaciones exteriores de España durante el siglo XIX. Apuntes para una historia diplomática (Madrid, Establecimiento Tipográfico de Jaime Ratés, 1924–1926, 3 vols.)*

developments that the establishment of the League had propitiated in the main theoretical international legal trends of the interwar period.

### The Re-Awakening of Universalism—The 'International Community' in the Interwar Doctrine

The great theoretical debates of the interwar years emanated from an international legal consciousness that was deeply shocked by the sheer magnitude of the horrors of the First World War. This period consequently saw the expansion of a greater diversity of doctrinal schools which were inspired by the promise of a new international community legal order under the auspices of the League of Nations.[154] As we have seen, the League promised, as noted by Anghie, 'in some way to replicate, even if very tenuously, the institutions found in domestic systems: a legislature, judiciary and executive'.[155] The overall impact of new international legal thought that accompanied this new international setting has been depicted as producing 'a break from classical to modern international law'.[156] Otherwise, the interwar period witnessed the cohabitation of 'classical international law', which, as noted by Becker, was 'based on the principles of absolute sovereignty, the standard of civilization and legal positivism,'[157] with a 'modern sensibility that criticized absolute sovereignty, foregrounded the interests of the international community and supported anti-formalist legal doctrines.'[158]

A continuation of the locus classicus' attempts at squaring the circle of statehood and international law, several interwar trends fitted in with a broad legalistic attempt to temper the 'excesses' of the late 19th century voluntarist theories of the positivist modern school and their 'absolutist' theoretical justification of the state's freedom to bind itself externally and accidentally to international law. Sharing a common programmatic spirit, the core theoretical debate among international legal scholars during these interwar years revolved around the nature and ultimate foundation of the binding character of international legal norms in a new international scenario more receptive to the pursuit of cooperation in the development of economic and social goals.

154 Kennedy, 'The Move to Institutions' (1987), 841.

155 Anghie, *Imperialism* 2004, 126.

156 Becker Lorca, *Mestizo International Law* 2015, 143.

157 Id.

158 Id.

The new doctrines sought above all to defend the primacy of international law over domestic law in order to smooth the accommodation of the 'unbridled sovereign autonomy' characterizing the pre-First World War era so that, as D. Kennedy notes, something akin to a 'social order among sovereigns could be achieved.'[159] This progressive doctrinal mood, which attempted to depart from an international legal order that had previously only been relatively tamed by the exigencies of a strategically-concerted balance of European imperial powers, led to the heyday of a 'foundational' debate on what was to be considered the 'ancillary stone of international law.'[160] Spreading in different versions over the European doctrinal stage, including, as we shall see, in a natural law form with Catholic underpinnings in Spain, this form of 'international legal consciousness' is today known, following Koskenniemi, as the interwar 'reconstructive doctrine.'[161]

With the common aim of much of the international legal writing being to reinforce the relevance of international law as a constraining factor in interstate relations at the service of the set of goals of the international community embodied in the League of Nations, constitutional analogies gained ground. The doctrinal relative decline of the contractualist and individualist conceptions underlying the earlier voluntarist Euro-centric positivist methodological dominance coincided with the partial reversion propitiated by the League of Nations of the long-standing dynamics of extra-European exclusion.[162] Although composed by great European Empires, the inclusion in the League of Nations of members from other continents marked an important stage on the path of the transition from the nineteenth century law of Christian and Christianized peoples underpinned by the *ius publicum europaeum* to a universalizing legal system.

The new doctrine followed various paths against the pre-eminence, as we saw in Chapter Two, of earlier voluntarist sovereigntist formulae of the late 19th and early 20th centuries, such as Hegel's 'state external law', G. Jellinek's principle of self-limitation, H.Triepel's Vereinbarung and forms of monist theory according

159 Id., 834.

160 J. B. Whitton, 'La règle pacta sunt servanda', Collected Courses of The Hague Academy of International Law (1934). 177.

161 Id., 159.

162 See the discussion of the Hague Conference 1907 and the Versailles Treaty from the perspective of the opposition between sovereign equality and legalized hegemony provided in Chapter V of Gerry Simpson, *Great Powers and Outlaw States: Unequal Sovereigns in the International Legal Order* (Cambridge: Cambridge University Press 2004), 132–164.

primacy to municipal law in order to overcome some of the refashioned dualist theories of the time. Prominent among the latter was D. Anzilotti's normativist theory,[163] which had paved an influential path since the publication of his Corso di Diritto Internazionale in 1912[164] by placing pacta sunt servanda as an a priori assumption to surpass voluntarism.[165] However, it was to be in German-speaking academic quarters[166] where the attempt to overcome positivism from within positivism itself would give way to one of the most influential efforts to come to grips with the 'sovereign question' from the perspective of an international constitutionalizing societal order. An analysis of international law's resulting self-constitutive bias towards community order as a monist—according primacy to international law—[167] grounding for an international constitutionalist perspective[168] was embedded in Kelsen's Pure Theory of Law.

Kelsen's monism in defence of the unity of national and international law as a single legal system was pursued as an 'epistemological postulate' to escape Austin's circularity problem.[169] In Kelsen, the derivation of the international legal system from a single normative non-will-based source becomes the core of its constitutional character. This explains why Kelsen could write about a 'constitution in a logical sense'[170] at the head of a system of legal validity, or otherwise as the ultimate basis of obligation in a legal system empirically approached as one grounded on a concept of legal imputation

163 Giorgio Gaja, 'Positivism and Dualism in Dionisio Anzilotti', European Journal of International Law 3 (1992), 123–138.

164 Truyol Serra, Histoire du droit international public 1998, 144.

165 On the longstanding influence of Anzilotti in Italy see finelly ironic, Luigi Condorelli 'Scholie sur l'idiome scellien des manuels francophones de droit international public' European Journal of International Law 1 (1990), 232–234.

166 Martti Koskenniemi, 'Georg Friedrich von Martens (1756–1821) and the Origins of Modern International Law' New York Institute of *International Law and Justice Working Papers* 1/2006, accesible at http://www.iilj.org/publications/documents/2006-1-ht-koskenniemi-web.pdf

167 Kelsen, Hans. General Theory of Law and the State (Cambridge: Harvard University Press, 1945), 386. Alexander Somek, 'Kelsen Lives', *European Journal of International Law* 18 (2007) 409–451, 422.

168 Danilo Zolo, *Cosmópolis, perspectiva y riesgos de un gobierno mundial* (Barcelona: Paidos 2000).

169 China Mieville, *Between Equal Rights, A Marxist Theory Of International Law* (Historical Materialism: 2007), 34–35.

170 Bardo Fassbender, *UN Security Council Reform And The Right Of Veto. A Constitutional Perspective* (The Hague: Martinus Nijjhof 1998).

that 'avoids identifying law in terms of an intuitive correspondence with an idea of right.'[171] By leaving the realm of social relations in his quest to isolate the autonomous scientific character of law, the father of the logical or normativist strand of positivism and neo-Kantian legal theorist attempted to de-psychologize the 'command theory' and its portrayal of international law as 'positive morality'. He did so, however, while remaining faithful to Austin's notion of law as effectively backed by sanctions, a notion that underlies Kelsen's view of positive law as a system of valid norms.[172] Furthermore, to counteract the hypothetical nature of an international legal order perennially at the whim of the changing sovereign will of the state and the ensuing existence of mutually exclusive domestic orders[173] pursuant to State solipsism, Kelsen depicted his opting for international law as superior to domestic law as being ethically grounded.

By theoretically dissolving the dogma of sovereignty—which he understood as the main instrument of the imperialist challenge to international law, in his view one of the more most important outcomes of Reine Rechtslehre—Kelsen believed that a hitherto insurmountable obstacle to any attempt at the progressive centralisation of international law had been surmounted.[174] His argument that in opting for international law as superior to national law he was choosing objectivism, altruism and pacifism over subjectivism, egoism and imperialism was, furthermore, consistent with the general representation of the telos of international law as a progressive and liberal one. The monist variant of international constitutionalism proposed by the Vienna School was paralleled by others which arose from traditions of domestic jurisprudence and political theory of the time. These included the one championed by an Italian school with S. Romano's theory of institution[175] at its core, which prolonged the tradition of Von Savigny's school in its identification of an international

171 Anthony Carty, 'The Continuous Influence of Kelsen on the General Perception of the Discipline of International Law', *European Journal of International Law* 9 (1998), 344–354.

172 Zolo, *Cosmópolis, perspectiva y riesgos* 2000, 143.

173 Hans Kelsen, *La Teoría Pura Del Derecho: Introducción a la Problemática Científica Del Derecho* (Madrid: Editorial Universitaria, 1979), 187.

174 Id., 199.

175 Santi Romano, *L'ordinamento Giuridico. Studi Sul Concetto, Le Fonti E I Caratteri Del Diritto* (1918) See also Filippo Fontanelli, 'Santi Romano and L'ordinamento giuridico: The Relevance of a Forgotten Masterpiece for Contemporary International, Transnational and Global Legal Relations', *Transnational Legal Theory* 2 (2011), 67–117.

constitution with a normative translation of the (international) community's fundamental structure as a social fact.[176]

Another strand of this critique of sovereignty joined, as M. Koskenniemi notes, 'French liberal solidarism with the sociological jurisprudence that developed in Germany in the 1920s.'[177] Indeed, the writings of several international law scholars mirrored the influence of sociology, which was characterized by an acuter sense of interdependence and the socialist-background influence of transnational solidarism, on the scientific spirit of the epoch. Transposing to the international realm the writings of Durkheim and Leon Duguit's 'droit naturel biologique,'[178] for which 'the basis of the law is the fact of 'solidarity' or of 'interdependence' between human beings,'[179] a number of authors, including among others Alejandro Alvarez, a highly influential promoter of debates on Latin-American regionalism, produced a peculiar hybrid of creole and socio-legal consciousness in international law.[180] This called on anti-formalist grounds for the study of a 'science of international relations' in which the combination of the study of law and international politics would further the practical realization of the social ends of the international system.[181] Nicolas Politis[182] and Georges Scelle contributed to this area by offering the 'first systematic treatment' of the sociological approach to international law.[183] This sociological strand in international law, which as Kolb notes was 'a means of fighting against state-centred and will-oriented positivism without giving up the anti-speculative and anti-metaphysical tradition,'[184] was particularly influential in France.

---

176 Robert Kolb, *Théorie Du Ius Cogens International: Essai De Relecture Du Concept* (2001), 103.

177 Martti Koskenniemi, 'History Of International Law, World War I To World War II' *Max Planck Encyclopedia of Public International Law* (2011) 10–12.

178 Truyol, *Histoire du droit international public* 1998, 145.

179 Robert Kolb, 'Politis and Sociological Jurisprudence of Inter-War International Law', *European Journal of International Law* 23 (2012), 237.

180 Liliana Obregon, 'Noted for Dissent: The International Life of Alejandro Alvarez' *Leiden Journal of International Law* 19 (2006), 983–1016.

181 Anghie, *Imperialism* 2005, 131.

182 Linos-Alexander Sicilianos/ Thomas Skouteris (eds) ' Symposium—The European Tradition in International Law: Nicolas Politis,' *European Journal of International Law* 23 (2012), 215–273.

183 Neff, *Justice Among Nations* 2014, 373.

184 Robert Kolb, 'Politis and Sociological Jurisprudence of Inter-War International Law' *European Journal of International Law* 23 (2012), 233–241, 236.

The most representative of the treatments that are often examined under the label of the solidarist (or sociological) school of international law was the consciously anti-positivist monism premised upon the lodestar of the 'objective law' of the international community of G. Scelle.[185] Inspired by a biological conception of the international system, Scelle's sociological approach to international law reconceived its fundamental rules as the 'constitution' of a global federalist legal system[186] in the making. The latter was bound to develop through institutionalized functional areas[187] in which state officials, in accordance with his 'theorie de dédoublement fonctionnel' ('role splitting') performed a functional dual role in fulfilling the competences that states obtain from international law in the service of the dynamic 'natural law of social development'[188] for the ultimate benefit of individuals. Individuals, according to Scelle's conception of 'methodological individualism', remained the true subjects of his 'droit des gens'.

In the United States, there was also an emerging anti-formalist American sociological jurisprudence of international law. This surged from the sociologically nurtured soil in the 1920s and 1930s and mirrored the parallel development of the theory of American legal realism, the building blocks of which lie in the sociological jurisprudence of Roscoe Pound[189] and the insights of Oliver W. Holmes[190] and Louis Brandeis before the war. The pre-war Lochner era[191] was only the opening stage of the sociological-based legal realist critique that emerged during what what Duncan Kennedy has called the beginning of the second 'globalization of the social in Law and Legal Thought' in the first decade of the twentieth century. This movement, which 'unsettle[d] the confidence of classical

185 Georges Scelle, *Precis de droits de gens: principes et systematique* (Paris: Editions Sirey 1932).

186 Emmanuelle Jouannet, 'L'idée de Communauté Humaine a La Croisée de La Communauté des Etats et de la Communauté Mondiale', *Archives De Philosophie Du Droit* 47 (2003) 191.

187 Rene-Jean Dupuy, 'Images de Georges Scelle', *European Journal of International Law* 2 (1990), 235–239.

188 Georges Scelle, 'Le Droit Constitutionnel International', In *Mélanges Carré De Malberg* (Paris: Sirey, 1933), 503.

189 Roscoe Pound, 'The Scope and Purpose Of Sociological Jurisprudence', *Harvard Law Review* 24 (1911), 591.

190 Oliver Wendell Holmes, 'The Path of the Law', *Harvard Law Review* 10 (1897) 457. See Also Justice Holmes' Dissenting Opinion In Lochner v. New York 198 U.S. (1905), 45.

191 For an analysis of the case as an exponent of classical legal thought in action, Kennedy *The Rise and Fall of Classical Legal Thought* (2006) 15 (noting how 'the case provides, in Harlan's dissent as well as in the majority opinion, good evidence about the structure of the legal consciousness of the period').

legal thought' that had already been decried earlier by R. Pound as formalism or mechanical jurisprudence,[192] or even as a conception of law akin (according to Holmes) to a 'brooding omnipresence in the skies',[193] reached its peak during the Great Depression in the United States when Karl Llewellyn,[194] influenced by Max Weber's sociology,[195] along with Jerome Frank,[196] and others would further 'unsettle the confidence of classical legal thought'. During the interwar period, in the United States, the 'legal realist' critique contributed to a 'new practical spirit, an orientation to process and policy at once contextual, purposive and functional.'[197] In its international legal version, this would posit 'an international law based on the social sciences [...] in the understanding that only by furthering social goals and developing a law that, far from being autonomous, was informed and shaped by social developments and that reflected the realities revealed by sociology and political science was international law able to operate effectively and ethically.'[198] This 'demand that orthodox international legal science transform itself into a functional, result-oriented approach' was according to Astorino, 'in full sway by the time World War II began',[199]

The influence of legal realists, who argued in more adamantly anti-formalist terms than their predecessors that 'juristic creativity was required to fill the deductive gaps with new tools for reasoning about what came to be known as policy—a loose umbrella for attending to social conditions, functional purposes, broad social goals and ethical commitments'[200]—, will be seen more clearly in the post- second World War's application of an

192 Roscoe Pound, 'Mechanical Jurisprudence', Columbia Law Review 8 (1908), 605–623, 605.

193 Oliver Wendell Holmes' opinion in Southern Pacific R.R. Co. v. Jensen, 244 U.S. 205, at 222 (1917).

194 Karl Llewellyn, 'Some Realism About Realism—Responding To Dean Pound', *Harvard Law Review* 44 (1931) 1222.

195 Duncan Kennedy, The Disenchantment of Logically Formal Legal Rationality or Max Weber's Sociology in the Genealogy of The Contemporary Mode of Western Legal Thought, *Hastings Law Journal* 55 (2004), 1169–1076, 1070.

196 E.G. Jerome Frank, *Law And The Modern Mind* (1930) 13 (Noting that the 'Widespread notion that law either is or can be made approximately stationary and certain' is 'irrational and should be classed as an illusion or a myth').

197 Id., 21.

198 Anghie, *Imperialism* 2005, 128.

199 Id., 291.

200 David Kennedy, 'Lon L. Fuller', in David Kennedy/ William W. Fisher III (eds) The Canon of American Legal Thought (Princenton: Princenton University Press 2006), 209.

alternative American jurisprudence of 'pragmatism' to international law.[201] After the second World War, the functional sociological jurisprudence, which was diagnosed as a cure for the ailments and the abstractly idealized legalism of international law of the interwar years combined with the development of a realist tradition in international law. Throughout the interwar period, and from different perspectives, the realist 'deniers' of international law[202] had continued to highlight the primitive character of the system that emerged at Versailles and the irreducibly political nature of an international legal system ultimately dominated by the realpolitik concerns of powerful states. After World War II, contributing to the development of 'international relations' as a separate academic discipline,[203] an influential retrospective realist interpretation[204] considered the interwar 'reconstructive doctrine' part and parcel of a 'legalistic-moralistic approach to international relations',[205] and bitterly decried the 'apparently fantastic constructions of a legalism or idealism that had been oblivious to the 'realities' of power in the international world.'[206]

However, whereas after two World Wars, the failure of the League of Nations as an international security organization to deliver international peace and security would generate a hard-nosed realist critique of what became retrospectively portrayed as the abstractly idealized legalism of international law, in the mid-1920s that same 'idealized legalism' became one of the forces for the renewal of the School of Salamanca in the interwar period.

H. Lauterpacht, a émigré scholar in Britain since the early 1920s,[207] acknowledged in his writings on the international community that the Spanish school

201 Roscoe Pound, *Philosophical Theory of International law*, Biblioteca Visseriana Dissertationum, Ius international ilustratum 1 (1923), 89.

202 Including Scandinavian realists by reference to Anders Vilhelm Lundstedt, Karl Olivecrona and other such as the hungarian Felix Somlo, see Truyol, *Histoire du droit international* 1998, 142–143.

203 See e.g. David Long, 'C. A. W. Manning and the Discipline of International Relations', *The Round Table* 94 (2005) 77–96.

204 For a refutal of the very existence of idealist paradigm in the interwar period, see e.g. Lucian M. Ashworth, 'Where are the Idealists in Interwar International Relations?', *Review of International Studies* 32 (2006), 291–308.

205 See George F. Kennan, *American Diplomacy: 1900–1950* (Chicago: University of Chicago Press, 1951), 79–89.

206 Koskenniemi, 'History of International Law, World War I to World War II' (2007), 19.

207 See Martti Koskenniemi, 'Hersch Lauterpacht 1897–1960', in Jack Beatson and Reihard Zimmermann (ed), *Jurists Uprooted: German-Speaking Emigré Lawyers in Twentieth-Century Britain*, (Oxford: Oxford University Press (2004), 601–661).

of Ius Gentium had 'laid the foundations of the jurisprudential treatment of the problem of the international community as a whole'.[208] Koskenniemi has approached H. Lauterpacht's contribution to the study of the science of international law as a hybrid of both 'traditionalism' and a modernist sensibility that arose immediately following the First World War.[209] Lauterpacht's leaning towards a value-loaded substratum for international law, and his open defence of 'peace' as a legal postulate in international law, which he understood 'as the law of the international community,'[210] made him differ starkly from the formalist value-free anti-sociolegal approach of Kelsen, one of his professors in Vienna, 'in regard to the place of natural law for legal construction.'[211] On the other hand, as Koskenniemi also notes, sharing 'Kelsen's modernist nominalism,' Lauterpacht, who embraced the central role of the judge in the common-law tradition and the detailed attention to judicial technique of his country of adoption, attempted to bring the anti-sovereign ethos of this epochal reconstructive doctrine to the terrain of an empirical critical approach to positivism as practice and, accordingly, to combat the 'scientific factuality'[212] of voluntarist positivism itself. Along these lines, Lauterpacht identified the problem of reliance on 'self-judgement' by sovereign states vis-à-vis international obligations as the basic obstacle to the realisation of a gradual transfer of the rule of law to the international plane. Lauterpacht's strong stance against a state-centred dogmatic voluntarism required him to demonstrate that this was at variance with both logic, through ad nauseam stressing of the regressive basis of the consensual principle, and facts, given that domestic maxims and general principles are key to filling the gaps between consensual norms.[213]

Indicative of this underlying consonance with the interwar strand of jurisprudential legalistic idealism was Lauterpacht's proposal for the establishment of domestic enforcement mechanisms in the administration of international law. Such mechanisms would, in his view, convert the absolute

208 Hersch Lauterpacht, 'The Grotian Tradition Of International Law', *British Yearbook Of International Law* 23 (1946) 1–53, 17. See also Randall Lesaffer, 'The Grotian Tradition Revisited: Change and Continuity in the History of International Law', *British Yearbook of International Law* 73 (2003),103–139.

209 Koskenniemi, *The Gentle Civilizer* 2001, 355–357.

210 Hersch Lauterpacht, *International Law. Collected Papers* (Cambridge: Cambridge University Press, 1979), 49.

211 Id., 356.

212 Koskenniemi, *The Gentle Civilizer* 2001, 355–357.

213 Id.

sovereign freedom exercised by states in their conduct of foreign policy into a limited discretion in consonance with the completeness and unity of the law and its 'priority over political will and political fact.'[214] Lauterpacht set out to jurisprudentially criticize the doctrines of non-justiciability in his 1933 'The Function of Law in the International Community', which, for Koskenniemi, is 'the most important English language book on international law in the 20th century,'[215] in order to show that '… all international disputes are, irrespective of their gravity, disputes of a legal character in the sense that, so long as the rule of law is recognized, they are capable of an answer by the application of legal rules',[216] and, therefore, require the completeness of the international legal system of which the international judge is the ultimate guarantor.[217] For Lauterpacht, 'the establishment and the binding force of international law as a whole' were both 'grounded in a factor superior to and independent of the will of states—a factor which gives validity to the law created by the will of the states. That superior rule is the objective fact of the existence of an interdependent community of states.'[218] This was, for him, in appropriate cases 'also a source which […] gives rise to legal rights and duties independently of the will of the states.'[219]

Recourse to constitutional analogies abounded, meanwhile, in doctrinal works that aimed to flesh out the notion of an ever universalizing 'international community' as the underlying necessary structure for an international legal order based on natural law. As the binding nature of international norms became for many the central and decisive question of the nature of international law, a revival of natural law, called upon to play the doctrinal function of a 'spiritualization of positivism' extended across various European countries, especially among Catholic circles. In doing so, it contributed to the revival of the Spanish School of the 16th century and the figure of Francisco de Vitoria. Alfred Verdross, an Austrian jurist educated in the Vienna School, became the 'outstanding natural-law advocate in the German-speaking world'.[220] Unlike

---

214 Id.

215 Herscht Lauterpacht, The Function of Law in the International Community (Oxford: Clarendon Press, 1933). See also Martti Koskenniemi, 'The Function of Law in the International Community: 75 Years After', *British Yearbook of International Law* 79 (2008), 353–366.

216 Lauterpacht, The Function of Law 1933, 1158.

217 Id., 363.

218 Id., 58.

219 Id.

220 Neff, Justice Among Nations 2014, 379.

the most conspicuous representative of the Vienna school, Verdross did not rely on an unverifiable scientific Grundnorm[221] resulting from an attack on the irrational ideal of justice as a 'subjective judgement of value.' By contrast, the Verdrossian approach, expounded in his 1927 course at The Hague on 'Le fondement du droit international,' amounted to a grounding of the theoretical foundations of international law on the normative idea of the moral unity of mankind, on a natural law conception of 'objective justice' as the ultimate source of law.[222] The abstract idea of the moral unity of mankind on which Verdross's monism was grounded found itself associated, through the notion of the international community, with the constitutional unity of a unique universal legal system. This system was originally posited as a hierarchical model constitutionally crowned by 'a series of fundamental principles of international law determining its sources, subjects, and execution, and the jurisdiction allocated to states,'[223] which, although based on the principle of pacta sunt servanda, referred back to 'material considerations susceptible to translating ideas of justice and common good.' For Verdross, the general principles of law, which in international law were for him a reflection of the legal conscience of the international community, were 'a bridge between pure natural law and pure positive law.'[224] The formal positivist Kelsenian self-constitutive bias of international law towards community order thus appears replaced in Verdross's thinking by an underlying theory of justice grounded on the realisation of universal communal values of Christian humanist inspiration.[225]

Verdross's conception, which was informed by a universalistic tradition retraceable to the Spanish legal theologians of the 16th century, benefitted from its recuperation, by a generation of Spanish international law scholars headed by Camilo Barcia Trelles and with the valuable help of James Brown Scott, of the Salamanca school. The marked relevance of anchoring the Christian community-oriented universalism of Vitoria, and especially that of Suarez,

---

221 Deborah Cass, *The Constitutionalisation Of The World Trade Organisation: Legitimacy, Democracy And Community In The International Trading System* (Oxford: Oxford University Press 2005), 32–39.

222 Robert Kolb, *Les Cours Généraux De Droit International Public de L'académie de La Haye* (Bruxelles: Bruylant 2004), 31.

223 See Bardo Fassbender *UN Security Council Reform* 1998, 37–45.

224 See Simma, The Contribution of Alfred Verdross 1995, 49.

225 Antonio Truyol Serra, 'Esbozo de una sociología del Derecho natural', *Revista de estudios políticos* 24 (1949), 15–38. Luis García Arias, 'Las concepciones iusnaturalistas sobre la fundamentación del derecho internacional' in Luis Garcia Arias, *Estudios de historia y doctrina del derecho internacional* (1964), 14.

in recovering the 'humanist' interpretation of the Salamanca school as the founding fathers of international law contributed to Verdross' neo-naturalist tendency, under which pacta sunt servanda 'n'est pas autre chose qu'un partie de la morale universelle.'[226] Verdross put the Spanish universal tradition at the service of the axiological foundation of the notion of the international community and, with it, through the notion of an international constitution, at the service of the binding character of international law.

The anti-sovereigntist ethos and the natural law tradition would also find other champions in different countries such as Cahtrein, Mausbach and Krabbe. In Austria, Kunz highlighted the emergence 'under our eyes' of a tendency which may take centuries to be realized but that ineluctably advanced towards a global legal system where all mankind would fuse under a single world state. In France, Louis Le Fur[227] wrote that 'les efforts de ceux qui veulent arriver à créer un droit international effectif, c'est-à-dire à affirmer la suprématie du droit sur la force, se résument en une lutte contre l'idée de souveraineté absolute'.[228] This struggle in Le Fur's view involved the recognition of a 'droit objectif à fondement moral.'[229] This universalist common tendency was identified by Barcia Trelles in speaking of a 'modern school of international law' as one of the sources of the 'renaissance of Vitoria and late Spanish scholasticism.' Meanwhile, in Spain, the second 'renaissance' of the 'Spanish classics of international law' was greatly encouraged, as we shall see, by the founding of the 'Association Francisco de Vitoria' in Madrid in 1926.[230]

## The Founding of the Association Francisco de Vitoria

In the interwar period, the sixteenth-century Dominican friar and prima professor of sacred theology at the University of Salamanca's idea of a 'universal' international legal order valid for all human societies inspired new theoretical attempts to square the circle of state sovereignty and the international legal community. These theoretical constructions were stimulated by an ius-naturalist Christian perspective that was, in its turn, made possible by the slow retrieval of the 'Spanish Classics of international law' since, as

226 Verdross, 'Le fondement du droit international' 1927, 257.

227 Louis Le Fur, 'La theorie du droit naturel depuis le xviième siecle', Recueil de cours de l'Academie de la Haye 27 (1927) 263.

228 Id., 548.

229 Id., 556.

230 Schmitt, The Nomos of the Earth 2003, 117.

we saw in earlier chapters, the mid-late nineteenth century. The revival of the Spanish universalist tradition fitted with the concepts, ideals and goals that the League of Nations had made fashionable as guidelines for an institutionalized international society, such as arbitration,'[231] just and unjust wars, universal peace and justice, the equality of nations and peoples, and the international right to trade. The fashionable doctrinal character acquired by a readaption of the Vitorian tradition to the conditions of the interwar years both mirrored, and further enhanced, the academic engagement with international law in Spain.

Most, if not all, interwar Spanish international legal scholars, some of whom occupied parliamentary and political posts, were Catholic, or otherwise had been educated and were sociologically embedded in a deeply Catholic cultural environment in Spain. However, this deep Catholic moral substratum, as Forcada explains, cohabited with a generational embrace of a 'modern scientism'[232] during the interwar years. Indeed, whereas for Forcada, 'the ius-philosophical origins and the appeal for historical knowledge became translated into a fixation with the doctrines of the Spanish theologians of the 16th century and, as a consequence, with a natural attraction towards a natural law with Christian roots,'[233] this religious influence was not an obstacle to the interwar Spanish doctrine of international law being, paradoxically enough, above all a 'clear example of a bourgeois modernity which attempted to confront the object of its study scientifically.'[234]

The new Spanish scientism was an offspring, as we saw in Chapter 2, of the Europeanizing tendencies and practical measures that had fostered the internationalization of research spurred by the 'regenerationist' movement and the intellectual liberalizing influence of the Free Institution of Teaching. This was also the product of the Spanish greater engagement with practical international problems with repercussions for Spain and the correlated gradual abandonment of abstract speculation in the field of international law. Scientific 'progress meant the specialized division of knowledge and the adoption of a scientific method to assure its progress and access to a truth devoid, to the

231 Mary Ellen O'Connell and Lenore Vander Zee, 'The History of International Adjudication' in Cesare P. R. Romano, Karen J. Alter, and Chrisanthi Avgerou (eds) The Oxford Handbook of International Adjudication (Oxford: Oxford University Press 2013), 42.

232 Ignacio Forcada Barona, 'La influencia de la religión católica en la doctrina internacionalista' 2012, 212–214.

233 Id., 212–214.

234 Id., 212.

extent possible, of revealed characters',[235] from which emerges the impression, as Del Arenal retrospectively noted, of the 'absolute primacy of the legal perspective in the Spanish academic approach to international problems.'[236] Despite this intellectual evolution, the religious and cultural national substratum was never really gone among Spanish international law scholars. The religious tradition was mirrored, according to Forcada, in their 'incapacity to unconditionally embrace the inevitable consequence of the scientific method in its legal application, positivism, which was instead replaced by a candid adhesion to an idealist ius-naturalism with Christian underpinnings'.[237]

As in other European settings, the second generation of international lawyers played the role of a 'hinge' between a mid-late nineteenth century discipline emerging from a magma of diplomatic history, ius-philosophical reflections and the history of international relations and another one that, as Forcada notes, 'had begun to cut its ties with legal philosophy and the history of international relations in order to adopt a technical legal style based on normative exegesis and the analysis of case law, which would allow it to be grouped with the hard core of legal disciplines.'[238] However, this process was slowed down in Spain by the strong Catholic cultural imprint of the Spanish tradition of international law and eventually brought almost to a halt by the Spanish Civil War. In particular, the deep divides brought about by the polarization of a social class struggle underlying the Spanish Civil War favoured the combination of the Catholic natural law tradition with a strong nationalist orientation, leading, as we shall see, most Spanish interwar international law scholars to support General Franco's coup d'état against the Second Spanish Republic.

A key driver for this intellectual substratum to develop in the interwar period in Spain was the foundation of the Association Francisco de Vitoria in 1926.[239] The new association was born with the object of 'spreading knowledge about the legacy of the classic Spanish ius-internationalists', and to 'update their doctrines.'[240] The idea for the Association—'a Spanish

---

235 id.

236 Del Arenal, 'El estudio de las relaciones internacionales en la España del siglo XIX' 1979, 50.

237 Id.

238 Forcada Barona, 'La influencia de la religión católica en la doctrina internacionalista' 2012.

239 Id., 189–190.

240 Ramón Hernández Marín. 'La cátedra 'francisco de Vitoria' de la universidad de salamanca', en actas del IV Seminario de Historia de la Filosofía Española (Salamanca: Ediciones Universidad de Salamanca/excma. Diputación provincial de salamanca, 1984), 335–336.

institution which could disseminate the Vitorian doctrine and would put it in contact with the current situation of the legal sciences and with the diverse schools and institutions of these sciences'[241]—was born in the context of a visit to Salamanca in 1925 by the Dutch Grotius Society[242] as part of the celebration of the tercentenary of the publication of *De Iure Belli ac Pacis*. The founding of the Association to honour the author who inaugurated the 'ius inter gentes' in his definition of *ius gentium* as 'Quod naturalis ratio inter omnes gentes constituit vocatur jus gentium'[243] saw an inter-generational confluence and combination of efforts by key figures from the first and second 'professional generation' of Spanish international law scholars across the political spectrum. In time, however, its appeal would be greater among the conservative and Catholic sectors.

Among the founders of the Association who belonged to the first generation were members of the Institution Libre de Enseñanza, such as Aniceto Sela Sampil who became the President of the Association (1929–1935), and Rafael Altamira, a historian and Americanist who sat as a judge at the Permanent Court of International Justice from 1919 to 1944. In the conservative aisle were Manuel González Hontoria, Minister of Foreign Affairs (1921–1922) who has served as representative at the Peace Conference in Paris, or the Marquis de Olivart, who had contributed to the first Vitorian revival by publishing the Latin versions of 'De Indis' and 'De Iure Belli' back in 1886 as an appendix to his treatise Manual de Derecho Internacional y Privado, one of Spain's earliest and leading works in the field through it several editions since 1886. The leading founder of the Association belonging to the second 'professional generation' was the 11th Viscount of Santa Clara de Avedillo and, at the time, Minister of Foreign Affairs of Spain, José Yanguas Messia (1890–1974). Yanguas, who played the leading role in the establishment of the Association was a chair of international law at the Central University of Madrid in 1920.

As in the case of Barcia Trelles, Yanguas Messia's formative years had benefitted from research stays abroad in the 1910s, studying in Paris in 1913–1914 following courses with Pillet and Weiss. Yanguas's works since his formative years, fitted a new pattern of study of international law in the light

241 id.

242 Anuario de la Asociación Francisco de Vitoria I (1927–1928), 44.

243 Vitoria replaced the word 'homines', thus transforming Gaius' classic definition of ius gentium from 'Quod naturalis ratio inter omnes homines constituit' by changing its subject from the individual (in the Roman conception) to peoples or nations, understood as 'grouping[s] of men organized in a superior entity'. Barcia Trelles, 'Francisco de Vitoria et l'école moderne', 1928.

of specific Spanish foreign policy areas of interest. This gradual abandonment of abstract speculation is discernible already in his doctoral dissertation on 'La neutralidad. Su concepto, derechos y deberes de los neutrales' (Neutrality: the concept, the rights and duties of neutrals) written during the First World War. Also from 1915 was his publication on 'La expansión colonial en África y el estatuto internacional de Marruecos' (The colonial expansion in Africa and the international legal status of Morocco),[244] a topic which mirror the weight that North Africa had in Spanish foreign policy. In 1919, Yanguas continued developing his international law scholarship on matters of international politics with practical repercussions for Spain with 'España y la Sociedad de Naciones' (Spain and the League of Nations).[245] In this work, Yanguas highlighted the League's role in strengthening 'international solidarity' by noting that 'it interests Spain as it interests all secondary states (…) the proletariat in the great international society, that this organization is democratic and equalizing.'[246] Yet, he warned that 'would be 'futile' to trust the external formulae of law the permanent solution of international problems'. For Yanguas 'those ritualistic formulae, those positive norms would be dead letters, words void of content, if from the bottom of the conscience of peoples and of their authorized organs of expression, the light of the immanent eternal justice would not irradiate as a 'vivifying' force.' Without the latter, the 'radiance' of which comes from above, the mankind of the future and the new international law that should regulate its life will change its external appearance, but not its substance.'[247] In 1923, again mirroring the cultural Americanist orientation of Spanish international law scholars in the early 1920s, Yanguas published 'El hispanoamericanismo en Ginebra', (Hispano-Americanism in Geneva).[248] Yanguas also developed a high-profile international role as legal adviser to the Spanish representation at the League of Nations (1920–1922), joining the Institut de Droit International in 1923, and serving as Judge at the Permanent Court of Arbitration (from 1925), in parallel with a prolific political career as Minister of Foreign Affairs (1925–1927) and, later, President of the Consultative National Assembly (1927–1929) during the dictatorship of Miguel Primo de Rivera in the late 1920s. As we shall later see, Yanguas Messia, exiled to France after the resignation of

244 Yanguas Messia, *La expansión colonial en áfrica y el estatuto internacional de marruecos* (Madrid: Imprenta Alianza Tipográfica 1915).

245 Yanguas Messia, *España y la Sociedad de Naciones* 1919.

246 Id. 26.

247 Id. 29.

248 Yanguas Messia, *El hispanoamericanismo en Ginebra* (Madrid: xxxx 1923).

Primo de Rivera, became one of the staunchest and more influential supporters of General Franco's coup d'état against the Second Spanish Republic.

After the founding of the Association in 1926, a Francisco de Vitoria Chair was created at the University of Salamanca in 1927 with the 'aim of developing courses and conferences on topics of international law, inspired by the doctrine of Vitoria and the great jurists, theologians and philosophers of the race that followed his magisterium'.[249] The time of the renewed academic glory of Vitoria coincided, as we have seen, with an increase in the strategic importance of the notion of 'Hispanidad' under Primo de Rivera's rule. 'Hispanidad', which had earlier developed in the context of Spanish-US competition for cultural influence in Latin America before 1898 and, afterwards, as part of a cultural anti-North American movement led by Latin Americans, had resurfaced in the context of the establishment of the League of Nations. Among Spanish international law scholars, Rafael Altamira Crevea (1866–1951), a member of the Free Institution of Teaching and a regenerationist of the 'circle of Oviedo', contributed as a historian to the fight against 'leyenda negra', the retrieval of 'Derecho Indiano'[250] reclaiming the Spanish civilizing legacy in the Americas,[251] and the 'Spanish collaboration in the common work of the Western civilization.'[252] In 1927, he articulated the position of the Spanish Americanists vis-à-vis the Spanish former colonies in 1927. As 'Americanistas', Altamira, noted, they reclaimed a 'special and exclusive camp, which is the one we have in common with the peoples of our civilization and our language.' 'In this field,' he stressed, 'we want neither intervention nor collaboration, which, in all likelihood, will perturb us. This is for the Spanish Americanists a dogma as intangible as the absolute domestic and international independence of all American republics.'[253] Spanish international lawyers in the mid-late 1920s also fostered 'Hispanidad' as part of reclaiming the intellectual legacy of the 'Spanish' school of Salamanca and to influence debates on the existence of an 'American international law' amidst the works on international codification then being prepared by Pan-American conferences. Barcia Trelles, who had published extensively

249 La gaceta de madrid, de 8 de marzo de 1927, 1438.

250 Luigi Nuzzo, 'Memoria, identità e uso pubblico della storia: l'invenzione del derecho indiano', *Forum Historiae Iuris*, Artikel vom 15 (2013) xxxx.

251 See among other works Rafael Altamira, *Historia de España y de la civilización española*, 4 vols. (Barcelona: impr. Juan Gili 1900–1911). Rafael Altamira, *Historia de la civilización española*, (Barcelona: Manuales Soler 1902).

252 Rafael Altamira, *España y el programa americanista* (Madrid: Ed. América 1917).

253 Rafael Altamira, 'España, los Estados Unidos y América', *Revista de las Españas* 7–8 (1927), 17–77.

on pan-Americanism and the Monroe Doctrine, noted that 'our brothers in America must turn their eyes to that Spain of the 16th century, that of the qualitative 'grandeurs' if they want to cement their international credo with a glorious tradition'[254] and explore how some of their current projects 'could be found embryonically in the theories of Vitoria.'[255]

Attention to Latin American affairs and the Hispanic world had also featured highly in the work of the multifaceted James Brown Scott. Retrospectively praised, as we have seen in Chapter Two, as 'the leading founder of the ASIL and its heart and soul for its first eighteen years'[256] and as the greatest figure in 'American universalism',[257] Brown Scott was also a prolific author of a very extensive body of scholarly work[258] that knew multiple editions and translations. Brown Scott's relationship with the Hispanic world had begun, as we saw in Chapter Two, back in the early 1910s. After the First World War and his participation as legal adviser at the Versailles Conference, James Brown Scott became professor of international law and international relations at the Georgetown School of Foreign Service since 1921 and continued at the forefront of international diplomacy.[259] Brown Scott's relationship with Spain would further consolidate after the foundation of the Association Francisco de Vitoria. Indeed, from 1926 onwards, Brown Scott, who from 1925 to 1929 was the President of the Institut de Droit

254 Barcia Trelles, 'Francisco de Vitoria et l'école moderne 1927, 331 noting 'Nos frères d'Amérique doivent donc forcément tourner leur regards vers cette Espagne du xvi siècle, celle des grandeurs qualitatives, s'ils veulent cimenter leur crédo international avec une glorieuse tradition'.

255 Barcia Trelles, 'Francisco de Vitoria et l'école moderne 1927, 200.

256 Frederic L. Kirgis, 'Elihu Root, James Brown Scott and the Early Years' 1996, 139.

257 Mark Weston Janis, 'International Law as Fundamental Justice: James Brown Scott, Harold Hongju Koh, And The American Universalist Tradition of International Law', *Saint Louis University Law Journal* 46 (2002), 346.

258 George A. Finch, 'James Brown Scott, 1866–1943', *American Journal of International Law* 38 (1944), 183–217, 217, mentioning that James Brown Scott was the 'author or editor of some thirty separate works and general editor of thirty-five titles in series, joint editor of ten more, writer of articles too numerous to mention, and speaker on hundreds of occasions for which he has left published or manuscript records'.

259 Hatsue Shinohara, *US International Lawyers in the Interwar Years. A Forgotten Crusade* (Cambridge: Cambridge University Press 2014) Scott continued to deliver official services as technical adviser to the US government at various international commissions and meetings. See Conference at Washington in 1921 on the Limitation of Armament and Pacific Questions the Third Pan American Scientific Congress at Lima in 1924, representative of the US at the Inter-American Commission of Jurists held at Rio de Janeiro 1927 et caetera, see further. Finch 'James Brown Scott, 1866–1943' 1944, 213–214.

International, began a period, that extended through his tenure as President of the American Society of International Law from 1929 to 1939, in which, as Carl Schmitt noted, he 'dedicated himself to becoming the official exponent of Vitoria's fame'.[260] Other than, as we shall later see, through a number of academic articles and books, Brown Scott promoted the Vitoria's cause by writing about the association in the American Journal of International Law[261] and by supporting Barcia Trelles through inter alia the Fellowship program of the Carnegie Endowment. In their turn, Spanish international law scholars, such as Luis Sela Sampil (1899–1990), chair-holder since 1933 at Universidad de Oviedo, like his father Aniceto Sela Sampil (1863–1935), who was by then the President of the Association Francisco de Vitoria (1929–1935), translated Brown's works into Spanish as 'Universalidad del Derecho de Gentes'[262] and wrote about him in 'Brown Scott, internacionalista.'[263] Brown Scott's 'El origen español del Derecho internacional moderno'[264] (The Spanish Origin of Modern International Law) was also published, with a prologue by Barcia Trelles, in Spanish in 1928, one year after he had received the title of doctor *honoris causa* from the University of Salamanca on the occasion of the inauguration of the Francisco de Vitoria chair.

Besides Brown Scott, the most internationally renowned contributor to the 'Vitorian restoration, was Camilo Barcia Trelles who noted that the revival of Vitoria was 'not only explained by the wish to repair an injustice, but because new times need new ideal paths through which they can reason'.[265] Barcia delivered his first course in French at The Hague Academy[266] on 'Francisco

260 Schmitt, The Nomos of the Earth 2003, 118.

261 Brown Scott, 'Asociación Francisco de Vitoria' 1928, 136.

262 James Brown Scott, 'Universalidad del Derecho de Gentes', *Revista de Legislación y Jurisprudencia* 76 (1927), 637–660.

263 Luis Sela Sampil. 'Brown Scott, internacionalista', *Revista de legislación y jurisprudencia* 75 (1927), 632–636.

264 Brown Scott, *El origen español del Derecho internacional moderno* 1928.

265 Camilo Barcia Trelles 'Francisco suarez (1548–1617): les théologiens espagnols du XVIe siècle et l'école moderne du droit international', Collected courses of the Hague Academy of International Law 43 (1933), 385–554, 415.

266 See respectively Camilo Barcia Trelles, 'Francisco de Vitoria et l'ecole moderne du droit international', Collected courses of the Hague Academy of International Law 17 (1928), 109–342. Camilo Barcia Trelles 'Francisco suarez (1548–1617): les théologiens espagnols du xvie siècle et l'école moderne du droit international', Collected courses of the Hague Academy of International Law 43 (1933), 385–554. Camilo Barcia Trelles 'Fernando Vázquez de Menchaca. L'école espagnole du droit international du xvie siécle', Collected courses of the Hague Academy of International Law 67 (1939), 430–534.

de Vitoria et l'ecole moderne de droit internationale' in 1927. In this course, Barcia particularly highlighted the ground-breaking role of Vitoria in his analysis in the *Relectiones* directly concerned with the 'American problem'. Barcia focused, in particular, on 'De Indis' by examining what Vitoria considered the seven 'illegitimate titles of acquisition' and eight 'legitimate titles of acquisition' respectively. For Barcia, in studying these titles, Vitoria 'formulated his immortal principles of international law'[267] and how the contemporary international tendencies—ranging from the international mandates established by the League of Nations[268] to international free trade[269] right up to the principle of collective intervention in the name of international solidarity[270]—were in conformity with Vitoria's thesis.

Meanwhile in Spain, an important vehicle for the international revitalisation of the 'humanist' interpretation of the Seconda Scholastica of the Spanish internationalists of the Sixteenth century[271] was the Anuario de la Asociación Francisco de Vitoria (The Yearbook of the Association Francisco de Vitoria). This began to be published in 1929[272] and continued, under the editorship of Luis G. Alonso Getino, also librarian of the Association, into five volumes until 1934, to reappear, after the Spanish civil war, in its sixth volume in 1946. An important role in this development was played by members of the Dominican order such as Vicente Beltran Heredia (1885–1973), the librarian of the Association, who published critical editions of the original texts 'Los manuscritos del Maestro Fray Francisco de Vitoria. Estudio Critico de introduccion a sus lecturas y reelecciones' in 1928 and edited the 'Comentarios del Maestro Francisco de Vitoria, O.P., a la Secunda Secundae de Santo Tomas' in 5 volumes in 1932. In 1929, Beltran de Heredia also examined the works of precursors of Vitoria, such as Matias de la Paz and his 'De dominio regum hispaniae super Indos',[273] and he produced a biography of Francisco de Vitoria

267 Id., 135.

268 Id., at 194

269 Id., 206–218. See also Koskenniemi Empire and International Law: The Real Spanish Contribution, The University of Toronto Law Journal, 61 (2011), 1–36.

270 Camilo Barcia Trelles, Francisco de Vitoria et l'ecole moderne 1928, 223.

271 Barcia Trelles, *Francisco de Vitoria, fundador del Derecho Internacional moderno*, 1928, 218.

272 Anuario de la Asociación Francisco de Vitoria (Salamanca: Imprenta Zoila Ascasibar, 1929).

273 Beltran de Heredia, Un Precursor del Maestro Vitoria. El P. Matias de Paz, O. P., y su tratado « De dominio regum hispaniae super Indos » (Salamanca: Calatrava 1929).

in 1939.[274] Other Dominicans continued this work with renewed impetus. One of them was Luis Alonso Getino (1877–1946), who was also among the original members of the Association and who had already contributed to the edition of Vitoria's work with a commentary in the 1910s. Getino had written essays in the journal 'La Ciencia Tomista,' of which he was the founder, and the first director, in nationalist overtones in line with the polemics over the 'Spanish science',[275] and in 1914 published 'El Maestro Fr. Francisco de Vitoria'.[276] In the 1930s, he published the monumental 'El Maestro Fray Francisco de Vitoria. Su vida, su doctrina y su influencia,'[277] and edited the critical edition of Vitoria's 'Relecciones' in 1933.[278] These new 'Vitorian' works added, as we shall see, to a climax in the production of works on the Spanish theologians of the 16th century, both nationally and internationally, against the background of Spain's convulsive domestic political situation, and the gradual crumbling of the League's system of collective security during the Second Spanish Republic.

## The Second Spanish Republic—A Principled Engagement with Internationalism

In 1927, Miguel Primo de Rivera established a National Consultative Assembly, which is considered the first parliament of corporatist character during the interwar period, and which drew up a pre-legislative project for an anti-liberal and authoritarian regime.[279] However, the popularity of his dictatorship was affected by the Wall Street Crash of October 1929 which, in fostering greater instability in Spain, led to his resignation in January 1930 and exile to France

---

274 Beltran de Heredia, The fundamental works of Beltran de Heredia on Francisco de Vitoria are gathered in Augusto sarmiento, 'Lecturas ineditas de Francisco de Vitoria: bases para la edicion critica' *Scripta Theologica* 12 (1980), 575–592.

275 See Francisco Castilla Urbano, *El pensamiento de Francisco de Vitoria: filosofía política e indio americano* (Barcelona: Anthropos Editorial, 1992).

276 Luis G. Alonso Getino, 'El Maestro Fr. Francisco de Vitoria y el renacimiento filosófico teológico del siglo XVI', Revista de archivos, bibliotecas y museos (1914).

277 Luis G. Alonso Getino, *El Maestro Fray Francisco de Vitoria. Su vida, su doctrina y su influencia* (Madrid: Imprenta Católica, 1930)

278 Luis G. Alonso Getino (ed.), Relecciones Vitorianas con textos en latin y su traduccion castellana, facsimiles de codices y ediciones principes, variantes, notas e introduccion (Madrid: Impr. La Rafa, 1933–35).

279 Gonzalo Alvarez Chillida, 'El fracaso de un proyecto autoritario: el debate constitucional en la asamblea nacional de Primo de Rivera' Revista de Estudios Políticos 93 (1996), 359–375.

where he died two months later. After two fleeting monarchical governments, King Alphonse XIII, deprived of the support of the army, also left for Paris some months later. The ground was ripe for the establishment of the Second Spanish Republic in April 1931. This brought in its wake a re-orientation of Spanish foreign policy toward the League.

The revisionist and prestige-seeking instrumentalist traditional axis of Spanish diplomacy associated with the logic of imperialism was replaced by a more finalist embracing of the values of the international system which emerged around the League in Geneva. The new Spanish foreign policy was founded on the post-1931 conviction that Spanish national interests would be better served by making the core of the foreign policy 'nothing other than an outward projection of the democratic and republican principles that inspired domestic policy.'[280] Conceived as a means to break Spain's traditional isolationism by reforming the 'traditional Spanish neutrality' in an 'active sense',[281] and attempting to lead it within the framework of the League, the new policy was assertively designed as a critical counterpoint to what was described as 'the past Monarchy's regime-survival-oriented and non-existent foreign policy.'[282]

The Republican alignment with the League of Nations was apparent in the Spanish Constitution of 1931, which in its article 1 established that 'Spain is a democratic republic of workers of all classes, organized under a regime of Freedom and Justice according to the principles of the League of Nations'. That building a 'new' international society and a 'new' Spain was a sea change[283] from the isolationism of the earlier regime was reflected in the constitution's embracing the League's policy of peace and the new government's active commitment to its goals. The fact that the new Republican 'Spain was among the League's firmest supporters'[284] of constitutional harmonization was reflected, as Quintana Navarro has concisely explained, in that in the new Spanish Constitution 'the renunciation of war as an instrument of foreign policy (article 6)

280 Ismael Saz, 'The Second Republic in the International Arena' in Sebastian Balfour/ Paul Preston (eds) *Spain and the Great Powers in the Twentieth Century* (London: Routledge 1999), 73–95, 75.

281 Id.

282 Zulueta quoted in Neila, 'La política exterior de la españa republicana' 2004, 48.

283 Yolanda Gamarra, 'Los lenguajes del derecho internacional en la Constitution de 1931' in Yolanda Gamarra & Ignacio de la Rasilla (eds.), Historia del pensamiento internacionalista español del siglo XX (Cizur Menor: Thomson Reuters Aranzadi, 2012) relying heavily, among others, on Francisco Quintana Navarro, *España en Europa 1931–1936. Del compromiso por la paz a la huida de la guerra* (Madrid: Nerea 1993), 36.

284 Francis O. Wilcox, 'The League of Nations and the Spanish Civil War' The Annals of the American Academy of Political and Social Science 198 (1938), 65–72, 68.

and respect for the universal norms of international law (article 7) was combined with recognition of the primacy of international treaties over domestic law (article 65), the compulsory publicity of treaties and the illegitimacy of secret agreements (article 76), the subordination of declaring war to the mechanisms of arbitration and conciliation (article 77), and finally, the declaration that Spain could only withdraw from the League of Nations through the passing of a special law voted by absolute majority and after giving the required notice according to the dispositions of the Covenant of the League of Nations (article 78).'[285]

This peaceful internationalism fitted within the broader domestic reformist trend that had made Spain a 'secular' multi-party democratic system based on equal rights for all citizens, with provisions for local and regional autonomy under the formula of the 'integral state', and the right to universal—including, for the first time in Spanish history, female—suffrage. The Spanish constitution received numerous positive international reactions. Among these were those of Toynbee, who saw it as a 'first signal' of the reaffirmation of liberalism in Europe at a time when Europe seemed to be advancing in the opposite direction.[286] Other authors, such as Mirkine-Guetzevitch, considered that it had crystallized for the 'first time in the constitutional history of post-war Europe' a 'complete harmonization of the rules of domestic public law and the Covenant of the League of Nations.'[287] International lawyers such as Manley O. Hudson,[288] and Paul de Visscher[289] also greeted the 'internationalism' of the new Spanish Constitution.

On the diplomatic plane, the new orientation of Spanish foreign policy was accompanied by a reform of the administrative structure under a new Minister of Foreign Affairs, A. Lerroux. During the 'progressive biennium' (1931–1933) of the Second Spanish Republic, Salvador de Madariaga (1886–1978) was selected to head the Spanish delegation to the League. Madariaga, an engineer by training and a literary man by vocation, worked for 'The Times' between

285 Francisco Quintana Navarro, *España en Europa, 1931–1936. Del compromiso de la paz a la huida de la guerra* (Ed. Nerea, 1993).

286 Ismael Saz, 'La política exterior de la segunda república en el primer bienio (1931–1933): una valoración' *Revista de Estudios Internacionales* 6 (1985), 843–858.

287 Boris Mirkine-Guetzevich, 'Ius Gentium Pacis', *Revista de Derecho Publico* I (1932) 264 quoted in Gamarra, 'Los lenguages de la Constitución' 2012, 193.

288 See e.g. Manley O. Hudson 'The Spanish Constitution of 1931', American Journal of International Law 26 (1932), 579–582.

289 Paul de Visscher, Les tendances internationales des constitutions modernes Collected Courses of the Hague Academy of International Law 80 (1952), 512–578.

1916 and 1921, in which capacity he covered the League in 1921–1922. He was also a civil servant at the League during the 1920s working as Secretary of the third Disarmament Commission between 1922–1927, an experience that served him when he published a work on Disarmament[290] after he moved to teach Spanish literature in Oxford. With the arrival of the Second Republic, Madariaga was appointed Ambassador to Washington in 1931 and, soon afterwards, Ambassador to Paris (1932–34) and Permanent Spanish Delegate at the League of Nations (1931–36), a post he combined with that of Minister for Instruction and Justice for a short period in 1934. Amidst much ministerial instability at the head of Foreign Affairs, with ten ministers in five years, Madariaga, the embodiment of the Europeanized elite intellectual who 'could live with his mind in Europe and his heart in Spain',[291] was the 'visible head of Spanish Diplomacy'[292] during the Second Spanish Republic. The new foreign policy style and the internationalist ideas enshrined in the Spanish Constitution of 1931—in the drafting of which Madariaga himself had participated—were embodied by Madariaga who appointed other Spaniards who had served at the League as his direct collaborators. Among the latter was P. de Azcarate, who had also actively participated in the work of the league, first from 1922 as civil servant and since 1931 as Director of the Department of Minority Protection Affairs, and who would later become the Deputy Secretary General of the League (1933–1936), and José Plá, and Spanish career diplomats such as Julio López Oliván.

To highlight the importance of the new orientation towards the League, the Spanish office of the League became dependent on the Political Section of the Ministry of Foreign Affairs, and a Commission for the League of Nations' Affairs was created including representatives in the different technical commissions. The activist re-implementation with a conscious effort to be at the avant-garde of the ideals of the League of Nations by the Spanish foreign policy elite gained it the support of small and medium powers. However, as the President of the Republic, Manuel Azaña, noted, this orientation was 'not only because of altruistic motives but because it provided solutions to the fundamental problems of the Spanish position in the world' as a 'disarmed nation, economically weak but on the way to progress and internal reconstruction'. Moreover, as Neila highlights, Madariaga's own famous 'Nota sobre política

290 Salvador de Madariaga, *Disarmement* (1929). Salvador de Madariaga, Desarmément (Geneva: ed. por la Société de Nations 1932).

291 Federico de Onís, Ensayos sobre el sentido de la cultura española (Madrid: Ed. Publicaciones de la Residencia de Estudiantes, 1932), 106.

292 Quintana Navarro, Salvador de Madariaga 1996, 107.

exterior de España' of 1932 illustrates a compromise between his embracing of the League's ideals and the 'assimilation of the goals and traditional interests of Spanish foreign policy,' such as its claim over Gibraltar, historical and cultural links with Latin America, the relationship between the Iberian states and the preference to gravitate around French and British guidelines in European and Mediterranean policy.[293]

The new Spanish orientation coincided with an interlude in the work of the League. As attention to war problems had receded into the background in the late 20ies, the League had steadily developed into branches of international and economic development. The great depression was a time of consolidation of the significance of the League, whose membership comprised all but eight of the self-governing countries in the world[294] in 'a new system of international relationships and its utility as a necessary organization for the transaction of much of the world's international business [was] generally acknowledged.'[295] The Spanish new turn coincided with a conjuncture in which Spain presided over the Council of the League and Japan invaded Manchuria. Madariaga gained the nickname of the 'Don Quixote of Manchuria' with his championing of a firm defence of the Covenant and his push for a resolution requesting the withdrawal of the Japanese troops and arguing that the future of the League was at stake. Eventually, the League did not impose sanctions and the enunciation of the Stimson doctrine did little to deter the creation of the puppet state of Manchukuo or the Japanese withdrawal from the League, but this did not detract from Madariaga's reputation. He had published utopian works, such as Disarmament in 1929, which John Simon, the chief British delegate to the Council of the League, called 'half ironically, half seriously, the conscience of the League of Nations,'[296] and gained further credibility in the light of Spain's attempt at leadership at the beginning of 1932 following article 8 of the Covenant, and earlier failed attempts to reach agreement in this department. A practical example of this policy was Spain's leadership as part of the 'Straight Eight' of minor European powers sharing democratic parliamentarism and peaceful societism (Belgium, Czechoslovakia, Denmark, Spain, The Netherlands, Norway, Sweden and Switzerland) in the Conference on the Reduction and Limitation of Armaments between 1932 and 1934. Spain, as a medium power, 'was neither ready to defend itself from an external attack or

293 Neila, 'La política exterior de la españa republicana' 2004, 58.

294 Afghanistan, Brazil, Costa Rica, Ecuador, Mexico, Russia, Turkey and the Unite d States.

295 The League of Nations—Ten Years. (1930).

296 René Wadlow, 'Salvador De Madariaga: Conscience of the League of Nations', *The Federalist Debate* 1 '(2009), 38–40.

possessed the economic capacity to invest in a powerful army.'[297] Its policy was oriented to pushing for a reduction in armaments that would reduce the risk of a war by proposing to suppress offensive weaponry, submit national armament stockpiling to an international legal regime and oblige publicizing of national arsenals and of the establishments where arms were manufactured.[298]

In Spain, the arrival of the Second Republic also engendered a reform of the law curriculum established during the dictatorship of Primo de Rivera.[299] The dictatorship of Primo de Rivera in 1923 had seen a strengthening of educational efforts to address a reform of universities and Spanish illiteracy, which remained a major problem. The facts were telling enough. By 1920, 52.35% of the Spanish population still could not read and write. Meanwhile, the total number of university students barely reached 25,000 out of a population of 23 million in the 1920s, and the budget for public instruction remained among the lowest in Europe.[300]

In 1919, a comprehensive university reform project put forward by the Minister of Public Instruction, Cesar Silio, had attempted to enhance the autonomy of the universities from state interference by setting the three goals of 'overcoming the bureaucratization of universities, improving the professional skills of the graduates and promoting scientific research.' Silio's ambitious reform proved too much of a stress test for the civil-servant-oriented and state-dependent Spanish universities and it proved short-lived. However, the road towards university autonomy that it proposed was followed in a more gradual scaled-back basis under the dictatorship of Miguel Primo de Rivera. The period of 'authoritarian modernization' that made education a 'priority of the state' proved itself to be particularly fruitful. A great public works policy with the construction of thousands of schools and a doubling of the budget for public instruction resulted in a doubling of the number of students who followed secondary education and a decrease in the illiteracy rate to 33% by 1930. Universities also benefited from major investment, which along with the spur given to secondary education led to an increase of 20% in matriculations after 1925, with the number of students in the twelve Spanish universities having increased to almost 60,000 by 1929–30. The number of law students more

297 Pedro Alguacil Cuenca 'España: de la sociedad de naciones a naciones unidas' Anales de derecho Universidad de Murcia. 24. (2006), 303–318, 309.

298 Id.

299 Decreto de 13 de mayo de 1931, por el que quedaban derogados los planes vigentes de segunda enseñanza y de enseñanza universitaria.

300 Eduardo Callejo de la Cuesta 'El plan de estudios de derecho en la universidad central (1923–1931)' *Cuadernos Del Instituto Antonio De Nebrija* 8 (2005) 281–358.

than doubled, from around 6,200 in 1922–23 (a third of them in the faculty of law at the Central University of Madrid) to almost 13,000 matriculated by 1929–1930. The reform gravitated around three axes that targeted the legal personality of universities to transform them into corporations of public interest and foster their economic autonomy by providing them with the control and management of 'colegios mayores' (university residence halls). There was also a reform of study plans which affected the legal curriculum. International law, for instance, became conceptualized as a 'practical subject,' which involved its teaching being complemented with practical cases, with a higher tuition fee and a larger salary for its professors.[301]

After the arrival of the Second Republic, the faculty of Law of the Central University of Madrid requested a division of the chair of international law into one of Public International Law and one of Private International law. It justified this division in view of 'the current development known by international legal studies, its considerable theoretical and practical potential that is evinced in so many institutions of the international society and other varied manifestations of the legislative and diplomatic activity of the various states'.[302] Furthermore, the proposal stressed the 'instrumental and technical complexity of its large respective programmes, and also the wide possibilities for research.'[303] The different scope and nature of the two disciplines was also highlighted by comparing the qualities of the 'juridical education, of rigorous analysis and precision' required for the private international law scholar and the fact that the public international law scholar, 'without prejudice to his qualities as a jurist, built his mains constructions on norms of high international politics which were pre-eminently influenced by economic and social factors that very often escape, at least in the international dimension, the specific functions of jurisprudence.'[304]

On the academic plane, the previous interest of Spanish scholars in the League of Nations and the international community continued to develop during the early 1930s. It attracted both Catholic universalist inquiries, such as Jose Maria Semprun's 'Sociedad Universal entre los hombres' (Universal Society Among Men), published in 1934 by the Catholic Union of International Studies, and socialist-inspired approaches, such as 'La comunidad internacional

301 Id.

302 José María Puyol Montero, 'El plan republicano en la facultad de Derecho de Madrid (1931–1934)', Cuadernos del Instituto Antonio de Nebrija 7 (2004) 197–234. 209–210. quoting 'Actas de la Junta de Facultad del 3 de noviembre de 1931, folios 268 s'.

303 Id.

304 Id.

y la sociedad de Naciones' (The International Community and the League of Nations), published by Fernando de los Rios[305] in 1935. As we have seen before, several Spanish legal scholars delivered courses at The Hague Academy during the mid-1920s and early 1930s. To them, we should add the courses taught on Spanish classics by Barcia Trelles, and by the last author be invited to teach at The Hague Academy before the outbreak of the Civil War.

Ramón Orue y Arregui (1894–1953) was a chair-holder in international law at the University of La Laguna (1923) and the University of Valencia (1926) and author of several works on the League of Nations[306] and textbooks on both private international law and public international law.[307] Very active in the Spanish internationalist associational movement of the late 1920s and early 1930s during which he produced a study on international law in the Spanish Constitution of 1931[308] he taught a course at The Hague Academy on 'Regionalism in the International Organization' in 1935. In his course, which was dedicated to Alejandro Alvarez, Orue provided a survey of the numerous doctrinal reflections penned by international law scholars on the subject of universalism and particularism in international law. This had been one of the central topics in the works of interwar doctrine and it reflected political and civil-society initiatives from the 1922 Grenoble session of the Institut de Droit international to the 'Union juridique internationale.' This latter session in 1926 occupied itself in studying the opportunity for a reform of the Covenant of the League of Nations on a continental or regional basis, together with other expert and civil society associations[309] such as the International Federation of League of Nations Societies in 1927.[310] Orue readily admitted 'the existence of particular

305 Fernando De los Rios (1879–1949) was the nephew of the founder of the Institution Libre de Enseñanza, Giner de los Rios. He was professor of constitutional law, and a prominent socialist leader who served as Minister of Justice, Minister of Education and Minister of Foreign Affairs during the Second Republic, and later during the Spanish Civil War as the ambassador to the United States.

306 See e.g. Jose Ramón Orue y Arregui *Sociedad de Naciones* (Madrid: ed. góngora, 1923).

307 Jose Ramón Orue y Arregui, *Derecho internacional privado* (Madrid: Editorial reus, 1ª ed 1928, 2ª ed. 1932, 3ª ed. corregida y aumentada, 1952) Jose Ramón Orue y Arregui, Manual de derecho internacional público, (Madrid: Editorial Reus, 1934).

308 Jose Ramón Orue y Arregui 'Preceptos internacionales en la constitución de la República española' (Madrid: Editorial Reus, 1932).

309 Jose Ramón Orue y Arregui, *Regionalism in the International Organization* Collected Courses of the Hague Academy of International Law 53 (1935), 1–95.

310 See e.g. Anne-Isabelle Richard 'Competition and complementarity: civil society networks and the question of decentralizing the League of Nations'. Journal of Global History 7 (2012), 233–256.

rules of international law'[311] which seemed to 'obviously imply a fractioning of the magna comunitas in as many particular communities as there are groups ruled by special rules not included in the general system.'[312] However, this fact did not challenge the 'co-existence between general law and particular law,' nor the process of gradual upgrading of particular rules into universal postulates insofar as 'a precise line of demarcation between the two' is drawn before attempting any 'durable work of codification.'[313] Orue transposed the problem of 'universalism or particularism' to the domain of the 'international organization' and, in particular, to the 'quasi-universality' of the League of Nations. The League, which despite its aspirations to universality was itself the matrix of the most notable 'particular system'[314] of the interwar period was, according to Orue, evolving towards a 'truly reduced internationalism' under the impact of fragmentation and 'the decentralizing movement, the new continentalist, and regionalist ideas.'[315] Against this background, Orue's efforts were aimed at demonstrating that the 'League of Nations and regionalism are not incompatible,'[316] but that regionalism could complement the League's universalism. Drawing on the distinction put forward by G. Scelle and other authors, he argued that the two general forms of 'decentralization' were compatible with both the unity of the League and that of international law.[317] The first of these was of political and geographical nature, in conformity with the criteria of regionalism, which itself was 'founded on a phenomenon of particular solidarity'[318] transcending an exclusively geographical conception, and the second was technical or services-based decentralization.[319]

On the internationalist associational plane, after the conservative social and cultural turn of the Vatican's Quadragesimo Anno (1931), the founding of the Association Francisco de Vitoria was followed by other internationalist associational initiatives in Spain during the Second Spanish Republic. Some members of the Association Francisco de Vitoria founded the Spanish Group of the Catholic Union of International Studies in 1933–1934. Its statutes defined it as 'an association of scientific character devoted to the study of international

311 Orue y Arregui, 'Regionalism in the International Organization' (1935), 12.
312 Id. 13
313 Id. 88
314 Id. 11
315 Id. 15
316 Id. 16
317 Id., 22
318 Id., 90
319 Id., 19

questions and informed by the doctrinal principles of Catholicism.'[320] Presided over by Pedro Sangro y Ros de Olano, among its mainly academic membership, especially of legal scholars, was Antonio de Luna (1901–1967) who was, years later, to become one of the most influential international lawyers of the Franco's regime. De Luna was a clear exponent of the interwar professional generation of Spanish international law scholars, benefiting from studies abroad in Freiburg, Paris and Oxford, he had obtained a doctorate from Bologna with a prize for the best doctoral thesis in 1925. He had been chair-holder of public international law at the Central University of Madrid since 1932, after having held chairs in Philosophy of Law at the universities of La Laguna, Salamanca, and Granada in the late twenties. He especially contributed through his teachings to the reception of the theoretical philosophical debates on the foundation of international law and was credited by A. Truyol y Serra with providing the 'Spanish doctrine of public international law with something as essential to any discipline as an updated general theory'.[321] De Luna carved out his intellectual reputation in an interwar period that he himself defined as the 'soteriological period' of international law, one of faith in 'normativism' and in the social engineering function of enlightened laws to modify the reality of international relations. He held several expert posts during the Second Republic at the Advising Legal Commission (1931–1934) and at the board of cultural relations of the Ministry of Foreign Affairs. De Luna also became the Director of the Institute of International and Economic Studies, founded in 1934. An initiative of the National Foundation for Scientific Research, this institution was to be coordinated by the Ministry of Foreign Affairs. In particular, the Instituto intended, as Neila highlights, to serve as a forum gathering Spanish and foreign researchers 'to study international matters related to Spanish interests and to prepare for Spanish participation in international conferences'[322] as well as a point of contact with Latin-American researchers 'in order to favour the search for convergent interests in the service of the development of the basis for future common action,'[323] in accordance with the transatlantic cultural community propitiated by Hispanidad.

Moreover, de Luna actively participated in the internationalist associational spirit that was in vogue in Spain in the early 1930s. Among others, he was the secretary of the Federation of Spanish Associations of International Studies,

---

320 Quoted Neila Hernández, 'La política exterior de la España republicana' 2004, 59.

321 See Antonio Truyol y Serra, 'Don Antonio de Luna García (1901–1967)' in *Estudios de Derecho Internacional Homenaje a D. Antonio de Luna* (1968).

322 Id.

323 Id.

created in 1933 and presided over by Judge Altamira in Geneva. The Federation reunited the Instituto de Derecho Comparado hispano-portugués-americano, the Asociación Española de Derecho Internacional y Legislacion Comparada,[324] (which was founded in 1928 and presided over by the Marquis de Olivart and, after his death, by the Marquis de Lema), and the Seminario de Estudios Internacionales, founded by Orue Arregui at the University of Valencia. Among the goals of the Federation supported by Luis Castillejos, the director of JAE (Board of Extension of Studies), was the training of post-graduate student specialists in the study of international relations[325] through a series of general and specialized courses, seminars and conferences on private and public international law, international history, politics and economics.[326]

In April 1933, following in the wake of the internationalist associationalist movement in Spain, the University of Salamanca authorized the creation of the 'Instituto Francisco de Vitoria', which emerged in the wake of the Association Francisco de Vitoria. Around this project to recover classical Spanish thought, there appeared as main associated or honorary members of the association, or speakers at their conferences, the names of all the internationalists of this generation 'who were more influenced by the ideas of cultural Catholicism,'[327] and who, a few years later, were to become some of the most pre-eminent international lawyers of Franquismo. Several of its members would also join the Sociedad de Estudios Internacionales y Coloniales (Society of International and Colonial Studies) founded in 1934. Among these was its founder, José Yanguas Messía, who had continued the Francophile orientation of his formative years in the 1930s during his exile after the proclamation of the Second Republic, with De La Pradelle, Noboyet and Le Fur, until he was restored to his chair in 1933–1934. The new society, also Catholic, 'but more conservative and less internationalist in orientation,'[328] was presided over by Gonzalo de Reparaz, with José Cordero Torres as its secretary, and consisted of international law scholars such as Fernando María Castiella, a chair-holder of international law at the university of La Laguna since 1935, who would become, as we shall later see, the longest-serving Minister of Foreign Affairs of General Franco. The society established that its goals were to 'pay preferential attention to questions of practical

324 Manuel Raventós Noguer, 'La Asociación Española de Derecho Internacional y Legislación Comparada', *Revista general de legislación y jurisprudencia* 77 (1928), 315–332.

325 Neila, 'La política exterior de la españa republicana', 2004.

326 Id.

327 Forcada Barona, 'La influencia de la religión católica en la doctrina internacionalista' 2012,

328 Neila, 'La política exterior de la españa republicana', 2004.

interest, defending with its own criteria the establishment of a fair international and colonial order, and international cooperation among Hispanic countries.' Echoing a terminology, already present in the foundational points of the Spanish Falange, which would become very familiar during the Franco era, among its goals was also 'the fulfilment of the universal mission of Spain.'[329]

On the academic plane, work on the School of Salamanca continued to thrive during the Second Spanish Republic. Barcia Trelles delivered his third course at The Hague Academy in 1933, on this occasion on 'Francisco Suarez (Les théologiens espagnols du XVIe siècle et l'Ecole moderne de droit international).' In this course, Barcia Trelles examined the contemporaneity of the thought of Francisco Suarez (1548–1617), thanks to whom, according to Pereña, 'one can find the scientific conquests of a century organically integrated, and through them, the (Spanish) School was incorporated into the European process of thought.'[330] In order to revisit the work of the author of a series of twenty books published in Coimbra, 'Tractatus de legibus ac Deo legislatore' (1612), and whose contemporaries called Papa Metaphysicorum et Anchora Papistaruni, Barcia needed to know, first, whether one could positively affirm the existence of a Spanish 'school' of internationalists by reference to the works of the Spanish legal theologians of the 16th century. These, according to Barcia, approached international questions from a perspective that presupposed the 'acceptance, more or less elaborated, of an international community.'[331] Barcia distinguished the Spanish 'internationalists' from the Spanish 'juristes-legistes' of the 16th century, which he qualifies as the 'emotional spokespersons of an imperial conception',[332] noting the impossibility 'of discovering in their theories the minimal sign that implies that it was their intention to transform themselves into agents of any political power'.[333] Barcia chose to use the title 'Spanish internationalists of the 16th century'[334] instead of the 'Spanish school'[335] because of a series of divergences among its authors

329 El programa de Falange Española de las J. O. N. S ABC diario ilustrado Madrid, número 9.834 (1934), 32–34 accesible at http://www.filosofia.org/hem/dep/abc/9341130.htm

330 Luciano Pereña, 'La tesis de la paz dinámica', in Luciano Pereña (ed.) Francisco de Vitoria, Relectio de iure belli o paz dinámica. Escuela española de la paz. Primera generación (1526–1560) Corpus Hispanorum de Pace Vol. VI (Madrid: Consejo Superior de Investigaciones Cientificas 1981), 67.

331 Barcia Trelles, *Francisco Suarez* (*Les théologiens espagnols du XVIe siècle*) 1933, 391.

332 Id., 391.

333 Id., 392.

334 Id., 396

335 Id., 396.

that make it impossible to positively affirm the existence of the latter despite their points in common. These points in common were that they all held that 'international relations must be ruled by moral laws and principles drawn from natural law', that 'these relations are not established at random, but they derive from exigencies of human nature' and that 'an international community is formed by a union of political societies' that 'are reciprocally dependent on each other,'[336]

Second, Barcia went on to examine the extent to which it was possible to draw a comparison between these Spanish 'internationalists' and the modern orientations of international law encompassed in what he termed 'The modern school of international law.'[337] This for Barcia was a reflection of the 'existence of a common anxiety,'[338] which he identifies in the work of his contemporaries as 'the effort to get rid of the criterion of sovereignty, the survival of which in its classic conception is considered incompatible with any attempt at coordination of international life.'[339] The 'revival of the theories of natural law, both in a constructive sense—although 'distinct from the birth of natural law in the sense that the new tendency does not consider natural law as immutable', but sees it as a 'natural law of variable nature'[340]—, and as a reaction to the abuse of the positivist-historical method,'[341] was for him an effort by the theorists of international law to catch up with 'the modern tendencies of international life.'[342] The inspiration for the establishment of the League of Nations itself, which he notes is often identified in 'the famous passage that Suarez left us in Chapter XIX of his De Legibus which is quoted every time that we speak of the international community and of its possible and desirable organization,'[343] is, nonetheless, for Barcia but the peak of Suarez's contribution. In order to prove this, he set Suarez's opus against the background of the evolution of ius gentium from the Roman tradition,[344] the Catholic thinkers of the Middle Ages,[345] including St. Isidoro de Sevilla and the analysis of the legal internationalists' conception of the ius gentium of Vitoria in Domingo de Soto's De justitiae et

336 Id., 395.
337 Id., 390–414.
338 Id., 397.
339 Id., 397.
340 Id., 399.
341 Id., 399.
342 Id., 400.
343 Id., 421.
344 Id., 424–426.
345 Id., 426–437.

jure (1553),[346] and Vazquez de Menchaca's Controversiarum Ilustrium.[347] He then exegetically examined Suarez's theoretical contributions to the determination of the scope and limits of ius inter gentes[348] between ius civilis and ius naturalis and also his analysis of the relationship between law and war.[349]

The fame of the contributions by Barcia Trelles, Alfred Verdross and, later, Carl Schmitt to the revival of Francisco de Vitoria and the so-called 'Spanish School of international law' pales, however, in comparison with the lasting popularity that championing Vitoria as the father of international law gave James Brown Scott.[350] As we have seen, J. Brown Scott, who from 1929 to 1939 served as President of the American Society of International Law, had supported the Association Francisco de Vitoria and its members, spoken at conferences and published on Francisco de Vitoria since 1926. He continued to actively support the cause of the Spanish legal theologians, including by fostering the publications of the Association internationale Vitoria-Suarez, which was created in 1932 by the Institut de Droit International to celebrate the 400th Anniversary of De Indis, through the Carnegie endowment in the 1930s.[351] In 1934, James Brown Scott published his own treatise in 'The Classics of international law': The Spanish Origins of International Law. Francisco de Vitoria and his Law of Nations.[352] In this book, which appeared under the aegis of the Division of International Law of the Carnegie Endowment for International Peace, Scott explicitly defends the thesis that 'there was a Spanish school of international law in the sixteenth century, within forty years of the discovery of America; that the founder of this school was Francisco de Vitoria, Prima Professor of Theology at the University of Salamanca; and that his two Relectiones, De Indis Noviter Inventis and De Jure Belli, set forth his law of nations, which was to become the international law not merely of Christendom

---

346 Id., 433–437.

347 Id., 437–440.

348 Id., 441–471.

349 Id., 473–531.

350 Still nowadays, it is common to note that 'Vitoria's position as the pionneer of international law is based on James Brown Scott's work' See e.g. Pekka Niemela, 'A Cosmopolitan World Order? Perspectives on Francisco de Vitoria and the United Nations' Max Planck Yearbook of United Nations Law 12 (2008) 301–334, 310.

351 Yves de La Brière, Vitoria et Suarez—Contribution des Théologiens au Droit International Moderne (Association internationale Vitoria-Suarez / Carnegie Endowment for International Peace; preface de James Brown Scott) (Paris: Pédone, 1939).

352 James Brown Scott. *The Spanish Origins of International Law. Francisco de Vitoria and his Law of Nations* (New York: Oxford University Press, 1934).

but of the world at large.'[353] The book first introduces an overview of what J. Brown Scott terms the era of discoveries and its effects on the tradition of humanist thinking. This is followed by an examination of the historical origins of the Spanish school. It then moves on to the leading events in the life of the Prima Professor of Theology at the University of Salamanca and provides a commentary on his relectiones in several chapters, in particular, on 'De Indis Noviter Inventis' (On the Recently Discovered Indians). There is also an analysis of Vitoria's conception of natural law and a study of the law of war in the scholastic tradition of St. Augustine and St. Thomas de Aquinas and a commentary on Vitoria's 'De Juri Belli'. This is complemented by a study of other relectiones by Vitoria: On Matrimony, On the Civil Power and On the Use of Reason. The book also contains an appendix of six relectiones translated into English.[354]

Brown Scott examines Vitoria's thought as a liberal in the tradition of the Dominican order, claiming that 'he was an internationalist by inheritance. And because he was both, his international law is a liberal law of nations.'[355] Brown Scott lists Vitoria's contributions to international law by retracing the origins of some of the contemporary institutions and fundamental principles of international law back to his teachings including the equality of states which he considers was 'the cornerstone of Vitoria's system.'[356] Brown Scott shows a remarkable faith in Vitoria's future legacy: 'Vitoria's law of nations and the Vitorian principles […] for four hundred years have pointed the path to an international law, still of the future, in which law and morality shall be one and inseparable, in which States are created by and for human beings, and every principle of international law and of international conduct is to be tested by the good of the international community and not by the selfish standards of its more powerful and erring members.'[357]

The Spanish Origins of International Law was conceived as the first of a series of three books culminating in H. Grotius. This, according to Brown Scott, should be relocated from the position often credited to him of 'father of the law of nations' to that of 'populariser in the best sense of the word,' and therefore 'a member of the Vitorian or, as it is more usually termed, the Spanish school, in that he derived his doctrine on the law of nature and of

---

353 Id. 9a, preface.

354 A. De Indis Noviter Inventis; B. De Jure Belli; C. De Potestate Civile; D. De Potestate Ecclesiae; E. De Jure Gentium et Natural; y F. De Bello.

355 Brown Scott. *The Spanish Origins of International Law* 1934, 280.

356 Id., 281.

357 11a preface.

nations, which formed the basis of his treatise On the Law of War and Peace of 1625, from members of the Spanish school'.[358] Rossi has interpreted Brown Scott's attempt to place 'international law in its true historical light' as one inspired by the aim 'to re-establish the moral basis of the modern law of nations, which he felt had been lost.'[359] But, overall, Brown Scott's reading of Vitoria is that of a liberal internationalist in the interwar period, seeing, as Quincy Wright notes, 'the germs of most of the system of international law'[360] in the conception of the system later followed by Grotius and Wolf which 'rests international law upon the assumption of a community of nations established by natural law.'[361] In 1934, further developing this line of thought, Brown Scott also published 'The Catholic Conception of International Law' (1934), which bore a manifesto-like subtitle: 'Francisco de Vitoria, Founder of the Modern Law of Nations, Francisco Suarez, Founder of the Modern Philosophy of Law in General and in Particular of the Law of Nations.'[362] Here, after introducing Vitoria's contribution—as expounder—to the intellectual foundations of international law in his relectiones, he summarizes the treatment by Francisco Suarez—as philosopher—of international law. He reviews Suarez's philosophy of natural law, the adaptability of custom and the role of sanctions, the state and his treatment of tyrannicide, 'as part and parcel of a general system of jurisprudence which in turn was conceived as a component of an all-embracing science of theology'.[363] This leads him to excursuses on the works of numerous other authors such as De rege et regis institutione, published by the Jesuit Mariana in 1599, and eventually on the question of war.

Brown Scott's ultimate objective was to demonstrate that the works of the Spanish authors contain 'the fundamental concepts of the modern law of nations—a law resting upon a Latin foundation and formulated in a Catholic atmosphere by Spanish theologians and publicists.' Brown Scott attempted, otherwise, to show that Suarez and Vitoria 'from a different approach [...]

---

358 10a, preface.

359 Rossi, *Broken Chain of Being* 1998, 4.

360 James Brown Scott, 'Francisco Suarez his Philosophy of Law and of Sanctions', Georgetown Law Journal 22(1933–1934), 405, 407.

361 Quincy Wright, Review of 'The Spanish Origins of International Law -Francisco De Vitoria and His Law of Nations', *American Journal of Sociology* 41 (1936), 539–540.

362 James Brown Scott, *The Catholic Conception Of International Law. Francisco De Vitoria, Founder Of The Modern Law Of Nations, Francisco Suarez, Founder of The Modern Philosophy Of Law In General and in Particular of the Law of Nations: A Critical Examination and a Justified Appreciation* (Washington, D.C.: Georgetown University Press, 1934).

363 John Dickinson, 'Review of Brown Scott's The Catholic Conception of International Law', Georgetown Law Journal 24 (1935–1936), 215–218, 216.

reached a common goal—the establishment of a single and universal standard of right and wrong in the relations between individuals within a state, in the relations of states with one another and in the relations of the international community composed of these individuals and of these states.'[364] In Brown Scott's opinion this led to the inevitable conclusion that Vitoria and Suarez 'justified once for all, in classical terms, the necessary and effective existence of the legal and moral international community.'[365]

On the political plane, the publication of Brown Scott's book 'The Catholic Conception of International law' coincided with a traditionalist re-orientation of Spanish foreign policy, following the victory of a coalition of conservative parties in the general election held in Spain in 1934. This reorientation gained ground in parallel to a series of developments which marked a gradual crumbling of the system of collective security and triggered a turn to neutrality among the small and medium powers. The League's policies would find a formidable foe in Hitler's rearmament policies. Japan's abandonment of the League in 1933 was accompanied by the withdrawal of Nazi Germany from the Disarmament Conference and the League of Nations in October 1933 and its parallel introduction of an intense programme of rearmament. This was a long-incubated reaction against article 231 of the Versailles Treaty, or what Germans had learnt to call the 'diktat of Versailles', and the accompanying sanctions, controls and demilitarization measures. The applications of the compensation agreements in the treaty of Versailles developed by the Dawes Plan (1924) and the Young Plan (1929–1930)[366] slowed down Germany's ability to reconstruct (and re-arm).

While in Germany the Hitlerian speeches added fuel to the fire of the works of racial doctrinaires, the notions of Gemeinschaft (community) or Gesellschaft (association), and the competition between Carl Schmitt's theory of Grossraum (a theory of great space with an attached prohibition on intervention by foreign powers) and the concept of Lebensraum[367] (vital space), started to gain ground as prototypical contributions to international law in the vision of the volklich-nationale.[368] Indeed, between Hitler being elected into power

364 Brown Scott, 'Francisco Suarez. His Philosophy' 1933–1934, 410.

365 Id. 420.

366 P Chandler Anderson, 'Final Liquidation of German War Reparations', *American Journal of International Law* 25 (1931), 97–101.

367 Detlev F. Vagts, International Law in the Third Reicht, 94 *American Journal of International Law* (1990) 661.

368 Virginia I. Gott, 'The National Socialist Theory of International Law' *American Journal Of International Law* 32 (1938), 704–718. See also Neff, *Justice Among Nations*, 2014, 387.

in 1933 and the beginning of the Blitzkrieg against Poland in September 1939, German international law auspicated a conceptual approach to the principle of equal sovereignty. This stress on formal equality and on the inalienability of a minimum of rights technically associated with it emphasised the fundamental rights of states was used against the 'normativist abstraction' of the 'reconstructive doctrine' with its constitutionalizing pretensions from the international legal order. The defence of the principle of the sovereign equality of states and its corollary of non-intervention in domestic affairs were carried through a biological-nationalist insertion in natural law doctrines. This was justified by the equivalence between the natural law of the community (Gemeinschaft) and a right to existence. This theoretical basis allowed the Nazi doctrine to maintain an ius-naturalist conception of international law based on the notion of Gessellschaft (association). This perspective became enshrined in 'three fundamental natural rights [...]: the right to self-preservation (from which the right to self-defence emerges) the right to equality and the right to sovereignty'[369] and in the corresponding exigency to re-adjust positive international law to this natural law of the international association of states.[370]

The Spanish general election of 1934 opened a two-year period in which the political spectrum in Spain swung to the right. Marked by much ministerial stability—six ministers of Foreign affairs in the biennium—this period saw a policy of rectification and distancing from the traditional alliances with Great Britain and France in the light of the risks inherent in such proximity in the case of a conflict with the German-Italian revisionist front. Spain stressed its neutrality in the 'group of six' or 'group of Neutrals'[371] after the split of the so-called 'Straight Eight' (Czechoslovakia and Belgium remained in the French orbit) that unsuccessfully tried to salvage the disarmament conference in 1934 through mediation, while certain sectors on the right began to display signs of a clear Germanophile orientation. Despite Spain voting in favour of sanctions against Italy under diplomatic pressure from Great Britain, the international climate brought about by the eruption of the Abyssinian crisis in 1935 led Spanish foreign policy to lean even further towards neutrality.

---

369 Id., 708

370 Meanwhile, semi-peripheral states like Turkey and China were attempting to free themselves from certain extra-territorial rights in what was to mark the sunset of the 'classical standard of civilization.' The Pan-American debates were also being crowned by the Montevideo Convention on the Rights and Duties of States, article 1 of which was to become the 'best known formulation of the basic criteria for statehood', James Crawford, *The Creation of States In International Law* (Oxford: Oxford University Press 1979), 36.

371 Neila, 'La política exterior de la España republicana' 2004, 64.

Although the USSR joining the League in 1934 had led to hopes after the withdrawal of Japan and Germany, the Abyssinian Crisis in 1935–36 and the British and French military passivity in March 1936 in the face of Hitler's remilitarization of the Rhineland in breach of the Versailles Treaty were subsequent milestones in the side-lining of the League and the slow crumbling of the interwar system despite some successes such as the imposition of feeble sanctions against Italy. The 'unfulfilled promise of the League' in the area of collective security, along with the policy of appeasement adopted by the British and French entente aimed at satisfying Italo-German pretensions 'without endangering vital British interests'[372] triggered, moreover, a 'tendency for states' such as Belgium and Switzerland and other small democracies 'that had previously been neutral to reassert that status.'[373] This turn to neutrality took place against the background of the rise of what K. Loewenstein in 1937 termed a 'Fascist International in the making', understood as 'a closer transnational alignment or bloc of fascist nations.' This Fascist International was 'transcending national borders and cutting across historical diversities of traditionally disjointed nationalisms', supported a 'pattern of a specific technique of fascist penetration and conquest' throughout the European continent.[374]

After the election in February 1936 of the 'Popular Front' government in Spain, the Spanish policy of renewed isolationism, neutrality and cautious appeasement of the revisionist and hegemonic policies of counter-revolutionary and totalitarian regimes became more inclusive within the framework of the League. The strict Spanish neutrality became more of a 'benevolent neutrality' towards the British and French positions. However, this late realignment, as we shall see in Chapter Four, could not prevent the Second Spanish Republic from being the first European victim of the 'turn to neutrality'[375] that accompanied the crumbling of the League of Nations, and marked the death knell of the system of international relations born with the Peace of Versailles.

372 Moradiellos 'The Allies and the Spanish Civil War' 1999, 100.

373 Stephen Neff, *Justice Among Nations* 2014, 390.

374 Karl Loewenstein, 'Militant Democracy and Fundamental Rights I', 31 The American Political Science Review 3 (1937), 417–432, 419.

375 Id., 92.

CHAPTER 4

# The Spanish Civil War—Inter Armas Pugnant Leges

## Non-Intervention in the 'Last Great Cause'

On July 18th 1936, a day that will be celebrated for four decades in Spain as the day of the 'glorious national uprising', Francisco Franco, the youngest European general of his day, who had already distinguished himself as a bold and cold-blooded officer in the Spanish colonial campaigns in North Africa,[1] joined a military uprising against the Second Spanish Republic. On 15th August 1936, less than a month after Franco launched his anti-Republican 'national crusade in defence of the Western Christian civilization and against Communist barbarism', Britain and France instituted with an exchange of notes an international agreement of non-intervention in Spain.[2] on 21st July 1936, the French Front Populaire government, led by Leon Blum, had responded favourably to the Spanish Republic's requests for importation of war material, but it provisionally halted exports to Spain on 27th July.[3] The non-intervention agreement of 15th August 1936 enshrined a French neutralist readjustment under the influence of both domestic political factors and British diplomatic pressure.[4] It was a hard blow for the besieged Spanish Republic. Despite the logistical aid the insurgents had received from Hitler's Germany on 26th July[5]

1 On General Francisco Franco, see e.g. Paul Preston, *Franco. A Bibliography* (London: Harper Press 1995).

2 See e.g. Fernando Schwartz, *La internacionalización de la guerra civil española*, (Barcelona: Ariel 1971).

3 The literature on the French 'change of mind' is very extensive e.g. M. D. Gallagher, 'Leon Blum and the Spanish Civil War', Journal of Contemporary History, 6 (1971), 56–64.

4 See W.N. Medlicott and D. Dakin (Eds) *Documents on British Foreign Policy, 1919–1939 Second Series Volume XVII, Western Pact Negotiations: Outbreak of Spanish Civil War June 1936—January 1937* (London: Her Majesty's Stationery Office, 1979).

5 For a account see e.g. M. Jean-François Berdah, 'L'Allemagne et le Royaume-Uni face à la question espagnole: reconnaissance de facto ou reconnaisance de jure? (1936–1939)' *Mélanges de la Casa de Velázquez* 29 (1993) 203–241. See also extended historical archival references in Enrique Moradiellos, 'El mundo ante el avispero español: intervencion y no intervencion extranjera en la Guerra Civil', in Santos Julia (ed) *Republica y Guerra en España (1931–1939)*, (Madrid: Espasa Calpe 2006), 305–310.

 | DOI 10.1163/9789004343238_006

and Mussolini's Italy[6] soon afterward, Franco's insurrection had fallen short of meeting its military objectives.

The Franco-British exchange of notes that sealed the fate of the Spanish Civil War made 'both countries' declarations contingent upon the adherence of the other government plus the governments of Germany, Italy, the Soviet Union and Portugal'.[7] Twenty-seven other governments soon jumped on the Anglo-French bandwagon and made similar declarations to those contained in the non-intervention agreement's preamble, whereby the original parties declared their resolution to 'abstain rigorously from all interference ('de toute ingérence') direct or indirect in the internal affairs of Spain.[8] The parties also subscribed to the agreement's 'three declarations of policy', aiming at the immediate implementation of a collective embargo on the sale of weapons to Spain. This extended to contracts that were already in course of execution with the Republican government.

The Spanish Civil War, then in its early stages, was to become a 'tertium genus'[9] in the history of the relationship between international law and civil strife on account of the 'anomalous'[10] collective non-intervention pact led by the United Kingdom. Despite the generalized use of the term 'international agreement' to describe it, the fact remains, however, that 'no agreement was legally binding on all' the state parties.[11] Several state parties did not sign the preamble of the non-intervention pact and some of them appended interpretations, qualifications, or reservations to its provisions. With the non-intervention agreement, thus, looking as 'merely a concert of policy' whose 'fulfilment depended entirely

6 On the decisive role played by the early intervention of Germany, see e.g. Neila, *España y el Mediterraneo en el siglo XX*, 2011, 220.

7 Norman P. Padeldorf, 'The International Non-Intervention Agreement and the Spanish Civil War', American Journal of International Law 31 (1937), 578–603, 580.

8 *International Committee for the Application of the Agreement regarding Non-Intervention in Spain, The Legislative and Other Measures Taken by the Participating Governments to Give Effect to the Agreement Regarding Non-intervention in Spain, and by the Swiss Government to Prohibit the Export of Arms and War Material from Switzerland to Spain*, HM Stationery Office, London (1936).

9 Antonio Cassesse, 'The Spanish Civil War and the Development of Customary Law Concerning Internal Armed Conflicts', in Antonio Cassese (ed.) *Current Problems of International Law. Essays on U.N. Law and on the Law of Armed Conflict.* (Milano: Dott. A. Giuffrè editore 1975).

10 See, among others, e.g. Herbert A. Smith 'Some Problems of the Spanish Civil War', *British Yearbook International Law* 18 (1937), 17–31.

11 Jill Edwards, *The British Government and the Spanish Civil War* (London: MacMillan Press 1979) 41.

upon the initiative of each state',[12] a 'Non-Intervention Committee' composed of diplomatic representatives of the non-intervening powers was, nonetheless, formed under the aegis of the British Foreign Office in London. Between the establishment of the London Committee and the end of the Spanish Civil War on 1st April 1939, '[t]here would be 30 meetings of the plenary committee and 93 of the Chairman's subcommittee, and seven further subcommittees dealt with technical problems as they arose'.[13] The ineffectual character of the non-intervention system, which the London Committee was charged with policing, had been soon obvious to its contemporaries.[14] This impression has largely been corroborated by historical data that leaves no doubt as to the failure of the strategy of British-led international 'localization' of the long drawn-out Spanish Civil War.[15]

It is, indeed, estimated that, over the next three years, more than 150,000 foreign troops, German and—especially—Italian Blackshirt militiamen served in the Rebel-Nationalist Army. Moreover, Germany and Italy supplied Franco's camp with some 10,000 technicians, military officials for training camps and a total of $505 million worth of war materials. Franco's crusade against the 'anti-Spain' also benefited from the logistical and diplomatic support of Salazar's Estado Novo.[16] The Republican Army, on the other hand, comprised 50,000 foreign troops—40,000 of which were in the 'international brigades', which included anti-fascist volunteers from over fifty countries,[17] while an estimated 10,000 volunteers fought directly with the Republican Army. Furthermore, the Soviet Union supplied up to 2000 technicians and $100 million worth of arms and weapons to the Spanish Republic. Comintern's aid to the loyalists—mainly in the form of war materials—has been estimated at $200 million, while other foreign military aid received has been estimated at $50 million.[18]

The non-intervention agreement soon spawned a series of legal debates between those who underwrote its 'international legality' and those who

---

12 Padeldorf, 'The International Non-Intervention Agreement', 1937, 580.

13 Edwards, The British Government and the Spanish Civil War 1979, 45.

14 D. Graham Hutton, 'British Policy Towards Spain', *Foreign Affairs* 15 (1936–1937), 661.

15 See among others e.g. Preston, The Spanish Holocaust 2012.

16 See e.g. Jose C. Jiménez Redondo, 'La política del bloque ibérico: las relaciones hispano-portuguesas (1936–1949)' *Mélanges de la Casa de Velázquez* 29 (1993), 175–201.

17 Hugh Thomas, The Spanish Civil War, (London: Penguin Books, 1977), 980–984.

18 See e.g. Van Wynen Thomas & Thomas, 'Non Intervention and the Spanish Civil War' American Society of International Law Proceedings XXX (1967) 1, 2.

denounced it as a 'legal monstrosity' that fatally impaired the right of the Republican democratically elected government to respond to a military putsch. The secular and democratic Spanish Constitution of 1931[19] which, as we have seen in Chapter Three, was fully aligned with the spirit of pacifism and legal internationalism of the League of Nations,[20] became the first of the many victims of a non-intervention agreement that proved ineffectual in preventing a massively deleterious foreign military intervention in a beleaguered Spain between 1936 and 1939. The demise of the Spanish Constitution of 1931 was followed by several decades of intellectual involution to an imagery of anti-liberal, nationalist[21] and ultra-Catholic references in Spanish political and cultural life and, by extension, as it will be shown in Chapter Five, in Spanish international legal thought. In the aftermath of the Spanish Civil war, Francisco de Vitoria and the School of Salamanca will transcend the realm of erudite circles to become enshrined as a Spanish nationalist identity symbol of the Francoist regime.[22] During the Spanish Civil War, the Association Francisco de Vitoria and the Institute Francisco de Vitoria in Salamanca already instrumentally employed, as we shall also see, the theories of the Spanish Theologians from the School of Salamanca to justify the 'just cause' of General Franco's troops.[23]

19 See e.g. Manley O. Hudson, 'The Spanish Constitution of 1931' 26 American Journal of International Law 3 (1932) 579–582. See also Gamarra, 'Los lenguajes del Derecho internacional en la Constitucion de 1931' (2012) Article 6 of the Spanish Republican Constitution of 1931 stated in the wake of the Kellogg-Briand Pact, Spain's 'renunciation to war as an instrument of national policy', and art. 7 established that 'The Spanish state will obey the universal normal of international law incorporating them into its positive law'.

20 Article 77 of the Spanish Constitution of 1931 went 'so far as to prohibit the President from signing a declaration of war 'except subject to the conditions prescribed in the Covenant of the League of Nations' and after the exhaustion of all peaceful means of procedure', See Wilcox, 'The League of Nations and the Spanish Civil War' 1938, 65.

21 See Agustin José Menendez, 'From Republicanism to Fascist Ideology under the Early Franquismo' in Joerges, Christian and Ghaleigh, Navraj Singh (eds.), *Darker Legacies of Law in Europe: The Shadow of National Socialism and Fascism over Europe and Its Legal Traditions,* (Oxford: Hart Publishers 2003), 337–360.

22 See Ignacio de la Rasilla del Moral, 'The Fascist Mimesis of Spanish International Law and its Vitorian Aftermath, 1939–1953', *The Journal of the History of International Law* 14 (2012), 207–236.

23 A detailed summary of the contents of Chapter 4 can be found in the 'Introduction'.

## Setting the Stage for the Localization of the Spanish Civil War and the League of Nations

Approved on the 12th November 1936, the first control plan of the London Committee established a system to control the entry of weapons and war materials into Spain. This first control plan was extended in mid-January 1937, soon after an Anglo-Italian Gentleman's Agreement by which Britain and Italy vowed to respect each other's rights in the Mediterranean Sea, to cover recruitment in, transit through, and departure from the territory of the signatories of persons of non-Spanish nationality intending to proceed to Spain for the purpose of taking part in the war. This supplementary measure was included at the request of the British government which, under a revived Foreign Enlistment Act of 1870, had made it illegal to recruit or volunteer for the armed forces of either side upon liability 'on conviction to imprisonment up to two years, or to a fine or to both a fine and imprisonment'.[24] A second control plan emerged from the London non-intervention Committee was approved on 8th March and entered into force on 20th April 1937. It provided for control of the land borders and a maritime control with neutral observers posted to Spanish ports and borders and the assignation of patrol zones to the United Kingdom, France, Germany, and Italy. Its application was, nonetheless, to lead to grave maritime incidents and, eventually, to the withdrawal of Italy and Germany from the non-intervention agreement. Despite the Committee being generally seen as 'a mutually consented institutionalized farce'[25] throughout 1937, British diplomacy used its influence to convince both countries to return to it to safeguard its formal maintenance. By then, the control plans had become toothless in terms of both policing and enforcement.[26] New measures, such as the setting up of an observation scheme, and a series of bodies and further measures to manage it, were added to the control plans in late 1937.[27] These measures were included in the 'Nyon Agreement'[28] signed off at a conference of Mediterranean and Black Sea states convened to set up a system of vigilance

---

24 See PRO, FO 371/21319, W906/7/41. Foreign Enlistment Act (1870), Bill (228) II. 61, Bill to Prevent Enlisting or Engagement of H.M. Subjects to Serve in Foreign Service, 1870.

25 Moradiellos Neutralidad Benevola 1990, 90.

26 Padeldorf, 'The International Non-Intervention Agreement' 1937, 587.

27 Id., 591–592.

28 Signatories were the countries of Bulgaria, Egypt, France, Greece, Romania, Turkey, the United Kingdom, the USSR and Yugoslavia. A second Agreement was signed on 17 September 1937 in Geneva. It extended the rules governing submarine warfare to surface vessels, and had the same signatories.

of the commercial shipping routes in the Mediterranean Sea to minimize the effects of the extensive Italian submarine warfare in support of Franco's army.

The massive foreign intervention in the Spanish Civil war was possible despite the parallel application of domestic legal deterrents in 'non-intervening' countries such as Britain. These, according to H. Graham, included the 'devastating efficacy of other initiatives instigated by the British which worked consistently and exclusively against the Republic, for example the effects of the merchant shipping act (carriage of munitions to Spain) passed in December 1936 (which made it illegal for British ships to carry war material from any port, including foreign ports, to any Spanish port—a trade which it was previously lawful for them to engage in), and the repeated blocking of the Republic's sterling export account by the British authorities'.[29] Indeed, in 1937, S. Baldwin's conservative government revived the Foreign Enlistment Act 1870—an example of a domestic legal deterrent addressed at limiting the role of the many British activists who, even to the detriment of other parallel causes, like the one, by then, fought in China against Japanese imperial policies,[30] were convinced that 'for Europe Republicans Spain was both a front and a frontier'[31] against the international rise of authoritarianism and fascism.

However, the re-enactment of the Foreign Enlistment Act proved to be relatively ineffective[32] in deterring circa 2,500 volunteers and their associated medical units from fleeing the British Isles to serve in the International Brigades.[33] The relative ineffectiveness of the Act, which became saddled with problems of legal applicability and enforcement, was related to the anomalous character of the international regime of non-intervention. From a domestic legal perspective, the wording of the 1870 Act required that '(a) Britain be at peace with both sides, and (b) that each contender be a de facto foreign state'—defined as 'any foreign country, colony, province, or part of any

29 Helen Graham, 'Spain and Europe: the View from the Periphery', The Historical Journal 35 (1992), 969–983, 971.

30 See e.g. Tom Buchanan, 'Shanghai-Madrid Axis'? Comparing British Responses to the Conficts in Spain and China, 1936–39, *Contemporary European History* 21 (2012), 533–552.

31 Graham, 'Spain and Europe: The View from the Periphery' 1992, 971.

32 S. P. Mackenzie, 'The Foreign Enlistment Act and the Spanish Civil War, 1936–1939' *Twentieth Century British History* 10 (1999), 52–66.

33 Bibliography is also extensive for the British volunteers, see e.g. James K. Hopkins, *Into the Heart of the Fire: The British in the Spanish Civil War* (Stanford: Standford University Press 1998) and Richard Baxell, *British Volunteers in the Spanish Civil War: The British Battalion in the International Brigades, 1936–1939* (London: Routledge 2004).

province or people, or any person or persons exercising or assuming to exercise the powers of government in or over any foreign country, colony, or province or part of any province or people'.[34] Thus, discussions arose as to whether the application of the 1870 Act was tantamount to a British formal recognition of Franco's regime. A related question, which also created uncertainty within the British Foreign office, was whether the 'Act was applicable without a formal declaration of neutrality to establish clearly that Britain was 'at peace' with both sides'.[35] Despite its relative ineffectiveness, the Foreign Enlistment Act, which remains a noted precedent for the disjuncture between official policies and acts of transnational solidarity in foreign civil strife, played an important symbolic function in the Spanish Civil War.

The 'localization' stance, which many states adopted under British leadership in relation to the Spanish Civil War, was, on the other hand, undertaken outside the institutional framework of the League of Nations. In light of the early support that Germany and Italy had provided Franco's troops and without which the Spanish Republic may well have successfully defeated Franco's rebellion in September 1936, the Spanish Minister of Foreign Affairs, Alvarez del Vayo, addressed the Assembly of the League to denounce that the so 'non-intervention agreement' amounted instead to 'foreign intervention' in Spain:

'The legal monstrosity of the formula of non-intervention is manifest. That formula ... places on the same footing the lawful Government of my country and the rebels, whom any Government worthy of the name is not only entitled but bound to suppress and punish. From the juridical point of view, non-intervention, as applied to Spain, represents an innovation in the traditional rules of international law, for it means withholding means of action from a lawful Government'.[36]

The Spanish government, furthermore, claimed that the foreign aid provided to the coup d'état was incompatible with the 'prescription of open, just and honourable relations between nations' included in the Preamble of the Covenant of the League of Nations. However, on 24th September the Assembly of the League of Nations[37] decided to declare its inability to deal with the Spanish Civil War under the pretext that it lacked competence on questions of internal order. To its declaration, the League added a delegation for the management of the Spanish conflict to the London Committee, which become categorized

34 Mackenzie The Foreign Enlistment Act 1999, 65.

35 Id.

36 League of Nations, Official Journal, Special Supplement no. 155, Records of the XVIIth Ordinary Session of the Assembly, Plenary Meetings, Geneva (1936) 49.

37 Tams, The League of Nations 2006.

as a sort of intergovernmental agency for the management of the Spanish conflict outside the competence of the League.[38] Desperate claims to the League of Nations by the Spanish Republic's government, which was excluded from participation in the London Committee, continued after Italy and Germany recognised General Franco's government as the de iure government of Spain on 18th November 1936. This recognition took place barely a few days before Germany and Japan signed the Anti-Comintern Pact—the cradle of the Second World War's Axis Powers—which Italy would join on 6th November 1937. On 27th November 1936, the Republican government 'appealed to the Council to consider the 'armed intervention' of Germany and Italy in Spain and the circumstances threatening to disturb international peace under the terms of Article 11 of the Covenant'.[39] Philip C. Jessup termed it, as we shall see in more detail below, an 'illegal intervention',[40] and even British international lawyers, such A.D. McNair, deemed it 'an act of war against Spain.'[41] However, on 12th December 1936 the League's Council adopted a resolution that did not condemn the military action of any state and, once again, gave moral support to the non-intervention plan by referring the matter to the London Committee.

Throughout 1937 and 1938, the status quo remained unchanged. With the documental support of a White Book containing 101 original documents, the Spanish government denounced, again in September 1937, the massive Italian intervention as a case of 'external aggression against ... [its] territorial integrity and existing political independence' based on Articles 10 and 16 of the Covenant. However, once again, despite all evidence to the contrary, 'the Council merely applauded the work of the Non-Intervention Committee, approved the international supervision of Spain, and urged the speedy withdrawal of volunteers'.[42] The League would again examine the 'Spanish case' in May and September 1938, at a time when, as we shall later see, many states had already recognized Franco's government over Spain, with the Council resolutions, consequently, going 'largely unheeded'.[43] Manuel Azaña, the President of the Second Spanish Republic, summarized the position of the Spanish government

38 Schwartz, *La internacionalización* 1971, 154–157.

39 Alfred de Zayas, 'Spanish Civil War', *Max Planck Encyclopedia of Public International* Law (2013) 1–10, 4.

40 Philip C. Jessup, 'The Spanish rebellion and International Law', *Foreign Affairs* 15 (1936–1937), 260–279, 270.

41 Arnold D McNair, 'The Law Relating to the Civil War in Spain', *Law Quarterly Review* 53 (1937), 471–500, 497.

42 See Wilcox, 'The League of Nations and the Spanish Civil War' 1938, 68.

43 De Zayas, 'Spanish Civil War' 2013, 1–10, 5.

toward the League of Nations's treatment of the Spanish question in a speech delivered in the summer of 1937. According to Azaña, the London Committee was 'not established in the arena of international law, in the juridical arena, but in the political and governmental one',[44] and it, therefore, 'examines the Spanish conflict not in the light of law and of international treaties, but as a factual question'.[45] The London Committee, Azaña concluded, 'does not replace the League of Nations, but only narcotizes it'.[46]

The Spanish Civil War sounded the death knell of the system of collective security established by the Versailles' Treaty. The rapid acceptance of the status quo regarding the Spanish Civil War and the non-intervention agreement should be seen, as examined in Chapter Three, in the context of the previous turn towards 'neutrality' adopted by European middle democratic powers in the face of the rise of fascism and authoritarianism. Many contemporaries viewed the British-led policy of localization of the conflict, through non-intervention and an arms embargo, as a remedy to avoid the extension of the war to the rest of Europe in the summer of 1936. This danger of escalation was surely present in Leon Blum's change of mind from 21 July 1936, (when the French President was determined to send support to the Republicans in Spain), through 27 July, (when, after a two-day trip to London, he provisionally halted the decision to send arms to Spain), to 8 August 1936 (when France proposed the Non-Intervention Pact.)[47] The danger of escalation was a major argument in the decisions of many European countries and, also, as we shall see, of the United States to support the non-intervention agreement. It was this fear of escalation that convinced them to stick to the anomalous non-intervention agreement sponsored by Britain and France, despite its apparent ineffectual character, and to a series of international legal positions that, as N. Berman noted, 'could be viewed as the 'nadir' of the traditional rules'.[48]

---

44 Manuel Azaña, 'Discurso en la Universidad de Valencia', in Manuel Azaña, *Los españoles en Guerra.* (Barcelona: Editorial Crítica, 1999) 58 quoted in Fernandez Liesa *La Guerra Civil española y el orden jurídico internacional* 2014, 60.

45 Id., 60.

46 Id., 60.

47 M.D. Gallagher, 'Leon Blum and the Spanish Civil War', *Journal of Contemporary History,* 6, 1 (1971), 58. As a journalist, contemporary of Blum, noted: 'Leon Blum is doing reluctantly but loyally what he judges to be best for peace. But history teaches us that it is always dangerous to turn one's back on justice, even with the best of intentions.' See Louis Martin-Chauffier: Editorial in Vendredi, 11 September 1936 quoted in Gallagher, 64.

48 Nathaniel Berman, 'Between 'Alliance' and 'Localization': Nationalism and the New Oscillationism', New York University Journal of International Law and Politics 26 (1993–1994), 449.

Laying behind this anomalous concerted international legal position[49] was a British foreign 'policy of appeasement' under the conservative governments of S. Baldwin (June 1935 to May 1937), and N. Chamberlain (May 1937 to May 1940). The earlier version of N. Chamberlain's 'peace for our time' speech[50] at the price of the sacrifice of Spain in 1936, was, however, not the only—or even the main—factor behind British foreign policy-making regarding non-intervention in the Spanish Civil War. Lurking behind what H. Lauterpacht would call, as we shall later see, 'the general interest of peace',[51] in Britain's championing of the non-intervention strategy in Spain there were a series of far less pacifist motives. These include, firstly, geostrategic concerns—including the protection of the Mediterranean 'imperial route' through the Strait of Gibraltar—and British long-term economic interests,[52] which, by 1936, amounted to 40% of the foreign investment in Spain.[53] The Western Mediterranean had, moreover, a long history of heightening tensions among European imperial powers as the Algeciras conference of 1906,[54] and the crisis of Agadir during the second Moroccan crisis[55] of 1911, examined in previous chapters, had shown. Barely a month before the outbreak of the Spanish Civil War, Britain had decided to unilaterally urge the abandonment of sanctions against

49 Which the future President of the International Court of Justice, Judge S.M. Schwebel would later decry as 'legally infirm (in the context of the obligations of the Covenant of the League of Nations) as it was politically cynical and craven', see Stephen M. Schwebel, 'Review of Sir Gerald Fitzmaurice and the World Crisis: A Legal Adviser in the Foreign Office by Anthony Carty and Richard A. Smith' The American Journal of International Law 97 (2003), 992–994, 994.

50 In defense of the Munich Agreement reached with A. Hitler in 1938, see Peace in our Time Speech given in Defence of the Munich Agreement, 1938 Neville Chamberlain Great Britain, Parliamentary Debates, Commons, Vol. 339 (October 3, 1938).

51 Hersch Lauterpacht, 'Recognition of Insurgents as a de Facto Government', *Modern Law Review* 3 (1939) 1–19, 1.

52 For an analysis of the Economic aspects of British Policy, see, Edwards, The British Government and the Spanish Civil War 1979, 64–100.

53 Id., at 65.

54 Carlos Jiménez Piernas and Millán Requena Casanova, 'Spain's Part in the 1906 Algeciras Conference: Internationalisation of the Moroccan Question and the Interests of Spain', Spanish Yearbook of International Law, XII (2008) 1–18, 4.

55 The partition of Morocco took place after the Second Moroccan Crisis, or the Agadir Crisis of 1911 spurred again by imperial competition by Germany which bargained its earlier position as defender of the sovereignty of the Sultan and of territorial independence of Morocco for territorial concessions in West Central Africa. See Neila *España y el Mediterraneo en el siglo XX,* 2011, 123.

Italy over Abyssinia,[56] thus setting the path for a strategy of rapprochement and conciliation toward Italy, which continued throughout the Spanish Civil War.[57]

The novel social aspects of the war also played a critical role in fostering the non-intervention agreement. At a time when new transnational social factors began to inform new perspectives on intervention, C.G. Fenwick, writing for the American Journal of International Law in 1938, approached the question of whether civil wars could be brought under the control of international law, and remarked: [What] we have been witnessing in Spain for the last two years is in a broad way a reversal of the earlier revolt of liberalism against monarchical legitimacy. For this time, it is the conservative groups that are the rebels; it is the army and the propertied interests that are questioning the authority of the de iure government; and in their challenge to the constitutional regime they are receiving the support of the clerics, who have normally been on the side of the established order'.[58] Inherently linked, indeed, to the historical causes behind the British decision to foster the quick alignment of neutral attitudes towards the Spanish Civil War was the fear of Bolshevism[59] of the British establishment elite.[60] In 1937, Loewenstein lucidly analysed how 'the hatred of communism and its kin, Marxism and socialism' was essential among 'the programmatic and ideological ingredients of the widely ramified movement of international fascism'.[61] The anti-communist element of British policy, which was fuelled by early reports to the Foreign Office from pro-Franco British

56 See Graham Hutton, 'British Policy Towards Spain' 1936–37, 661

57 See e.g. 'Memoradum on Itallan Foreign Policy in the Spanish Civil War' drawn up by the Foreign Office and circulated to the Foreign Policy Committee of the Cabinet. Included in 'Note by Mr, Eden (W9885/9549/41) August, 19, 1936', W.N. Medlicott and D. Dakin (Eds) *Documents on British Foreign Policy, 1919–1939 Second Series Volume XVII, Western Pact Negotiations: Outbreak of Spanish Civil War June 1936—January 1937* (1979) 136.

58 See interestingly C.G. Fenwick 'Can Civil Wars be brought under the Control of International Law?' *American Journal of International Law* 32 (1938) 538–542, 540.

59 See e.g. Douglas Little, 'Red Scare 1936: Anti-Bolshevism and the Origins of British Non-intervention in the Spanish Civil War', *Journal of Contemporary History* 28 (1988), 291–311, 291 (suggesting that 'Whitehall imposed an arms embargo on the Spanish Republic primarily to prevent the emergence of a communist Spain, and more broadly, to check the spread of Bolshevism in western and southern Europe').

60 This was acute in figures such as Winston Churchill, see e.g. Dorothy Boyd Rush, 'Winston Churchill and the Spanish Civil War' *Social Science* 54 (1979), 86–92.

61 Loewenstein, 'Militant Democracy and Fundamental Rights' 1937, 421.

diplomats in Spain,[62] remained an important factor in Britain's determination to prevent, as the foreign office noted, 'France by hook or by crook from going 'Bolshevik' under the influence of the Spanish Civil War'.[63] The ideological class-background motivation behind the British appeasement has been stressed by several authors, such as D. Little, who noted that 'Britain quickly adopted a 'better Franco than Stalin' approach, which probably helped shape the strategy of appeasement over the following two years.'[64]

Moreover, in Spain, anti-communism allied itself with a religious fervour which borrowed from the crusade-like ultra-Catholic credentials of the Spanish imperial Christianising and Counter-Reformation past. The portrayal of Franco as the 'sentinel of Western civilization' and Christianity was supported, as we shall later see, by several Spanish international lawyers. These went as far as to argumentatively justify Franco's 'glorious national uprising' with reference to the works of the Spanish founders of international law[65] including Francisco de Vitoria the academic status of whom had risen exponentially in the interwar years, partly, as we saw in Chapter three, due to the zealous support of the President of the American Society of International law.[66] Supporters of Franco's coup d'état included, as we shall later see, noted Spanish international lawyers such as J. Yanguas Messia, the co-founder of the Association Francisco de Vitoria in 1926,[67] who drafted the Junta decree of 29 September 1936 that

62 Such as the British ambassador in Madrid informing Eden on 18 August 'Spanish Government has not authority and law and order is in reality inexistent. Anarchists and communists and advanced socialist elements are in de facto charge of the situation'. See Mr Ogilvie- Forbes to Mr. Eden (received August 18, 9.30 am) No. 9 Telegraphic (W 8973/62/41) in W.N. Medlicott and D. Dakin (Eds) Documents on British Foreign Policy, 1919–1939 Second Series Volume XVII, Western Pact Negotiations: Outbreak of Spanish Civil War June 1936—January 1937 1979, at 107. For recent research on the role of British diplomats in Spain, see Tom Buchanan, 'Edge of Darkness: British 'Front-Line' Diplomacy in the Spanish Civil War, 1936–1937' *Contemporary European History* 12 (2003), 279–303, 279.

63 See signed on August 12, 1936 'Minute by Mr Sargent on the danger of a creation of rival ideological blocs in Europe (W 9331/62/41)' in Medlicott and D. Dakin (Eds) op.cit., 91.

64 Little, 'Red Scare 1936: Anti-Bolshevism' 1988, 307.

65 Forcada Barona, 'La influencia de la religión católica en la doctrina internacionalista' 2012.

66 Brown Scott, *The Spanish Origins of International Law,* 1932, and Brown Scott, *The Catholic Conception of International Law. Francisco de Vitoria, Founder of the Modern Law of Nations* 1934.

67 Brown Scott, 'Asociación Francisco de Vitoria', 22 American Journal International Law 1 (1928), 136–139.

proclaimed General Franco Head of the government of the Spanish State. By holding 'up a mirror to class tensions and imperialist rivalries in Europe',[68] the vaunted Catholic and anti-communist credentials of the nationalists arguably played also a role in F.D. Rooselvelt's decision to follow the British lead against the letter of the US' own traditional policy of aiding a legally recognised democratic government, even if this meant forcing the US Congress to enact a specially Amended Neutrality Act in May 1937 to the Spanish Civil War.

## International Legal Aspects of the Spanish Civil War

International lawyers have traditionally understood the 'non-intervention' system in the Spanish Civil War in terms of 'its conformity with, or divergence from, the traditional rules'[69] regulating intervention in foreign wars at the time. Several contemporary authors considered the non-intervention system to greatly diverge from traditional rules and criticized it as a mask for intervention. A second group supported the position that the 'non-intervention' system was in 'conformity with the traditional rules' regulating intervention in foreign wars, but highlighted its sui generis character.[70] Recognition of the 'anomalous' character of the non-intervention pact was pervasive in all cases.

British international lawyers, in particular, were at pains to fit the non-intervention policy into traditional categories of international law. Their analysis of the international legal aspects raised by the Spanish Civil War can be divided into two main stages. Between 1937 and early 1938, these international lawyers mainly focused their attention on the legal justification of the policy of non-intervention and the management of its anomalous international legal framework. From early 1938 to the end of the Spanish Civil War, analysis by the British courts of cases arising from the conflict came to the fore. The apologetic stage aimed to tame the anomalies of the course of action adopted by the British Conservative government into technically debatable international legal categories; the second stage was presided over by a classical British 'practitioner's approach' to the tragedy of the Spanish Civil War.

Many contemporary international lawyers agreed with the Spanish government that non-intervention was simply a mask for intervention on Franco's side. They concurred that the official Spanish Republic's characterization

68 Graham Hutton, 'British Policy Towards Spain' 1936–37, 689.

69 Berman 'Between 'Alliance' and 'Localization'' 1993–1994, 461.

70 Id.

of it as a 'legal monstrosity' was a fair portrayal of the non-intervention agreement. By depriving the lawful (and democratically legitimate) government of Spain of its customary entitlements under international law, the non-intervention agreement forced the Republic 'to seek arms in the murky world of the private market'[71] at astronomical prices. For Georges Scelle, who decried the inaction of the League of Nations, the non-intervention system meant the illegal withholding from a member State of the League of Nations of the 'free and complete exercise of the normal competences which it derives from international law'.[72]

In the United States, Philip C. Jessup, who denounced the anomaly of an intervention pact for which there were no precedents,[73] also stressed the customary status of the Spanish Republic's right to maintain its normal commercial relations unchanged. Jessup highlighted that the Pan-American Convention on the Duties and Rights of States in the Event of Civil Strife,[74] signed in Havana in 1928, had codified this entitlement in the Americas and pointed out that 'the Arms Traffic Convention of 1925, if it had come into force, would have served somewhat the same purpose'.[75] The Resolution of the *Institut de droit International* on 'Duties of Foreign Powers toward the Government which is fighting the Insurrection' had already made it plain in 1900 that 'every third Power, at peace with an independent nation, is bound' (...) 'not to furnish to the insurgents either arms, munitions, military goods, or financial aid' and 'not to interfere with the measures which this nation takes for the re-establishing of internal peace'.[76] The fact that the US State Department could not enforce

71 Balfour, 'Spain from 1931 to the Present' in Raymond Carr (ed.) *Spain. A History* (2001), 243–283, 264.

72 Georges Scelle, 'La guerre civile espagnole et le Droit des gens', *Revue Generale de Droit International Public* 45 (1938) 265 and Georges Scelle, 'La guerre civile espagnole et le Droit des gens' *Revue Generale de Droit International Public* 46 (1939), 197–228.

73 The only one, albeit only indirectly, took place during the Third Carlist War (1872–76).

74 Jessup, 'The Spanish rebellion and International Law', 1936–1937, 266.

75 Id.

76 Institut de droit International, Duties of Foreign Powers towards the Government which is fighting the Insurrection. Article 2. -Section 1. Every third Power, at peace with an independent nation, is bound not to interfere with the measures which this nation takes for the re-establishing of internal peace. Section 2. It is bound not to furnish to the insurgents either arms, munitions, military goods, or financial aid. Section 3. It is especially forbidden for any third Power to allow a hostile military expedition against an established and recognized government to be organized within its domain.

its policy of 'moral embargo'[77] towards the Republican government against private parties in 1936 further illustrates the fact that the Republican government's consuetudinary expectations under the international law of the period were anomalously quashed in the summer of 1936.

More subdued was the analysis of Fenwick, also from the United States, for whom answers to foreign intervention in domestic conflicts had ebbed and flowed since the principle of legitimacy had supported foreign intervention on behalf of absolute monarchs against liberal revolts[78] in the aftermath of the Napoleonic Empire. Fenwick hinted at a sort of international federal solution inspired against the background of the 'failure of international law to develop any general rule expressing the right of the community of nations to intervene between the parties to a civil war',[79] and the consequent 'assertion on the part of individual states of a right to take the law into their own hands'.[80] However, Fenwick considered that although 'the method by which the United States has met the problem within the scope of its federal constitution',[81] was suggestive in domestic terms, it was not 'sufficiently parallel to the international problem to permit inferences to be drawn from it.'[82]

By contrast, another group of authors, which included the cream of British international lawyers, attempted to carve out the view that the non-intervention system was in accordance with traditional rules or, as Charles Rousseau noted, that 'it is neither legal nor illegal, since it develops in a zone of competence which remains, in many respects, a sort of legal no man's land.'[83]

---

77 See Michael E. Chapman, *Arguing Americanism. Franco Lobbyists, Roosevelt's Foreign Policy and the Spanish Civil War* (Kent: Kent State University Press, 2011). See also e.g. Ana Bosch, *Miedo a la democracia. Estados Unidos ante la Segunda República y la guerra civil española*, (Barcelona: Editorial Crítica 2012).

78 In Spain itself, for instance, the intervention of the so-called 'one hundred thousand sons of Saint Louis', accorded in the Congress of Verona in 1922, put an end to the 'liberal triennium' of 1820–1823 during which the official study of 'natural law and the law of nations' was, as we saw in Chapter 1, briefly restored in Spain.

79 Fenwick 'Can Civil Wars be brought under the Control of International Law' 1938, 539.

80 Id., 539.

81 Id., 541. This In accordance with Section 4 of Article IV of the Constitution, the United States (using the plural) 'shall guarantee to every State in this Union a republican form of government, and shall protect each of them against invasion; and on application of the Legislature, or of the Executive (when the Legislature cannot be convened) against domestic violence.'

82 Id., 541.

83 Charles Rousseau, 'La Non-intervention en Espagne', 19 *Revue de droit international et legislation comparée* 19 (1938), 217, 228.

For most British international lawyers the non-intervention in Spain was but a collective application of a rigorous version of the traditional doctrine of neutrality. This was, in fact, the departure point of H.A. Smith's contribution to its study at the British Yearbook of International Law in 1937.[84] Smith, who was a professor of International law at the London School of Economics, assimilated the non-intervention agreement to a 'collective declaration of neutrality, although presented in an unusual form'.[85] Smith, nonetheless, took issue with the technical deviations from the resulting international legal scheme that the subsequent British policy of non-recognition of belligerent rights to the parties brought with it. This legal technical deviation alone impelled him to cast a shadow over the justificatory enterprise: 'my hope is that future lawyers will be able to regard the policy pursued in this war as an anomaly. My fear is that future politicians will regard it as a precedent'.[86] H.A. Smith also invoked the figure of the 'historian of the future', noting that he 'will be better able than we are to appreciate the value of the causes which have led to a departure from these rules (the accepted rules which govern the attitude of foreign powers in the event of a civil war) in the case of the Spanish Civil War'.[87]

In 1975, after almost forty years of Franco's continuous dictatorship in Spain, a young A. Cassese agreed with the common point of departure of the British justificatory perspective by noting that 'the behaviour of the States parties to the non-intervention agreements was impeccable from a legal point of view'.[88] According to Cassese: 'customary international law merely confers a right on States to help the lawful Government. States are therefore at liberty to waive this right by mutual agreement. Moreover, by agreeing not to help the rebels, they merely confirmed an obligation deriving from customary law'.[89] By the time of the signature of the legally 'impeccable' non-intervention agreement to which Cassesse referred, respect for the customary legal obligation to not help the rebels was already being blatantly breached by Germany and Italy which military intervention in Spain only continued to escalate throughout the war.

If there was, indeed, a line to be drawn between the right of some states to promote a collective arms embargo outside the framework of the League of Nations against the Spanish Republic in defiance of the obligation that 'every

84 Smith, 'Some Problems of the Spanish Civil War' 1937, 28.
85 Id., 28.
86 Id., 30.
87 Id., 31.
88 Cassesse, 'The Spanish Civil War and the Development of Customary Law' 1975, 131.
89 Id.

third power, at peace with an independent nation' had to not interfere 'with the measures which this nation takes for the re-establishing of internal peace',[90] such a line appeared completely blurred in the apologetic contribution penned in 1937 by the first British Judge and President of the International Court of Justice (1946–1955), Arnold D. McNair.[91] Writing for the Law Quarterly Review in 1937, at the time of his transition from the Whewell Professorship of International Law at Cambridge to the post of Vice-Chancellor of Liverpool University, McNair instead presented an unflinching defence of the strategic course of action adopted by the British government regarding the Spanish Civil War. McNair, who focused his contribution 'on the law applying between each of the contending parties and foreign States',[92] began his article by providing arguments to justify the British policy of denying any assistance to the Spanish Republican government in dealing with General Franco's uprising. McNair considered that the duty of the United Kingdom as a foreign power in peace with Spain 'to not interfere with the measures which this nation takes for the re-establishing of internal peace' was equivalent to the guiding principle that 'the conduct of foreign States towards their unhappy neighbour suffering from civil strife is merely a continuance of the normal duty of non-interference in the domestic affairs of another State.'[93] Moreover, he argued that he was 'not aware of any rule of customary international law which imposes any duty upon the United Kingdom to sell implements of warfare to the Spanish Government to enable it to suppress an insurrection or to permit British or foreign traders in the United Kingdom to do so'.[94]

Having discarded any customary basis 'for any active duty to assist' the democratic Republican government, McNair then went on to review the treaty law in vigour between Spain and Great Britain, in particular the British-Spanish Commercial Treaty of 31 October 1922 and the Exchange of Notes dated 4 and 5 April 1927. He put stress on the bilateral agreements in order to argue against the view expressed 'in some quarters, that we have broken them by not allowing implements of war to be sold to the Spanish Government, or at any rate that we have evaded them by improperly resorting to an exception contained

90 The Resolution of the *Institut de droit International* on 'Duties of Foreign Powers toward the Government which is fighting the Insurrection' had enshrined this perspective back in 1900.

91 Arnold D McNair, 'The Law Relating to the Civil War in Spain', *Law Quarterly Review* 53 (1937) 471–500, 497.

92 Id., 472.

93 Id.

94 Id., 472.

in them'.[95] McNair reaffirmed the exception the British government used to evade the applicability of the Commercial Treaty (including 'weapons, ammunition and war material and, under exceptional circumstances, also in respect of other materials needed in war') in vigour between Spain and the United Kingdom 'to protect itself from being depleted of war materials.' McNair, who maintained that 'there cannot be any doubt that the United Kingdom was and is legally justified in prohibiting the export to Spain of these materials, as it did as from August 19 1936, either because we could not spare these materials or for any other reason,'[96] and went even further. He invoked the 'maintenance of the peace in Europe' as a legal ground 'by virtue of a condition to be implied in the treaty to issue such a prohibition'.[97]

However, the persuasive attempt by McNair—who, years later, became the First President of the European Court of Human Rights (1956–1965)—to justify the international legal 'impeccability' of the British policy in the event of the military coup d'état supported by Nazi Germany and Fascist Italy in the summer of 1936 in a member state of the League of Nations with a secular multi-party democratic system based on equal rights for all citizens, with provisions for regional autonomy, and with the right to universal—including, for the first time in Spanish history, female—suffrage,[98] had to confront a number of further technical difficulties. The first of these had to do with the use of the term 'neutrality', and the second one with the question of the implicit triggering of belligerent rights to the contending parties by the non-intervention agreement as well as with the consequences of the early recognition by Germany and Italy of Franco's government as the de iure government of Spain. Finally, the British de facto recognition of the fact of insurgency also triggered further legal difficulties.

Indeed, as N. Berman notes, the first difficulty for McNair had to do with the 'misuse' of the term 'neutrality', or at the very least the anomalous enlargement to which it had to be subjected at the time for it to be able to indicate that the non-intervention system could (then) be seen as the 'application of a stringent version of the duties of neutrals.'[99] The issue of neutrality also considerably coloured the American contributors' approach to the first stage of the international legal debate on the Spanish Civil War. P.C. Jessup remarked on the US Acting Secretary of State's reticence to use 'neutrality' terminology in a circular instruction

95 Id., 473.
96 Id.
97 Id., 474.
98 Universal female suffrage was not restored until the Spanish Constitution of 1978 in Spain.
99 Nathaniel Berman 'Between 'Alliance' and 'Localization'', 1993–1994, 461.

of August 7 1936 that 'it is clear that our Neutrality Law with respect to embargo of arms, ammunition and implements of war has no application in the present situation, since that applies only in the event of war between or among nations'.[100] Another U.S. legal scholar, N.P. Padeldorf, highlighted as well that 'neutrality and non-intervention in times of unrecognized insurgency and in times of international warfare involve very different propositions. To apply to unrecognized and irresponsible rebels the same principles that are applicable to sovereign states and established governments is to encourage rebellion and disorder and to weaken public law and authority. The law cannot long afford to do this'.[101]

The legitimate expectations of the Republican government to be able to arm itself to curb an internal insurrection are further illustrated by the fact that in December 1936, at the request of a US private exporter, the US Department of State issued two licenses[102] for the 'exportation of a shipment of airplanes and engines to the port of Bilbao in Spain, which is the principal port of entry held by the forces of the Spanish Government.'[103] The US government sent a telegram to a series of European governments to justify its legal obligation in view of the fact that this private party had not 'patriotically refrained from requesting licenses for such shipments upon receiving an explanation of this Government's attitude and policy of scrupulous non-intervention in the Spanish situation'.[104] The private exporter, instead, insisted 'upon his legal right' to have such licences granted because, as the telegram from the US government readily admitted, the US Neutrality Law 'providing for an embargo against the shipment of arms, ammunition and implements of war to 'belligerent countries' does not apply to the present civil strife in Spain as it is applicable to wars between nations'.[105]

---

100 Jessup, 'The Spanish rebellion and International Law', 1936–1937, 263.

101 Norman J. Padelford, 'Remarks', *Proceedings of the American Society of International* Law 31 (1937) 154.

102 Subsequently on Jan. 5 the US State Department made also known that it was obliged to grant licenses to another exporter to ship war supplies valued at $4,500,000 to the port of Valencia.

103 State Dept. Press Release, Dec. 30, 1936 quoted in George A. Finch, 'The United States and the Spanish Civil War' *American Journal of International Law* 31 (1937) 74–81, 75.

104 Id.

105 On January 8, 1937, after a request by the US President to Congress of 'an addition to the existing Neutrality Act to cover specific points raised by the unfortunate civil strife in Spain' the Congress approved the Pittman Resolution. For an immediate criticism that the Pittman Spanish Civil War Resolution reversed the legal order 'by placing unrecognized rebels and the constituent government in Spain on the same footing' see E. Borchard, 'Neutrality' and Civil Wars', the American Journal of International Law 31 (1937) 304–306.

Many authors engaged with a second related difficulty of the justificatory scheme put forward by the British government. This resulted from the fact that the non-intervention agreement implicitly recognized the existence of a war between the parties, and it therefore implicitly entailed the recognition of belligerent rights to the rebels.[106] Writing in 1937, G. Balladore Pallieri,[107] also a later President of the European Human Rights Commission (1974–1980), highlighted that 'if one did not interpret the states participating in the non-intervention system as having implicitly recognized a state of belligerency, the system would be illegal because it would have disabled a State at peace seeking to vanquish a revolt.'[108] A. Smith too, who, as we saw, initially assimilated the non-intervention agreement to a 'collective declaration of neutrality, although presented in an unusual form,'[109] made the recognition of belligerence a post-facto pre-condition of the international legality of the non-intervention agreement itself: 'if the powers concerned did not recognize the existence of a war, then the Non-Intervention Agreement was singularly misnamed. If the rebellion was no more than an internal disorder, then the agreement was a grave act of intervention in the internal affairs of Spain, for it was an attempt to prevent the Spanish Government from obtaining the supplies which it needed for the restoration of order in its own dominions'.[110]

However, and remarkably enough in this context, the British Foreign Office, which had orchestrated the non-intervention agreement, decided to have it both ways by resisting the recognition of belligerent rights to the contending parties.[111] Against this background, H.A. Smith's position was that of a plea for international legal coherence with familiar established categories by recognising belligerence and belligerent rights.[112] As early as 1937, H.A. Smith stressed the double standards of the British Foreign Office, which had 'recognized the authority of the insurgent government throughout the territories which the latter controls', and highlighted that 'belligerent recognition is a matter of conduct and not of words'.[113]

106 And that, it should be highlighted, barely a month after Franco's 'glorious national uprising' against the Spanish Republic.

107 Balladore served as President of the ECtHR between 1974 and 1980.

108 Giorgio Balladore Pallieri, 'Quelques aspects juridiques de la non-intervention en Espagne', *Revue de droit international et de legislation comparee* 18 (1937) 285, 293.

109 Smith, 'Some Problems of the Spanish Civil War' 1937, 18.

110 Id., 28.

111 Berdah, L'Allemagne et le Royaume-Uni face à la question espagnole, 1993, 221.

112 Id.

113 Smith, 'Some Problems of the Spanish Civil War' 1937, 28.

The nominal British policy of non-recognition of a belligerent status of the parties, and on the bandwagon of this the non-recognition of belligerence by other states would lead A. Cassese to retrospectively consider that the Spanish Civil War 'was, rather, regarded as a conflict belonging to a tertium genus, intermediate between mere 'civil wars' and those civil wars where the contending parties are recognized as belligerents'.[114] However, Cassese's retrospective perspective, which he reached on the basis that 'the behaviour of third States towards the contending parties in Spain never amounted to a recognition of belligerency'[115] must, once again, however, be qualified in the light of the fact the several states went far beyond recognizing the belligerent status of Franco's camp during the Spanish Civil War. Indeed, as early as November 18 1936, barely two months after the establishment under the aegis of the British Foreign Office of the Non-Intervention Committee in London, Mussolini's Italy and Hitler's Germany already granted de iure official recognition to Franco's government as the established government of Spain. In doing so, Germany and Italy were completely reversing the international legal status of the leaders of the forces who in orchestrating a military coup d'etat had committed a crime of rebellion against the high organs of the Spanish nation and the democratically elected Republican government. The Republican government reacted, as noted before, to this recognition *de iure* of the anti-Republican forces by denouncing a 'foreign intervention' under article 11 before the League of Nations in November 1936.

Jessup agreed with the position adopted by the Republican government, highlighting that 'international law does brand as an illegal intervention in the domestic affairs of another state a recognition prematurely accorded to an insurrectionary group with a view to aiding that group in ousting the established government'.[116] Moreover, on the 8th of June 1937, the insurgents' camp issued a diplomatic note claiming that Franco's Salamanca government had already been recognized by six countries: Guatemala, El Salvador, Nicaragua, Albania, Germany and Italy. These were followed in 1937 by both Japan and the Holy See, and by many others in 1938, either *de iure* (such as Portugal, Turkey, Austria and Hungary), or *de facto* (such as Belgium, Denmark, Norway, Sweden and Finland)[117] through the establishment of diplomatic relationships with the Franco's camp in the last months of 1938. In early 1939, following its recognition of the Nationalist Government, the

---

114 Cassesse, The Spanish Civil War and the Development of Customary Law 1975, 130.

115 Id., 132.

116 Jessup, 'The Spanish rebellion and International Law', 1936–1937, 263–279.

117 See Fernandez Liesa, La Guerra Civil española y el orden jurídico internacional 2014, 84.

Swiss Government forcibly closed and sealed the office of the Permanent Delegation of Spain to the League of Nations.[118]

The recognition by Germany and Italy in 1936 of the nationalist army, 'not provisionally as belligerents, but as the permanent and legitimate government of Spain,'[119] is reflected in the writings of British international lawyers. McNair, whose legal analysis appears, as we have seen, to strikingly coincide with the course of the policy decisions adopted by the British Foreign Office regarding the Spanish Civil War, devoted considerable attention to the question of whether there was what he termed 'a tertium quid between a state of peace and Recognition of Belligerency.'[120]

McNair agreed with Jessup's view about the illegality of the German and Italian recognition of Franco's camp: 'there is no doubt that recognition of legitimacy at that stage of the conflict constituted an illegal intervention and an international wrong upon Spain'[121] However, Mc Nair went further by highlighting that the de iure recognition of Franco's government by Italy and Germany in November 1936 amounted to an implicit recognition of belligerence and that, therefore, Italian and German military interventions, in breach of the law of neutrality, 'against the Spanish Government amounted to acts of war against Spain'.[122] This derived from Article 7 of the Resolution of the Institut de Droit International on 'the Consequences of the Grant of Recognition of Belligerency by another State', according to which, as echoed by McNair, 'recognition entails all the usual consequences of neutrality', or in other words, 'it automatically brings into force as between each belligerent party and the recognizing State the corpus of the law of neutrality'.[123]

However, the admission that Germany and Italy had engaged in a war of aggression against Spain, as the Republican government declared before the League of Nations in late 1936, did not lead McNair to conclude that the anomalous international non-intervention agreement heralded by the United Kingdom and France, to which Germany and Italy were parties, was moot. Neither did it lead McNair to advise the recognition of belligerent rights to the contending parties. By contrast, McNair, denied that the UK actions should be interpreted as constituting a *de facto* recognition of belligerent rights of the

118 Norman J. Padelford, 'Closure of the Office of the Permanent Delegation of Spain to the League of Nations', *The American Journal of International Law*, 33 (1939), 563–566.

119 Smith 'Some Problems of the Spanish Civil War' 1937, 29.

120 McNair 'The Law Relating to the Civil War in Spain' 1937, 484.

121 Id., 497.

122 Id.

123 Id.

contending parties. McNair continued, indeed, to focus on justifying the original British policy on the grounds that 'I cannot see that there is any well-settled practice which fetters the discretion of the United Kingdom in deciding whether or not it is politic to grant or to deny recognition of belligerency'.[124] Moreover, he insisted on the stated practice according to which 'our Ministers have frequently repeated that we have granted belligerent rights to neither side',[125] and decided to focus on how the non-recognition of belligerence specifically affected the UK 'with special reference to a maritime power like ourselves'.[126] McNair also showed, once again, his great ability to excel in the lawyer-like practice of argumentative reversion when he highlighted the non-applicability of the rules of belligerence. McNair stressed in particular the non-applicability of those which may affect a maritime power like the UK, such as those that confer 'upon both belligerent parties the right of visit and search of the merchant ships of the recognizing State, the right of intercepting contraband, the right of establishing blockades, and the right of setting up Prize Courts and condemning merchant ships for carriage of contraband, breach of blockade, un-neutral service etc.'[127] McNair's contribution to study of the law relating to the civil war in Spain concluded with him characterizing the legal regime adopted by the UK as one in which 'we were compelled by the exigencies of the situation to recognize the fact of insurgency in Spain and thus to embark upon the comparatively uncharted sea of a relationship to both parties of which the rules are ill-defined and still in course of development.'[128] The overall character of McNair's apologetical contribution to the Spanish Civil War, and McNair's own decision not to engage with the work of any other author[129] on the subject—including that of Smith—reinforces the impression that Mc Nair, who occupied the Whewell Professorship of International Law at Cambridge University until 1937, might have acted as a shadow legal advisor of sorts to the British Foreign Office regarding the international legal position to adopt regarding the Spanish Civil War.

---

124 Id., at 484.

125 Id.

126 Id., 476.

127 Id.

128 Id., 498.

129 Id., 500. 'I do not wish to be thought to be lacking in courtesy because I have not dealt with the literature now growing up round the subject of this article, notably Professor Smith's article in the British Year Book of International Law of this year and articles and comments in the American Journal of International Law. I have only refrained because I wanted to state my own view upon the materials available to me, and my article is already long enough.

A number of states followed the UK into the 'unchartered sea' described by Mc Nair and 'adopted the intermediate legal institution of recognition of insurgency.'[130] According to another leading British (-assimilated) international lawyer, H. Lauterpacht writing in 1939: 'the condition of insurgency in international law is one of considerable elasticity. It is a factual relation in the meaning that legal rights and duties as between insurgents and third states exist only in so far as they are expressly conceded and agreed upon for reasons of convenience, of humanity, or of economic interests'.[131] This is the legal position on the basis of which the British government developed greater ties with Franco's Salamanca government from the last third of 1937. This rapprochement, which included the signature of commercial agreements, led to the exchange of diplomatic agents—headed by the Duke of Alba in London from 16th November 1937.[132] The British rapprochement to Franco, which coincided with a parallel British rapprochement to Italy, led to a change in the British position. The subsequent 'recognition of the government of General Franco as an insurgent government exercising de facto control over a considerable portion of Spain'[133] influenced, as we shall see, the legal position adopted by the British courts in several cases in 1938 and 1939.

## H. Lauterpacht and the Practitioner's Approach to the Spanish Civil War

The literature on the Spanish Civil War, a conflict 'which abounded in anomalous situations',[134] adopted a new character in 1938, the year Europe witnessed the Anschluss of Austria in March 1938, and the Munich Agreement, which permitted the German annexation of the Sudetenland from Czechoslovakia,

130 De Zayas, 'Spanish Civil War' 2013, 4.

131 Hersch Lauterpacht, 'Recognition of Insurgents' 1939, 3.

132 See e.g. Berdah, L'Allemagne et le Royaume-Uni face à la question espagnole, 1993, 228. See on the evolution of French foreign policy regarding recognition of Franco's camp in 1938 e.g. Michel Catala, 'L'attitude de la France face à la Guerre d'Espagne: l'échec des négociations pour la reconnaissance du gouvernement franquiste en 1938' *Mélanges de la Casa de Velázquez* 29 (1993) 243–262.

133 Lauterpacht, 'Recognition of Insurgents as a de Facto Government', 1939, 8 quoting a communication from the British Foreign Office to the Court of Appeals in the case *Banco de Bilbao v Rey* (1938).

134 Lawrence Preuss, 'State Immunity and the Requisition of Ships during the Spanish Civil War: I. Before the British Courts' *The American Journal of International Law* 35 (1941), 263–281, 281.

in September 1938. The authors devoting their attention to the Spanish Civil War gradually abandoned the areas of non-intervention and the recognition of belligerency to give way to a focus on several other interrelated questions raised by the conduct of the hostilities.

In the French language, Louis Le Fur,[135] an ardent Catholic conservative and defender of natural law,[136] who heartily supported the legitimacy of Franco's cause and, by extension, the legality of the non-intervention agreement, was among those who had already included aspects related to maritime warfare in their legal analysis of the conflict back in 1936 and 1937.[137] From early 1938, a number of contributions in the English language also began to tackle the legal anomalies arising from the non-application of the regime of maritime neutrality to issues of maritime warfare.[138] These legal peculiarities included discussions on matters such as the reconceptualization of the terminology of piracy in the light of blockade actions and submarine warfare[139] carried out principally by Italy.

J.L. Brierly, who held the Chichele Professorship of International Law at Oxford at the time, briefly dealt with the debates surrounding the Spanish Civil War in a short intervention broadcast in 1938. Brierly was mainly worried by the bombing of British ships[140] in Spanish ports and puzzled over the effects of the absence of a formal recognition of belligerence on the jurisdiction of prize courts, the rights of the parties in conflict to conduct searches to identify contraband goods and the right of seizure. Brierly identified the looming danger of war in Europe as 'the invisible part of the iceberg'[141] lurking beneath the anomalous status quo in Spain. Air strikes by officially non-intervening

135 See consecrating some pages to deconstruct how opposite ideological positions conditioned the international legal analysis of two French authors, Louis Le Fur and G. Scelle, regarding the Spanish Civil War, Koskenniemi, The Gentle Civilizer of Nations 2001, 338–342.

136 Louis Le Fur, 'La théorie du droit naturel depuis le XVIIIe siècle et la doctrine moderne', Courses of the Hague Academy XVIII, 1928, 259–442.

137 See e.g. Louis Le Fur, 'La guerre civile d'espagne et le droit international', Revue politique et parlamentaire (1936) 385–598 and Raoul Genet, 'La qualification de 'pirates' et le dilemme de la guerre civile,' 3 Revue international francaise du droit des gens (1937) 13–25.

138 See e.g. N.J. Padelford, 'Foreign Shipping during the Spanish Civil War' American Journal of International Law 32 (1938) 264.

139 Raoul Genet, 'The Charge of Piracy in the Spanish Civil War' American Journal of International Law 32 (1938) 253–263.

140 Delivered June 20, 1938 over British Broadcasting System, James L. Brierly, 'Bombs and the Law. An English Viewpoint', Vital Speeches of the Day 19. 4 (1938), 605.

141 Id.

powers on the civil population also attracted wide doctrinal attention among international lawyers following the destruction of the town of Guernica by the German Condor Legion in April 1937 and the indiscriminate massive Italian bombardments of Barcelona on March 1938.[142]

In 1937, the conduct of hostilities brought one case before the Permanent Court of International Justice (PCIJ). Belgium's signing of the non-intervention agreement did not prevent it from invoking before the PCIJ the international responsibility[143]of the Republican government after the death of the Belgian ambassador Baron Jacques de Borchgrave in Madrid. However, the PCIJ never rendered a judgement on the Borchgrave case. The proceedings were eventually discontinued at the request of the parties. The Spanish Republican government, stressing the exceptional circumstances of a Madrid under siege, presented its excuses to the Belgian government. The Belgian government recognised that, given the lack of proof of any engagement of a governmental agent in the act, the responsibility of the Spanish government had not been compromised.[144]

The conduct of hostilities also brought numerous other cases to the attention of different national courts.[145] British ones in particular focused on a series of cases involving 'measures of expropriation and requisition enacted during the Spanish conflict by both the Republican and the Nationalist Governments'.[146] These measures of requisition involved 'fundamental questions relating to state immunity, the effect of the acts of foreign states and governments, and the consequences of de facto recognition by the British government[147] of Franco's insurgence'. Hersch Lauterpacht examined the matter of 'the recognition of insurgents as a government' in the light of what he considered to be 'perhaps the most significant case decided by English Courts during the Spanish Civil War, namely, Arantzadu Mendi'.[148] This was Lauterpacht's only direct contribution to the study of the Spanish Civil War.

---

142 See Carlos Fernandez Liesa, *La Guerra Civil española y el orden jurídico internacional* 2014, 134–141.

143 Borchgrave case (Belgium v. Spain) (1937) P.C.I.J., Ser. A/B, Nos. 72.

144 See Fernandez Liesa, *La Guerra Civil española y el orden jurídico internacional* 2014, 61–62.

145 Including but not limited to the American courts, Lawrence Preuss 'State Immunity and the Requisition of Ships during the Spanish Civil War: I. Before US Courts', *The American Journal of International Law* 36 (1942) 37–55.

146 Preuss, 'State Immunity and the Requisition of Ships' 1941, 281.

147 De Zayas, 'Spanish Civil War' 2013, 4.

148 Lauterpacht, 'Recognition of Insurgents as a de Facto Government' 1939, 3.

The House of Lords, in the case of the Government of Republic of Spain v ss Arantzazu Mendi and Others, on 23rd February 1939 had confirmed the decision of the Court of Appeal which had found that the insurgent nationalist government had the status of the government of a foreign sovereign state.[149] Against the background of the British de iure judicial recognition of Franco's Burgos government, which had been the position of Hitler's Germany from 18th November 1936, H. Lauterpacht critically examined whether 'the nature and degree of recognition stated in the (earlier) answer of the foreign office irresistibly led to the conclusion arrived at by the British courts'.[150] Lauterpacht opposed this conclusion of the House of Lords on the basis of the need to differentiate between the right of a state to 'recognize the insurgents as a government exercising de facto authority over the territory under its control', which, being the British position, was, in Lauterpacht's view, 'not contrary to international law', and the fact, as he stressed, that 'such recognition is limited in its effects and cannot properly be assimilated to recognition de iure'.[151] For Lauterpacht, the distinction derived from what he considered 'the established principle that so long as the civil war lasts the recognition of the insurgents, whether recognized as belligerents or not, as a de iure government is contrary to international law'.[152] Until that moment arrived, Lauterpacht was of the view, *contra* the interpretation adopted by the British courts (on the basis of their interpretation of the answer they received from the British Foreign Office), that recognition of the insurgent government 'while obliging courts to acknowledge the validity of the legislation of the de facto insurgent authority within its territory, it does not transform the authority thus recognized into an independent government of a foreign sovereign state outside its territory to jurisdictional immunities, in particular as against the government recognized de iure, in respect of its property or its representatives'.[153]

The neglect of the study among historians of the contribution of British international lawyers to the Spanish Civil War may account for the lack of attention by the, otherwise extensive number of commentators on H. Lauterpacht's

149 In a previous case, the Banco de Bilbao v Sancha and Rey Case, the British court held that the British government had granted the insurgent authorities recognition as an insurgent government exercising de facto control over a considerable part of Spain (at 257). Banco de Bilbao v Rey (Court of Appeal) (17 March 1938) [1938].

150 Lauterpacht, 'Recognition of Insurgents as a de Facto Government' 1939, 5.

151 Id.

152 Id.

153 Ibid., 21.

doctrinal opus[154] to the influence of Lauterpacht's doctrinal position in this case for his 'Recognition in International Law'.[155] This contrasts with the fact, as Elihu Lauterpacht briefly records in his biography of his father, that 'although no direct trace has been found of H. Lauterpacht's views, a letter to him from Mr Pilcher QC, leading counsel for the Republican government, suggests that H Lauterpacht' (...) 'has given him some assistance in the form of a note supportive of the view that the nationalist government did not constitute a state and was not entitled to immunity'[156] in the Arantzazu Mendi case before the English courts.

Lauterpacht's contribution to the study of the international legal questions raised by the Spanish Civil War remains within the strictest confines of a professionally detached doctrinal technical work. Lauterpacht was supportive of the right to remedy, which the Spanish Republican government as the de iure government of Spain had been deprived of by the jurisdictional immunity granted by the British courts in the light of the judicially sanctioned assimilation of the insurgent de facto Franco government to the de iure government of Spain. The character of his contribution is in perfect consonance with what A. Carty has termed the 'practitioner's approach',[157] characteristic of the 'greats' of the 'discipline in the 1920s and 1930s, in particular ... Oppenheim, McNair, Brierly and even Lauterpacht'.[158] This 'practitioner's approach' coincides with what M. Koskenniemi considers to be the common programme that McNair and Lauterpacht 'shared: to bring international law out of its isolation as a branch of suspect moral or jurisprudential theory by presenting it as an object of legal technique no different from the domestic'.[159]

---

154 Since e.g. recently Patrick Capps, 'Lauterpacht's Method', *British Yearbook of International Law* 82 (2012) 248–280

155 According to Elihu Lauterpacht, 'of all his writings this is the one that has given rise to most controversy' (...) 'since its basic doctrine of the legal character of recognition has been largely abandoned in state practice over the half-century that has followed', Elihu Lauterpacht, 'Sir Hersch Lauterpacht: 1897–1960' European Journal of International Law 8 (1998) 313–315.

156 Elihu Lauterpacht, *The Life of H. Lauterpacht*, Cambridge University Press, Cambridge (2012) 98.

157 Anthony Carty, 'Why Theory?—The Implications for International Law Teaching', in British Institute of International Law (ed.), Theory and International Law: An Introduction (1991), 75, 77.

158 Crawford, 'Public International Law in 20th Century England' 2014, 685.

159 Martti Koskenniemi, 'Hersch Lauterpacht (1897–1960)' in Jack Beatson/ Reinhard Zimmermann (eds.) *Jurists Uprooted: German-Speaking Emigré Lawyers in Twentieth Century Britain*. Oxford University Press, Oxford (2004) 602–662, 617.

The assertion of the professional relevance of international law within the British common law tradition appears almost programmatically present in several works penned by British international lawyers in the 1920s and 1930s. Writing in 1928, P. Higgins highlighted 'the scarcely veiled contempt with which international law was viewed by practising members of the Bar and the legal profession in general'. Higgins concluded that 'it was extraordinary that, in a country with so many worldwide commitments, so few people were trained in international law' and that it was not even considered 'an essential qualification' in the Foreign Office, the Diplomatic Service or the Service Departments.[160] A year later in 1929, partly thanks to the influence of H. Lauterpacht, by then a Lecturer in International Law at the London School of Economics under the mentorship of A.D. McNair, The Annual Digest of Public International Law began to publish a digest of cases in international tribunals and in national tribunals on points of international law.

Like elsewhere in Europe, the independent academic study of international law in England benefited from the First World War, during which, in 1915, the Grotius Society was founded,[161] and began to publish an annual volume of its Transactions, and took hold in its aftermath in the wake of the establishment of the League of Nations. This engendered a greater academic engagement with international law, or, as J.L. Brierly remarked, 'a quickening of interest in the subject in this country and others'.[162] The new interest in international studies was also reflected in the establishment of the Royal Institute of International Affairs in London in 1919 and found an academic parallelism in the first chairs in international relations established in Aberystwyth and the LSE in the early 20ies.

In 1920, the British Yearbook of International Law added itself to the prewar batch of new international law journals which 'had broken the pattern (if it was such)'[163] of earlier nineteenth-century journals on international law of 'not

160 A. Pearce Higgins 'Remarks' Law Quarterly Review 39 (1928) 507, quoted in D. H. N. Johnson 'The English Tradition of International Law' International and Comparative Law Quarterly 11 (1962) pp. 416–445, 426.

161 In the Introduction to Volume I of the Proceedings of the Grotius Society, Professor Goudy wrote that 'the object of founding the Society has been to afford an opportunity to those interested in International Law of discussing from a cosmopolitan point of view the acts of the belligerent and neutral States in the present war and the problems to which it almost daily is giving birth'.

162 James L. Brierly, 'International Law in England', *Law Quarterly Review* 51 (1935), 24–35, 34–35.

163 Martti Koskenniemi, 'The Case for Comparative International Law' 2009, 1.

pointing to any national and regional allegiance' in their title.[164] However, the academic appeal of international law in England in the early interwar period should be seen in relative terms: as of 1921, there were only 10 public teachers of international law in the United Kingdom.[165] This was no great force to academically manage what has retrospectively been called 'the modern foundational period of contemporary international law'.[166] According to Crawford, the reason for the lack of a university international law tradition can be found in the nineteenth century, when, although 'international law was a developed study in the English-speaking world' (...) 'in England this had relatively little to do with the universities, and it was based on no new theoretical underpinnings or insights'. Instead, whereas 'international law was a developed system of practice for dealing with certain classes of relations beyond the state', (...) its 'local focus was the Foreign Office and the embassies and lawyers' chambers in London rather than the universities'.[167]

Indeed, although scattered chairs of international law (eo nomine) had been established in England before the 1880s it was not until the period 1888–1908 that one of them, the Whewell Chair in international law filled by an international legal scholar of stature[168] John Westlake. From being the domain of early 19th century's practice dominated by the Doctors Commons, a cast of civilian lawyers who practiced in a series of non-common law jurisdictions—ecclesiastical courts and the Court of the Admiralty—and gave diplomatic advice, by the second half of the 19th century, international law become 'more the

164 As we saw in previous chapters, this trend has been inaugurated by the Spanish Revista de Derecho Internacional y Politica Exterior in 1905 and the *American Journal of International Law* in 1907. This was followed an earlier geographical expansion and consolidation of 'national' allegiance in the title of international law journals in the Americas, which was promoted by J. Brown Scott and J. Alvarez throughout the 1910s, as shown by both Revista Mexicana de Derecho Internacional (1919) and Revista Argentina de Derecho Internacional (1920).

165 Editorial note, (1921) 27 LQR 8.

166 Andreas Paulus, 'The International Legal System as a Constitution' in J.L. Dunoff/J.P. Trachtman (eds), Ruling the World? Constitutionalism, International Law, and Global Governance (Oxford: Oxford University Press 2009), 69–112.

167 See James Crawford 'Public International Law in 20th Century England' in Jack Beatson and Reinhard Zimmermann (eds.) *Jurists Uprooted: German-Speaking Emigré Lawyers in Twentieth Century Britain.* Oxford University Press, Oxford (2004) 681–70, 691–692. See also, Michael Lobban English Approaches to International law in the Nineteenth Century, in Matthew Craven, Malgosia Fitzmaurice and Maria Vogiatzi (eds.)Time, History and International Law (The Hague: M Nijhoff, 2007), 65–90, 70.

168 See Crawford, Public International Law in 20th Century England (2014), 691–692.

preserve of a set of academic jurists', whose views 'were far more dominated by a common law approach than had been the case before'[169] and who 'focused less on the litigation of Admiralty Courts and more on political issues'.[170] According to J Crawford, indeed, 'the notable British contribution to the development of international law in the nineteenth century occurred through public life rather than scholarly work, so to speak',[171]otherwise, 'the university teaching and writing of international law, had little or no connection' (…) to either 'the profession of international law outside the Foreign Office' (…) nor 'to the way in which the British Government approached the subject and was informed of it'.[172] Against this background, it would take the next four decades and the fundamental role of émigrés, such as, in this period, L. Oppenheim (1858–1919), who came to England in 1895 and, after publishing in 1905/6 what has been often described the 'probably the most influential English textbook of international law',[173] took the Whewell chair of international law at Cambridge University in 1908,[174] for the academic organization of the discipline of international law in England to get foot.

Against this background, Lauterpacht's generational focus on the importance of judicial practice in international law is apparent in a series of his writings in the early 1930s. In 1931, for instance, he attempted to prove 'that there is no substance in the doctrine of 'two schools of thought', an Anglo-American and Continental one, in international law' by taking issue respectively with, first, 'differences between the 'two schools of thought' on specific matters of international law'; second, the question of 'Anglo-American and continental rules and doctrines of municipal law of possible relevance in international law'; and, third, the question of 'general differences in legal approach and legal philosophy'.[175] He concluded that contemporary statements on the alleged contrast between Anglo-American and Continental schools of

169 Lobban, English Approaches to International law in the Nineteenth Century 2007, 66.

170 Id., 70.

171 Crawford, 'Public International Law in 20th Century England' 2014, 691–692. Noting 'how the notable British contribution to the development of international law in the nineteenth century occurred through public life rather than scholarly work, so to speak'.

172 Crawford, 'Public International Law in 20th Century England' 2014, 691–692.

173 Arthur Nussbaum. *A Concise History of the Law of Nations* (Macmillan 1947), 247.

174 Mathias Schmoeckel, 'Lassa Oppenheim (1858–1919)' in Jack Beatson and Reinhard Zimmermann (eds) *Jurists Uprooted: German-Speaking Emigré Lawyers in Twentieth Century Britain* (2014), 583–599.

175 Herscht Lauterpacht, 'The so-called Anglo-American and Continental Schools of Thought in International Law' *British Yearbook of International Law* 12 (1931), 32.

thought in international law 'did not find support in any of the above meanings of the term'[176] and that they should be discarded both on the ground of scientific accuracy (because 'it is essentially no more than a phrase'),[177] and because of 'the ultimate uniformity of the sense of right and justice which is the foundation of the legal ordering of the relations between states'.[178]

J.L. Brierly defended the same perspective in his overview of 'International Law in England' in 1935, stressing that court decisions were 'one of the sources of the raw materials out of which the international system is constructed'.[179] Brierly principally focused on a series of areas (namely the law of prize) through which decisions of the English Courts had contributed to the development of international law. Like Lauterpacht, Brierly also considered British judicial practice 'an important source, both because of the weight which the views of a great country properly carry in international affairs, and particularly because of the high prestige of our Courts'.[180] However, despite acknowledging the progress that the study of international law in England had experienced during the interwar period, Brierly held that 'international law would be stronger, and those who are especially concerned with its study would be encouraged, if the interest of English lawyers in it were more widespread than it yet is.'[181]

This common perception among the reduced group of interwar British international lawyers of a comparative professional irrelevance of international law in the highly court-ridden British legal system[182] also transpires from the rather gloomy picture that W.E. Beckett offered in 1939 of 'the position in England of international law as a subject of scientific study and practice'.[183] Beckett, who served as the 'Second Legal Adviser' to the Legal Department of the Foreign Office, was involved in Spanish affairs during the conflict, along with Gerald Fitzmaurice, who by then was 'Third Legal Adviser', and as his former professor in Cambridge, A.D. McNair, also a future British judge at the International Court of Justice (1960–1973) and the European Court of Human Rights.[184] According to Beckett, the situation in England was still one of 'little general interest in, and much general ignorance of, international law—public

176 Id.
177 Id., 62.
178 Id.
179 J.L. Brierly, 'International Law in England' 1935, 24.
180 Id., 25.
181 Id., 34–35.
182 See on this evolution Crawford, 'Public International Law in 20th Century England' 2014.
183 W.E. Beckett 'International law in England', 55 Law Quarterly Review (1939) 257, 258.
184 Edwards, The British Government and the Spanish Civil War 1979, 44.

and private'. Beckett noted that these 'two factors, indifference and ignorance, operate in a vicious progression, one producing increased states of the other'.[185]

In coherence with this doctrinal background, Lauterpacht's only contribution to the debate on the Spanish Civil War focused on the practice of domestic tribunals regarding the conflict. Lauterpacht, who in 1937 had replaced A.D. McNair as Whewell professor of International law at Cambridge, and would go on to replace him again as British judge on the bench of the International Court of Justice from 1955 to 1960, was solely interested in disputing the precedential 'authority' of the Arantzazu Mendi case because of its finding that there is no distinction between de facto and de iure recognition before British Courts. The only deferential contextual reference to the horrifying events behind Lauterpacht's parochial technical dissection of the case—a legal dissection that never put into question either the legality or the opportuneness of the non-intervention agreement in Spain—was a sweeping reference to the Spanish Civil War as 'a period when breaches of international law on a wide scale were committed by some states and tolerated by others in what was assumed to be the general interest of peace'.[186]

However, Lauterpacht's views on the justification of the non-intervention agreement have not resisted well the passing of time. The Archives of the British Foreign Office have amply demonstrated that the Non-Intervention Agreement and the establishment of a supervisory committee in London served the principal British diplomatic objectives in the conflict well as it entailed 'restriction of the war to Spain, restraining the intervention of her French ally, avoiding any alignment with the Soviet Union, and any confrontation with Italy and Germany over their support for the rebels'.[187] The basic coincidence between these British foreign policy goals and the insurgents' strategy clearly appears from the archives of the Spanish Ministry of Foreign Affairs under Franco in 1939:

'Our principal and the almost exclusive task was to localize the war in Spanish territory, avoiding in this way, by all means, an international war out of which we would have little to gain and much to lose. At the same time, however, we had to ensure that we would still be able to obtain the aid we needed from our foreign friends while ensuring at all costs that our enemy received no aid or at least that this aid was minimized'.[188]

---

185 Beckett, op.cit. 258.

186 Lauterpacht, 'Recognition of Insurgents as a de Facto Government' 1939, 1.

187 Id.

188 AMAE R834/31, memo by Gines Vidal (Director of the European Section, Spanish Ministry of Foreign Affairs) 28 January 1939 quoted in Moradiellos 'The Allies and the Spanish Civil War' 1999, 45–46.

This coincidence of interests was confirmed by (Sir) Robert Vansittart, Chief Diplomatic Adviser to the Foreign Office, for whom, writing in a memo in 1939 'the whole course of our policy of non-intervention—which has effectively, as we know, worked in an entirely one-sided manner—has been putting a premium on Franco's victory'.[189]

The British government's covert pro-Francoism expressed in a non-intervention strategy which some did not hesitate early on to term a policy of British 'malevolent neutrality',[190] had the effect of tilting the balance against the Second Spanish Republic in the Spanish Civil War. Support for the non-intervention agreement de facto neutralized the role of the League of Nations vis à vis the early German and Italian interventions in the conflict, and amounted to the imperial guardian of the system of collective security preventing many third countries from legally assisting the incumbent Republican government. In this process, British international lawyers served as handmaidens to the strategic design of the British Foreign Office at a time when international law, as Crawford notes, provided 'part of the language in which international debates were conducted, the conduct of politicians criticized, proposals for settlement or change put forward and rejected or agreed'.[191]

The British-led non-intervention agreement in the Spanish Civil War marked the death knell of the system of collective security established by the League of Nations and became the revolving door for Europe's entry into the Second World War. Its legacy for the history of international law and civil wars is that it provides a cautionary tale about the role of international lawyers, who work as a two-way bridge between international policymaking

189 *Sir Robert Vansittart, Chief Diplomatic Adviser to the Foreign Office* PRO *FO371724115, W973, memo by (Sir) Robert Vansittart, 16 January 1939*

190 See Douglas Little, Malevolent Neutrality: The United States, Great Britain and the Origins of the Spanish Civil War, (Ithaca: Cornell University Press 1985) indicating that the term 'malevolent neutrality' was coined by Lord Strabolgi, a Labour Peer, in an article critical of British policy in Spain which appeared in the Daily Herald, 10 August 1936.

191 Crawford, 'Public International Law in 20th Century England' 2014, 693. However, Crawford notes 'But one must be careful not to draw too much from this in terms of the influence of particular scholars, or even of international lawyers in general. To take an analogy, art critics may influence the development of painting in a variety of ways, but it would be misleading to write a history of art by reference to their work. For the most part the product of international law scholarship is a similarly secondary literature'. James Crawford, also a former Whewell professor of International Law at the University of Cambridge followed the footsteps of A.D. McNair and H. Lauterpacht and became judge of the International Court of Justice in 2014.

and international law,[192] under the 'gravitational or other effects' of those 'black holes'[193] to which the repercussions of the 'secret life of international law' on the 'visible life of international law'[194] have been aptly compared. Its legacy for the cultivation of the study of international law in Spain was a Spanish international law academia that remained for the next decades a loyal fellow-traveller of the authoritarian rule born from the ashes of a civil war that was soon to be legislatively defined as 'a popular revolt to prevent a criminal conspiracy from making Spain a slave to the Soviet tyranny'.[195] The interwar appeal of the League of Nations, and 'modern scientism' in tune with the value system of a bourgeois liberal modern mentality, vanished across most of the Spanish international law academia almost as soon as the Spanish Civil War erupted.

### Francisco de Vitoria and the Spanish Civil War

Since the beginning of the Civil War, Franco's General Headquarters and the State Delegation for Press and Propaganda, which included among its tasks international propaganda in support of the non-intervention regime and the international recognition of Franco's government, was established in Salamanca. In September 1936, a 'Message from the University of Salamanca to the universities and academies of the world concerning the Spanish Civil War' was unanimously signed by the Senate of Salamanca University.[196] The 'Message' defined the civil war as the dire struggle that is being fought in defence of our Western

192 Particularly acute in the international legal adviser, the duplicity of whom appears to be as old as the function. This duplicity is echoed by the very nick-name of 'the first Legal Assistant appointed to the British Foreign office—in effect the post of Legal Adviser' in 1886, E. Davidson. This, according to J. Crawford, 'was apparently known as '*Quoad*' Davidson for his habit of advising '*quoad* legal adviser' one thing, and '*quoad* Davidson' another'. Crawford, 'Public International Law in 20th Century England' 2014, 687.

193 Daniel Bethlehem, 'The Secret Life of International Law,' *Cambridge Journal of International and Comparative Law* 1 (2012) 23–36.

194 Id., 36. Daniel Bethlehem held the position of principal Legal Adviser of the United Kingdom Foreign & Commonwealth Office between 2006–2011.

195 Ley 1 de marzo de 1.940 (B.O.E. nº 12.667) para la Represión del Comunismo y la Masonería. See, further, Julius Ruiz, *Franco's Justice. Repression in Madrid after the Spanish Civil War*, (Oxford: Oxford University Press 2005).

196 Vid. LGR, 8-X-1936, p. 1. Quoted in Pérez Delgado/ Fuentes Labrador, *De rebeldes a cruzados* 1986, 250.

Christian civilization'. It was widely interpreted as a sign of the University of Salamanca's intellectual moral support for the Francoist camp.

Within the University of Salamanca, the Salamanca's Faculty of Law would be particularly adamant in its doctrinal support of the uprising. This included among its most pro-Franco supporting members, I. Beato Sala,[197] (1868–1954) the chair-holder in international law in Salamanca University since 1911, and a member of the Association Francisco de Vitoria since 1927. In 1932, he had published a work on 'The Propaganda of the Christian Religion as a Title of Conquest according to the Teachings of Master Vitoria'[198] in the Yearbook of the Association of Francisco de Vitoria. Beato did not hesitate to transpose the same principle to the circumstances of the Spanish Civil War. The University of Salamanca also included several international lawyers belonging to the Instituto Francisco de Vitoria and the Association Francisco de Vitoria.[199] These immediately became an 'essential centre of legitimizers of the 1936 Rebellion, using Thomism and the theories of the Spanish Theologians from Salamanca in the Sixteenth century to generate a discourse (…) against tyranny, a holy war, a crusade, a fight against believers and those without God to save the motherland from communism.'[200] At a meeting of the association Francisco de Vitoria in Salamanca, which included some of the greatest experts on Vitoria, such as the Dominican father Getino, it was decided that new courses were to be organized in which the doctrines of the Spanish school of the 16th century would be applied to the 'historical moment.'

Yanguas Messia, the founder of the Association Francisco de Vitoria in 1926, when he was the Minister of Foreign Affairs, and later President of the Consultative Assembly during General Primo de Rivera's dictatorship, became one of the most engaged supporters of Franco's rebellion in the Spanish Civil War. After the fall of Primo de Rivera, he had followed the footsteps of General Primo de Rivera in exile to Paris in 1930. There, he rekindled his ties with French conservative Catholic international law scholars like L. Le Fur, who,

---

197 Tomás Pérez Delgado/ Antonio Fuentes Labrador 'De rebeldes a cruzados. Pioneros del discurso legitimador del movimiento nacional. Salamanca julio-octubre de 1936' Studia Historica 4 (1986), 235–266, 250.

198 Isidro Beato Sala "La propaganda de la religion Cristiana, como título de conquista, según las enseñanzas del Mro. Vitoria", III *Anuario de la Asociación Francisco de Vitoria* (1932).

199 Tomás Pérez Delgado, 'Francisco de Vitoria: institucionalización de su memoria en Salamanca (1926–1936)', en Estudios históricos salmantinos. Homenaje al P. Benigno Hernández Montes (Salamanca: Ediciones Universidad de Salamanca, 1999) 539–571.

200 Forcada Barona, 'La influencia de la religión católica en la doctrina internacionalista' 2012.

as we have seen, vigorously supported the Francoist cause during the civil strife in Spain. In 1931, Yanguas joined the group of Catholic monarchist intellectuals of proto-fascist orientation around the journal Acción Española, which was founded by Ramiro de Maeztu. Since the outbreak of the Civil War, Yanguas who during the 'conservative turn' in the Spanish Republic had been re-appointed to a chair of private international law at the Central University of Madrid, participated in the drafting of the Junta's decree of 29 September 1936 that proclaimed Franco Chief of the Government of the Spanish State. In 1937, Yanguas also organized a series of conferences in the framework of the Association Francisco de Vitoria in which, building on Vitoria's relectiones, he defended 'the legitimacy or even the compulsory character of the uprising.'[201] An active member of the Francoist Burgos government's Junta de Defensa Nacional during the Civil War, in 1938, he was appointed to the key post of ambassador to the Holy See which he held until 1942.

In his service of Franco's rebellion in the 'war of propaganda' to justify the legitimacy of the military uprising and later the legality of General Franco's regime, Yanguas Messia was not alone. The active liberal reformist support for international institutions that several Spanish legal scholars had shown during the interwar period, did not prevent them from actively supporting or actively sympathizing with the cause of Franco's army. In particular, most of the international lawyers affiliated to the Association Francisco de Vitoria aligned themselves with Franco's camp. One of the most notable ones was Jose Maria Trias de Bes, (1891–1965), the author of a course on private international law at The Hague Academy in 1930[202] who, immediately exiled himself to Italy from his chair in Barcelona at the beginning of the Civil War, and offered his services to the National Movement.[203] In 1937, he returned to Salamanca, the unofficial capital of the rebels, to work on the legal advisory diplomatic committee of the rebel government. Despite the Civil War, Trias de Bes visited The Hague once again to teach a course on the 'Règles générales des conflits de lois' (General Rules on Conflicts of Laws)[204] in 1937.

201 Id.

202 Jose Maria Trias De Bes, *Conception Du Droit International* 1930, 623.

203 María Pilar Hernando Serra, Jose Maria Trias de Bes, Diccionario de catedráticos españoles de derecho (1847–1943) (Madrid: Universidad Carlos III de Madrid. Instituto Figuerola de Historia y Ciencias Sociales, 2011).

204 Jose Maria Trias De Bes. *Règles générales des conflits de lois*, Collected Courses of the Hague Academy of International Law 62 (1937) 1–93. He presented his excuses regarding the 'incomplete character of the study and the annexed bibliography' because 'amidst the revolutionary events that cover Spain in blood' his 's library has been 'ransacked and all his papers have been burnt.'

He also joined the University of Salamanca, where he delivered lectures defending the legitimacy of the military insurrection against the Republic to restore the 'universal order God wanted'. By the end of Spanish Civil War, Trias became the chief international legal advisor of the Ministry of Foreign Affairs of the first Francoist government.

Another former lecturer at The Hague Academy, who also sided with Franco's cause was Jose Gascón y Marín (1875–1962). Gascón, a former Minister of Public Instruction, and Vice-President of the Association Francisco de Vitoria, was one of the leading lights in the field of administrative international law and international civil service, on which, as examined in Chapter Three, he taught twice at The Hague Academy in the early 1930s. Another notable international lawyer affiliated to the Association who also aligned himself with Franco's camp. Joaquin Fernandez-Prida (1863–1942), Fernandez Prida, a member of the Institut de Droit International, who had served in different ministerial positions, including as Minister of Foreign Affairs in 1922, and had contributed to the Vitorian renaissance in 1929 with his book on the 'Influence of the Spanish Treatisers on the Science of Public International Law'[205] also became an active collaborator of the Association Francisco de Vitoria during the war in Salamanca.[206]

Among the Franco's supporters, there were also members of the 'third' professional generation of international lawyers. A case in point is that of Antonio de Luna (1901–1967), chair-holder in public international law at the Central University of Madrid from 1932 who, as we had seen in Chapter Three, had actively participated in the internationalist associational movement in the early 1930s. However, from 1937 to 1939, de Luna served as the first holder of the National Delegation of Justice and Law of the unified Phalangist Party under the supreme command of Franco. The program of the National Delegation under the leadership of de Luna was to bring about the 'judicial revolution' as part of the 'national revolution' defended by the Spanish Phalange. This, which become embodied in a series of legislative projects affecting of realms of juridical life (from the criminal code to the penitentiary code to civil and penal procedural law) would mark a 'radical change of

205 He died of natural causes soon afterwards in 1942. Joaquin Fernandez-Prida, Influencia de los tratadistas españoles en la formacion de la ciencia del derecho internacional publico (Madrid: Imprenta Artistica Saez Hermanos 1929).

206 José María Puyol Montero, Joaquin Fernandez-Prida, Diccionario de catedráticos españoles de derecho (1847–1943) Universidad Carlos III de Madrid. Instituto Figuerola de Historia y Ciencias Sociales, 2011- accesible at.

vision' from the Republican legislation. The ultimate goal of these projects was to bring about an 'extremely hierarchized judicial personalist structure, independent from the executive and greatly influenced by the Phalanx'.[207] As we shall see in more detail in Chapter Five, after the civil war, this future member of the International Law Commission of the United Nations (1962–1966) became President of the Commission for the Depuration of Madrid's University Personnel, joined the activities of the main 'Falange' think tank, and was appointed to the board of the National Council for Scientific Research on which the 'Instituto Francisco de Vitoria,' of which he became the director in 1940, was organically dependent.

Another key member of the 'third' professional generation of Spanish international lawyers who supported Franco's uprising was the chair-holder in International Law at La Laguna in 1935, Fernando Maria Castiella (1907–1976). He would become, along with de Luna, the co-founder in 1948 of Revista Española de Derecho Internacional, and later the longest-serving Spanish Minister of Foreign Affairs in the 20th century. The future course of the works of international lawyers in Spain, and the importance of Francisco de Vitoria and the Spanish classics among international lawyers, will be influenced, as we shall see in more detail in Chapter Five, for decades to come by de Luna, Castiella and, others such as Luis Legaz Lacambra (1906–1980). Legaz Lacambra, who was also a member of the Association Francisco de Vitoria, collaborated during the Civil War with the Section of Studies of the Ministry of Organization and Unionist Action, established by Franco's Government in Burgos,[208] as well as with Jerarquía (1937–1938), the so-called 'black journal of the Falange'.

The doctrines of Francisco de Vitoria and the Salamanca School were also used by Yanguas Messia, Trias de Bes, Gascon y Marín and Fernandez Prida who served on the committee of twenty-one jurists who drafted the 'Advisory Opinion on the Illegitimacy of the Acting Powers on the 18th of July 1936' (Dictamen sobre la ilegitimidad de los poderes actuantes el 18 de julio de 1936).[209] The commission, which was known as the 'Commission

---

207 See i.e. Abel Téllez Aguilera, 'La proyectada Ley de Prisiones de 1938 y la figura de D. Federico Castejón Historia de un conato legislativo' Revista de Estudios Penitenciarios 157 (2014) 9–31.

208 During the war, Legaz collaborated with the Section of Studies of the Ministry of Organization and Unionist Action established in Santander. Of this period is his Cuatro estudios sobre sindicalismo vertical, Zaragoza (1938).

209 Dictamen sobre la ilegitimidad de los poderes actuantes el 18 de julio de 1936 (Madrid: Editora Nacional 1939).

of the 21 Just Men', was established by Franco's government in December 1938, at a time when many European governments had already recognized Franco's government as the legitimate government of Spain. Building on the Salamanca School, the commission argued that the rebels had on their side 'the indestructible titles, without a doubt a hundred times stronger (than the legal ones) before God and history, which can propel a country in a decisive moment to liberate itself, to remain truthful to itself and save Mankind, in order to distance a certain and terrible danger'. Those who subscribed to this view '[came] to that conviction through the path of the teachings of the theologians, who since Saint Thomas and Mariana, with Vitoria and Suarez, proclaim[ed] as sanctified the right to oppose the tyrant that usurped his power, by means of including the faculty of resisting oppression among the most sacred rights of the citizen.'[210] The Advisory Opinion ended up declaring that Franco's coup d'état and subsequent war had 'not constituted any act of rebellion against authority or the law.'

Whereas services to the Franco's cause on the part of legal scholars during the war were, as we shall see in Chapter Five, recompensated with academic honours and political posts in its aftermath, some of those who supported Franco, or who, otherwise, appeared to have a political or ideological affinity with the rebels paid it with their own lives during the civil war. Among these was Quintiliano Saldaña (1878–1938), one of the interwar pioneers, as seen in Chapter Three, of international criminal justice and the first Spanish author to be invited to lecture at The Hague Academy in 1925. Professor of criminal anthropology and advanced criminal studies at the University Central of Madrid since 1911, Saldaña, like Yanguas Messia, had been a member of the National Consultative Assembly where, as the leading sponsor in Spain of the notion of 'social defence', he had contributed prominently to the project of the Spanish Criminal Code of 1928, considered one of the proto 'fascist' criminal codes in Europe. At the outbreak of the Spanish Civil War, Saldaña had sought political asylum at the Cuban embassy fearing for his life in a besieged Madrid of internecine struggles between socialist, anarchist and communist factions. Despite all diplomatic efforts made on his behalf over the next two years, the government of the second Spanish Republic repetitively denied Saldaña a salvo-conduct to leave Spain or to, alternatively, cross over to the rebel General Franco's camp. Suspended from his chair at Madrid University by the Republican government, his house looted and his library, one of the

210 Id. 18.

most complete in Spain, destroyed, Saldaña eventually died of malnutrition as a political refugee in the Cuban embassy in Madrid in October 1938.[211]

Another victim of the civil conflict was Roman Riaza Martinez-Osorio (1899–1936), the Secretary General of the Association Francisco de Vitoria. Riaza had written his doctoral dissertation on the interpretation of the laws and doctrine of Francisco de Suarez,[212] and had delivered lectures on 'The First Challenger of Vitoria, Gregorio Lopez' in the framework Francisco de Vitoria chair in 1932.[213] He was also the co-author with A. Garcia Gallo of a lengthy 'Manual on the History of Spanish Law'.[214] At the time of the outbreak of the civil war, he was the professor in charge of the Chair of the History of International Law, replacing Fernandez Prida at the time of his retirement. In 1940, his widow officially declared, in order to to be awarded a war pension[215] that 'the martyr and wise man D. Román Riaza Martínez-Ossorio' was assassinated by the 'red hordes' at the end of 1936 in Madrid.

However, not all Spanish members of the Association Francisco de Vitoria supported Franco's uprising against the Second Spanish Republic. The PCIJ Judge Rafael de Altamira, a member of the Institucion Libre de Enseñanza (ILE), was in Segovia, which was occupied by the rebels in the early days of the uprising. After fleeing to Vitoria, he was detained and only allowed to return to The Hague because of the mediation of Yanguas Messia who gave him diplomatic immunity as a PCIJ judge.[216] Altamira spent the

---

211 José María Puyol Montero. Saldaña Garcia Rubio, Quintiliano (1878–1938) Diccionario de catedráticos españoles de derecho (1847–1943) (Madrid: Universidad Carlos III de Madrid. Instituto Figuerola de Historia y Ciencias Sociales, 2011). See further, Ignacio de la Rasilla del Moral 'International Criminal Justice as Universal Social Defence, Quintiliano Saldaña (1878–1938)', in F. Megret and I. Talgrenn (eds), The Dawn of a Discipline—International Criminal Justice and Its Early Exponents (Cambridge: Cambridge University Press, forthcoming, 2018).

212 Roman Riaza Martinez-Osório 'La interpretación de las leyes y la doctrina de Francisco Suárez', Revista de Archivos, Bibliografía y Museos 385 (1925).

213 Roman Riaza Martinez-Osorio, 'El primer impugnador de Vitoria' in Gregorio López (ed) Conferencias pronunciadas en la cátedra Francisco de Vitoria de la U. de Salamanca 27 y 28 de enero (Salamanca: AFV, 1932) p. 21.

214 Alfonso García Gallo/ Roman Riaza Martinez-Osorio, *Manual de Historia del Derecho Español* (Madrid: imp. Góngora 1934–1935).

215 Braulio Díaz Sampedro, 'Roman Riaza Martinez-Osorio', in *Diccionario de catedráticos españoles de derecho, 1847–1943* (Madrid: Universidad Carlos III de Madrid. Instituto Figuerola de Historia y Ciencias Sociales, 2011) accesible at http://www.uc3m.es/diccionariodecatedraticos.

216 Gamarra, *The Judge as Gentle Civilizer* 2011, 103.

civil war at The Hague and stayed until the occupation of The Hague by German troops in mid-1940 after which he was exiled to Bayonne and, after sojourns at Lisbon and Columbia universities, eventually to Mexico where he reconnected with the Spanish government in exile.[217] Another member of the Association who did not support Franco's uprising was Salvador de Madariaga (1886–1978) who had led the Spanish foreign policy before the League of Nations during the Second Spanish Republic. He returned to Oxford during the Spanish Civil War where he maintained a posture of critical inhibition equally equidistant from the two camps and gave himself to writing with publications such as 'Theory and Practice of International Relations',[218] which is considered the 'first Spanish contribution to the field of international relations',[219] in 1937.

On the other hand, some members of the interwar generation who belonged to the Association Francisco de Vitoria suffered, nonetheless, Francoist persecution. One of them was Adolfo Miaja de la Muela (1908–1981), a disciple of

217 Disappointed and bitter at the futility of pacifism and his belief in civilized progressin his late works, he died, never to return to Spain, in 1951.

218 Madariaga, Theory and Practice of International Relations 1937.

219 During the civil war, Madariaga transited from the idealism of the 1920s and his support for the constructive pacifist role of the League to a more realist-pragmatic approach after his government experience. In Oxford, he developed a considerable intellectual activity. Other than his 'Theory and Practice of International Relations,' published in 1937, he published 'Unanimous Organic Democracy' and 'Anarchy or Hierarchy' both of 1937. The ideas for the latter work are to be found in a pamphlet published in 1935 'Anarquía o jerarquía. Ideario para la Constitución de la III República,' in which he proposed for Spain 'a system of organic government that, without renouncing democracy and liberalism, could be grounded on order and hierarchy'. In 1938, he also published 'The World's design,' which devotes 'its final chapters to the analysis of the role of international law in the world system.' After the Second World War, Madariaga's more important works are of historical character, such as 'El auge del imperio español en América' of 1955 and 'La decadencia del imperio español en América'. He also remained an engaged liberal activist against communism and in favour of European federalism founding the College of Bruges and working to favour democratic politics in Spain. However, he would only return briefly to Spain in 1976 after the death of Franco to occupy his post, vacant since 1936, at the Spanish Royal Academy. He died in Locarno, barely some days of the ratification of the Spanish Constitution of 1978, at a very old age. See among others, Salvador de Madariaga, El auge del imperio español en América (Buenos Aires: Ed. Sudamericana 1955) Salvador de Madariaga, El auge y ocaso del imperio español en América (Madrid: Espasa Calpe 1977) Salvador de Madariaga, Bosquejo de Europa (Méjico, Ed. Hermes, Buenos Aires, Cía. Imp. Argentina, 1951) Salvador de Madariaga, Democracy versus Liberty. The faith of a liberal heretic (London: Pall Malí 1958).

Barcia Trelles at Valladolid University and also a fellow of the JAE in Holland and Paris in 1931–32. Miaja, who was a member of the association since 1934, had taught as Professor at the 'Instituto Francisco de Vitoria' at the University of Salamanca[220] in 1933 on 'American International Law'. He also published several celebrated works on Vazquez de Menchaca[221] and Serafin de Freitas[222] in the 1930s. Miaja, the youngest Spanish catedratico of international law in the twentieth century, when he became chair-holder at Santiago de Compostela in 1934, was condemned to 12 years in prison some days after the outbreak of the Civil war. He was accused o 'crimes of induction to revolution' based on his membership of the 'Republican Left' party (Izquierda Repúblicana). When he was released in 1941 after five years in prison, he found himself expelled from the bar and de-habilitated as chair-holder of international law.[223]

The Spanish Civil War also reserved a paradoxical fate for Camilo Barcia Trelles, the man that C. Schmitt credited with having provided 'the strongest breakthrough for the world at large regarding Francisco de Vitoria'. Professor of International Law at the University of Valladolid, a city which fell to the rebel camp, Barcia Trelles was immediately detained (his brother Augusto

---

220 Pilar Hernando/ Carlos Petit, Adolfo Miaja de la Muela, Diccionario de catedráticos españoles de derecho (1847–1943) Universidad Carlos III de Madrid. Instituto Figuerola de Historia y Ciencias Sociales, 2011- accesible at http://www.uc3m.es/diccionariodecatedraticos.

221 Adolfo Miaja de la Muela, *Internacionalistas españoles del siglo XVI. Fernando Vázquez de Menchaca* (Valladolid: Talleres tipográficos Cuesta 1932).

222 Adolfo Miaja de la Muela, Las ideas fundamentales del Derecho de Gentes en la obra de Fray Serafín de Freitas (Madrid: Imprenta la RAFA, 1933).

223 Constrained to survive as a private teacher for more than a decade, during which he produced works on the history of international law in Spain, after his rehabilitation to a chair at the University of Valencia in 1952 he delivered a course at The Hague Academy in 1972, and retired from his chair at Valencia University at the dawn of the democratic period as the most prolific Spanish international lawyer of the 20th century. Among the ranks of Spanish ius-internationalist academics, his case is exemplary of the effects of university purges, which were to be defined years later by P. Laín Entralgo, one of the most distinguished Falange intellectuals, as an 'atrocious pollarding' of Spanish universities. See Manuel Diez de Velasco. 'El profesor Miaja de la Muela: ensayo biográfico' in Homenaje al profesor Adolfo Miaja de la Muela (Madrid: Ed. Tecnos 1979), 18–29, 22–27. See Adolfo Miaja de la Muela, 'Les principes directeurs des règles de compétence territoriale des tribunaux internes en matière de litiges comportant un élément international', Collected Courses of the Hague Academy of International Law 135 (1972), 1–96 A chronological list of his publications can be found in Enrique Pecourt García,' El pensamiento internacionalista del prof. Miaja de la Muela », en aa vv, estudios de derecho internacional. libro-homenaje al prof. a. miaja de la muela (Madrid: Tecnos, 1979) pp. 49 y ss.

Barcia Trelles (1881–1961) was serving as Minister of Foreign Affairs of the Spanish Republic on the day of General Franco's uprising) and was subjected to a criminal a process on the grounds of being a 'mason, a-catholic, anti-national and anti-hierarchical.' However, Barcia received the support of notable members of the Association of Francisco de Vitoria and noted supporters of Franco, such Yanguas Messia, and Trias de Bes.[224] This helped him to survive the civil war with only a suspension of employment and salary for two years, the prohibition from applying for vacant posts for five years, and the de-habilitation for the exercise of directive positions, or ones of trust. Nonetheless, as we shall see in Chapter Five, Barcia Trelles would soon gain the favour of the new Francoist regime carrying on for several more decades a prolific academic author in Spain. In 1939, he completed the feat of being the scholar who delivered more courses at The Hague Academy in the interwar period, with his final course on 'Vazquez de Menchaca et l'école espagnole du droit international du XVIe siècle'.[225] His extensive contribution to the interwar renaissance of Francisco de Vitoria and the Spanish legal theologians of the 16th century's Salamanca School had definitively become the 'Spanish School of International Law'.

---

In 2015, the Spanish association of Professors of international law established the first edition of the Prize 'Adolfo Miaja de la Muela' to the best Ph.D. in Public International Law defended in Spanish universities defended at all Spanish Universities between 2013–2015. See also Pedro Laín Entralgo, *Desgargo de conciencia (1930–1960)* (Barcelona: Ed. Barral 1970)

224 Jaume Claret Miranda, *El atroz desmoche. La destrucción de la Universidad española por el franquismo, 1936–1945* (Barcelona, Ed. Crítica, 2006), 184.

225 Barcia Trelles, 'Fernando Vazquez de Menchaca (1512–1569)' 1939.

CHAPTER 5

# Noli Foras Ire. In Hispaniae Habitat Veritas

## Unity of Fate in the Universal

'We are not going to argue with the regulars over the tasteless spoils of a dirty banquet. Our place is outside in the open air, under the cloudless heavens, with our weapons pointing starward over our shoulders. Let others continue with their feasts. Here, outside, in tense, fervent and sure vigilance, we already anticipate the dawn in the joy of our entrails'.[1]

Less than six years, half a million deaths and more than a million exiles lie between the last paragraph of the founding speech of the Spanish Falange in 1933 and Generalísimo Franco's signature of his last war dispatch: 'On this day, with the Red Army captured and disarmed, the national troops have reached their ultimate military objectives. The war has ended'. By the 1st April 1939, José Antonio Primo de Rivera,[2] the man who had feverishly pronounced the ominous words of the founding speech of the Spanish Falange in Madrid's Teatro de la Comedia in October 1933 had long been shot dead by a firing squad in a Republican prison at the onset of the Civil War.

The Spanish Falange Primo de Rivera founded soon merged with a far-right wing faction of the 'Assemblies of the National Syndicalist Offensive' of R. Ledesma and O. Redondo in 1934, and became known by the acronym FE of the JONS. In 1937, General Franco, who was the militarily undisputed leader of the rebellion against the Second Spanish Republic, but who lacked a strong social base of popular support, unified under his leadership the ultra-traditionalist Carlist movement (Requetes) and the Spanish Falange,[3] an

1 José Antonio Primo de Rivera, 'Discurso de la Fundación de Falange Española' in Jose Antonio Primo de Rivera, *Escritos y discursos. Obras Completas 1922–1936* (recopilación de Agustín del Río Cisneros) (Madrid: Delegación Nacional de la Sección Femenina de F. E. T. y de las J. O. N. S., 1959) 189–198.

2 Jose Antonio Primo de Rivera was the 3rd Marquis of Estella and 7th Marquis of Sobremonte and the notorious son of the Spanish military dictator who had ruled Spain, as we saw in Chapter 3, from 1923 to 1930. On his figure, see e.g. Julio Gil Pecharromán. *José Antonio Primo de Rivera, Retrato de un visionario* (Barcelona: Editorial Planeta 2003).

3 'The Spanish Falange and Carlists, with their present organization and members, shall join together, under my leadership, in one single political entity of national character which, for the time being, will be called Spanish Traditionalist Falange and of the Jons ... All other political organizations and parties are dissolved.' Decree for Unification, Art. 1, B.O. April 29, 1937.

 DOI 10.1163/9789004343238_007

acephalous organization since the loss of its leader. The new party became known as FET y de las JONS, otherwise: 'The Spanish Traditionalist Falange and of the Assemblies of the National Syndicalist Offensive.'[4] From the end of the Civil War onwards, FET y de las JONS, by then already commonly known as 'The National Movement,' or merely 'The Movement,' became the ideological arm of the Franquoist regime. It remained the sole official party in Spain until 1977.[5]

In the aftermath of the Spanish Civil War, the ranks of Spanish academia appeared decimated by death and exile.[6] Imprisonment and university purges[7] were soon to complete the elimination of all vestiges of Republicanism from the twelve universities that existed in the country. Only those 'addicted to the regime', some of whom benefitted from vacant chairs as booty for their services in the 'crusade' against the 'Anti-Spain,' saw their careers boost. Among those rehabilitated to their chairs in the areas occupied by the Republican forces during the war were included several members of the Association Francisco de Vitoria who, as we saw in Chapter Four, actively supported Franco's uprising and went to enjoy a bright future in Franco's Spain.[8] The atmosphere of forced

---

4 On the occasion of the Decree of Unification with the Carlist *requetes*, the original programmatic 27 points of the Spanish Falange were reduced to 26 so as to eliminate point 27 in which the original Falange had vowed to not engage in any sort of political alliances to conquer the state.

5 See Stanley G. Payne, *Fascism in Spain, 1923–1977*, (Madison: The University of Wisconsin Press 1999).

6 See Henry Kamen, *The Disinherited: Exile and the Making of Spanish Culture (1492–1975)* (New York: Harper Collins, 2007).

7 Claret Miranda, *El atroz desmoche* 2006. See also, as part of a growing line of historical research on the Spanish university under Franquismo, in this case with particular attention to criminal law professors: Juan Carlos Ferré Olivé. Universidad y Guerra Civil: Lección inaugural Curso Académico 2009–2010 (Huelva: Servicio de Publicaciones Universidad de Huelva, 2009).

8 The judicial instructor of the university depuration commission that restored Trias de Bes to his chair of international law at Barcelona University highlighted the 'unconditional adhesion' made evident 'by our government in appointing him to different political posts'. Among many other honours received during the Franco's period in subsequent years, Trias de Bes became a member of the Royal Academy of Moral and Political Sciences and held, until near his death, the role of director and chief international legal advisor at the Spanish Ministry of Foreign Affairs. Gascon y Marín, the author of two courses at The Hague Academy on the administrative international law and international civil service received numerous honours after the war including that of as President of the Association Francisco de Vitoria (…) and from 1953 to the time of his death in 1962 served as President of the Spanish Royal Academy of Moral and Political Sciences.

entanglement in an imagery of anti-liberal, nationalist and ultra-catholic references was intensified by a wave of exaltation of the fatherland, any attack on which was portrayed as the continuation of the deleterious effects of foreign intellectual mimesis on Spanish traditionalist thought, or else as crude Marxism. This ideology found its ultimate propagandist expression in the barely caricatural myth of the existence of a nebulous 'Judean-Masonic-Marxist' international conspiracy against Spain. For the new ruling Falangist intelligentsia, Marxism had to be portrayed as the 'antithesis' of the 'Spanish genius' and a 'fairly uncomfortable waiting room to hell'.[9]

This political and cultural climate was mirrored in the the first university law of the new totalitarian state, the University Law of 1943.[10] This decreed that the Spanish university would have as its 'supreme guidance, Christian dogma and morals'[11] while commanding 'the faithful service of the university to the ideals of the Falange which inspire the State.'[12] The law, furthermore,

---

Another a member of the Association Francisco de Vitoria, the author of course at The Hague Academy on 'Regionalism in the International Organization' in 1935, just before the Spanish Civil War erupted, was Jose Ramón Orue y Arregui (1894–1953) was 'rehabilitated without sanction' by the Tribunal for the Depuration of University professors in his university post in the Republican Valencia from which he had been suspended after a satisfactory study of his 'ideology, conduct and adhesion to the glorious National movement.' Other members of the Association will, as we shall see, developed successful careers. See i.e. AGA, secció Educación, IDD 1.08, lligall 32/45/15054, expediente personal de Josep Maria Trias de Bes Giró (núm. 6) quoted in Jaume Claret Miranda, la repressió franquista a la universitat española. Tesis Doctorales en Xarxa http://www.tdx.cat/handle/10803/7463 124. See also, Jose Maria Trias de Bes y Giro, 'La Organización Internacional. Discurso leído en el acto de su recepción como académico de número contestación del Académico de número Excmo. Sr. D. José de Yanguas y Messía' (Madrid: Imprenta Viuda de Galo Sáez 1947). See also Luis Jordana de Pozas, 'El profesor Gascón y Marín y su obra' Revista de Estudios de la Vida Local 125 (1962) 641–672 and Maria Fernanda Mancebo, 'Consecuencias de la guerra civil en la universidad valencia: depuraciones y exilios' Cuadernos del instituto Antonio de Nebrija 4 (2001), 165–188.

9 José Cortes Grau 'Nuestro anti-comunismo' *Revista de Estudios Políticos* 35–36 (1947) 129–137.

10 Ley de 9 de julio de 1943 sobre ordenación de la Universidad Española. Boletín Oficial del Estado, Numero 2012, 7406–7431, 31 de Julio 1943.

11 Preamble. Id.

12 Ley de 9 de julio de 1943 Artículo tercero 'La Universidad inspirándose en el sentido católico, consubstancial a la tradición universitaria española, acomodará sus enseñanzas a las del dogma y de la moral católica y a las normas del Derecho canónico vigente'. Artículo cuarto 'La Universidad española, en armonía con los ideales del Estado nacionalsindicalista, ajustará sus enseñanzas y sus tareas educativas a los puntos programáticos del Movimiento'

proclaimed that after the 'crusade that has saved Western civilization,' the University Law must "embody a deep mutation of spirits in the transformation of the university order which, while tying itself to the glorious Hispanic tradition, adapts itself to the norms and the statute of a new State. This is the antithesis of liberalism and the implacable executor of the sacred trust of the dead: to bring back to Spain its unity, its greatness, and its freedom."[13] This purist Spanish re-foundation was asserted against the background of what the law describes as 'generations of decadence' in Spanish universities fostered by academic freedom, foreign intellectualism, and secularism, culminating in the arrival of the Second Spanish Republic, 'which threw universities well down the path toward annihilation and denationalization to the point that the most monstrous national denials surged from their own entrails'.[14] The national academic re-foundation was to be inspired by the classical model of the Universidad de Salamanca which 'at a time of the advent of national unity and the sounding of the universal hour of Spain,'[15] became, according to the law, the 'creator of a teleological army that is willing to enter into battle against heresy to defend the religious unity of Europe and the missionary Falange that must affirm the Catholic unity of the globe.' From the classrooms of Salamanca—the 1943 University Law went on—emerged 'the doctrine that forged humanism in the national soul, Christianizing the paganism of the Renaissance [...] the definition of the law of peoples [...], science; in sum, a Spain one and universal in the Catholic spirit through which it was possible to dominate the world with the greatest empire in history.'[16]

The doctrine of 'National-Catholicism', which was a Spanish variant of interwar 'clerical Fascism',[17] became the ever-impregnating ideological basis of the Spanish state and, by extension, of all Spanish universities. The doctrine was enshrined in the 1943 Law 'in harmony with the ideals of the national-syndicalist state,' which decreed that the university should 'adapt its teaching and educational plan to the programmatic points of The Movement.'[18] Accordingly, all Spanish universities were presided over by a member of the Spanish Falange for the next decades. Moreover, during the Franco's period, all generations of Spanish lecturers and professors in all university ranks, including

---

13 Preamble, Id.

14 Id.

15 Id.

16 Ley de 9 de julio de 1943, Preface.

17 See comparatively Matthew Feldman/ Marius Turda/ Tudor Georgescu (eds.) *Clerical Fascism in Interwar Europe* (London: Routledge 2013).

18 Ley de 9 de julio de 1943, Article 4.

all Spanish international law professors, were requested to sign an official document declaring 'their firm adhesion to the fundamental principles of the State accredited by a certificate of the General Secretary of The Movement.'[19] These obligations were also extended to students, all of whom should 'belong to the University Syndicate of the Traditionalist Spanish Falange and of the Assemblies of the National Syndicalist Offensive'[20] according to the new Spanish University Law of 1943.[21]

## The Fascist Mimesis of International Law in Spain and the Axis Temptation

In 1941, the inaugural editorial of Revista de Estudios Políticos, flagship of the Franco regime's think-tank, Instituto de Estudios Políticos,[22] pledged the journal to be at the service of the 'whole and radical truth' of the Movimiento Nacional in the construction of a functional knowledge that 'now more than ever is required from us to be urgently sure'.[23] The first issue of Revista de Estudios Políticos also contained a translation of Carl Schmitt's 'The concept of Empire in International Law'[24] where he celebrated how 'the action of the Führer has provided political reality, historical truth and a splendid future to the idea of our empire in International Law'.[25] The Schmittian defense of the 'concept of empire as the cornerstone of international law'[26] was theoretically grounded on the notion of *Weltanschauung*[27] and on the related claim that any domestic political changes in a State should result in changes in the international legal community. The latter was a corollary of Schmitt's critique of the liberal international legal order epitomized by the Versailles' model of international law, which Schmitt decried as one stemming from abstract normativism. Its publication in the flagship of the

19 Ley de 9 de julio de 1943, Articles 58.4, articles 62 b) and articles 64.

20 Ley de 9 de julio de 1943, Article 70.

21 A detailed summary of the contents of Chapter 5 can be found in the 'Introduction'.

22 José Menendez, 'From Republicanism to Fascist Ideology' 2003.

23 Alfonso García Valdecasas, 'Editorial' 1 *Revista de Estudios Políticos* (1941), 5–6, at 6.

24 Carl Schmitt, 'El concepto de imperio en el Derecho internacional' (trad. de Javier F. Conde) 1 *Revista de Estudios Políticos*, (1941), 83–101.

25 Schmitt, 'El concepto de imperio en el Derecho internacional' 1941, 100.

26 Id., 99.

27 See Anthony Carty, 'Carl Schmitt's critique of Liberal International Legal Order Between 1933 and 1945', *Leiden Journal of International Law* 14 (2001), 25–36.

Franco regime's think-tank, Instituto de Estudios Políticos,[28] mirrored the ascendancy of the fascist mimesis in Spanish international legal thought. Schmitt's reflections were, indeed, presented to the Falangist intelligentsia as an illustration of 'how the profound transformations of the world we are living through are accompanied by the renovation of political concepts'.[29] This was in consonance with the Spanish own 'will of Empire' proclaimed in the Falange's twenty-seven program points.[30]

In the aftermath of the Spanish Civil War, Schmitt's intellectual relationship to Spain was already long-standing. As early as the late 1920s, prominent Spanish intellectual figures had commented upon Schmitt's political thought, and some of his fundamental books had been translated into Spanish in the 1930s.[31] Moreover, Schmitt himself had engaged in a dialogue in the late 1920s with the 'theologized politics of dictatorship'[32] of a mid-19th century reactionary Spanish philosopher, Juan Donoso Cortes whose reputation, as well as the role that his works played in the Francoist intelligentsia's debates,[33] owes considerably to this Schmittian affiliation.[34] Schmitt's enduring relationship with Spain, which has been portrayed as one of 'reciprocal effect',[35] continued far

28 José Menendez, 'From Republicanism to Fascist Ideology' 2003.

29 Id., 83.

30 The third point of the Phalanx program points reads in Spanish as follows: 'Tenemos voluntad de imperio. Afirmamos que la plenitud histórica de España es el Imperio. Reclamamos para España un puesto preeminente en Europa. No soportamos ni el aislamiento internacional ni la mediatización extranjera. Respecto de los países de Hispanoamérica, tendemos a la unificación de cultura, de intereses económicos y de poder. España alega su eje espiritual del mundo hispánico como título de preeminencia en las empresas universales'.

31 Vid, among others, C. Schmitt, *La defensa de la constitución,* (trad. M.Sánchez Sarto) (Barcelona: Ed. Labor, 1931). C. Schmitt, *La Teoría de la Constitucion* (trad. F. Ayala) (Madrid: Editorial Revista de Derecho Internacional Privado 1934).

32 See Jan Werner Muller, *A Dangerous Mind: Carl Schmitt in Post-War European Thought,* (New Haven and London: Yale University Press 2003), 133.

33 Jose Corts Grau, 'Perfil actual de Donoso Cortés', Revista de Estudios Políticos 19–20 (1945) 74–120. Especially thanks to their re-interpretation through monarchical traditionalist lenses by Alvaro d'Ors, See José Antonio López García, 'La presencia de Carl Schmitt en España', *Revista de estudios políticos* 91 (1996), 139–168, 140.

34 This long relationship would culminate in his book C. Schmitt, *Donoso Cortés in gesamteuropäischer Interpretation,* (Cologne: Greven Verlag 1950).

35 José María Beneyto, *Politische Theologie ais politische Theorie. Eine Untersuchung zur Rechts- und Staatstheorie Cari Schmitts und zu ihrer Wirkungsgeschichte in Spanien,* (Berlin: Dunckcr und Humblot 1983), 18. See also A.Truyol y Serra, *Historia de la Filosofía del Derecho y del Estado* 2004, 313–319.

beyond the Second World War at both the affective[36] and intellectual levels.[37] However, in the early 1940s, the Spanish political-academic elites, who were invested in laying the foundations of a totalitarian state, were mostly interested in the possibilities that Schmitt's works offered for the theoretical legitimatization of the Franco regime.

During this early Franquoist period, in which as López García noted 'Carl Schmitt's theoretical positions are not simply assumed, but yet will serve as inexcusable reference for the legal-political debate of the epoch',[38] Schmitt's main works were mainly translated into Spanish by his foremost Spanish disciple, Francisco Javier Conde (1908–1974). Conde attempted in his own work to 'glocalise'[39] Schmitt's theoretical foundations to better allow their adaptation to the conforming features of the new Spanish political regime. Adapted to the transcendental theological legitimacy basis—'*creatio a Deo*'—of the Francos's regime, Schmitt's conceptual schemes played a pivotal role in the regime's political theory. This was in urgent need of a solid theoretical basis to legitimize from a totalitarian perspective its *coup d'état* against the democratic second Spanish Republic. This was a task to which, as we saw in Chapter Four, several Spanish international lawyers, such as Yanguas Messia and Trias de Bes, actively contributed in 1939, through inter alia their re-interpretations of the Spanish classics of international law, as members of the Committee of twenty-one jurists who drafted the 'Advisory Opinion on the Illegitimacy of the Acting Powers on the 18th of July 1936'.[40] Conde also became the main theorist of the concept of 'caudillaje.' The ideological justification of this Spanish variant of absolute leadership was theoretically premised in his work on the 'transcendence/immanence dichotomy' with the former overcoming the latter, so as to underpin the legitimization of the

36 See the very interesting Truyol's personal recollections and doctrinal considerations on Carl Schmitt in Antonio Truyol y Serra, *Historia de la Filosofía del Derecho y del Estado, vol. 3. Idealismo y positivismo* (Madrid: Alianza Ed 2004) 313–319.

37 See Piet Tommissen, 'Miroir de Carl Schmitt', 16 *Cahiers Vilfredo Pareto* (1978) 220–275. The longstanding nature of this relationship is evidenced by the fact that by the dawn of the democratic period in 1978 Spain occupied the top post of the international ranking by number of translations of the Schmitt's opus. Of the 85 works of C. Schmitt referred by Tommissen, 34 were translated in Spanish (of which 31 in Spain). The second country in translations of C. Schmitt was by that date Italy with 15 of his works translated.

38 López García, 'La presencia de Carl Schmitt' 1996, 140.

39 See, as the most representative, Francisco Javier Conde, *Teoría y sistema de las formas políticas*, (Madrid: Instituto de Estudios Políticos, 1944).

40 Dictamen de la Comisión sobre ilegitimidad de poderes actuantes en 18 de julio de 1936 (Madrid: Editora Naciona, 1939), 18.

leader using a genuine updated source from the Spanish historical tradition. This theoretical construction derives from the Schmittian critique of Kelsen's attempt to construct an order of abstract norms and it was fundamental to provide Franco, the 'caudillo' of Spain 'by the grace of God and only accountable to God and History' with an elaborate legitimizing political theory equivalent to those that crowned the Duce and the Führer's totalitarian regimes.

Conde's familiarity with Schmitt owed much to the fellowship he obtained from the Council of Extension of Studies and Scientific Research (the JAE) to study in Berlin in the early 30s.[41] During the Spanish Civil War, the JAE disappeared. It was provisionally replaced in 1938 by the Instituto de España, and from 1939 by the Consejo Superior de Investigaciones Cientificas (Spanish High Council of Scientific Research) under the control of Phalanx. In this, he was not alone. However, the work of Conde, as well as, we have seen in earlier chapters, the work of other legal scholars who also went to contribute to legitimizing the Franco regime's political regime, stemmed, paradoxically enough, from an institutional attempt at modernizing Spanish science inspired by the Krausism of the Institución de Libre Enseñanza[42] (1876–1936). In this he was not alone. The intellectual work of Kelsen's main disciple and translator into Spanish, Luis Legaz Lacambra (1906–1980), a beneficiary in the 1930s as well of JAE's academic support in a country with a staggering 32% illiteracy rate in 1930, was also directly relevant to the evolution of Spanish international legal academia during this period.

Legaz Lacambra was one of the Spanish legal philosophers of this academic generation who developed a keener interest in international legal matters.[43] He became also, along with Conde, one of most remarkable political and legal theorists of early Franquismo.[44] In 1939, Legaz made appear the name of the founder of Phalange on a par with Hans Kelsen[45] in 'La théorie pure du droit

41 See Alberto Reig Tapia, 'Aproximación a la teoría del caudillaje en Francisco Javier Conde' 69 *Revista de Estudios Políticos* (nueva época), (1990), 61–81.

42 For an introduction, see Elías Díaz, *La filosofía social del krausismo español*, (Madrid: Edicusa 1973).

43 See, e.g., Luis Legaz Lacambra 'El Derecho internacional en el pensamiento de Ortega y Gasset' 111 *Revista de Estudios Políticos* (1960) 5–41.

44 See Luis García Arias, 'Perfil humano, universitario y científico del profesor Legaz y Lacambra' in *Estudios Jurídico-Sociales, Homenaje al profesor Luis Legaz y Lacambra*, (Santiago: Universidad de Santiago de Compostela, 1960) 15–81, 17.

45 At the time an émigré law scholar in Geneva, see briefly Nicoletta Bersier Ladavac, 'Hans Kelsen (1881–1973) Biographical Note and Bibliography' European Journal of International Law 9 (1998), 391–400.

et la pensée politique de José Antonio Primo de Rivera'[46] published in La révue internationale de la théorie du droit. In the early 1940s, Legaz Lacambra became the main Spanish theoretician of the single party with his 'Introduction to the Theory of the Syndicalist-National State', in which he builds on the crisis of the liberal State to defend the theorization of the single party as a militant ecclesia.[47]

Luis García Arias, one of the most noted representatives of the post-Spanish Civil War generation and its neo-naturalist international law revival in the 1940s, provided a retrospective intellectual portrait of Legaz Lacambra in the early 1940s. Garcia Arias described Legaz 'as one of the most authoritative theorists of Spanish legal, philosophical and political thought, the mission of which is to come up with a precise synthesis of Hispanic thought and thus contribute to forming a new order of concepts where the state and the man, the person and the country, are not merely reciprocally implicated in an indestructible unity. Instead—as Legaz himself argued—they could not be understood outside their service to norms and moral values which constitute the patrimony of mankind.'[48] In his panegyric, Garcia Arias also stressed that a 'common political orientation around the meaning of the National Movement and the possibilities it offered for the greatness of the country' united him, then a young professor at the University of Zaragoza, and others with Legaz at a time of the return to the universities 'of the students who exchanged books for weapons to liberate Spain from spiritual and material disintegration.'[49]

Less than ten years before, however, Legaz Lacambra had mainly been known for being a gifted student of the father of the normativist strand of legal positivism to whose work he had devoted his doctoral dissertation.[50] He soon distinguished himself as the prologue writer and translator into Spanish of an abridged version of Reine Rechtslehre in 1933[51] and, soon afterwards,

---

46 Luis Legaz Lacambra, 'La théorie pure du droit et la pensée politique de José Antonio Primo de Rivera', *Révue internationale de la théorie du droit* (1939).

47 Luis Aurelio Gónzalez Prieto, 'La concreción teórica del partido único español franquista' 141 *Revista Estudios Políticos* (2008), 41–68.

48 García Arias, 'Perfil humano, universitario y científico del profesor Legaz' 1960, 15–81.

49 Id., 17.

50 Luis Legaz Lacambra, *Kelsen. Estudio crítico de la teoría pura del Derecho y del Estado en la Escuela de Viena*, (Prol. Luis Recaséns Siches), (Barcelona: Casa Bosch 1933).

51 Hans Kelsen, *El método y los conceptos fundamentales de la teoría pura del Derecho*, (trad. Luis Legaz Lacambra) (Madrid: Ed. Revista de Derecho Privado 1933).

of Kelsen's General Theory of Law, among others.[52] By the outbreak of the Spanish Civil War in 1936, Legaz had also already published various essays on international legal issues. The themes of these essays ranged from an examination of the validity of international law in defense of the unity of the universal legal order, following Alfred Verdross,[53] to a long commentary arguably written under the scholarly inspiration of the works of Francisco Suárez[54] on the primacy of international law over domestic law pursuant to Article 7 of the 1931 Spanish Constitution. In 1934, his essay 'The Primacy of the Spiritual in the Construction of International Law: the Sociological-axiological Basis of Nationalism and Internationalism' appeared.[55] It was published in an edited volume that gathered together a number of works that emerged from a Conference celebrating the Founding Act of the Catholic Union of International Studies of the Spanish Group of the Union of Fribourg[56] in the early 30ies; a period, as we saw in the previous chapter, when the associational internationalist movement thrived in Spain. Legaz, who was by then the Vice-President of the International Catholic Student Association, contributed a piercing analysis of a series of inter-war authors and international legal debates. These fitted in perfect consonance in a book where the Spanish expression 'entrechocar de civilizaciones' (meaning literally 'clash of civilizations') is employed to refer to the looming threat posed by the crisis of the League of Nations[57] in view of the rise of East Asia, North America and other regions of the world. Although conservative in orientation, Legaz had kept himself in the early 30ies at a prudent distance from the legal philosophy of National-Socialism, a subject to which he had devoted an essay published

52 By the 30s and early 40s, Legaz's contribution to scientific translations into Spanish was considerable. This includes his prologues, epilogues and 'additions' to works by Kelsen, Mirkine-Guetzèvitch, Sauer, Mayer, Holstein, Larenz or Mosca among others.

53 Luis Legaz Lacambra, 'La validez del Derecho Internacional (Estudio de teoría jurídica pura)' *Universidad* 8 (1931).

54 Luis Legaz Lacambra 'Las garantías constitucionales del Derecho internacional' *Revista de Derecho Público*, Madrid (1933).

55 Luis Legaz Lacambra 'Las primacía de lo espiritual en la construcción jurídica internacional. Las bases sociológico-axiológicas del nacionalismo y del internacionalismo' in *Estudios Internacionales*. (Madrid: Publicaciones del Grupo Español de la Unión de Friburgo, 1934).

56 See Pedro Sangro y Ros de Olano, 'La unión católica de estudios internacionales' in *Estudios Internacionales*. (Madrid: Publicaciones del Grupo Español de la Unión de Friburgo 1934), 9–26.

57 Id., 20.

in 1934 noting that 'one cannot applaud with a rigorous ethical criterion the curious mix that [National-Socialism] engenders between trans-personalism of a high idealist connotation and the infra-personalism of biological taints'.[58]

However, the influence of National-Socialist legal theory would become apparent in Legaz's academic production during the Civil War. This found Legaz collaborating with the Section of Studies of the Ministry of Organization and Unionist Action, established by Franco's Government in Burgos,[59] as well as with Jerarquía (1937–1938), the so-called 'black journal of the Falange'. Profoundly embedded in the doctrine of the 'Movimiento Nacional', Legaz's work in the aftermath of the Civil War was depicted by its own author as an evolution of 'the theory of justice to the question of 'personalism' and 'trans-personalism', taking a 'personalist' position combined with a sociological universalism'.[60] Such a sociological orientation may be the result of the influence on Legaz's output of José Ortega y Gasset (1883–1955), to whose perspective of 'international law as an ensemble of norms which usurp the real international law', Legaz would dedicate a long study some years later.[61] This sociological perspective became dominant in Legaz's work during the first half of the 1940s leading him, partly under the inspiration of the works of G. Gentile,[62] to the realm of social organicism. Moreover, it led to his interest in the philosophical underpinnings of Labor Law and social policy,[63] which was Legaz's main contribution to the construction of the new Spanish state in the very early years of Franquismo. The influence of Legaz, who also became the President of the Association Francisco de Vitoria, continued to partly undergird the philosophical orientation, and the related selection of topics,[64] including through his own subsequent works on Francisco de Vitoria and the

58 Luis Legaz Lacambra, 'La filosofía jurídica del Nacional-Socialismo', 1 *Universidad* XI (1934).

59 During the war, Legaz collaborated with the Section of Studies of the Ministry of Organization and Unionist Action established in Santander. Of this period is his Cuatro estudios sobre sindicalismo vertical, Zaragoza (1938).

60 Aditional note to Sauer's Filosofía Jurídica y Social quoted in Garcia Arias 'Adiciones sobre la historia de la doctrina hispánica' 1949, 28.

61 Luis Legaz Lacambra, 'El Derecho internacional en el pensamiento de Ortega y Gasset' 111 *Revista de Estudios Políticos* (1960) 5–41 at 24.

62 Luis Legaz Lacambra 'La filosofía jurídica de Giovanni Gentile' *Revista de la Universidad de Santiago*, 1941.

63 Luis Legaz Lacambra, *Introducción a la teoría del Estado nacionalsindicalista*, (Barcelona: Casa Bosch, 1940) Barcelona (1940).

64 Vid section II (infra).

School of Salamanca,[65] of the new Spanish doctrine of international law which was forged in the aftermath of the Spanish Civil War.

The early reception of Schmitt, which as Lopez Garcia has noted, was 'not comparable to the reception of any other European intellectual associated with the European fascist regimes',[66] marks the peak of the 1939–1942 period of 'fascist mimesis' in the Spanish international legal academia. A number of essays on international themes appeared in the pages of the scholarly journal of the Falange's brain trust, Revista de Estudios Políticos, during this period of maximum exposure to the ideological underpinnings of the New Order. This internationalist scholarly production combined news of legal developments in foreign jurisdictions with articles tackling 'the radical transformation of Spanish law and essays on totalitarian legal scholarship'.[67] This was consonant with the Spanish foreign policy's 'Axis temptation'[68] during World War II.

Although heavily supported by ideologically-close regimes in Germany, Italy, and Portugal during the Civil War, Franco's foreign policy maintained a strategy of 'double diplomacy,' aimed at preserving the international British-led regime of non-intervention in Spain during the Civil War and achieving the recognition of Franco's new state by most European powers. However, a shift in strategy became apparent in a number of Franco's pro-Axis alignment steps in the last months of the Civil War and its immediate aftermath. These included the signing of a cultural agreement with Germany in January 1939, a Spanish-German treaty of Friendship in March 1939, the Spanish incorporation in the Antikominternpakt (March 1939) and Spain's definitive withdrawal from the League of Nations in May 1939. The substitution of the traditionalist pro-British General Jordana as Minister of Foreign Affairs by J.L. Beigbeder, a colonel of the North African Spanish army and Military Governor of North Morocco, in August 1939, confirmed the ascendancy of the Falangist conception of an 'external variant' of the Spanish triumphal national revolution. These foreign policy measures, despite being wrapped in an official declaration of strict neutrality in World War II, signaled General Franco's clear preference for a pro-Axis foreign tilt and both mirrored and further nurtured the fascistization of Spanish international legal academia in the aftermath of the Spanish Civil War. The climax of this academic fascistization reached its

65 See e.g. Luis Legaz Lacambra, 'Lo medieval y lo moderno en Francisco de Vitoria' (Santiago de Compostela: Universidad de Santiago 1947), 297–333.

66 Jose Luis Lopez García, 'La presencia de Carl Schmitt' 1996, 140.

67 Menendez 'From Republicanism to Fascist Ideology' 2003, 345.

68 Paul Preston, *The Politics of Revenge. Fascism and the Military in 20th Century Spain*, Routledge, London (1995) at 51–84.

peak with the military defeat of France. This was soon followed in June 1940 by a Spanish declaration of non-belligerency and the appointment of the head of the Falange, R. Serrano Suñer, Franco's own brother-in-law, who was known for his pro-Third Reich stance, as Minister of Foreign Affairs in September 1940.[69]

Consonant with the defining international and domestic political atmosphere of the time is how the leading article of the first issue of Revista de Estudios Politicos featured the Prologue to 'Reivindicaciones de España' alongside the translation of Schmitt's work in 1941.[70] 'Reivindicaciones de España' was a book that had been awarded the Spanish National Prize for Literature in 1941 for elaborating in extenso on the legal-historical titles that supported the Franco regime's neo-colonialist pretensions. In this republished Prologue, one of the founders of the Spanish Falange, Alfonso García Valdecasas (1904–1993), who was also the first director of the Instituto de Estudios Politicos, strongly criticizes 'sinister groups of increasing influence who are systematically opposed to anything meaning Spanish affirmation: Marxists, republicans, separatists, all of them joined by the same idea: abandoning all foreign enterprise.'[71] Instead, Valdecasas highlighted the importance of the book in the current 'experimental period in the constitution of the State',[72] itself conceived of as a 'totalitarian instrument at the service of the integrity of the motherland'[73] based on the 'the original characters of the Spanish political conception,'[74] one that is 'for us not only physical, territorial or geographic, but also a moral one'.[75]

The two coauthors of 'Reivindicaciones de España' became Ministers of Foreign Affairs of Spain in the following decades. One of them, Fernando María Castiella (1907–1976) who was the chair-holder of international law at University of La Laguna since 1935, and had been appointed a member of The Hague Permanent Court of Arbitration in 1939, was the Director of the Spanish Society of International and Colonial Studies at the time he co-wrote 'Reivindicaciones de España'. Soon thereafter, in 1942–43, Castiella enlisted as a volunteer in the Wehrmacht's Einheit Spanischer Freiwillliger, best known

69 Vid. e.g. Jose Luis Neila Hernández, 'La sublevación y la improvisación de una política exterior de Guerra, 1936–1939' in J. Tussell, J. Aviles & R. Pardo (eds.) La política exterior de España en el siglo XX (Madrid: Ed. Biblioteca nueva, 2000), 263–297, 289.

70 Alfonso García Valdecasas, 'Política Exterior' *Revista de Estudios Políticos,* 1 (1941) 7–16.

71 Id., 11.

72 Alfonso García Valdecasas, 'Los estados totalitarios y el Estado español', Revista de estudios políticos 4 (1942) 5–32, 24.

73 Id., at 26.

74 Id., at 32.

75 Id., at 27.

as the Blue Division—a military contingent which assembled more than 47,000 Spanish volunteers, for whom the fight against communism, especially, in the siege of Leningrad during the 2nd World War was a continuation of the crusading spirit of the Spanish Civil War. Castiella's long influential shadow, as the longest serving Spanish Minister of Foreign Affairs (1957–1969) in the 20th century, appears inextricably linked, as we shall later see, to the organic evolution of Spanish international legal academia during the different adaptive phases of Franco's foreign policy. The other co-author of Reivindicaciones de España, José Maria de Areilza (1909–1998), after a long career, which thrived during the ministerial tenure of Castiella, as a Spanish Ambassador of the Francoist state, became Minister of Foreign Affairs at the dawn of the Spanish Democratic Transition (1975–1976). Four decades earlier, the Spanish territorial claims on Western North Africa contained in Castiella and Areilza's book, which attributed domestic decadence to the Spanish 'humiliating subjugation' to British and French influence in foreign affairs, constituted the *casus belli* for the Franco regime's negotiations to enter the Second World War alongside the Axis powers.

After Spain's forced withdrawal from its last overseas colonies in the aftermath of the 1898 Spanish-American war, the substitute North-African orientation of Spanish foreign policy was, as we saw in Chapters Two and Three, initially facilitated by Spain's role as an equilibrium factor in England and France's contest for the Western Mediterranean.[76] Spain's long-standing competition with France in North Africa extended over a period of three decades and underwent various fluctuations, including a military struggle against Abd-el-Krim, the leader of a nationalist uprising in the Rif province in the 1920s. This contributed, as we saw in earlier chapters, to the crisis that triggered the pronunciamiento in 1923 by General Miguel Primo de Rivera—the father of the charismatic founder of the Spanish Falange. The arrival of the Second Republic, which had been seen with deep mistrust by the Africanist and isolated military elite-like special forces in Morocco occurred after 'the pacification of the Spanish zone had been completed and colonization plans became effective.'[77] Azaña's government's decision to 'review the privileges awarded during the dictatorship' to Africanists constituted 'a turning point'[78] in the relationship between the Second Republic and the Spanish military forces

76 See Susana Sueiro Seona, 'La política exterior de España en los años 20: una política mediterránea con proyección africana' in Javier Tussell/ J.Aviles/ Rosa Pardo (Eds.) La política exterior de España en el siglo XX, (Madrid: Ed. Biblioteca Nueva 2000), 135–157.

77 La Porte, 'Civil Military Relations in the Spanish Protectorate in Morocco' 2011, 220.

78 Id.

deployed in North Africa. The heightening of domestic tensions was illustrated by José Sanjurjo, the director of the Alhucemas' campaign[79] who plotted a coup against the Second Republic in 1932, and in the severe repression suffered by the Asturian miners in their uprising (known as the Revolution of Asturias) in 1934 with the deployment of legionnaires from Morocco. This historical background was deeply felt by the Africanist General Franco and paved the way for the Spanish neo-colonial claims during the period of fascist mimesis.

The Spanish territorial demands examined in 'Reivindicaciones de España' included the return of Gibraltar, the extension of Spanish sovereignty over French Morocco and Tangiers, and the expansion of the Spanish Sahara, the Oran region of Algeria, territories around the Red Sea and Conchinchina, and Spanish Guinea. During the long, and well-documented, Spanish-German negotiations over entering World War II,[80] these colonialist pretensions were mainly addressed to the bargaining chip of French Morocco. Confronted with the dilemma of needing to reconcile conflicting demands by potential allies, these plans were ultimately halted by Hitler's strategic calculation of a likely risk of the French colonies deserting from Vichy's Metropolitan France[81] if Germany agreed to the Spanish demands.[82] Paradoxically enough, the very same Spanish imperialist pretensions contained in Areilza and Castiella's book were later used by the regime to spread the myth of one of Franco's greatest historical triumphs in Spanish public opinion. Franco was, then, portrayed as the leader who, by conditioning his belligerence to the fulfillment of those neo-imperialist demands, 'was able to say no to Hitler,' or at least 'not yet,' and thus helped to cunningly preserve the shattered Spain from the horrors of World War II. The historically hushing up of the Spanish 'pragmatic enthusiasm'[83] for collaborating with the New Order would keep

---

79 Jose Sanjurjo died in a plane crash when he was to assume the leadership of the rebellion against the Spanish Republic initiated in the North of Morocco on the 17th of July 1936.

80 See e.g. Stanley G. Payne, Franco and Hitler, Spain, Germany and World War II, (New Haven: Yale University Press 2008).

81 See Norman J.W. Goda 'Franco's Bid for Empire: Spain, Germany and the Western Mediterranean in World War II' in Raanan Rein (ed.) *Spain and the Mediterranean since 1898*, (London & Portland: Franck Cass 1999), 168–194 and e.g. Wayne H. Bowen *Spaniards and Nazi Germany. Collaboration in the New Order* (Columbia and London, University of Missouri Press 2000).

82 Reported as one of the various junctures that might have decided the fate of the Second World War, these failed negotiations were soon to be followed by a new focus of the Axis' war effort on the Russian front.

83 Wayne H. Bowen Spaniards and Nazi Germany. Collaboration in the New Order (Columbia and London: University of Missouri Press 2000), 229.

the phalangist propaganda[84] busy at different reprises during the following decades.[85] However, this did not prevent Garcia Arias, one of the paramount defenders of the natural law tradition of the 'Spanish Classics' of international law, to consider in 1949 'Reivindicaciones de España' as 'the fundamental work on our foreign policy in over a hundred years'.[86]

'Reivindicaciones de España' was, however, far from being the only work produced by Spanish international lawyers that put itself at the service of an imperially oriented Spanish foreign policy agenda in this period of ideological affinity with the Axis powers. This ideological affinity was compounded by Franco's gratitude for Italian and German military aid during the recent Civil War[87] and Spain's onerous external financial debt to its civil war allies. Some Spanish international lawyers, such as José Yanguas Messía[88] were particularly keen to contribute to the nationalist front and the exaltation of Spanishness. The founder of the Association Francisco de Vitoria in 1926 during his term as Minister of Foreign Affairs in Miguel Primo de Rivera's regime was, as we saw in Chapter Three and Four, an active member of the Francoist Burgos government's Junta de Defensa Nacional during the Civil War. In the 1940s and 1950s, after leaving his post as Ambassador to the Holy See, he continued to develop a career marked with honours as member of the National Council of the Spanish Falange. Yanguas presided over several Spanish Royal Academies, such as those of Moral and Political Sciences and Law and Jurisprudence and, *ad maiorem gloriam* to his long-standing 'devotion to the cause of international law', he also presided over the Institut de Droit International in 1956.

Other Spanish international legal academics produced a range of similarly assertive works on foreign policy issues. In 1939, Camilo Barcia Trelles,

---

84 The dogmatic truth was flagged on the capitulation day of 8th May 1945 in the Editorial of the Spanish mainstream journal ABC: 'Franco appears to be chosen by God's Providence. When everything was obscure, he saw through it (...) and kept and defended the Spanish neutrality Quoted in Julio Gil Pecharromán, La política exterior del franquismo: Entre Hendaya y El Aaiún. (Barcelona: Ed. Flor de Viento 2008) at 131.

85 Also in the panegyric published in Revista de Estudios Políticos on the occasion of Castiella's appointment as Spain's foreign affairs Minister in 1957 Jan Werner Muller, A Dangerous Mind: A Carl Schmitt in Post-War European Thought, (New Haven and London: Yale University Press 2003), 133.

86 Garcia Arias 'Adiciones sobre la historia de la doctrina hispánica' 1949, 511.

87 See e.g. Nathaniel Berman, 'Le clivage de l'internationalisme face aux guerres d'Espagne et de Bosnie: entre 'alliance' et 'localization' in N. Berman, *Passions et Ambivalences. Le colonialisme, le nationalisme et le droit international* (Paris: A. Pédone, 2008), 235–275.

88 Adolfo Miaja de la Muela, 'In Memoriam: José de Yanguas Messia (1890–1974)' 2 *Revista de instituciones europeas*, 1 (1975), 5–10.

the coiner of title of 'founder of modern international law' for Francisco de Vitoria who had barely escaped from Franco's repression during the civil war, published 'Puntos cardinales de la politica exterior española'[89] in support of the 'national cause'. Other works such as 'Aspects of the Universal Mission of Spain'[90] written by J. Cordero Torres, the first secretary of the Spanish Society of International and Colonial Studies (SICS), which headquarters had been transferred to the Institute Francisco de Vitoria, relied explicitly on the notion of Spanish *lebensraum*. Early nazification was also apparent in a future prominent international law scholar, Mariano Aguilar Navarro who published in 1944 an article in the flagship think tank of Phalange in which he qualified a conference pronounced in Madrid by Schmitt 'as the instance in which with greater intellectual authority has been defended the theory of *Lebensraum* in Spain'.[91] Aguilar also declared that 'political and military necessity has brought Schmitt to the position we defend by conviction, independently of the avatars of war'.[92]

By 1942, the entry of the United States in the Second World War and the British victories in North Africa had led the Caudillo to accept that 'there was no territorial compensation which could justify the risks now involved in going to war'.[93] Although Franco continued, nevertheless, to reserve the possibility to be exercised 'after the worst of the fighting was over, but before the division of the spoils',[94] the appointment as new Minister of Foreign Affairs of F. Gómez-Jordana[95] in September 1942 initiated a gradual re-orientation of the regime, and a slow move towards neutrality, ultra-Catholicism and fierce anti-communism as defining features of Spanish foreign policy. This resulted in the 'traditional right' progressively taking over from the decline of the 'new right' of the Falange. The ultimate nature of the Spanish regime as a 'fascist-ised

---

89 Camilo Barcia Trelles, Puntos cardinales de la politica exterior española, (Barcelona: Editorial Fe 1939).

90 José María Cordero Torres, *Aspectos de la misión universal de España*, (Madrid: Vicesecretaria de Educación popular 1942) See also Zacarías García Villada, *El destino de España en la Historia Universal*, (Madrid: Ed. Cultura Española 1940).

91 See Carl Schmitt, *Cambio de estructura del Derecho Internacional* (included in a supplementary sheet to *Revista de Estudios Políticos*), Madrid, junio (1943), 1–36.

92 Mariano Aguilar Navarro, 'La guerra en el orden internacional' 13 *Revista de Estudios Políticos* (1944) 23–88, at 33.

93 Paul Preston, *The Politics of Revenge. Fascism and the Military in 20th Century Spain*, Routledge, London (1995), at 78.

94 Ibid., at 62.

95 See Gil Pecharromán La política exterior del franquismo 2008, 91–95 on the *Begoña* bombings and the reform of the Ministry of Foreign Affairs introduced by Gómez-Jordana.

dictatorship' or, if preferred, as the 'missing link between fascist dictatorships and authoritarian regimes'[96] is shown by the ulterior process of introversion and ultra-catholic-oriented de-fascistization that accompanied the evolution of the Franco regime under the influence of both domestic political tensions and an ever-changing international stage.

In 1943, reflecting this change of orientation, the National Delegation of Propaganda issued a series of intellectual directive guidelines that to remind the Spanish academia in peremptory terms that 'the Spanish state is exclusively grounded on principles, political norms and a philosophical basis with a strict national character. In no circumstance will it be allowed to compare our State with other States which might appear similar, and even less to extract consequences of supposed foreign adaptations to our country'.[97] At a time when the Second World War was turning in favor of the allies, these instructions were oriented at warning the Falange's pro-Axis intelligentsia of the convenience of turning their attention towards a purist traditional Spanishness very much along the lines of the 'noli foras ire … in interiore Hispania habitat veritas' of the classic work of Angel Ganivet.

Indeed, the work of this Spanish diplomat, who had penned the Spanish Idearium (1898) published the same year as the Spanish-American war,[98] became one of the inspiring pillars of the new regime's rhetorical architecture. This 'essentialist' rhetoric was based on the discursive articulation of a gradual process of cultural reinvention of a strengthened Spanish national identity. The intellectual precedents lie in the debates on the 'Spanish science' animated by M. Menéndez Pelayo in the framework of which, as we saw in Chapter One, the figure of Francisco de Vitoria resurfaced in the late nineteenth century. It began to take its modern form at the beginning of the twentieth century[99] during the crisis of national identity that deeply influenced the political and intellectual life of the country and, as we saw in Chapter Two, also the study of international law in Spain, in the aftermath of the 'Disaster of 1898.' This historical background would, in time, contribute to the radicalization of a series of conservative and traditionalist ideological notions, some of which had seeped into Spanish rightist ideology from the discourse of the disillusioned

96 Ismael Saz Campos, *Fascismo y Franquismo,* Publicaciones de la Universidad de Valencia (2004) at 90.

97 Fernando Díaz-Plaja. *La España franquista en sus documentos.* (Barcelona: Plaza & Janés 1976), 139–140.

98 And soon before Ganivet committed suicide by throwing himself into the frozen waters of the river Dvina in Riga in 1898.

99 Id., 213.

post-1898 'regenerationism'. With the triumph of the Second Spanish Republic in the early 1930s, Catholic nationalism and the exaltation of a 'purist' intellectual tradition became reinforced by the Fascist core aim of national regeneration. This was channeled along the vectors of 'Spain's universal spiritual mission and the belief in an essential and unitary, as opposed to plural, Spain, whose roots lay in Castile and Catholicism.'[100] This ideological imagery found a political echo in the second of the Falange's 27 program points, in which Primo de Rivera portrayed Spain as having a 'unity of fate in the universal.' An enraged militant post-Civil War anti-Marxism came to complete the ideological triad of pillars sustaining the early Franco regime's constituency.[101]

The slow post-1943 political-ideological turn, which accompanied the decline of the Axis' war efforts, was reflected in the works of Spain's intellectual elites. It is clearly illustrated by the evolution of the most emblematic Falangist cultural journal, El Escorial. Managed by a group of high-profile intellectuals under the direction of Pedro Laín Entralgo,[102] since its establishment in 1940, the purpose of El Escorial had been that of contributing to the search for theoretical, ideological and cultural foundations for the new Spanish totalitarian state under the inspiration of the 'supreme director of our enterprises',[103] José Antonio Primo de Rivera. This intellectual endeavor involved the journal's editorial lobbying in favor of Spanish entry into the Second World War in defense of the New Order, the upholding of the Spanish neo-colonialist territorial claims and its defense of a national syndicalist community to construct a totalitarianism which, by blending existing ideas, would contribute to forging a new 'synthesis unclassifiable as either right or left'. However, by the mid-40s, El Escorial began to leave the political realm and to re-orientate its work towards literary and historical topics. This reorientation went hand in glove with the new prominence acquired by the perspectives of a revamped Catholic fundamentalism that claimed to find inspiration in the works of Francisco de Vitoria, Luis Vives, and Francisco Suarez.[104] This line of pure Spanish 'national thought'

100 See Sebastian Balfour, 'The Loss of Empire, Regenerationism, and the Forging of a Myth of National Identity' in ed. by Helen Graham and Jo Labanyi (eds) *Oxford Spanish Cultural Studies: An Introduction. The Struggle for Modernity*, (London: University Press 1995), 25–39, 29.

101 See Pedro Carlos González Cuevas, *Historia de las Derechas españolas. De la Ilustración a nuestros días.* Ed. (Madrid: Biblioteca Nueva 2000), 372–384.

102 See Pedro Laín Entralgo, *Desgargo de conciencia* (1930–1960) (Barcelona: Barral, 1970).

103 See e.g. Santos Juliá Díaz, Falange Liberal o Intelectuales Fascistas? Claves de razón práctica 121 (2002) 4–13. See also e.g. Manuel Jesus Lopez Baroni, El falangismo liberal y la transicion española 1, Revista Internacional de Pensamiento Politico 7 (2012), 467–490.

104 González Cuevas, *Historia de las Derechas españolas* 2000, 374–378.

would find, as the next section examines, a fertile soil in the works of the Spanish doctrine of international law.

Although, as Griffin noted, 'para-fascism and true phalangism would become increasingly peripheral to what remained at heart an authoritarian conservative system',[105] the intellectual activity of the Instituto de Estudios Políticos (IEP) and other parallel satellite think-tanks of the Movimiento continued to set the highest academic standards and to influence the regime's most important legislative emanations. Two of the key figures of the period of fascist mimesis, Francisco J. Conde—the main Spanish disciple of C. Schmitt who as someone well-versed in fascist and Nazi theories 'could push forward the half-baked ideas of Spanish reactionary thought into a more coherent (…) canon',[106] and Luis Legaz Lacambra—the gifted disciple of H. Kelsen in the 30s—served in the following years as directors of the Instituto de Estudios Políticos. The think tank of Phalanx, with which noted Spanish international lawyers collaborated, continued to play a key role through its various journals, reports, legal opinions and pre-legislative projects of political and legal transcendence during the next four decades of Franco's regime.

### The 'Vitorian' Aftermath and Autarchic Ostracism

With the fascist dream of the New Order and the New Europe[107] vanishing after the success of the D-Day landings in June 1944, and the increasing threat of an extension of the liberation struggle to communist guerrilla warfare and partisan activity in Spain,[108] the later stages of the Second World War witnessed a cautious Spanish diplomatic realignment with the Allies. 'Order, unity, and endurance'—such was the strategic formula that Luis Carrero Blanco,[109] by then Sub-Secretary of the Spanish Presidency, suggested to Franco in 1945 to

105 Roger Griffin (Ed.), *Fascism*, (Oxford: Oxford University Press 1995), 185.

106 See José Menendez, 'From Republicanism to Fascist Ideology' 2003, 350.

107 See Rafael García Pérez, 'La idea de la 'Nueva Europa' en el pensamiento nacionalista español de la inmediata posguerra 1939–1944' *Revista del Centro de Estudios Constitucionales* 5, (1990), 203–240.

108 See Geoffrey Swain, 'Stalin and Spain, 1944–1948' in Christian Leitz and David J. Dunthorn *Spain in an International Co*ntext, 1936–1959, (New York-Oxford: Berghahn Books 1999), 245–131.

109 Admiral Luis Carrero Blanco was killed in a terrorist bombing orchestrated by E.T.A. under the name 'Operation Ogre' when he was Spain's Prime Minister in 1973.

countervail the growing international hostility towards the only pro-Axis regime that had survived the end of the Second World War.[110] These guidelines, which coincided with the new management of Spanish foreign policy by Catholic elites under the direction of a new Spanish Minister of Foreign Affairs, Alberto Martín Artajo (1945–1957), had a profound influence on the thematic choices of Spanish international law scholars during the oft-called 'autarchic' Spanish period between 1945 and 1953.

The first stage of the period of Spain's international ostracism crystallized in the Potsdam Final Declaration of July 1945 which did not grant support for Spain's application to join the United Nations. Instead, it was agreed that a united front of the post-war allies should aim at a quarantine-like international isolation of Franco's regime. The allied goal was to weaken Franco's rule because of 'its origins, its nature, its record and its close association with the aggressor states,'[111] ideally so as to make possible a peaceful transition to democratic rule from within the regime. The aggressive diplomatic character of this initial stage was premised on an assessment that the geopolitical situation in the aftermath of the Second World War ruled out any possible direct foreign military intervention in Spain. This stage was presided over by the USSR-led diplomatic insistence on 'liquidating the last remnants of Fascism'. It reached its climax with the UN Security Council Res. 4 of 29 April 1946. This Resolution stressed the 'unanimous moral condemnation of the Franco regime in the Security Council'[112] and created a special subcommittee to conduct an investigation into any potential threat to international peace and security from the Franco regime. The Monitoring of the Spanish situation by the Security Council continued until Res. 10 of 4 November 1946 which referred the matter to the General Assembly. The subsequent GA Res. 39 (I) of 12 December 1946 imposed a regime of international sanctions against Spain.

In the text of this resolution, the Assembly declared itself 'convinced that the Fascist Franco Government of Spain, which was imposed by force upon the Spanish people with the aid of the Axis Powers and which gave material assistance to the Axis Powers in the war, does not represent the Spanish people and by its continued control of Spain is making the participation of the Spanish

---

110 Note of the 29th August 1945 in Alberto Martín Artajo's archives: Luis Carrero Blanco, 'Notas sobre la situación política' quoted in Florentino Portero 'Spain, Britain and the Cold War' in Sebastian Balfour and Paul Preston (eds) *Spain and the Great Powers in the 20$^{th}$ Century* (London and New York: Routledge, 1999) 210–228, 216.

111 Article IX, The Berlin (Potsdam) Conference, July 17-August 2, 1945 (a) Protocol of the Proceedings, August l, 1945.

112 Security Council Resolution 4 of April 29, 1946 on 'The Spanish Question'.

people with the peoples of the United Nations in international affairs impossible.'[113] Resolution 39 (I) also recommended that 'the Franco Government of Spain be debarred from membership in international agencies established by or brought into relationship with the United Nations, and from participation in conferences or other activities which may be arranged by the United Nations or by these agencies, until a new and acceptable government is formed in Spain' and requested all UN Members 'to immediately recall from Madrid all ambassadors and Ministers plenipotentiary accredited there.'[114]

Against the background of the international Spanish stigmatized ostracism in the post-war period, the re-reorientation in anti-foreign intellectual grounds previously ordered by the guidelines of the National Delegation of Propaganda in 1943 was to combine well with the strategic of 'endurance' preconized by Carrero Blanco to support the Franco's effort to 'escape the Axis stigma'.[115] Their combined impact was to fostering further the study of neo-scholasticism, the Spanish Catholic-bounded imperial past and the Spanish 'autochthonous' forms of thinking during this 'autarky period' by Spanish international lawyers. This scholarly orientation, which benefitted from the availability of both primary and secondary academic sources in a period of international scientific isolation and internal censorship, was, moreover, the most convenient theme from the perspective of an unproblematic professional development of academic activities in Franco's new Spain of the 1940s under the parameters of the University Law of 1943. A good exemplification of this epochal shift of focus from the period of 'fascist mimesis' to that of Spanish autarky can be found in Legaz Lacambra's work from the early-mid-40s onwards. In this period, Legaz's interest in international legal issues partially replaced the focus on labor law and social policy, which had characterized his intellectual production during the Civil war and its immediate aftermath in support of the social national-syndicalist underpinnings of the Spanish totalitarian state. Although without abandoning the 'totalitarian humanism' that he proudly proclaimed that characterized his work, Legaz went to pay more attention to the international legal historical realm. Representative of this re-orientation are Legaz's book Man and War (1944), which revisits the notion of just war in the Spanish classics, and his articles 'The Modern and the Medieval in Vitoria'[116] (1946)

113 General Assembly Res 39 (I) of 12th December 1946.

114 Id.

115 David Wingeate Pike, *Franco and the Axis Stigma*, (London: Palgrave MacMillan, 2008).

116 Luis Legaz Lacambra, 'Lo moderno y lo medieval en Vitoria' in Luis Legaz Lacambra, Horizontes del Pensamiento Juridico (Barcelona: Casa Bosch 1947).

and, published, in the inaugural issue of Revista Española de Derecho Internacional in 1948, 'The Foundation of ius gentium in Suarez.'[117]

The new third professional generation of Spanish international law scholars, those who surged in the 30ies, and had ended up not killed, into exile or imprisoned, in the aftermath of the civil war, strictly followed the new guidelines. Particularly representative among them is Antonio Truyol y Serra (1913–2003), the translator of Alfred Verdross' textbook on international law in its different editions from 1955,[118] who played an important role in the cultivation of the Salamanca school in this autarchic period of Spanish international law.[119] The work of the young Truyol, which Koskenniemi has referred to as work that 'decried the spiritual poverty of positivism and advocated a turn to metaphysics and morality',[120] was mainly historical and almost exclusively Catholic ius-naturalist in orientation engaged with the works of Saint Augustine,[121] Vitoria,[122] Suarez,[123] the sources of natural law,[124] and Medieval scholarship[125] during the 40s and early 50s. The character of the intellectual production of an author who had written on 'The State in Rousseau and Lenin'[126] just before the outbreak of the Spanish Civil War, is a reminder that

117 Luis Legaz Lacambra, La fundamentación del ius gentium en Suarez, Revista Española de Derecho Internacional I (1948) 11–44.

118 Alfred Verdross, *Derecho internacional público* (transl., bibliography and additional notes by A. Truyol y Serra), (Madrid: Ed. Aguilar, 1955).

119 Truyol, who later became Judge of the Spanish Constitutional Court (1981–1990), was the only Spanish catedrático of the 20th century to have successively held chairs of philosophy of law (1940–1957), international relations (the first ever in Spain, established in 1957) and public international law (also since 1957).

120 Koskenniemi, *The Gentle Civilizer of Nations* 2001, 350.

121 See e.g. Antonio Truyol y Serra, *El derecho y el Estado en San Agustín*, Editorial Revista de Derecho Privado Madrid (1944).

122 See e.g. Antonio Truyol y Serra, *Los principios del derecho público en Francisco de Vitoria (selección de textos, con introducción y notas)*, Ediciones de Cultura Hispánica, Madrid (1946).

123 See e.g. Antonio Truyol y Serra, 'El objetivismo ético de Francisco Suarez y su influencia en la historia del pensamiento', in Actas IV Centenario de Francisco Suarez (1548–1948) (Madrid: Dirección General de Propaganda, Madrid, 1949) 107–209.

124 See for example Antonio Truyol y Serra, *Fundamentos del Derecho Natural*, (Barcelona: F. Seix 1949).

125 See for example Antonio Truyol y Serra, 'La filosofía jurídica y social en la crisis del mundo medieval', *Revista Internacional de Sociología* V (1947), 135–153.

126 Manuel Medina, 'El pensamiento internacionalista del profesor Truyol y Serra', in Pensamiento jurídico y sociedad internacional: libro-homenaje al profesor Antonio Truyol Serra (Madrid: Centro de Estudios Constitucionales: Universidad Complutense 1986), 15–28, 20.

the intellectual soil nurtured by earlier generations of Spanish international legal scholars remained a doctrinal land tilled by a maimed farmer for a great part of Franco period. In this revival of the Catholic natural law tradition and the Spanish classics of international law, he was accompanied by many other others.

Among these was Carl Schmitt himself, whose works on international law in the 40ies and early 50ies abound in references to Spain as the last guardian of the 'great Christian European tradition' preserved in the tradition of ius gentium of the School of Salamanca.[127] Indeed, Schmitt, in his 'Der Nomos der Erde', published in 1950 celebrates Vitoria and Suarez as the true exponents of a religious-based universalism that he contrasted with the 'nihilist' morality of secular values that informed the post-Versailles system of humanitarian internationalism.[128] Schmitt also decries the 'especially widespread and improper use of Vitoria's thinking' represented by 'the transposition of his moral-theological doctrines into a context centuries later where [...] jurists of neutral (with respect to religion) powers developed arguments in international law.'[129] Although a medieval 'scholastic' interpretation of Vitoria was at the heart of Schmitt's reconstruction of the ius publicum europaeum that he yearned for, his existentialism would, nonetheless, become tempered on Christian ius-naturalist grounds in its domestic political reception in Spain.[130] The warm reception in Spain of C. Schmitt's works on the history of international law coincided with a time when the Francoist ideological spiritual model was being mirrored by an internationalist imaginary that had made the same traditional ultra-national-Catholicism flagged by the regime one of defining central elements. This orientation went hand in glove with the, by then, prevailing atmosphere of Spanish nationalist atavistic and middle-aged cultural forms drawn from the mythology of Spanish Reconquista, Counter-Reformation, and Empire. It was furthermore in consonance with the recent 'Crusade' against the 'anti-Spain' for the purpose of national reunification against disaggregating regionalisms, such as the proclamation by the President of the Generalitat of Catalonia of the Catalonian State of the Federal Spanish Republic in October

---

127 See further José Antonio López García, 'La presencia de Carl Schmitt' 1996, 142 and 146–149. See further José Menendez, 'From Republicanism to Fascist Ideology' 2003.

128 See Martti Koskenniemi, International Law as Political Theology: How to Read der Nomos der Erde? Forum Historiae Iuris, Artikel vom 31 (2006), 1–20, 6.

129 See Carl Schmitt, *The Nomos of the Earth* 2003, 115.

130 For the influence of Carl Schmitt's interpretation of Vitoria in the domestic debate over the weight of the Spanish tradition as an explanation of the international isolationism of Spain, see López García, 'La presencia de Carl Schmitt' 1996, 147.

of 1934. Combined with political repression and economic autarky, Spanish international law scholars both accommodated to, and contributed, with their work, to a cultural mood that paved the way domestically along what the Franco's regime saw as a 'healthy road to modernity'.[131]

The cultivation of a neo-Scholastic natural law and of the study of the Spanish priests who had 'founded' international law was, moreover, perfectly consonant with the need to identify new forms of historically autochthonous legitimacy for Franco's regime in the internationally isolated position that the military defeat of totalitarianism across Europe has left Spain in. The new international isolation fostered a series of adaptative domestic legislative reforms—including the passing of a Bill of Rights contained in the 'Charter of the Spaniards'[132] of 1945. These rights were, nonetheless, limited, among other caveats, in their exercise to not opposing the 'fundamental principles of the State' and were accompanied by other parallel forms of totalitarian legislation which made the enjoyment of the rights contained in the Bill mostly illusory.[133] The post-war period also saw a step in the gradual consolidation of the image of Franco's regime as an 'organic democracy', the cosmetic formula that evolved from the 'totalitarian and corporative' state embodied in the Labour Charter of 1938. The latter was the first of the eight 'Fundamental Laws' of the regime and became concretized in Catholic organicist terms in the Law of the Congress of 1942/43 and further developed in the Law of National Referendum of 1945. This supplemented the aim of 'opening to all Spaniards their collaboration in the tasks of the state through the natural organisms constituted by the family, the municipality and the syndicate'[134] by 'direct consultation with the nation in public referendum in those cases when due to the transcendence of the laws or uncertainties of opinions the Head of State considers such consultation to be opportune and convenient.'[135]

Along with these legislative measures, which were oriented towards a softening of the external image of Franco's dictatorial political regime, these years also witnessed a parallel continuation of the search for a historically-rooted purist Spanish legitimacy free from the intellectual infections of the

---

131 See Mike Richards, 'The Material Reality of Power' in Helen Graham and Jo Labanyi (eds.) *Spanish Cultural Studies: An Introduction. The Struggle for Modernity,* Oxford University Press, London (1995), 173–182.

132 B.O. July 18, 1945.

133 For a critical analysis of the Jesus Galindez, 'Spain', *Columbia Law Review* 54 (1954), 809–820.

134 Ley de Referéndum de 1945 (22 de octubre de 1945).

135 Id.

eighteenth-century Enlightenment. This movement which replicates the late eighteenth-century origins of the cultivation of international legal studies in Spain examined in Chapter 1, is one the circumstantial factors that, as Perez Luño has noted, 'explain a favorable context for an invocation and manipulation of the Salamanca School as it had never been known before.'[136] During the 40s, the cultivation by Spanish international law scholars of the Salamanca School, which as we have seen in Chapter Three had acquired much fame in international legal academic circles during the interwar era, greatly contributed to the preferred external image projected by the Francoist foreign policy of Spain as an Catholic neo-scholastic natural-law oriented, and anti-Marxist, stronghold.

The immediate aftermath of the Second World War witnessed a series of institutional events celebrate the figure of Francisco de Vitoria. The institutionalization of Vitorian studies, initiated with the setting up of the Association Francisco de Vitoria in 1926, and followed by the creation of a Francisco de Vitoria Chair at the University of Salamanca in 1927, had continued in the 1930s with the creation, also in Salamanca, of the Institute of International Law Francisco de Vitoria. This was born in 1933 with the 'ambition of becoming one day an autonomous organism with the rank of a faculty and able to award its own degrees.'[137] In 1940, after his service to the Franco's cause during the Civil War, Antonio de Luna, after a brief stint presiding over university depuration commissions at the Central University of Madrid,[138] became the director of the Instituto Francisco de Vitoria de Derecho Internacional. The Instituto Francisco de Vitoria had been a fundamental centre for justifiers of

136 Pérez Luño *Natural Law Theory in Spain and Portugal* 2013, 1–24, 7. As perez-luno has noted, 'it would clearly be an overstatement to sustain that the political regime established in Spain by Franco after the Civil War pretended to support a 'revival' of the Spanish Natural Law Classics. It is obvious that the so-called Movimiento Nacional (National Movement) had to address more urgent issues, culture not being among their primary concerns'.

137 Ibid. Actas de 27-IV-1933, fols. 271–74; de 13-V-33, fols. 274–78 y de 20-V-33, fols. 278–79. Quoted in Tomás Pérez Delgado/ Antonio Fuentes Labrador, 'De rebeldes a cruzados. Pioneros del discurso legitimador del movimiento nacional. Salamanca julio-octubre de 1936' *Studia Historica* 4 (1986), 235–266, 250.

138 As we saw in Chapter Three, Antonio de Luna had been excluded at the outbreak of the civil war by the Republican authorities from the Chair of Public International law that he had occupied at the Central University of Madrid since 1932 and had spent the rest of conflict in the besieged Spanish capital as a member of the fifth column as an agent for the First Corps of the Franco National Army.

Franco's rebellion and legitimizers of the new totalitarian system during the Spanish Civil War.

In 1946, the Instituto Francisco de Vitoria played a leading role in the organization of the celebration of the 400th anniversary of the death of Francisco de Vitoria. This coincided with the nineteenth Congress of Pax Romana, which was inaugurated in Salamanca with hundreds of participants from thirty different countries under the presidency of Joaquín Ruiz-Giménez, in late June 1946.[139] This Congress was an occasion for an homage to James Brown Scoot by the then president of the Association Francisco de Vitoria, Gascón y Marín, another of the authors who had delivered courses at the Hague Academy and who had signed the 'Advisory Opinion on the Illegitimacy of the Acting Powers on the 18th of July 1936.' Gascón y Marín announced a gold medal of the Association in honor of James Brown Scott, who had died in 1943.[140]

In 1946, the city of Vitoria also erected a national monument to Francisco de Vitoria.[141] This statue, which had been a long-standing aim of the Association Francisco de Vitoria was inaugurated by General Franco, the papal ambassador to Spain, several ministers and representatives of the foreign diplomatic corps. Evidencing once more the nationalist symbolism acquired by Francisco de Vitoria, in the book that gathered together the discourses given on that occasion, Barcia Trelles, the most published author by The Hague Academy in the interwar period, wrote: 'I will only tell you this: in twenty-five years of academic labour, everything I did, I always did it with a consciousness of Spain, which I always wanted to serve, and of the university. And now I can show with pride my own poverty. God gave me the opportunity to vindicate my motherland across three worlds, bringing to my lips this great truth: that the origin of modern international law is, indisputably, Catholic and Spanish.'[142] A year later, 'the James Brown Scott Chair' (1947 to 1965) was inaugurated in the summer courses of the University of Valladolid –where J. Brown Scott had published his first book on Vitoria in the framework of the Section of Americanist Studies founded in the early 1920s by Barcia Trelles. Several international lawyers attended the

---

139 Congreso de la Pax Romana 1946, available at filosofia.org/mfb/1946pax.htm

140 La Vanguardia Española, Barcelona, martes 25 de junio de 1946, 3. Quoted in Forcada Barona, 'La influencia de la religión católica en la doctrina internacionalista' 2012.

141 Ana Barredi Barandiaran, ' El Monumento a Francisco de Vitoria, Historia de su construccion', Sancho el Sabio 25 (2006) 165–179.

142 Camilo Barcia Trelles, 'Fray Francisco de Vitoria y la Carta orgánica de San Francisco', in AA VV, Fray Francisco de Vitoria, fundador del Derecho internacional moderno 1546–1946 (Conferencias pronunciadas en la inauguración de su Monumento Nacional en la ciudad de Vitoria) (Madrid: Ediciones Cultura Hispánica 1946), 91.

event held in the city of Vitoria in homage to Scott and deposited flowers before the statue to Francisco de Vitoria while the Spanish national anthem was played.[143] The introduction by the Bank of Spain of a 500-peseta banknote with Vitoria's effigy on one side and the Plateresque facade of the University of Salamanca, dating from 1529–1533, on the other, completed the official events of the 400th anniversary of the death of Francisco de Vitoria in 1946.

## Hispanidad, International Law and International Re-Alignment

The enshrinement of Francisco de Vitoria as a symbol of the 'universal mission of Spain' within the 'collective consciousness' of the Spanish people was connected with specific Spanish foreign policy goals. The aims served by the revival of neo-scholastic studies that characterized the 1940s in Spain included the defense of Hispanidad. This regained importance as part of the Spanish diplomatic policy towards South America during the period of international ostracism of Spain. The Hispanidad, whose origins lay in the competition between Spain and the United States for the cultural and spiritual terrain in Latin America since the late-nineteenth century, had been revived during the interwar years when it was supported by all the different regimes. In the last years of the Restoration system (1876–1923) following a proposal by Américo Castro, the Office of Cultural Relations of Spain at the Ministry of Foreign Affairs was established. During the dictatorship of Primo de Rivera (1923–1930), the pan-Hispanic inspiration found different expressions, including legislative ones such as the limited Sephardic Citizenship decree of 20 December 1924. With the arrival of the Second Republic, the republican 1931 Constitution facilitated terms of double citizenship for Latin Americans and the opportunity of citizenship for all people of Spanish origin living abroad.[144]

The early 1930s also saw the beginning of the Fascist coloring of the notion of Hispanidad.This had already fostered numerous reflections on the elements of the hybridity of the Hispanic world with spiritual and Catholic underpinnings against the background of U.S. policies in its regional courtyard. In Spain, the Hispanidad had also encouraged a renewal of traditional views about Spanish history and the nature of Spanishness. The successive linking of the Hispanidad with a nostalgia for the Spanish colonial and imperial

143 Details of the press-coverage can be found on the website that the proyecto de filosofía en español devotes to James Brown Scott 1866–1943 at http://www.filosofia.org/ave/001/a355.htm

144 Payne *Franco and Hitler, Spain, Germany* 2008, 212.

past was theorized by the most emblematic intellectuals of Franco's regime. Ramiro de Maeztu, a member of the intellectual Generation of 1898, who was incarcerated in a Republican prison, and executed soon after Franco's coup d'état, was one of them. De Maeztu, who in 1931 founded[145] Acción Española,[146] an ultra-nationalist publication to which Spanish international law scholars like Yanguas Messia contributed to, gave in his influential book 'En Defensa de la Hispanidad' (In Defence of Hispanidad), a conservative-reactionary turn to the notion of 'Hispanidad' inspired by fascist ideals in 1934.[147] This book nurtured the soil for what some 'Spanish rhetorical patriots call[ed] the empire of the culture and of the language'.[148] The founder of the Spanish Falange, José Antonio Primo de Rivera, would be inspired by this background in designing the programmatic points of the Falangist manifesto: 'Regarding the Hispano-American countries, we tend to the unification of culture, of economic interests and power. Spain claims its condition as the spiritual axis of the Hispanic world as a title of pre-eminence in universal enterprises.'[149]

Since its very origins, Francoism made 'Hispanidad' a key rhetorical aspect of its foreign policy. This orientation was akin to the mystique of the new Spanish imperial vision spurred by the Spanish Falange under the banner 'Through Empire to God.' This was a slogan aiming to portray Spain as a moral supervisor and a cultural and religious guide to its ancient colonies under the fraternal cloak of Hispanidad. The establishment of The Council of the Hispanidad in 1940[150] shows the importance that the new regime attributed to this vector of its foreign policy. The new Council, which was an initiative of the 'Foreign branch of the Falange', was charged with the mission of 'studying and resolving the common spiritual and material needs of the Peoples of our lineage'.[151] The very term Hispanidad was trademarked by the Spanish Ministry of Foreign Affairs in a single-articled Ministerial Order in May 1941. According to this telling example of how ideological notions can become normatively conceptualized, 'While [Hispanidad] means the ensemble of nations that integrate the Hispanic world,

145 Claret Miranda, *El atroz desmoche. La destrucción de la Universidad Española* 2006.
146 See Forcada Barona, 'La influencia de la religión católica en la doctrina internacionalista' 2012.
147 Celestino del arenal, *Politica exterior de España y relaciones con America Latin. Iberoamericanidad, europeización y atlantismo en la política exterior española*, (Madrid: Fundacion Carolina, 2011), 31–33.
148 Madariaga, Theory and Practice 1939, 37.
149 El programa de Falange Española de las J. O. N. S., 1934.
150 Delgado Gómez-Escalonilla, 'Un siglo de diplomacia cultural Española', 2014.
151 Julio Gil Pecharromán, *La política exterior del franquismo* 2008, 87.

it also embodies their peculiar spirit and their understanding of life as well as their common historical tradition and superior universal destiny. It is thereby forbidden to freely use the term 'Hispanidad,' which cannot be employed as a trademark in industrial terms or for commercial establishments'.[152]

As we have seen, the General Assembly Resolution 39 (I) of 12 December 1946 opened a new era in Spain's international isolation. It also marked the abandonment of the Spanish imperial ambitions of the period of 'fascist mimesis', and fostered the design of 'policies of substitution' to allow the Franco regime to cope with the new foreign policy realities of the autarchic period. Consonant with Carrero Blanco's guidelines of 'unity, resistance and endurance', these 'policies of substitution' were designed for the diplomatic privileging of certain regions and allies to advance the 'Spanish question' at the United Nations through the gradual scratching of votes from the Arab world and Latin America. In this new context, one of the first measures adopted by the Catholic-oriented new Ministry of Foreign Affairs under the direction of A. Martín Artajo was suppressing the Council of Hispanidad in 1945 because its 'imperialist aura' created discomfort in Latin America. Although the Council was replaced by the more diplomatically correct Institute of Hispanic Culture in October 1946, a new Ministerial order of 1947 extended the trademark of the term Hispanidad to prohibiting the expressions 'Hispanic world, Hispanic culture and any other term of analogous meaning that makes reference to the spiritual community of the peoples of Spanish language'.[153]

During the early epoch of the Franco's regime, Spanish international lawyers continued to play a key role at the Instituto de Estudios Políticos—the think-tank of Phalanx. One of the authors of Reivindicaciones de España, and future Spanish Minister of Foreign affairs, F.M. Castiella, was appointed as its second Director (1944–1948). The international plane was covered by an international chronicle in Revista de Estudios Políticos (REP). One of the authors of the conspicuous Falangist hymn 'Cara al Sol', Pedro Mourlane Michelena, and two noted international lawyers, Luis García Arias and Camilo Barcia Trelles,[154] were successively charged with the responsibility for it from 1945 to 1949. During his tenure at the helm of the flagship of the Falange's 'brain trust',[155] Castiella co-founded what remains the Spanish international

152 Orden Ministerial Mayo 1941.

153 See Pecharromán, La política exterior del franquismo 2008, 162.

154 See Pedro Mourlane Michelena 24 *Revista de Estudios Políticos,* November-December (1945). The last international chronicle was penned in issue 44 March/April (1949) by Camilo Barcia Trelles.

155 Stanley G. Payne, *Falange. Historia del fascismo español,* (Paris: Ed. Ruedo Ibérico, 1965), 217.

legal doctrine's main scientific organ of expression, the Revista Española de Derecho Internacional, in 1948.

Revista Española de Derecho Internacional walked in the footsteps of a series of short-lived international law journals that had existed in Spain during the late nineteenth and early twentieth centuries. As we have seen in earlier chapters, A. Garcia Montero founded Revista de Derecho Internacional, Legislación y Jurisprudencia Comparadas in 1887, and the Marquis de Olivart launched Revista de Derecho Internacional y Política Exterior[156] in 1905. During the interwar years, there was no specialized journal of international law in Spain although articles on international law themes were regularly published in 'general' law journals and in other periodical publications such as the Yearbook of the Association Francisco de Vitoria. In 1948, the same year of the launching of the Jahrbuch für Internationales Recht in Germany, Revista Española de Derecho Internacional (REDI) was founded. The second co-founder of REDI and its first managing director (until 1963) was the Director of Instituto Francisco de Vitoria (1940–1963), Antonio de Luna. De Luna was also directly connected with Instituto de Estudios Politicos, where he has served as the director of its own division of international politics, and had extensively contributed with articles of an ultra-nationalistic orientation to the pages of its intellectual flagship, Revista de Estudios Políticos.[157] When Spain gained entrance to the United Nations in 1955, de Luna became the chief legal adviser to the Minister of Foreign Affairs. He was also the first Spanish member of the International Law Commission (1962–1966) where he participated in the drafting of the Vienna Convention on the Law of Treaties. Completing the eminent founding triumvirate as the REDI's third co-founder was Federico de Castro (1903–1983), a reputed civil law professor, who, in time, became the first—and only—Spaniard to sit as a permanent judge (1970–1979) on the bench of the principal judicial organ of the United Nations.[158]

In its first period (1948–1963), REDI followed the guidelines established by Antonio de Luna, who together with Castiella, and De Castro occupied its board of directors. This board oversaw an editorial board onto which all newly appointed Spanish catedráticos of international law were automatically

156 On the foundation of Revista de Derecho Internacional, Legislación y Jurisprudencia Comparadas, see also available in English Ignacio de la Rasilla, 'The Study of the History of International Law in the Short Spanish Nineteenth Century' Chicago-Kent Journal of International and Comparative Law 13 (2013), 122–150.

157 Antonio de Luna, 'España, Europa y la Cristiandad', *Revista de Estudios Políticos* 9–10 (1943), 41–98.

158 On Altamira, see e.g. Gamarra Chopo, 'Rafael Altamira y Crevea (1866–1951)', 2012.

incorporated alongside several representative catedráticos from other legal disciplines, such as Legaz Lacambra and Antonio Truyol Serra.[159] For its first fifteen first years (1948–1963), under the direction of A. de Luna, REDI was biannual.[160] In terms of its internal structure, REDI was, at the time, composed of four separate sections. The most extensive of them,[161] 'doctrinal studies', was divided into the subsections of 'Studies' and 'Notes'. Two hundred and fifteen works of a 'markedly speculative'[162] character were published in both categories[163] including thirty-five contributions by foreign authors (of which twenty-two, written by not native authors, were translated into Spanish). The foreign contributions were inaugurated in 1949[164] by Carl Schmitt, the first foreign author to be published in REDI, with, perhaps, not surprisingly, a work justifying the occupation of the New World, following Vitoria's doctrine, in 1949.[165] This cultivation of traditional historical themes, which echoed the imperial past, the delving into natural law schools of international legal thought, and the Spanish classics of international law, would find an echo on the 'marked thematic centers of doctrinal interest during the first epoch'[166] of REDI. During the period 1948–1963, these mainly included 'studies on the Spanish school of ius gentium, essays on war and peace' and also 'the problematic of criminality of war and crimes against humanity',[167] an area of studies that Quintiliano Saldaña had pioneered in the interwar period.

After 1948, the bulk of the specialized Spanish academic production in international law was channeled into the new main organ of expression along with Revista de Política Internacional in 1950, one of the new scientific periodicals associated with the Instituto de Estudios Políticos, the flagship of the Falange's think-tank.[168] The beginning of the publication of REDI in 1948 coincided with the beginning of the second stage of Spain's international ostracism.

159 See Antonio Remiro Brotons, 'El discreto encanto—y desencanto—de la Revista Española del Derecho Internacional (1948–1978)' in *Estudios de Derecho Internacional. Libro-homenaje al Prof. A. Miaja de la Muela,* (Madrid: Ed. Tecnos 1979), 123–124.

160 Except for the period 1949–1952 when it was four-monthly Id., 124.

161 Id., 23–27.

162 Id., 124.

163 Id., 124.

164 Id., 125.

165 Carl Schmitt, 'La justificación de la ocupación de un nuevo mundo (Francisco de Vitoria)', *Revista Española de Derecho internacional* II (1949), 13–44.

166 Remiro Brotons, 'El discreto encanto—y desencanto' 1979, 129.

167 Id., 129.

168 These also included Revista de Administración Pública (1950), Revista de Economía Política (1945–1983) and Revista de Política Social (1949–1985).

This was marked by a shift in the US position vis-à-vis Spain[169] coinciding with the beginning of the Cold War and the enunciation of the Truman Doctrine on 12 March 1947—soon followed by both the 'Kennan Report' in October 1947 and the National Security Council Report 'NSC3' in December 1947. These enshrined the definitive official position that it was in the US' national interest to modify its policy vis-à-vis Spain and to work towards both political and economic normalization with the Franco regime. The establishment of Revista de Política Internacional in 1950 was a response by the Instituto de Estudios Políticos to the growing need for specialized Spanish journals on international affairs at a time when Spain's international isolation was gradually coming to an end.[170]

The key turning point for the end of Spain's post-war isolation was the 'rehabilitating' General Assembly Resolution 386 (V) of 4 November 1950 which gave Franco's government the possibility of reestablishing diplomatic relations and join the UN's specialized agencies.[171] Setting a rare precedent, Res. 386 (V) of 4 November 1950 repealed Res. 39 I of 12 December 1946. This had imposed a regime of international sanctions against Spain after the Assembly had declared itself 'convinced that the Fascist Franco Government of Spain (...) does not represent the Spanish people and by its continued control of Spain is making the participation of the Spanish people with the peoples of the United Nations in international affairs impossible.'[172] Proof of this regained Spanish international assertiveness, in one of the first issues of Revista de Política Internacional in 1950, José Sebastian de Erice y O'Shea, author of two volumes of Diplomatic Law,[173] examined what he termed 'the monstrously anti-juridical

169 A precedent for this shift can be found in George Kennan's reference to the Russian position regarding Spain in his influential Long Telegram of 3rd Feb. 1946: 'As far as Spain is concerned, Russia has learned nothing and forgotten nothing since the Civil War. Their only programme is to return to that struggle unabashed by the chaos which might ensue.'

170 The launching of Revista Española de Derecho Internacional (1948) and Revista de Política Internacional (1950) gradually relieved Revista de Estudios Politicos (REP) of its editorial mandate to cover both foreign policy and legal international relations. Many Spanish international lawyers, including Barcia Trelles, continued to contribute articles and essays on international themes to the Phalange's intellectual flagship. See e.g. Camilo Barcia Trelles, 'El ayer, el hoy y el mañana internacionales' *Revista de Estudios Políticos* 50 (1950), 135–156.

171 Paula María Vernet 'Decolonization: Spanish Territories' Max Planck Encyclopedia of Public International Law (2010).

172 General Assembly Res 39 (I) of 12th December 1946.

173 José Sebastián de Erice O'Shea, *Derecho Diplomático* (Madrid: Instituto de estudios políticos, 1954).

unfolding between 1945 and 1950 of the so-called 'Spanish case'[174] at the United Nations.[175] De Erice retraces the UN's obscure 'gambling and deals in corridors'[176] that induced what he terms the 'Western historical mistake' of falling into the trap of the 'completely mendacious and injurious'[177] diplomatic strategy designed by Russia and its satellites against the only country that had effectively proven itself able to resist as a 'European stronghold against Russian imperialism'. The work of De Erice, the future first Spanish Ambassador to the United Nations in 1955, presents in detail the gradual evolution of the votes diplomatically scratched by Spain[178] in favor of the 'recognition of the truth of our motherland'[179] as a great success of the Spanish policies of diplomatic substitution towards both South America and the Arab world against the odds of the fierce anti-Spanish international strategy led by international communist forces.[180]

---

174 José Sebastián de Erice O'Shea, 'España y las Naciones Unidas' 1 *Revista de Política Internacional* 4 (1950), 9–49, 9.

175 See: Pedro Antonio Martínez Lillo, 'La política exterior de España en el marco de la Guerra Fría: del aislamiento limitado a la integración parcial en la sociedad internacional, 1945–1953' in Javier Tussell, J. Aviles & Rosa Pardo (Eds.) *La política exterior de España en el siglo XX,* (Madrid: Ed. Biblioteca Nueva 2000),323–369. Gil Pecharromán, La política exterior del franquismo 2008, 137–185. Swain, 'Stalin and Spain, 1944–1948' 1999, quoting the Pravda's Editorial of the 13th January 1946—'It is time, it has long been time, to move from words to action on the Spanish question. Liquidating the last remnants of fascism—that is the most urgent task which must be resolved by creating a post-war system of peace and security'—at 245. Vid. also Boris N. Liedtke 'Compromising with the Dictatorship' U.S.-Spanish Relations in the Late 1940s and Early 1950s'in Christian Leitz and David J. Dunthorn, Spain in an International Legal Context: 1936–1959, (New York & Oxford: Berghahn Books 1999), 265–275, 270–274.

176 De Erice O'Shea, 'España y las Naciones Unidas', 15.

177 Id., 11.

178 Id., Documentary Annexes; from 51 states against Spain in 1945 to 6 votes in favor in 1946, 16 in 1947, 26 in 1949 and 38 in 1950.

179 Id., 29.

180 The same propagandist insistence on anti-Marxism and Hispanidad shall be a dogmatic truth in the book commemorating 25 years of the National Movement, with a prologue by General Franco himself. Here, the Spanish diplomat Gonzalo, organic intellectual, and later Minister of Public Works (1970–1974), Fernandez de la Mora (1924–2002) presents a balance sheet of a quarter of a century of Spanish foreign policy, which he portrays as 'always ancillary to domestic policies'. After stressing, once again, the 'blinding evidence' of Spanish neutrality in World War II and defending the strategic nature of Franco's appeasement policy vis-à-vis Hitler, he notes that 'Spanish foreign policy in the last quarter of a century has not been pragmatic but founded on spiritual and

The adhesion of Spanish professors of international law to the fundamental guidelines of the new state continued to go hand in glove with the Spanish foreign policy as this confronted an international sphere that was undergoing swift and radical transformations. By the time of Franco regime's gradual diplomatic realignment with the West, the work of Camilo Barcia Trelles, the author who had more contributed to the 'cause of Vitoria' in the interwar period, was focused on geopolitical analyses of the foreign policies of the USSR and the US. Barcia's critical approach, in accordance to the regime's official line, to the USSR and Marxism is illustrated by the leading article in the first issue of Revista de Política Internacional,[181] which he wrote on the occasion of the establishment of the Atlantic Pact. Barcia's essay, which is highly influenced by the geopolitics of H. Mackinder,[182] and reminiscent of Schmitt's Der Nomos der Erde, develops a detailed historical analysis of Russia as a 'geocratical power' vis-à-vis the US, which he conceptualizes as a 'talasocracia'. This geopolitical framework portrays the limited 'dissuasive value of the Atlantic Pact' against an 'ideological soviet tactic,' which Barcia conceived as a mere 'instrument of execution of the great Russian historical geopolitical designs which originated in the times of Peter the Great'.[183] In contrast to what Barcia judged to be a temporarily disorientated U.S. foreign policy, he devoted his analysis to warn about the danger posed to Western civilization by a 'messianic' Russia, which at that historical juncture had the 'international initiative on its side' and that, according to Barcia, knew perfectly well where it was 'orientating its steps'[184] in perfect compliance 'with certain indeclinable geopolitical laws'.[185] Barcia distinguished 'between communism as an instrument of expansion and Russian imperialism as the final goal of the former',[186] before putting forward a

historical affinities—the Hispanidad, the Iberian Bloc, Hispanic-Arab friendship—and inspired by a fundamental ideological position: anti-communism'. Twenty five years of Spanish foreign policy become by this dint officially subsumed under one single emblem: 'Spain, which has not maintained diplomatic relations with the USSR since the killing of the Tzar Nicholas II, configured his current State in its fight against the Marxist conception of man and the world' Gónzalo Fernández de la Mora, 'La política exterior de España' in *El nuevo Estado español. Veinticinco años de Movimiento Nacional. 1936–1961*. (Madrid: Ed. Instituto de Estudios Políticos 1961), 65–92, 70–71.

181 Camilo Barcia Trelles, 'El pacto Atlántico y las inclinaciones geopolíticas de la URSS' *Revista de Política Internacional* 4 (1950), 13–52.

182 Id., 38.

183 Id., 52.

184 Id., 48.

185 Id., 38.

186 Id., 40.

number of foreign policy recommendations for U.S. foreign policy makers in Asia.[187] These would, according to Barcia, to supplement the 'incomplete vision of unity of those who articulated the Atlantic Pact,'[188] which he considered the 'United States' dialectical suit of armor'[189] at 'this culminating stage of the fight between the World Island and the Periphery world'.[190]

Consonant with the bipolar international background described by Barcia Trelles, the final stage of the Spanish realignment with the West[191] witnessed the definitive enshrinement of a Western 'Realpolitik' mindset towards Spain. This was exemplified in the reopening of foreign embassies in Madrid (18 accreditations of ambassadors in 1951 plus 5 more in 1952) and the gradual integration of Spain in international institutions (OMM, FAO, OMS, UIT in 1951 and UNESCO in 1952). The Western re-alignment will find its corollary in the signature of a Concordat with the Vatican in August 1953 and of three important economic-military Pacts of Spain with the U.S. in September 1953. These included the provision of extensive financial aid in exchange for the establishment of U.S. military bases in Spain. The Concordat with the Vatican and the economic-military agreements with the U.S. defined the two fundamental key safeguards of Franco's regime on the international plane and marked the axis of the evolution of Spanish foreign policy until the death of General Franco in 1975.[192] Two years later, Spain was eventually admitted as a member of the United Nations in 1955, where due to Franco's anticommunist policy, it became a strategic partner within the group of countries under US leadership.

The 'Vitorian' aftermath of the 'fascist mimesis' of Spanish international law lived on, however, far beyond the date that marks the Spanish re-alignment

---

187 Id., 45–48.

188 Id., 52.

189 Id., 32.

190 Id., 36.

191 Alberto J. Lleonart y Amsélem *España y ONU. La Cuestión española* Tomo VI (1952–1955). Estudios introductivos y corpus documental (Madrid, Consejo Superior de Investigaciones Cientificas, 2002).

192 Spain was finally admitted in 1955, during the Cold War (1947–91), when, due to Franco's anticommunist policy, it became part of the group of countries under US leadership despite the first paragraph of Res. 39 (I) Relations of Members of the United Nations with Spain: 'The peoples of the United Nations, at San Francisco, Potsdam and London, condemned the Franco regime in Spain and decided that, as long as that regime remains, Spain may not be admitted to the United Nations' (Res. 39 (I) has already been repealed by Res. 386 (V) of 4 November 1950, something that would not happen again until 1991).

with the West in the early stages of the Cold War. Apart from a short period, between 1964 and 1968,[193] the very cover of the Revista Española de Derecho Internacional featured, throughout the whole period of General Franco's dictatorship, the effigy of Francisco de Vitoria ambivalently transmogrified into the enduring symbol of the Phalangist project of Spain as a 'unity of fate in the universal'.[194]

---

193 This coincided with the attempt by a new generation of Spanish International lawyers to set 'new premises and partly different problems and methodologies' in the study of international law in Spain. These new premises included a fleeting awakening of the study of the history of international law throughout the nineteenth and early part of the twentieth century in Spain. See Mariano Aguilar Navarro, 'Tareas de la doctrina española de Derecho internacional público', Revista Española de Derecho Internacional 17 (1964) 501–515, 502.

194 El programa de Falange Española de las J. O. N. S. ABC diario ilustrado Madrid, viernes 30 de noviembre de 1934 año 30, número 9.834 páginas 32–34. Also known as the 27 puntos de La Falange Española. Punto II: 'España es una unidad de destino en lo universal'.

# Conclusion

## 1.

The history of the study of international law in Spain during the nineteenth century and the first half of the twentieth century contained in this book began in 1770, when the study of public law, natural law and the law of peoples was included for the first time in a Spanish curriculum at the Royal School of Studies of San Isidro in Madrid. It ended in 1953 when Spain reintegrated with the Western bloc in the early stages of the Cold War. The signature of the Concordat with the Holy See and the strategic military pacts with the United States marked the beginning of the end of the post-war period of international ostracism of Spain as a relic of the interwar rise of fascist ideologies in Europe. Despite the survival of the Franco regime and the key role played by international lawyers supporting that regime in the broader international law profession over the following decades, the book's lengthy historical journey concludes in 1953 to mark the end of a historical cycle in the history of international law in Spain.

Historians understand 'periodization' as the 'process or study of categorizing the past into discrete, quantified named blocks of time in order to facilitate the study and analysis of History'. The equivalent of the square and triangle in the historians' tool-kit, periodizations are used as a conceptual tool to tear History's 'seamless web'.[1] In developing their historical craft, scholars interested in the study of the history of international law continually make use of multiple periodizations. Occasionally, they also propose alternative ones. In this case, the relative linear chronology pursued throughout the book was methodologically designed to provide a 'historiographical' backbone in a neglected area of studies. This historiographical backbone shall surely be gradually fleshed out by future historical research on the history of international law in Spain for each of the different periods covered in the present volume, and, hopefully, also for both previous and subsequent ones. However, in order to contribute to the "formation of new, formerly unknown periods", a task that is considered "an essential part of historiographical innovation,"[2] the book also proposes the period 1770 to 1953 as a suitable temporal framework to examine the historical evolution of the study of international law in Spain. This historical

1 The expression is from F Pollock and F. W. Maitland, *The History of English Law,* (Indianapolis: Liberty Fund, 2nd ed. 1898) at 1. "Such is the unity of all history that everyone who endeavours to tell a piece of it must feel that his first sentence tears a seamless web".

2 Ibid., 898

 | DOI 10.1163/9789004343238_008

cycle began in 1770, during the latest stages of the decadent 'first empire in history on which the sun never set' at a time when this was cautiously opening itself to an 'absolutist' form of enlightenment which, through a series of reforms, including of university studies, attempted to modernize Spain without breaking its ties with the Catholic historical tradition. Paradoxically enough, this early offspring of 'enlightened despotism', which was epitomized by the search of an autochthonous Spanish natural law and law of peoples free of protestant influences, attained its climax within a diminished and beleaguered fascistized National-Catholicist state in the aftermath of the Spanish Civil War. As the dream of the 'New Order' vanished across Europe, Franco's regime wrapped itself in the rags of the ideological glorification of a pre-enlightened Spanish tradition of Catholicism and Counter-Reformation with the School of Salamanca at one of its epicentres. The year 1953, by marking the end of the climax of this second *ius* internationalist legal cultural atavistic period, signals, as well, the end of a historical cycle in the history of international law in Spain.

## 2.

In the practice of history writing, however, the choice of the departure point and ending point of a narrative are only one of the many necessary engagements with the multiple existing periodizations that any author encounters as he develops his narrative structure. Any narrative is built on the goal of 'informing the reader of what happened'. This 'story-telling function' of history writing is combined with, a more or less implicit, or explicit, 'persuasive and rhetorical purpose.'[3] An open-ended historical narrative which, in its own flow conveys itself to the reader is, in this author's view, preferable to one where the supposed 'lessons of history' unearthed by it appear in the form of maximalist clear-cut conceptual statements. The subtlety of the illocutionary impact in the reader's understanding triggered by the knowledge-creation process carried by history writing should be enough to convey its ultimate educational purpose or nothing else will do.

Nonetheless, a *longue durée* perspective of the history of international law in Spain over almost two hundred years has shown, among other aspects, which can be found broadly summarized in the 'Introduction', that the enthusiasm for international law and commitment to its study came in ebbs and flows for

3 Anna Green and Kathleen Troup, *The Houses of History. A Critical Reader in History and Theory* (Manchester: Manchester University Press 1999) 205.

almost 200 years in Spain. The intensity of these internationalist waves varied greatly depending on both domestic and external circumstances. Since the late 18$^{th}$ century, and throughout the nineteenth century, the development of international law in Spain accompanied the rise and consolidation of the liberal constitutional state, becoming submerged during periods of absolutist rule. This tendency repeated itself during the twentieth century as the liberal state became prey of authoritarian ideologies and international law turned into a propagandist companion of Spanish foreign policies. A *longue durée* perspective of the history of international law in Spain has also shown the importance of national universalist symbols and of their reinterpretation over time as well as the limits of internationalism in critical historical junctures. The first rediscovery of the School of Salamanca among international law scholars took place in the late 19th century at a time when the new academically organized profession was looking to set up a genealogy of the origins of the science of international law which accompanied the justification of a new strand of 'civilizing' European formal imperialism. The second and definitive renaissance of Francisco de Vitoria, and the ensuing consolidation of the international reputation of the 'Spanish classics of international law' as the founders of international law materialised in the mid-1920s and early 1930s against the background of the renewal of cultural and linguistic ties under the cloak of Hispanidad between Spanish and Latin-American nations spurred by the establishment of the League of Nations. This propitious diplomatic backdrop coincided, as the book has explained, with an intellectual re-alignment and updating of the doctrines of Francisco de Vitoria and the Spanish classics of the Seconda Scholastica at a time when the international legal doctrine across Europe was looking in an anti-sovereigntist vein for a natural law-based ancillary stone of the 'international community' to further legitimize the appeal of the League of Nations and the binding force of international law.

Along with these international 'renaissances' of Vitoria and the Salamanca School, there was, as the book has examined, an 'ideological glorification' of the Spanish classics of international law during the civil war and early Franco's years. Francisco de Vitoria and the Salamanca School—almost caricaturally portrayed by Spanish international lawyers as champions of the defence of Catholicism and the right to rebellion against tyranny by a military uprising supported by Nazi Germany and Fascist Italy against a democratic liberal government—became intellectual pawns in an atmosphere of forced entanglement to an imagery of anti-liberal, nationalist and ultra-catholic references in the name of a glorious imperial past which was portrayed as the antithesis of foreign mimetic intellectualism. While the book does not pass any judgement on historical figures, whose ideas and attitudes are placed 'in the context' of their own polarized and critical times, it does, nonetheless, contain an implicit warning from the Spanish history of international law regarding the risks of manipulation of symbolic intellectual myths and the feeble nature of the legal internationalism of national intellectual elites at critical historical junctures.

## 3.

The history of the study of international law in Spain during the nineteenth century and the first half of the twentieth century contained in this book is finally, like any other history, an imperfect and always incomplete sum of multiple histories. It is also a fragment of the infinite whole of the history of international law. This, like the 'Poem' in Jorge Luis Borges' 'Another Poem of the Gifts', is 'inexhaustible and becomes one with the sum of all created things, and will never reach its last verse, and varies according to its writers'.[4]

---

4 Jorge Luis Borges, 'El otro poema de los dones', Jorge Luis Borges, *El otro, el mismo* (1964), in *Obras Completas de Jorge Luis Borges* Vol. II (Barcelona: Emecé, 1989).

# Bibliography


Abad y Cavia, Fidel. 'El dominico español Sr. Francisco de Vitoria and los principios modernos sobre el derecho de la guerra', Revista de Derecho Internacional y Política Exterior 4 (1909), 241–292.

Aguilar Navarro, Mariano. 'La guerra en el orden internacional' 13 Revista de Estudios Políticos 13 (1944), 23–88.

Aguilar Navarro, Mariano. 'Tareas de la doctrina española de Derecho internacional público', Revista Española de Derecho Internacional 17 (1964), 501–515.

Aguilera de la Arena, Rafael. El Tratado de Versalles y el Pacto de 5 de noviembre de 1918 ante el derecho internacional contemporaneo (Madrid: Imprenta y encuadernación de Julio Cosano, 1930).

Ainsa, Fernando. 'El centenario de Ariel: una lectura para el 2000', Cuadernos Americanos 85 (2001), 18–35.

Alfredo Liebana Collado. La educación en España en el primer tercio del siglo XX: la situación del analfabetismo y la escolarización (Madrid: Universidad de Mayores de Experiencia Recíproca, 2009).

Alguacil Cuenca, Pedro. 'España: de la Sociedad de Naciones a Naciones Unidas', Anales de derecho de la Universidad de Murcia 24 (2006), 303–318.

Allen Coates, Benjamin. Legalist Empire. International Law and American Foreign Relations in the Early Twentieth Century (Oxford: Oxford University Press, 2016).

Allue Salvador, Miguel. La condicion juridica de los consules (Zaragoza: Mariano Salas, 1909).

Alonso Getino, Luis G. (ed.) Relecciones vitorianas con textos en latin y su traducción castellana, facsimiles de codices y ediciones principes, variantes, notas e introduccion (Madrid: Impr. La Rafa, 1933–35).

Alonso Getino, Luis G. El Maestro Fr. Francisco de Vitoria y el renacimiento filosófico teológico del siglo XVI. Revista. de archivos, bibliotecas y museos (1914).

Alonso Getino, Luis G. El Maestro Fray Francisco de Vitoria. Su vida, su doctrina y su influencia. (Madrid: Imprenta Católica, 1930).

Alonso y Pesquera, Eusebio. Historia de las relaciones internacionales de España (Madrid: Impr. de José M. Ducazca, 1856).

Altamira, Rafael Historia de la civilización española (Barcelona: Manuales Soler, 1902).

Altamira, Rafael. 'España, los Estados Unidos y América', Revista de las Españas 7–8 (1927), 17–77.

Altamira, Rafael. 'La Organización comunal de todos los Estados', Revista de derecho internacional, legislación y jurisprudencia comparadas 27 (1887), 39.

Altamira, Rafael. España y el programa americanista (Madrid: Ed. América, 1917).

Altamira, Rafael. Historia de España y de la civilización española, 4 vols. (Barcelona: impr. Juan Gili, 1900–1911).

Altamira, Rafael. La Guerra actual y la opinión española (Barcelona: Araluce, 1915) (republ. Pamplona: Editorial Analecta, 2015).

Altwicker, Tilmann and Oliver Diggelmann, 'How is Progress Constructed in International Legal Scholarship?' 25 European Journal of International Law (2014), 425–444.

Alvarez Chillida, Gonzalo. 'El fracaso de un proyecto autoritario: el debate constitucional en la asamblea nacional de Primo de Rivera', Revista de Estudios Políticos 93 (1996), 359–375.

Álvarez de los Corrales y Melgarejo, Diego. Breves consideraciones sobre las doctrinas de los escritores españoles de derecho internacional del siglo XVI (Madrid: Universidad Central, 1855).

Alvarez de Morales, Antonio 'La enseñanza del derecho natural y de gentes: el libro de Heinecio', in Manuel Bermejo Castrillo (Ed), Manuales y textos de enseñanza en la universidad liberal (Madrid: Dykinson, 2004), 365–382.

Álvarez de Morales, Antonio. 'La difusión del derecho natural y de gentes europeo en la universidad española de los siglos XVIII y XIX', in Doctores y escolares. II Congreso internacional de Historia de las universidades Hispánicas (Valencia: Editorial Universidad de Vàlencia 1995), 49–60.

Alvarez, Alejandro. 'Latin-America and International Law', American Journal of International Law 3 (1909), 269–353.

Alvarez, Alejandro. 'The New International Law', Transactions of The Grotius Society 15 (1929), 35–51.

Alvarez, Alejandro. Le droit international américain: Son Fondement, sa Nature d'apres L'Histoire Diplomatique des Etats du Nouveau Monde et leur Vie Politique et Economique (Paris: Pedone 1910).

Alvarez, José E. 'Between Gallipoli and D-Day: Alhucemas, 1925', The Journal of Military History 63 (1999), 75–98.

Amado, Luis. 'La Opinión española y la política exterior (cont.)', Revista de Derecho Internacional y Politica Exterior 3 (1908), 62–70.

Amado, Luis. 'La Opinión española y la política exterior', Revista de Derecho Internacional y Politica Exterior 2 (1907), 61–71.

Amorosa, Paolo. 'James Brown Scott's International Adjudication between Tradition and Progress in the United States', Journal of the History of International Law 17 (2015), 15–46.

Amunátegui, Miguel Luis. Vida de don Andrés Bello (Santiago de Chile: Imprenta de PG Ramirez, 1882).

Anderson, P. Chandler. 'Final Liquidation of German War Reparations', American Journal of International Law 25 (1931), 97–101.

Anghie, Antony. 'Finding the Peripheries. Sovereignty and Colonialism in Nineteenth Century International Law', Harvard International Law Journal 40 (1999), 1–80.

Anghie, Antony. 'Nationalism, Development and the Postcolonial State: The Legacies of the League of Nations' Texas International Law Journal (2006), 447–463.

Anghie, Antony. 'On Critique and the Other', in Anne Orford (ed.), International Law and Its Others (Cambridge: Cambridge University Press, 2009), 389–400.

Anghie, Antony. Imperialism, Sovereignty and the Making of International Law, (Cambridge: Cambridge University Press, 2005).

Anónimo, 'Relacion del Sitio de Melilla' Revista de Derecho Internacional y de Politica Exterior 4 (1908) 293–315.

Armitage, David. Foundations of Modern International Thought, (Cambridge: Cambridge University Press, 2013).

Arnabat i Mata, Ramón. 'El impacto europeo y americano de la proclamación de la Constitución de Cádiz en 1820', Revista de historia moderna y contemporánea 24 (2012), 47–64.

Ashworth, Lucian M. 'Where are the Idealists in Interwar International Relations?', Review of International Studies 32 (2006), 291–308.

Austin, John. 'Province of Jurisprudence Determined: The First Part of a Series of Lectures on Jurisprudence, or, the Philosophy of Law' (London: John Murray, 1832).

Azaña, Manuel. 'Discurso en la Universidad de Valencia' in Manuel Azaña, Los españoles en Guerra. (Barcelona: Editorial Crítica, 1999).

Azaña, Manuel. 'Los motivos de la germanofilia'. (Madrid: Imprenta Helénica, 1917).

Balfour, Sebastian. 'Spain and the Great Powers in the Aftermath of the Disaster of 1898', in Sebastian Balfour / Paul Preston (eds.), Spain and the Great Powers in the Twentieth Century (London: Routledge 1999), 13–31.

Balfour, Sebastian. 'Spain from 1931 to the Present', in Raymond Carr (ed.) Spain. A History (2001), 243–283.

Balfour, Sebastian. 'The Loss of Empire, Regenerationism, and the Forging of a Myth of National Identity', in Helen Graham and Jo Labanyi (eds.), Oxford Spanish Cultural Studies: An Introduction. The Struggle for Modernity (London: University Press 1995), 25–39.

Balladore Pallieri, Giorgio. 'Quelques aspects juridiques de la non-intervention en Espagne', Revue de droit international et de la législation comparée 18 (1937) 285.

Barcia Trelles, Camilo. 'El ayer, el hoy y el mañana internacionales', Revista de Estudios Políticos 50 (1950), 135–156.

Barcia Trelles, Camilo. 'El pacto Atlántico y las inclinaciones geopolíticas de la URSS', Revista de Política Internacional 4 (1950), 13–52.

Barcia Trelles, Camilo. 'Fernando Vázquez de Menchaca. L'école espagnole du droit international du xvie siécle', Collected courses of the Hague Academy of International Law 67 (1939), 430–534.

Barcia Trelles, Camilo. 'Francisco suarez (1548–1617): les théologiens espagnols du xvie siècle et l'école moderne du droit international', Collected courses of the Hague Academy of International Law 43 (1933), 385–554.

Barcia Trelles, Camilo. 'Fray Francisco de Vitoria y la Carta orgánica de San Francisco', in AA VV, Fray Francisco de Vitoria, fundador del Derecho internacional moderno 1546–1946 (Madrid: Ediciones Cultura Hispánica 1946), 91.

Barcia Trelles, Camilo. 'La Constitución Americana y la Sociedad de Naciones' (Valladolid: talleres tipográficos Cuesta, 1930).

Barcia Trelles, Camilo. 'La Doctrina Monroe y el problema de la cooperación internacional' (Madrid: Ed. Mundo Latino, 1931).

Barcia Trelles, Camilo. 'La doctrine de monroe dans son développement historique particulièrement en ce qui concerne les relations interamericaines' Collected Courses of the Hague Academy of International Law 32 (1930), 391–603.

Barcia Trelles, Camilo. El imperialismo del petróleo y la paz mundial, (Valladolid: talleres tipográficos Cuesta, 1925).

Barcia Trelles, Camilo. 'Francisco de vitoria et l'ecole moderne du droit international', Collected courses of the Hague Academy of International Law 17 (1928), 109–342.

Barcia Trelles,Camilo. La política exterior norteamericana de la postguerra, (Valladolid: talleres tipográficos Cuesta 1925).

Barcia Trelles, Camilo. Puntos cardinales de la politica exterior española, (Barcelona: Editorial Fe, 1939).

Baron Kaltenborn, Carl. Die Vorläufer des Hugo Grotius auf dem Gebiete des jus naturae et gentium sowie der Politik im Reformationszeitalter (Leipzig: Verlag von Gustav Mayer, 1848).

Barredi Barandiaran, Ana. 'El Monumento a Francisco de Vitoria, Historia de su construccion', Sancho el Sabio 25 (2006), 165–179.

Barthelemy, Jean. François de Vitoria, in A. Pillet (ed.), Les fondateurs du droit international, leurs œuvres, leurs doctrines (Paris: V. Giard & E. Brière, 1904), 1–36.

Bartolomé de las Casas, 'Historia de las Indias', in Juan Pérez de Tudela (ed.), Obras escogidas de Bartolomé de las Casas. vol. I (Madrid: Ed. Atlas. 1957).

Baxell, Richard. British Volunteers in the Spanish Civil War: The British Battalion in the International Brigades, 1936–1939 (London: Routledge, 2004).

Bayly, Christopher A. The Birth of the Modern World (1790–1914) (Oxford: Blackwell, 2004).

Beato Sala, Isidro. 'La propaganda de la religión cristiana, como título de conquista, según las enseñanzas del Maestro Vitoria', Anuario de la Asociación Francisco de Vitoria III (1932).

Becker Gonzalez, Jerónimo. Historia de las relaciones exteriores de España durante el siglo xix. Apuntes para una historia diplomática (Madrid, Establecimiento Tipográfico de Jaime Ratés, 1924–1926, 3 vols.)

Becker Lorca, Arnulf. 'International Law in Latin America or Latin American International Law? Rise, Fall, and Retrieval of a Tradition of Legal Thinking and Political Imagination', Harvard International Law Journal 47 (2006), 283–305.

Becker Lorca, Arnulf. 'Universal International Law: Nineteenth-Century Histories of Imposition and Appropiation', Harvard International Law Journal 51 (2010), 475–552.

Becker Lorca, Arnulf. Mestizo International Law. A Global Intellectual History, 1842–1933 (Cambridge: Cambridge University Press, 2015).

Beckett, W.E. 'International law in England', Law Quarterly Review 55 (1939) 257–258.

Bello, Andrés. Principios de derecho de gentes (Santiago de Chile: Impr. de la Opinión, 1832).

Bello, Andrés. Principios de derecho internacional (Madrid: Viuda de Calleja e hijos, 1844).

Beneyto, José María, Politische Theologie ais politische Theorie. Eine Untersuchung zur Rechts- und Staatstheorie Cari Schmitts und zu ihrer Wirkungsgeschichte in Spanien, (Berlin: Dunckcr und Humblot, 1983).

Bentham, Jeremy. Tratados de legislación civil y penal (traducción de Ramón Salas) (Madrid: Imprenta de Fermín Villalpando, 1821).

Bentley, Jerry H. 'Cross-Cultural Interaction and Periodization in World History' American Historical Review 101 (1996), 749–770.

Berdah, Jean-François M. 'L'Allemagne et le Royaume-Uni face à la question espagnole: reconnaissance de facto ou reconnaisance de jure? (1936–1939)', Mélanges de la Casa de Velázquez 29 (1993), 203–241.

Berman, Nathaniel. 'Between 'Alliance' and 'Localization': Nationalism and the New Oscillationism' New York University Journal of International Law and Politics 26 (1993–1994), 449.

Berman, Nathaniel. 'Le clivage de l'internationalisme face aux guerres d'Espagne et de Bosnie: entre 'alliance' et 'localization' in Nathaniel Berman, Passions et Ambivalences. Le colonialisme, le nationalisme et le droit international (Paris: A. Pédone, 2008), 235–275.

Bersier Ladavac, Nicoletta. 'Hans Kelsen (1881–1973) Biographical Note and Bibliography', European Journal of International Law 9 (1998), 391–400.

Bethlehem, Daniel. 'The Secret Life of International Law', Cambridge Journal of International and Comparative Law 1 (2012), 23–36.

Blanc Altemir, Antonio. El marquès d'olivart i el dret international (1861–1928). Societat internacional i aportació científica (Lleida: Institut d'Estudis Ilerdencs, 2000).

Boast, R.B. 'The Spanish Origins of International Human Rights Law: A Historiographical Review', Victoria University of Wellington Law Review 41(2010), 235–272.

Bonfiglio, Florencia. 'Los principios hispanoamericanos: la crítica de José Enrique Rodó y la literatura peninsular', in Raquel Macciuci (ed) Huellas de la Constitución de Cádiz; Diálogos transatlánticos (La Plata: Mercado Editorial 2011).

Borchard, Edwin. 'Neutrality' and Civil Wars', the American Journal of International Law 31 (1937), 304–306.

Bosch, Ana. Miedo a la democracia. Estados Unidos ante la Segunda República y la guerra civil española, (Barcelona: Editorial Crítica, 2012).

Bourgeois, Émile. Manuel historique de politique étrangère. (Paris: Librairie classique Eugène Belin, 1898).

Bowen, Wayne H. Spaniards and Nazi Germany. Collaboration in the New Order (Columbia and London: University of Missouri Press 2000).

Boyd Rush, Dorothy. 'Winston Churchill and the Spanish Civil War', Social Science 54 (1979), 86–92.

Boyle, Francis Anthony. Foundations of World Order Foundations of World Order, The Legalist Approach to International Relations (1898–1922) (Durham N.C.: Duke University Press, 1999).

Breña, Roberto. 'Un momento clave en la historia política moderna de la América hispana, Cadiz, 1812', in Josefina Zoraida Vázquez (ed), El nacimiento de las naciones iberoamericanas—síntesis histórica (Madrid: Ed. Fundación Mapfre Tavera, 2002), 63–98. 58.

Brierly, James L. 'Bombs and the Law. An English Viewpoint' (delivered June 20, 1938 over British Broadcasting System), Vital Speeches of the Day 19. 4 (1938), 605.

Brierly, James L. 'International Law in England', Law Quarterly Review 51 (1935), 24–35.

Brown Scott, James. 'American Institute of International Law', University of Pennsylvania Law Review 61 (1913), 580–587.

Brown Scott, James. 'Asociación Francisco de Vitoria', 22 American Journal International Law 1 (1928), 136–139.

Brown Scott, James. 'Francisco Suarez: His Philosophy of Law and of Sanctions', Georgetown Law Journal 22 (1933–1934), 405.

Brown Scott, James. 'International Organization: Executive and Administrative', Proceedings of the American Society of International Law 11 (1917), 91–107.

Brown Scott, James. 'Preface', in Thomas Erskine Holland (ed.), The Classics of International Law, Richard Zouche, Iuris et iudicii fecialis, sive, iuris inter gentes, et quaestionum de eodem explication (Washington: Division of International Law, Carnegie Endowment for International Peace, 1911).

Brown Scott, James. 'The American Institute of International Law', Advocate of Peace 78 (1916), 8–10.

Brown Scott, James. 'The Hague Academy of International Law', American Journal of International Law 17 (1923), 746–751.

Brown Scott, James. 'The Revista de Derecho Internacional', The American Journal of Iinternational Law 16 (1922), 437–438.
Brown Scott, James. 'Universalidad del Derecho de Gentes', Revista de Legislación y Jurisprudencia 76 (1927), 637–660.
Brown Scott, James. Cases on International Law (St.Paul: West Publishing Company, 1926).
Brown Scott, James. Cases on International Law: Selected from Decisions of English and American Courts (St. Paul: West Publishing Company, 1906).
Brown Scott, James. El origen español del Derecho internacional moderno (Valladolid: Talleres Tipográficos Cuesta, 1928).
Brown Scott, James. El origen español del Derecho internacional moderno (Valladolid: talleres tipográficos Cuesta, 1928).
Brown Scott, James. The Catholic Conception Of International Law. Francisco De Vitoria, Founder of The Modern Law of Nations, Francisco Suarez, Founder of The Modern Philosophy of Law in General and in Particular of the Law of Nations: A Critical Examination and a Justified Appreciation (Washington, D. C.: Georgetown University Press, 1934).
Brown Scott, James. The Spanish Origin of International Law. Francisco de Vitoria and his Law of Nations (New York: Oxford University Press, 1934).
Brown Scott, James. The United States: A Study in International Organization (Oxford: Oxford University Press, 1920).
Brown, Chris. Terry Nardin, Nicholas Rengger (eds) International Relations in Political Thought: Texts from the Ancient Greeks to the First World War (Cambridge: Cambridge University Press, 2002).
Bryce, James. The american Commonwealth (London: Macmillan and Company, 1889).
Buchanan, Tom. 'Edge of Darkness: British 'Front-Line' Diplomacy in the Spanish Civil War, 1936–1937', Contemporary European History 12 (2003), 279–303.
Buchanan, Tom. 'Shanghai-Madrid Axis'? Comparing British Responses to the Conficts in Spain and China, 1936–39, Contemporary European History 21 (2012), 533–552.
Butler, William. 'Periodization and International Law', in Alexander Orakhelashvili (Ed) Research Handbook on the Theory and History of International Law (Cheltenham and Camberley: Edward Elgar, 2011), 379–393.
Cacho Viú, Vicente. La institución libre de enseñanza, orígenes y etapa universitaria, 1860–1881 (Madrid: Sociedad Estatal de conmemoraciones culturales, 2010).
Cádiz Deleito, Francisco. España y el Tribunal de La Haya: El Tribunal Permanente de Justicia Internacional y el Tribunal Internacional de Justicia (Madrid: Imprenta del Ministerio de Asuntos Exteriores, 1968).
Cadwalader, John Lambert. Digest of the Published Opinions of the Attorneys General, and of the Leading Decisions of the Federal Courts with Reference to International Law, Treaties and Kindred Subjects (Washington: Government printing office, 1877).

Callejo de la Cuesta, Eduardo. 'El plan de estudios de derecho en la universidad central (1923–1931)', Cuadernos Del Instituto Antonio De Nebrija 8 (2005), 281–358.

Calvo, Carlos. Colección completa de los tratados, convenciones, capitulaciones, armisticios y otros actos diplomáticos de todos los estados de la América Latina desde el año 1493 hasta nuestros días precedidos de una memoria sobre el estado actual de América, de cuadros estadísticas, de un diccionario diplomático y de una noticia histórica sobre cada uno de los tratados más importantes (Paris: A. Durand, 1862).

Calvo, Carlos. Derecho Internacional teórico y práctico de Europa y América (Paris: D'Amyot 1868).

Capps, Patrick. 'Lauterpacht's Method', British Yearbook of International Law 82 (2012), 248–280.

Carr, Raymond. 'Liberalism and Reaction 1833–1931', in Raymond Carr (ed), Spain: A History (Oxford, Oxford University Press 2000), 205–242.

Carr, Raymond. Spain, 1808–1936 (Oxford: Oxford University Press, 1966).

Carrillo Salcedo, Juan Antonio. El Derecho Internacional en perspectiva histórica (Madrid: Editorial Tecnos, 1997).

Carty, Anthony. 'Carl Schmitt's critique of Liberal International Legal Order Between 1933 and 1945', Leiden Journal of International Law 14 (2001), 25–36.

Carty, Anthony. 'The Continuous Influence of Kelsen on the General Perception of the Discipline of International Law', European Journal of International Law 9 (1998), 344–354.

Carty, Anthony. 'Why Theory? The Implications for International Law Teaching', in British Institute of International and Comparative Law (ed.), Theory and International Law: An Introduction (London: BIICL, 1991), 75.

Casanovas y la Rosa, Oriol. 'A Debate over International Economic Law: The Discussion between Miaja de la Muela, Adolfo. and Mariano Aguilar Navarro in 1971/72', Spanish Yearbook of International Law 19 (2015), 1–21.

Cass, Deborah. The Constitutionalisation of the World Trade Organisation: Legitimacy, Democracy and Community in the International Trading System (Oxford: Oxford University Press 2005).

Cassesse, Antonio. 'The Spanish Civil War and the Development of Customary Law Concerning Internal Armed Conflicts', in Antonio Cassese (ed.), Current Problems of International Law. Essays on U.N. Law and on the Law of Armed Conflict. (Milano: Dott.A. Giuffrè editore, 1975).

Castilla Urbano, Francisco. El pensamiento de Francisco de Vitoria: filosofía política e indio americano (Barcelona: Anthropos Editorial, 1992).

Catala, Michel. 'L'attitude de la France face à la Guerre d'Espagne: l'échec des négociations pour la reconnaissance du gouvernement franquiste en 1938', Mélanges de la Casa de Velázquez 29 (1993), 243–262.

Cauchy, Eugène. Le droit maritime international consideré dans ses origines et dans ses rapports avec le progrès de la civilisation (Paris: Ed. Guillaumin, 1862).
Chapman, Michael E. Arguing Americanism. Franco Lobbyists, Rooselvelt's Foreign Policy and the Spanish Civil War (Kent: Kent State University Press, 2011).
Chernilo, Daniel. 'The critique of methodological nationalism: Theory and History', Thesis Eleven 106 (2011), 98–117.
Chetail, Vincent. 'Vattel and the American Dream: An Inquiry into the Reception of the Law of Nations', in Vincent Chetail / Pierre Marie Dupuy (eds.), The Roots of International Law. Liber Amicorum Peter Haggenmacher (Leiden: Martinus Nijhoff 2013), 251–300.
Claret Miranda, Jaume. El atroz desmoche. La destrucción de la Universidad española por el Franquismo, 1936–1945 (Barcelona: Ed. Crítica, 2006).
Coates, Ken. 'North American Indigenous Peoples' Encounters', in Bardo Fassbender/ Anne Peters (eds.), The Oxford Handbook of the History of International Law (Oxford: Oxford University Press 2012), 787–810.
Cohen, Felix S. 'The Spanish Origin of Indian Rights in the Law of the United States' 31 Georgetown Law Journal 1 (1942–1943), 1.
Condorelli, Luigi. 'Scholie sur l'idiome scellien des manuels francophones de droit international public', European Journal of International Law 1 (1990), 232–234.
Conrotte, Manuel. La Intervencion de España en la Independencia de Los Estados Unidos, (Madrid: Libreria general de Victoriano Suarez, 1920).
Conrotte, Manuel. Manual de Derecho internacional para uso de Jefes y Oficiales del Ejército y Armada (Madrid: Imprenta del Patronato de Huérfanos de Administración Militar, 1906).
Conrotte, Manuel. Un proyecto de Tratado entre Turquia y España en el reinado de Felipe V, Revista de Derecho Internacional y Politica Exterior 3 (1907), 223–267.
Cordero Torres, José María. Aspectos de la misión universal de España (Madrid: Vicesecretaria de Educación popular, 1942).
Crawford, James. 'Public International Law in 20th Century England', in Jack Beatson and Reinhard Zimmermann (eds.) Jurists Uprooted: German-Speaking Emigré Lawyers in Twentieth Century Britain (Oxford: Oxford University Press, 2004) 681–701.
Crawford, James. The Creation of States in International Law (Oxford: Oxford University Press 1979).
Dalmau de Olivart, Ramón. 'De la Dislocacion de la política exterior española en Marruecos' Revista de Derecho Internacional y Politica Exterior 5 (1909–1910), 107–137.
Dalmau de Olivart, Ramón. 'Origen y desarrollo de la doctrina de Drago y su aceptación parcial por la segunda Conferencia de la Paz', Revista de Derecho Internacional y Politica Exterior 3 (1907) 232.

Dalmau de Olivart, Ramón. Colección de tratados, convenios y documentos internacionales concluidos o ratificados por nuestros gobiernos con los estados extranjeros desde el reinado de doña Isabel II hasta nuestros días (Madrid: Fernando Fé, 1902).

Dalmau de Olivart, Ramón. El Derecho internacional público en los últimos veinticinco años (Madrid: Espasa Calpe, 1927).

Dalmau de Olivart, Ramón. Francisco de Vitoria, Reelecciones de indios y del derecho de la guerra con trozos referentes a la potestad civil, texto latino y versión al español (Madrid: Espasa Calpe, 1928)

Dalmau de Olivart, Ramón. La posesión: apuntes y fragmentos de una nueva teoría posesoria. noción en el derecho abstracto. etimología, carácter jurídico, base de su protección (Barcelona: J. Jepus, 1884).

Dalmau de Olivart, Ramón. La sesión de Gante del Instituto de Derecho internacional, Revista de Derecho Internacional y de Politica Exterior 3 (1907), 142.

Dalmau de Olivart, Ramón. La Sociedad de Naciones (Madrid: Imprenta Patronato de huerfanos de la intendencia e intervencion militares, 1919).

Dalmau de Olivart, Ramón. Manual de derecho internacional público y privado: extractado y traducido de las obras de Calvo, Bar, Neumann etc., con extensas notas y un bosquejo del derecho internacional privado español. Tomo I (Madrid: Fernando Fe, 1886).

Dalmau de Olivart, Ramón. Tratado elemental de Derecho Internacional Público. Segunda edición con un apendice del autor sobre el estado de la ciencia (Madrid: Impr. Los hijos de R. Álvarez, 1900).

Dalmau de Olivart, Ramón. Tratado y notas de derecho internacional público (Madrid: Manuel Murillo, 1887).

Dalmau de Olivart, Ramón. Tratado y notas de derecho internacional público (Madrid: Manuel Murillo, 1899).

De Abreu y Bertodano, Joseph Antonio. Colección de Tratados de Paz, 12 vols. (Madrid: Antonio Marin, 1840–1852).

De Azcarate y Florez, Pablo. League of Nations and National Minorities: an Experiment (Washington: Carnegie endowment for international peace, 1945).

De Blas Guerrero, Andrés. 'Regeneracionismo español y cuestion nacional', in Antonio Morales Moya et al. (eds) Historia de la nacion y del nacionalismo español (Barcelona: Galaxia Gutenberg, 2013), 638–650.

De Calatayud, Antonio. La condición jurídica del espacio aéreo ante el derecho internacional (Valencia: Est. tip. hijos de F. Vives Mora, 1913).

De Erice O'Shea, José Sebastián. 'España y las Naciones Unidas' 1 Revista de Política Internacional 4 (1950), 9–49.

De Erice O'Shea, José Sebastián. Derecho Diplomático. (Madrid: Instituto de estudios políticos, 1954).

De Felice, Fortunato Bartolomeo. Lecciones de Derecho natural y de gentes (Madrid: Impr. Nueva Bernardo Marin, 1841).

De Ferrater, Esteban. Código de derecho internacional, o sea, Colección metódica de los tratados de paz, amistad y comercio entre España y las demás naciones tomo primero (Barcelona: Impr. Ramón Martín Indar, 1846).

De Heredia, Beltrán. Un Precursor del Maestro Vitoria. El P. Matias de Paz, O. P., y su tratado "De dominio regum hispaniae super Indos" (Salamanca: Calatrava, 1929).

De Herrera, Cristobal Martín. Discurso sobre el verdadero fin del Derecho internacional (Madrid: Impr. de J. Compañel, 1855).

De Hinojosa y Naveros, Eduardo. Historia general del derecho español. Tomo I. (Madrid Tip. de los Huérfanos, 1887).

De Hinojosa y Naveros, Eduardo. 'De la influencia que tuvieron en el Derecho público de su patria, y singularmente en el derecho penal, los filósofos y teólogos españoles anteriores a nuestro siglo' (Madrid: Tipografía de los Huérfanos, 1890).

De La Brière, Yves. Vitoria et Suarez—Contribution des Théologiens au Droit International Moderne (Paris: Pédone, 1939).

De la Rasilla del Moral, 'El estudio de la historia del Derecho internacional en el corto siglo XIX español' Zeitschrift des Max-Planck-Instituts für europäische Rechtsgeschichte 23 (2013), 48–65.

De la Rasilla del Moral, 'The Unexpected Transformations and Reintepretations of Francisco de Vitoria for International Law', International Community Law Review 15 (2013), 287–318.

De la Rasilla del Moral, Ignacio / Yolanda Gamarra (eds) Historia del Pensamiento Iusinternacionalista español del siglo XX (Cizur Menor: Thompson-Reuters Aranzadi, 2012).

De la Rasilla del Moral, Ignacio, 'The Zero Years of Spanish International Law' in Emmanuelle Jouannet and Iulia Motoc (eds.) Les doctrines internationalistes durant les annees du communisme reel' (Paris: Société de législation comparée, 2012), 237–276.

De la Rasilla del Moral, Ignacio. / Yolanda Gamarra (eds.) Historia del pensamiento internacionalista español del siglo XX, (Cizur Menor: Thompson Reuters Aranzadi, 2012).

De la Rasilla del Moral, Ignacio. 'Beyond the Spanish Classics—The Ephemeral Awakening of the History of International Law in Pre-Democratic Spain', Monde(s), Histoires, Relations 7 (2015), 137–157.

De la Rasilla del Moral, Ignacio. 'In the General Interest of Peace? British International Lawyers and the Spanish Civil War', Journal of the History of International Law 18 (2016), 197–238.

De la Rasilla del Moral, Ignacio. 'International Criminal Justice as Universal Social Defence, Quintiliano Saldaña (1878–1938)', in F. Megret and I. Talgrenn (eds), The

Dawn of a Discipline—International Criminal Justice and Its Early Exponents (Cambridge: Cambridge University Press, forthcoming, 2018).

De la Rasilla del Moral, Ignacio. 'The Fascist Mimesis of Spanish International Law and its Vitorian Aftermath, 1939–1953', The Journal of the History of International Law 14 (2012), 207–236.

De la Rasilla del Moral, Ignacio. 'History of International Law 1550–1700', in Oxford Bibliographies of International Law (Oxford: Oxford University Press, 2014), 1–25.

De la Rasilla del Moral, Ignacio. 'The Study of the History of International Law in the Short Spanish Nineteenth Century', Chicago-Kent Journal of International and Comparative Law 13 (2013), 122–150.

De Labra, Rafael María. 'Marruecos y la Conferencia de Algeciras', Revista de Derecho Internacional y de Politica Exterior 2 (1906), 274–321.

De Labra, Rafael María. El Derecho internacional y los Estados Unidos de América (Madrid: Impr. A. J. Alaria, 1877).

De Labra, Rafael Maria. La colonización en la Historia (Madrid: Editorial San Martín, 1877).

De Labra, Rafael María. La política colonial y la revolución española de 1868 (Madrid: Tipografia Sindicato de Publicidad, 1916).

De Landa y Alvarez de Carvallo, Nicasio. El derecho de la Guerra conforme à la moral (Pamplona: Imprenta de Joaquín Lorda, 1867).

De Lapradelle, Albert Geouffre, and Nicolas Politis (eds.) Recueil des arbitrages internationaux, Vol. I. (Paris: Les editions internationales, 1905).

De Llauder, Fernando M. Rápida ojeada sobre el Derecho internacional antiguo y moderno (Madrid: Imprenta de Tejado, 1855).

De Luna, Antonio. 'España, Europa y la Cristiandad', Revista de Estudios Políticos 9–10 (1943), 41–98.

De Madariaga, Salvador. Desarmément (Geneva: ed. por la Société de Nations, 1932)

De Madariaga, Salvador. Theory and Practice of International Relations, (Filadelfia: Swarthmore College, 1937)

De Martens, Jorge Federico. Tratado de Derecho internacional, prólogo y notas de J. Fernández Prida, 4 vols., (Madrid: 1882).

De Martens, Jorge Federico. Tratado de diplomática, o estado de relaciones de las potencias de Europa entre sí, y con los demás pueblos del globo (prologo y traducción de Joaquín Rodrigo Campuzano) (Madrid: Imprenta Real 1835).

De Olmeda y León, José. Elementos de derecho público de la paz y de la guerra, ilustrados con noticias históricas, leyes y doctrinas del derecho español (Madrid: Impr. Viuda de Manuel Hernandez, 1771).

De Onís, Federico. Ensayos sobre el sentido de la cultura española (Madrid: Ed. Publicaciones de la Residencia de Estudiantes, 1932).

De Ortega y Cotes, Ignacio Joseph. Questiones del derecho publico en interpretación de los tratados de paces (Madrid: Impr. Antonio Marin, 1747).

De Poó, Antonio Rafael. Necesidad imprescindible de adoptar un método único en el estudio del Derecho internacional (Madrid: Impr. de D. Eusebio Aguado, 1858).

De Vattel, Emeric. El Derecho de gentes, o principios de la Ley Natural aplicados a la conducta y a los negocios de las naciones y de los soberanos (Traducción de M. Pascual Fernandez) (Madrid: Imprenta de I. Sancha, 1820).

De Visscher, Paul. Les tendances internationales des constitutions modernes, Collected Courses of the Hague Academy of International Law 80 (1952), 512–578.

De Vitoria, Francisco, Political Writings, in Anthony Pagden, Jeremy Lawrance (eds.) (Cambridge University Press, 2001).

De Vitoria, Francisco. De Indis et De iure belli relectiones (Classics of International Law. Preface, by J.B. Scott. Introduction, by Ernest Nys) (Washington: The Carnegie Endowment, 1917).

De Vitoria, Francisco. De Potestate Civili (1528), in Luis G.A. Getino (ed.) Relecciones Teologicas del Maestro Fray Fr. De Vitoria (Madrid: Editorial FEDA, 1934).

De Vitoria, Francisco. Relectio de jure belli, o, Paz dinámica: Escuela Española de la Paz primera generación, 1526–1560 Luciano Pereña (ed.) (Madrid: Editorial CSIC-CSIC 1981).

De Zayas, Alfred. 'Spanish Civil War', Max Planck Encyclopedia of Public International Law (2013) 1–10.

Del Arenal, Celestino. 'El estudio de las relaciones internacionales en la España del siglo XIX', Revista de Estudios Políticos 163 (1979), 7–45.

Del Arenal, Celestino. 'La génesis de las relaciones internacionales como disciplina científica', Revista de Estudios Internacionales 4 (1981), 849–892.

Del Arenal, Celestino. La teoría de las Relaciones Internacionales en España (Madrid: Sección Española de la Internacional Law Association, 1979).

Del Arenal, Celestino. Politica exterior de España y relaciones con America Latin. Iberoamericanidad, europeización y atlantismo en la política exterior española, (Madrid: Fundación Carolina, 2011).

Del Arenal, Concepción. Ensayo sobre el derecho de gentes (Madrid: Sucesores de Rivadeneyra, 1879).

Del Cantillo, Alejandro. Tratados, convenios y declaraciones de paz, 1700–1840 (Madrid: 1843).

Delgado Gómez-Escalonilla, Lorenzo. 'Un siglo de diplomacia cultural española: de la Junta para Ampliación de Estudios al Instituto Cervantes', Real Instituto Elcano, Documento de Trabajo 12 (2014), 11–42.

Dezalay, Yves/Bryant G. Garth, 'Law, Lawyers and Empire', in Michael Grossberg / Christopher L. Tomlins (eds), Cambridge History of Law in America. The Twentieth Century and After (1920-) (Cambridge: Cambridge University Press 2011), 718–758.

Díaz Sampedro, Braulio. 'Román Riaza Martinez-Osorio', Diccionario de catedráticos españoles de derecho (1847–1943) (Madrid: Universidad Carlos III de Madrid. Instituto Figuerola de Historia y Ciencias Sociales, 2011).

Díaz, Elías. La filosofía social del krausismo español, (Madrid: Edicusa, 1973).

Díaz-Plaja, Fernando. La España franquista en sus documentos. (Barcelona: Plaza & Janés 1976).

Dicey, Albert Venn. Introduction to the Study of the Law of the Constitution (London: Macmillan and Company, 1915).

Dicey, Albert Venn. Lectures on the Relation between Law and Public Opinion in England during the Nineteenth Century (London: Macmillan and Company, 1905).

Dickinson, John. 'Review of Brown Scott's The Catholic Conception of International Law', Georgetown Law Journal 24 (1935–1936), 215–218.

Diez de Velasco Vallejo, Manuel. 'El profesor Miaja de la Muela: Ensayo biográfico' in libro homenaje al profesor A. Miaja de la Muela (Madrid: ed. Tecnos 1979), 18–29.

Domingo Acebrón, Maria Dolores. 'Rafael Maria de Labra ante la cuestion de Cuba, 1898', Anuario de Estudios Americanos LV (1998), 153–164.

Dupuy, René-Jean. 'Images de Georges Scelle', European Journal of International Law 2 (1990), 235–239.

Duverdy, Carlos. 'Derecho Internacional. Derecho de los neutrales. Contrabando de guerra. Decreto de 24 de febrero de 1854. Corsarios neutrales'. Revista general de legislación y jurisprudencia 3 (1855), 686–97.

Duverdy, Carlos. 'Derecho Internacional: Cuestión de Mr. Soulé', Revista general de legislación y jurisprudencia 2 (1854), 132–138.

Edward Kerr, James. The Insular Cases. The Role of the Judiciary in American Expansionism (Port Washington, N.Y.: Kennikat Press, 1982).

Edwards, Jill. The British Government and the Spanish Civil War (London: MacMillan Press, 1979).

Espaliu Berdud, Carlos. La junta de ampliación de estudios e investigaciones científicas y el derecho internacional in Ignacio de la Rasilla / Yolanda Gamarra (eds.) Historia del pensamiento internacionalista español del siglo XX (Cizur Menor: Thomson Reuters Aranzadi, 2012), 153–184.

Esquirol, Jorge L. 'Latin America', in Bardo Fassbender / Anne Peters (eds) Oxford Handbook of the History of International Law (Oxford: Oxford University Press 2012), 553–577.

Esteban De Vega, Mariano. / Francisco de Luis / Antonio Morales Moya (eds.) Jirones de hispanidad: España, Cuba, Puerto Rico y Filipinas en la perspectiva de dos siglos (Salamanca: ediciones de la Universidad de Salamanca, 2004).

Esteve y Vila, Antonio. Desarrollo histórico-científico del Derecho internacional (Madrid, Impr. de José Ducazcal, 1855).

Evans Darby, William. International arbitration. International Tribunals. A Collection of the Various Schemes which have been Propounded and of Instances in the Nineteenth Century (London: Peace Society, 1899).

Fabra Rivas, Antonio, La organización internacional del trabajo (Madrid: Ed. Javier Morata Pedreño, 1925).

Fassbender, Bardo. UN Security Council Reform and the Right of Veto. A Constitutional Perspective, (Leiden: Martinus Nijhoff 1998), 37–45.

Feldman, Matthew / Marius Turda / Tudor Georgescu (eds.) Clerical Fascism in Interwar Europe (London: Routledge 2013).

Fenwick, Charles G. 'Can Civil Wars be brought under the Control of International Law?' American Journal of International Law 32 (1938), 538–542.

Fernandez de Cordoba, Gónzalo. La solución jurídica de los conflictos internacionales (Madrid: Imprenta de La revista de legislación, 1903).

Fernández de la Mora, Gónzalo. 'La política exterior de España', in El nuevo Estado español. Veinticinco años de Movimiento Nacional, 1936-1961 (Madrid: Ed. Instituto de Estudios Políticos 1961), 65–92.

Fernandez Liesa, Carlos. 'La cuestion de Olivenza a la luz del Derecho Internacional Publico', Encontros, Revista luso-española de investigadores en Ciencias Humanas y Sociales 4 (2004), 230–281.

Fernandez Liesa, Carlos. El Derecho internacional de los derechos humanos en perspectiva histórica, (Madrid: S.L. Civitas Ediciones 2013).

Fernandez Liesa, Carlos. La Guerra Civil española y el orden jurídico internacional, (Madrid: Thompson Reuters Aranzadi, 2014).

Fernandez Liesa, Carlos. 'La Constitución de Cádiz de 1812 en perspectiva internacional', in M. Aznar Gómez/J. Cardona Llorens/J. Pueyo Losa/J.L. Rodríguez-Villasante/J.M. Sobrino Heredia/M. Pérez González (eds.) Estudios de Derecho internacional y de derecho europeo en Homenaje al Profesor Manuel Pérez González, (Barcelona: Tirant Lo Blanc 2012), 585–596.

Fernandez Novoa, José. Del llamado derecho de naufragio y su abolición por la cvilizacion contemporánea (Madrid: RDIPE, 1911).

Fernandez Rozas, José Carlos. /Paz Andrés Sáenz de Santa María. 'La aportación de la Facultad de Derecho de la Universidad de Oviedo al progreso del Derecho internacional', in Santos Coronas González (ed.) Historia de la Facultad de Derecho, 1608–2008 (Oviedo: Servicio de Publicaciones de la Universidad de Oviedo, 2010), 495–570.

Fernández Sola, Natividad. El pensamiento internacionalista del Profesor Miaja de la Muela. Su contribución al Derecho internacional público y al Derecho europeo (Zaragoza: Mira Editores, 1999).

Fernandez-Prida, Joaquín. Influencia de los tratadistas españoles en la formacion de la ciencia del derecho international publico (Madrid: Imprenta Artistica Saez Hermanos, 1929).

Ferré Olivé, Juan Carlos. Universidad y Guerra Civil: Lección inaugural Curso Académico 2009–2010 (Huelva: Servicio de Publicaciones Universidad de Huelva, 2009).

Fidler, David P. 'The Return of the Standard of Civilization', Chicago Journal of International Law 2 (2001), 137–157.

Finch, George A. 'The United States and the Spanish Civil War' American Journal of International Law 31 (1937), 74–81.

Finch, George A. Adventures in Internationalism: A Biography of James Brown Scott (William E. Butler ed.) (Pennsylvania: The Law Book Exchange, 2012).

Finch, George. 'Brown Scott, James. 1866–1943', American Journal of International Law 38 (1944), 183–217.

Fiocchi Malaspina, Elisabetta. 'La circulación de Le droit de gens de Vattel en los Países hispánicos', Coloquio de Historia Canario-Americana XX (2012), 1074–1080.

Fiore, Pasquale. Tratado de Derecho Internacional público vertido al castellano (de la tercera edición italiana) y aumentada con notas y un apéndice con los tratados entre España y las demás naciones por Alejo García Moreno (Madrid: Centro Editorial de Góngora, 1894).

Fischer, Thomas. 'El español en el mundo: hispanoamericanismo en la Liga de las Naciones Iberoamericana', Iberoamericana 13 (2013), 119–131.

Fontanelli, Filippo. 'Santi Romano and L'ordinamento giuridico: The Relevance of a Forgotten Masterpiece for Contemporary International, Transnational and Global Legal Relations', Transnational Legal Theory 2 (2011), 67–117.

Forcada Barona, Ignacio. 'La influencia de la religión católica en la doctrina internacionalista española del período de entreguerras (1918–1939)' in Ignacio de la Rasilla / Yolanda Gamarra (eds.) Historia del pensamiento internacionalista español del siglo XX, (Cizur Menor: Thompson Reuters Aranzadi 2012), 212–285.

Friedrich Krause, Christian. El ideal de la humanidad para la vida (con introducción y comentarios de Julian Sanz del Río) (Alicante: Biblioteca Virtual Miguel de Cervantes, 1999).

Fusi, Juan P. 'Ortega y España', in Antonio Morales Moya et al. (eds) Historia de la nación y del nacionalismo español (Barcelona: Galaxia Gutenberg. Circulo de Lectores 2013), 638–650.

Gaja, Giorgio. 'Positivism and Dualism in Dionisio Anzilotti', European Journal of International Law 3 (1992), 123–138.

Galindez, Jesús. 'Spain', Columbia Law Review 54 (1954), 809–820.

Gallagher, M. D. 'Leon Blum and the Spanish Civil War', Journal of Contemporary History 6 (1971), 56–64.

Gamarra, Yolanda. 'Los lenguajes del derecho internacional en la Constitution de 1931' in Ignacio de la Rasilla / Yolanda Gamarra (eds.), Historia del pensamiento internacionalista español del siglo XX (Cizur Menor: Thomson Reuters Aranzadi, 2012).

Gamarra, Yolanda. 'Rafael Altamira Crevea. The International Judge as Gentle Civilizer', Journal of the History of International Law 14 (2012) 1–49.

Gamarra, Yolanda. 'Rafael Altamira, un historiador del derecho en el tribunal permanente de justicia internacional (1921–1939)', Revista Internacional de Pensamiento Político 6 (2011), 287–300.

García Arias, Luis. 'Adiciones sobre la historia de la doctrina hispánica del Derecho internacional' in Arthur Nussbaum Historia del Derecho Internacional (transl. by F.J. Osset) (Madrid: Editorial Revista de Derecho Privado, 1949).

García Arias, Luis. 'Fichero de Derecho Internacional Público de la REDI', Anuario hispano-luso-americano de derecho internacional 3 (1967), 257.

García Arias, Luis. 'Las concepciones iusnaturalistas sobre la fundamentación del derecho internacional', in Luis Garcia Arias, Estudios de historia y doctrina del derecho internacional (Madrid: Instituto de Estudios Políticos, 1964).

García Arias, Luis. 'Perfil humano, universitario y científico del profesor Legaz y Lacambra' in Estudios Jurídico-Sociales, Homenaje al profesor Luis Legaz y Lacambra, (Santiago: Universidad de Santiago de Compostela, 1960) 15–81.

García Delgado, José Luis/ Santiago Roldán/ Juan Muñoz (eds.) La consolidación del capitalismo en España, 1914–1920 (Madrid: Confederación Española de Cajas de Ahorros 1974).

García Montero, Alejo. Editorial, Revista de Derecho Internacional, Legislación y Jurisprudencia Comparadas 1 (1887) 1.

Garcia Mora, Luis Miguel. 'El Ateneo de Madrid y el problema colonial en las vísperas de la guerra de independencia cubana', Revista de Indias LVI (1996), 429–449.

García Sanz, Fernando. España en la Gran Guerra. Espías, diplomáticos y traficantes (Barcelona: Galaxia Gutenberg, 2014).

García Valdecasas, Alfonso. 'Editorial' Revista de Estudios Políticos 1 (1941), 5–6.

García Valdecasas, Alfonso. 'Los estados totalitarios y el Estado español', Revista de estudios políticos 4 (1942) 5–32.

García Valdecasas, Alfonso. 'Política Exterior', Revista de Estudios Políticos 1 (1941), 7–16.

García Villada, Zacarías. El destino de España en la Historia Universal (Madrid: Ed. Cultura Española, 1940).

Garcia-Salmones, Mónica. The Project of Positivism in International Law (Oxford: Oxford University Press, 2013).

Garrido Muro, Luis. 'Esta estúpida nación. La nación moderada', in Antonio Morales Moya/Juan Pablo Fusi/Andres de Blas (eds.) Historia de la nación y del nacionalismo español (Madrid, Galaxia Gutenberg 2013), 277–292.

Gascón y Marin, José. Les fonctionnaires internationaux, Collected Courses of The Hague Academy of International Law 41 (1932), 721–798.

Gascón y Marín, José. Les transformations du droit administrative international, Collected Courses of The Hague Academy of International Law 34 (1930), 1–74.

Gathii, James Thuo. War, Commerce and International Law (Oxford: Oxford University Press, 2010).

Genet, Raoul. 'La qualification de 'pirates' et le dilemme de la guerre civile,' Revue international francaise du droit des gens 3 (1937), 13–25.

Genet, Raoul. 'The Charge of Piracy in the Spanish Civil War' American Journal of International Law 32 (1938), 253–263.

Gérard de Rayneval, Mathias-Joseph. Instituciones de derecho natural y de gentes (Traduccion de M. Antonio López, Vol. 1) (Madrid: D. L B. Masson é hijo, 1821).

Gerry Simpson, Great Powers and Outlaw States: Unequal Sovereigns in the International Legal Order (Cambridge: Cambridge University Press, 2004).

Gestoso Acosta, Luis. Curso elemental de Derecho internacional público e Historia de los tratados (Madrid: Imprenta Domenech, 1897).

Gestoso Acosta, Luis. Resumen de Derecho Internacional Público (Madrid: Imprenta Domenech, 1893).

Gil Pecharromán, Julio. José Antonio Primo de Rivera. Retrato de un visionario (Barcelona: Editorial Planeta, 2003).

Gil Pecharromán, Julio. La política exterior del franquismo: Entre Hendaya y El Aaiún. (Barcelona: Ed. Flor de Viento 2008).

Giner de los Rios, Francisco. Escritos sobre la Universidad española (Madrid: S.L.U. Espasa Libros, 1990).

Giner de los Rios, Francisco. Memoria de 1877, Boletín de la Institución Libre de Enseñanza I (1877) 21.

Goda, Norman J.W. 'Franco's Bid for Empire: Spain, Germany and the Western Mediterranean in World War II', in Raanan Rein (ed.) Spain and the Mediterranean since 1898 (London & Portland: Franck Cass 1999), 168–194.

Gong, Gerrit W. The Standard of Civilization and the international Society (Oxford: Clarendon Press, 1984).

González Campos, Julio. / Mesa, Roberto. / Pecourt, Enrique. 'Notas para la historia del pensamiento internacionalista español: Aniceto Sela Sampil (1863–1935)', Revista Española de Derecho Internacional XVII (1964), 561–583.

González Cuevas, Pedro Carlos. Historia de las Derechas españolas. De la Ilustración a nuestros días. (Madrid: Biblioteca Nueva 2000), 372–384.

Gónzalez Prieto, Luis Aurelio. 'La concreción teórica del partido único español franquista' Revista Estudios Políticos 141 (2008), 41–68.

Gonzalez-Hontoria, Manuel. Tratado de derecho internacional publico (Madrid: Voluntad, 1928).

Goñi, Facundo. 'De la filosofía de la historia y sus principales escuelas', Revista española de ambos mundos 5 (1854), 613–615.

Goñi, Facundo. Tratado de las Relaciones Exteriores de España (Madrid: Impr. Ramón Rodríguez de Rivera, 1848).

Gott, Virginia I. 'The National Socialist Theory of International Law' American Journal of International Law 32 (1938), 704–718.

Gottlieb Heineccio, Johann. Elementa Iuris Naturae et Gentium Castigationibus ex Catholicorum Doctrinae et Iuris Historia aucta ab J. Marin et Mendoza (Madrid: 1776).

Gottlieb Heineccio, Johann. Elementos de derecho natural y de gentes. Corregido y reformado por el profesor Don Mariano Lucas Garrido, a los que se añadió los de filosofía moral del mismo autor y traducción al castellano por el bachiller en leyes D.J. A. Ojea. (Madrid: imprenta de Fuentenebro, 1837).

Gozzi, Gustavo. 'The Particularistic Universalism of International Law in the Nineteenth Century' Harvard International Law Journal—online 52 (2010), 73–86.

Graham, Helen. 'Spain and Europe: The View from the Periphery', The Historical Journal 35 (1992), 969–983.

Grau Corts, José. 'Nuestro anti-comunismo', Revista de Estudios Políticos 35–36 (1947) 129–137.

Grau Corts, José. 'Perfil actual de Donoso Cortés', Revista de Estudios Políticos 19–20 (1945) 74–120.

Green, Anna / Kathleen Troup, The Houses of History. A Critical Reader in History and Theory (Manchester: Manchester University Press, 1999).

Gregory, Charles Noble. 'The Study of International Law in Law Schools', American Law School Review 2 (1907) 41.

Grewe, Wilhem. The Epochs of International Law (translated and revised by Michael Byers) (Berlin: De Gruyter 2000).

Griffin, Roger (ed.), Fascism (Oxford: Oxford University Press, 1995).

Gutiérrez Sobral, José. 'Conferencia de Algeciras y España', Revista de Derecho Internacional y Politica Exterior 2 (1906), 268–273.

Gutierrez Vega, Pablo. 'Vattel Larva Detracta. Reflexiones sobre la recepcion del ius publicum europaeum en la universidad preliberal española', in Manuel Angel Bermejo Castrillo (ed.) Manuales y textos de la ensenanza en la universidad liberal (Madrid: Ed. Dykinson, 2004), 537–578.

Haggenmacher, Peter. 'La place de Francisco de Vitoria parmi les fondateurs du droit international', in Antonio Truyol et al. (eds.) Actualité de la pensée juridique de Francisco de Vitoria (Bruxelles: Bruylant, 1988), 27–36.

Hérmida de Blas, Fernando. 'La primera escuela de Madrid', Lecciones del Curso 'Cincuenta años de Ortega y Gasset (1955–2005)', (Madrid: Asociación de Hispanismo Filosófico, Biblioteca Virtual, 2005), 1–33.

Hernandez Marín, Ramón. 'La cátedra 'francisco de vitoria' de la universidad de salamanca', en actas del IV Seminario de Historia de la Filosofía Española (Salamanca: Ediciones Universidad de Salamanca/excma. Diputación provincial de salamanca, 1984), 335–336.

Herrero Rubio, Alejandro. 'Le droit des gens dans l'Espagne du XVIII siècle', Collected Courses of the Hague Academy of International Law 81 (1952), 309–450.

Higgins, A. Pearce. 'Remarks', Law Quarterly Review 39 (1928), 507.

Hilpold, Peter. 'The League of Nations and the Protection of Minorities—Rediscovering a Great Experiment', Max Planck Yearbook of United Nations Law 17 (2013), 87–124.

Hobsbawm, Eric. The Age of Capital, 1848–1875 (London: Hachette, 1975).

Hobsbawm, Eric. The Age of Empire 1874–1914 (London: Abacus, 1987).

Hobsbawm, Eric. The Age of Revolution, 1789–1848 (London: Weidenfeld & Nicolson, World Publishing Company, 1962).

Holland, T.E. Les devoirs des neutres dans la guerre maritime et les evenements recents, Revista de Derecho Internacional y Politica Exterior 2 (1906), 97–118.

Holmes, Oliver Wendell. 'The Path of the Law', Harvard Law Review 10 (1897), 457.

Hopkins, James K. Into the Heart of the Fire: The British in the Spanish Civil War (Stanford: Standford University Press, 1998).

Hudson, Manley O. 'Portrait of Dr. Brown Scott, James. Harvard Alumni Bulletin xxiii' (1931), 419.

Hudson, Manley O. 'The Spanish Constitution of 1931' American Journal of International Law 26 (1932), 579–582.

Huici Miranda, Ambrosio. 'Los estudios árabes y el africanismo español' Revista de Derecho Internacional y Politica Exterior 5 (1910), 94–106.

Hunt, Gaillard. / Brown, James. (eds.) The Debates in the Federal Convention of 1787 which Framed the Constitution of the United States of America reported by James Madison (Oxford: Oxford University Press, 1920).

Hutton, D. Graham. 'British Policy Towards Spain', Foreign Affairs 15 (1936–1937), 661.

Isern, Damian. 'Las alianzas de España' Revista de Derecho Internacional y Politica Exterior I (1905), 169.

Jacobini, Horace B. A Study of the Philosophy of International Law as Seen in Works of Latin American Writers (The Hague: Martinus Nijhoff, 1954).

Janis, Marc Weston. America and the Law of Nations 1776–1939 (Oxford: Oxford University Press, 2010).

Janis, Marc Weston. Jeremy Bentham and the Fashioning of International Law, American Journal of International Law 78 (1984), 405.

Janis, Marc Weston. The American Tradition of International Law, Great Expectations, 1789—1914, (Oxford: Oxford University Press, 2004).

Janis, Marc Weston. The Quest for an Ethical International Law, West Virginia Law Review 109 (2006–2007) 571.

Janis, Mark Weston. 'International Law as Fundamental Justice: Brown Scott, James. Harold Hongju Koh, and the American Universalist Tradition of International Law', Saint Louis University Law Journal 46 (2002), 346.

Janis, Mark Weston. 'Jeremy Bentham and the Fashioning of International Law', American Journal of International Law 78 (1984), 405–418.

Javier Conde, Francisco. Teoría y sistema de las formas políticas (Madrid: Instituto de Estudios Políticos, 1944).

Jeremy Bentham, An Introduction to the Principles of Morals and Legislation (Oxford: Clarendon Press, 1907).

Jessup, Philip C. 'The Spanish rebellion and International Law', Foreign Affairs 15 (1936–1937), 260–279.

Jiménez Piernas, Carlos. / Enrique Crespo Navarro, 'La organización de la paz y la limitación del uso de la fuerza en pleno apogeo del imperialismo: las Conferencias de Paz de La Haya', in Gregorio Peces Barba / E. Fernández García / R. de Asís Roig, (eds.), Historia de los Derechos Fundamentales (Madrid: Dyckinson, 2005).

Jimenez Piernas, Carlos. 'El papel de España en la conferencia de la Haya de 1899', Revista Española de Derecho Internacional LI (1999), 775–782.

Jimenez Piernas, Carlos. 'The Role of Spain in The Hague Peace Conferences of 1899', in Fritz Kalshoven (ed.), The Centennial of the First International Peace Conference, Reports and Conclusions, (The Hague: Kluwer Law International), 1–8.

Jiménez Piernas, Carlos. and Millán Requena Casanova, 'Spain's Part in the 1906 Algeciras Conference: Internationalisation of the Moroccan Question and the Interests of Spain', Spanish Yearbook of International Law, XII (2008) 1–18, 4.

Jiménez Piernas, Carlos. y Millán Requena Casanova, 'Spain's Part in the 1906 Algeciras Conference: Internationalisation of the Moroccan Question and the Interests of Spain', Spanish Yearbook of International Law XII (2008), 1–18.

Jiménez Torres, David. 'Journalists at the Front: Ramiro de Maeztu, Inglaterra en armas and Spanish Intellectuals during the First World War', Bulletin of Spanish Studies 90 (2013), 1291–1311.

Jiménez Torres, David. 'What is an Intellectual? The Spanish Debate during the First World War' Hispanic Research Journal 15 (2014), 515–529.

Joerges, Christian/Navraj Singh Ghaleigh/ Michael Stolleis (eds), Darker Legacies of Law in Europe: The Shadow of National Socialism and Fascism Over Europe and Its Legal Traditions (Oxford: Hart, 2003)

Johns, Fleur, Thomas Skouteris, and Wouter Werner. 'The League of Nations and the Construction of the Periphery Introduction', Leiden Journal of International Law 24 (2011), 797–798.

Johnson, D. H. N. 'The English Tradition of International Law', International and Comparative Law Quarterly 11 (1962), 416–445.

Johnston, Douglas M. The Historical Foundations of World Order. The Tower and the Arena, (Leiden: Martinus Nijjhoff, 2008).

Jordana de Pozas, Luis. 'El profesor Gascón y Marín y su obra' Revista de Estudios de la Vida Local 125 (1962), 641–672.

Jouannet, Emmanuelle / Anne Peters, 'The Journal of the History of International Law: A Forum for New Research', Journal of the History of International Law 16 (2014), 1–8.

Jouannet, Emmanuelle. 'L'idée de Communauté Humaine a La Croisée de La Communauté des Etats et de la Communauté Mondiale', Archives De Philosophie Du Droit 47 (2003), 191.

Jouannet, Emmanuellle. Emmer de Vattel et l'émergence doctrinale du droit international classique (Paris: Pedone, 1998).

Juliá, Santos. "La nueva generación: de neutrales a antigermanófilos pasando por aliadófilos" Ayer: Revista de Historia Contemporánea 91 (2013), 121–144.

Juliá, Santos. '¿Falange liberal o intelectuales fascistas?' Claves de razón práctica 121 (2002), 4–13.

Kamen, Henry. The Disinherited: Exile and the Making of Spanish Culture (1492–1975) (New York: Harper Collins 2007).

Kaufmann, Erich. Das wesen des völkerrechts und die clausula rebus sic stantibus (Berlin: J. C. B. Mohr, 1911).

Kelsen, Hans. El método y los conceptos fundamentales de la teoría pura del Derecho, (traducción de Luis Legaz Lacambra) (Madrid: Ed. Revista de Derecho Privado, 1933).

Kelsen, Hans. General Theory of Law and the State (Cambridge: Harvard University Press, 1945).

Kelsen, Hans. La Teoría Pura Del Derecho: Introducción a La Problemática Científica Del Derecho (Madrid: Editorial Universitaria, 1979).

Kennan, George F. American Diplomacy: 1900–1950 (Chicago: University of Chicago Press, 1951).

Kennedy, David. 'Lon L. Fuller', in David Kennedy and William W. Fisher III (eds.), The Canon of American Legal Thought (Princeton: Princenton University Press, 2006), 209.

Kennedy, David. International Law and the Nineteenth Century: History of an Illusion, Quinnipiac Law Review 17 (1997), 99–136.

Kennedy, David/ William Fisher III (eds.), The Canon of American Legal Thought (Princeton: Princeton University Press 2006).

Kennedy, Duncan. 'Savigny's Family/Patrimony Distinction and its Place in the Global Genealogy of Classical Legal Thought', American Journal of Comparative Law 58 (2010) 811–842.

Kennedy, Duncan. 'Three Globalizations of Law and Legal Thought', in David Trubek/Alvaro Santos (eds.), The New Law and Economic Development: A Critical Appraisal (Cambridge: Cambridge University Press, 2006), 19.

Kennedy, Duncan. The Disenchantment of Logically Formal Legal Rationality or Max Weber's Sociology in the Genealogy of The Contemporary Mode of Western Legal Thought, Hastings Law Journal 55 (2004), 1169–1076.

Kennedy, Duncan. The Rise & Fall of Classical Legal Thought: With a New Preface by the Author, 'Thirty Years Later' (Washington: Beard Books 2006).

King, Willlard L. Melville Weston Fuller, Chief Justice of the United States 1888–1910 (New York: The MacMillan Company 1950).

Kirgis, Frederic L. 'Elihu Root, James Brown Scott and the Early Years of the ASIL', Proceedings of the Annual Meeting of the American Society of International Law 90 (1996), 139–143.

Kolb, Robert. (ed.), Commentaire sur le Pacte de la Société des Nations (Bruxelles: Bruylant, 2015).

Kolb, Robert. 'Politis and Sociological Jurisprudence of Inter-War International Law', European Journal of International Law 23 (2012), 237–241.

Kolb, Robert. Advanced Introduction to International Humanitarian Law (Cheltelham: Edward Elgar, 2014).

Kolb, Robert. Les Cours Généraux De Droit International Public de L'académie de La Haye (Bruxelles: Bruylant, 2004), 31.

Koskenniemi, Martti. 'Book review of Mark Janis: The American Tradition in International Law', 100 American Journal of International Law (2006), 266–270.

Koskenniemi, Martti. 'Empire and International Law: The Real Spanish Contribution', University of Toronto Law Journal 61 (2011), 1–36.

Koskenniemi, Martti. 'Expanding Histories of International Law', American Journal of Legal History 56 (2016), 104–112.

Koskenniemi, Martti. 'Georg Friedrich von Martens (1756–1821) and the Origins of Modern International Law' New York Institute of International Law and Justice Working Papers 1 (2006).

Koskenniemi, Martti. 'Hersch Lauterpacht (1897–1960)', in Jack Beatson/ Reinhard Zimmermann (eds.), Jurists Uprooted: German-Speaking Emigré Lawyers in Twentieth Century Britain (Oxford: Oxford University Press, 2004), 601–662.

Koskenniemi, Martti. 'History of International Law Histories', in Bardo Fassbender / Anne Peters (eds.), Oxford Handbook of the History of International Law (Oxford: Oxford University Press 2012), 943–971.

Koskenniemi, Martti. 'History of International Law, World War I To World War II' Max Planck Encyclopedia of Public International Law (2011).

Koskenniemi, Martti. 'International Law in a Post-Realist Era' Australian Yearbook of International Law 16 (1995), 1.

Koskenniemi, Martti. 'Race, Hierarchy and International Law: Lorimer's Legal Science' European Journal of International Law 27 (2016), 415–429.

Koskenniemi, Martti. 'The Case for Comparative International Law', Finnish Yearbook of International Law 20 (2009), 1–8.

Koskenniemi, Martti. 'The Function of Law in the International Community: 75 Years After', British Yearbook of International Law 79 (2008), 353–366.

Koskenniemi, Martti. 'The Ideology of International Adjudication and the 1907 Hague Conference', in Yves Daudet (Ed) Topicality of the 1907 Hague Conference, the Second Peace Conference/ Actualité de la Conférence de La Haye de 1907, Deuxième Conférence de la paix (Leiden/Boston: Brill, 2008), 137.

Koskenniemi, Martti. 'Vitoria and Us. Thoughts on Critical Histories of International Law', 22 Rechtsgeschichte (2014) 119.

Koskenniemi, Martti. 'Why History of International Law Today?' Rechtsgeschichte—Legal History 4 (2004), 61–66.

Koskenniemi, Martti. From Apology to Utopia. The Structure of the International Legal Argument (Cambridge: Cambridge University Press, 2006).

Koskenniemi, Martti. International Law as Political Theology: How to Read Der Nomos der Erde?, Forum Historiae Iuris, Artikel vom 31 (2006), 1–20.

Koskenniemi, Martti. The Gentle Civilizer of Nations: The Rise and Fall of International Law, 1870–1960 (Cambridge: Cambridge University Press, 2001).

La Porte, Pablo. 'Civil-military relations in the Spanish protectorate in Morocco: The road to the Spanish Civil War, 1912–1936'. Armed Forces & Society 30 (2004), 203–226.

La Porte, Pablo. 'Rien a` ajouter': The League of Nations and the Rif War (1921–1926)' European History Quarterly 41 (2011), 66–87.

Lachs, Manfred. 'The development and general trends of international law in our time' Collected Courses of the Hague Academy of International Law 169 (1980), 320.

Laín Entralgo, Pedro. Desgargo de conciencia (1930–1960) (Barcelona: Ed. Barral, 1970)

Lasala y Villanova, Mateo. Sobre la influencia de la civilización en el derecho internacional (Madrid: Universidad Central, 1855)

Lauterpacht, Elihu. 'Sir Hersch Lauterpacht: 1897–1960' European Journal of International Law 8 (1998), 313–315.

Lauterpacht, Elihu. The Life of H. Lauterpacht (Cambridge: Cambridge University Press, 2012).

Lauterpacht, Hersch. 'Recognition of Insurgents as a de Facto Government', Modern Law Review 3 (1939), 1–19.

Lauterpacht, Hersch. 'The Function of Law in the International Community' (Oxford: Clarendon Press, 1933)

Lauterpacht, Hersch. 'The Grotian Tradition of International Law', British Yearbook Of International Law 23 (1946), 1–53.

Lauterpacht, Hersch. 'The so-called Anglo-American and Continental Schools of Thought in International Law', British Yearbook of International Law 12 (1931), 32.

Lauterpacht, Hersch. International Law. Collected Papers (Cambridge: Cambridge University Press, 1979).

Le Fur, Louis. 'La guerre civile d'espagne et le droit international', Revue politique et parlamentaire XXX (1936), 385–598.

Le Fur, Louis. 'La théorie du droit naturel depuis le XVIIIe siècle et la doctrine moderne', Collected Courses of the Hague Academy 18 (1928), 259–442.

Legaz Lacambra, Luis. 'El Derecho internacional en el pensamiento de Ortega y Gasset' Revista de Estudios Políticos 111 (1960), 5–41.

Legaz Lacambra, Luis. 'La filosofía jurídica del nacionalsocialismo', Universidad XI (1934).

Legaz Lacambra, Luis. 'La primacía de lo espiritual en la construcción jurídica internacional. Las bases sociológico-axiológicas del nacionalismo y del internacionalismo' in Estudios Internacionales. (Madrid: Publicaciones del Grupo Español de la Unión de Friburgo, 1934).

Legaz Lacambra, Luis. 'La théorie pure du droit et la pensée politique de José Antonio Primo de Rivera', Révue internationale de la théorie du droit (1939).

Legaz Lacambra, Luis. 'La validez del Derecho Internacional (Estudio de teoría jurídica pura)' Universidad 8 (1931).

Legaz Lacambra, Luis. 'Las garantías constitucionales del Derecho internacional' Revista de Derecho Público (1933).

Legaz Lacambra, Luis. 'Lo medieval y lo moderno en Francisco de Vitoria' (Santiago de Compostela: Universidad de Santiago, 1947).

Legaz Lacambra, Luis. 'Lo moderno y lo medieval en Vitoria', in Luis Legaz Lacambra, Horizontes del Pensamiento Juridico (Barcelona: Casa Bosch 1947)

Legaz Lacambra, Luis. Introducción a la teoría del Estado nacionalsindicalista (Barcelona: Casa Bosch, 1940)

Legaz Lacambra, Luis. Kelsen. Estudio crítico de la teoría pura del Derecho y del Estado en la Escuela de Viena (Barcelona: Casa Bosch, 1933).

Legaz Lacambra, Luis. La fundamentación del ius gentium en Suarez, Revista Española de Derecho Internacional I (1948), 11–44.

Legg, Stephen. 'The Life of Individuals as well as of Nations': International Law and the League of Nations' Anti-Trafficking Governmentalities' Leiden Journal of International Law 25 (2012), 647–664.

Leroy, Maxime. 'La Societe des Nations', Revista de Derecho Internacional y Politica Exterior 4 (1908).

Leroy, Maxime. La Societe des Nations, Revista de Derecho Internacional y Politica Exterior 3 (1907).

Leroy, Maxime. La Societe des Nations, Revista de Derecho Internacional y Politica Exterior Tome 5 (1909–10).

Leroy, Maxime. La Societe des Nations, Revista de Derecho Internacional y Politica Exterior 6 (1909–10).

Lesaffer, Randall. 'International Law and Its History: The Story of an Unrequited Love', Matthew Craven/ Malgosia Fitzmaurice/ Maria Vogiatzi (eds.) Time, History and International Law (Leiden/Boston: Martinus Nijjhoff, 2006), 27–41.

Lesaffer, Randall. 'Peace Treaties and the Formation of International Law' in Bardo Fassbender / Anne Peters (eds.), Oxford Handbook of the History of International Law (Oxford: Oxford University Press 2012), 71–94.

Lesaffer, Randall. 'The Grotian Tradition Revisited: Change and Continuity in the History of International Law', British Yearbook of International Law 73 (2003), 103–139.

Lesaffer, Randall. 'The Temple of Peace The Hague Peace Conferences, Andrew Carnegie and the Building of the Peace Palace' in Mededelingen van de Koninklijke Nederlandse Vereniging voor Internationaal Recht, Preadviezen, 140 (2013), 1–38.

Lewis, Mark. The Birth of the New Justice (Oxford: Oxford University Press, 2014).

Liedtke, Boris N. 'Compromising with the Dictatorship' U.S.-Spanish Relations in the Late 1940s and Early 1950s', in Christian Leitz and David J. Dunthorn, Spain in an International Legal Context: 1936–1959, (New York & Oxford: Berghahn Books 1999), 265–275.

Little, Douglas. Malevolent Neutrality: The United States, Great Britain and the Origins of the Spanish Civil War, (Ithaca: Cornell University Press, 1985).

Little, Douglas. 'Red Scare 1936: Anti-Bolshevism and the Origins of British Non-intervention in the Spanish Civil War', Journal of Contemporary History 28 (1988), 291–311.

Lleonart y Amsélem, Alberto J. (ed.). España y ONU. La Cuestión española Tomo VI (1952–1955). Estudios introductivos y corpus documental (Madrid, Consejo Superior de Investigaciones Cientificas, 2002).

Llewellyn, Karl. 'Some Realism About Realism- Responding To Dean Pound', Harvard Law Review 44 (1931), 1222.

Lobban, Michael. 'English Approaches to International law in the Nineteenth Century', in Matthew Craven/Malgosia Fitzmaurice/Maria Vogiatzi (Eds) Time, History and International Law (Leiden: Martinus Nijjhoff, 2007), 65–90.

Loewenstein, Karl. 'Militant Democracy and Fundamental Rights I', 31 The American Political Science Review 3 (1937), 417–432.

Long, David. 'C. A. W. Manning and the Discipline of International Relations', The Round Table 94 (2005), 77–96.

Lopez Baroni, Manuel Jesús. El falangismo liberal y la transición española, Revista Internacional de Pensamiento Politico 7 (2012), 467–490.

López Cordón, Maria Victoria. 'España en las Conferencias de la Haya de 1899 y 1907' Revista de Esludios Internacionales 3 (1982), 703–756.

López García, José Antonio. 'La presencia de Carl Schmitt en España', Revista de Estudios Políticos 91 (1996), 139–169.
López-Sánchez, Pedro. Elementos de Derecho internacional público precedidos de una introducción a su estudio bajo los aspectos de su desarrollo histórico o positivo y de su teoría, (Madrid: Impr. de la Revista de Legislación, 1866).
Lorimer, James. The Institutes of the Law of Nations: a Treatise of the Jural Relations of Separate Political Communities. (Edinburgh & London: William Blackwood & Sons, 1883).
Luis Garcia Arias, Estudios de historia y doctrina del derecho internacional (Madrid: Instituto de Estudios Políticos, 1964).
Mackenzie, S. P. 'The Foreign Enlistment Act and the Spanish Civil War, 1936–1939' Twentieth Century British History 10 (1999), 52–66.
Mancebo, María Fernanda. 'Consecuencias de la guerra civil en la universidad valencia: depuraciones y exilios', Cuadernos del Instituto Antonio de Nebrija 4 (2001), 165–188.
Marfil Garcia, Mariano. 'Relaciones entre España y la Gran Bretaña, desde las paces de Utrecht hasta nuestros días', Revista de Derecho Internacional y Politica Exterior 2 (1906), 8.
Marfil Garcia, Mariano. 'Relaciones entre España y la Gran Bretaña, desde las paces de Utrecht hasta nuestros días' Revista de Derecho Internacional y Politica Exterior 3 (1907), 100.
María Pilar Hernando Serra, 'José María Trias de Bes', Diccionario de catedráticos españoles de derecho (1847–1943) (Madrid: Universidad Carlos III de Madrid. Instituto Figuerola de Historia y Ciencias Sociales, 2011).
Marín López, Antonio. 'Notas para la historia del pensamiento internacionalista español: Manuel Torres Campos, 1850–1918', Revista de Derecho español y americano 12 (1966), 125–154.
Marín y Mendoza, Joaquín. Historia del derecho natural y de gentes, 1776 (Introduccion, edición y notas de Salvador Rus Rufino) (Valencia: Ed. Diputación de Valencia, Institución Alfonso el Magnanimo, 1999).
Marshall, Alfred. 'Whewell Scholarships: Letter 871 to Courtney Stanhope Kenny, 29 April 1907' in John K. XXX Whitaker (ed.) The Correspondence of Alfred Marshall, Economist: Volume 3, Towards the Close, 1903–1924 (Cambridge: Cambridge University Press 1996) 155–156.
Martin, Percy Alvin. 'Latin America and the League of Nations', The American Political Science Review 20 (1926), 14–30.
Martínez Lillo, Pedro Antonio. 'La política exterior de España en el marco de la Guerra Fría: del aislamiento limitado a la integración parcial en la sociedad internacional, 1945–1953', in Javier Tussell, J. Aviles & Rosa Pardo (eds.) La política exterior de España en el siglo XX, (Madrid: Ed. Biblioteca Nueva 2000), 323–369.

Martínez Neira, Manuel. '¿Una supresión ficticia? Notas sobre la enseñanza del Derecho en el reinado de Carlos IV', Anuario de Historia del Derecho español 68 (1998), 532–544.

Martínez Neira, Manuel. La creación del cuerpo de catedráticos de universidad (1812–1857) Estudio histórico-jurídico (Madrid: Editorial Dykinson, 2013).

Martinez, Jenny. The Slave Trade and the Origins of International Human Rights Law (Oxford: Oxford University Press 2012).

Maura Gamazo, Gabriel. La neutralidad en la guerra marítima (Madrid: 1910).

McNair, Arnold D. 'The Law Relating to the Civil War in Spain', Law Quarterly Review 53 (1937), 471–500.

Medina, Manuel. 'El pensamiento internacionalista del profesor Truyol y Serra', in Pensamiento jurídico y sociedad internacional: libro-homenaje al profesor Antonio Truyol Serra (Madrid: Centro de Estudios Constitucionales: Universidad Complutense 1986) 15–28.

Medina, Manuel. 'Notas para la historia del pensamiento internacional español: La teoría de las relaciones internacionales de Ortega y Gasset', Anuario de Derecho Internacional III (1976), 349–375.

Medlicott, W.N. and D. Dakin (eds.) Documents on British Foreign Policy, 1919–1939 Second Series Volume XVII, Western Pact Negotiations: Outbreak of Spanish Civil War June 1936–January 1937 (London: Her Majesty's Stationery Office, 1979).

Megret, Frederic. 'The Rise and Fall of 'International Man'', in Prabhakar Singh/Benoît Maye (eds.) Critical International Law (Oxford: Oxford University Press 2014).

Menéndez Pelayo, Marcelino. Discurso leído ante la Academia de la Historia (1879) in Menéndez Pelayo, Marcelino. Edición Nacional de las Obras Completas de Marcelino Menéndez Pelayo, 65 Vols. (Madrid: Consejo Superior de Investigaciones Cientificas, 1940–1959).

Menéndez Pelayo, Marcelino. Edición Nacional de las Obras Completas de Marcelino Menéndez Pelayo, 65 Vols. (Madrid: Consejo Superior de Investigaciones Cientificas, 1940–1959).

Menendez Pelayo, Marcelino. Historia de los heterodoxos españoles (1880–1882), in Menéndez Pelayo, Marcelino. Edición Nacional de las Obras Completas de Marcelino Menéndez Pelayo, 65 Vols. (Madrid: Consejo Superior de Investigaciones Cientificas, 1940–1959).

Menendez Pelayo, Marcelino. La ciencia española (1876) in Menéndez Pelayo, Marcelino. Edición Nacional de las Obras Completas de Marcelino Menéndez Pelayo, 65 Vols. (Madrid: Consejo Superior de Investigaciones Cientificas, 1940–1959).

Menendez, Agustín. 'From Republicanism to Fascist Ideology Under the Early Franquismo' in Joerges, Christian and Ghaleigh, Navraj Singh (eds.) Darker Legacies of Law in Europe: The Shadow of National Socialism and Fascism Over Europe and Its Legal Traditions (Oxford: Hart Publishers 2003), 337–360.

Merino, Abelardo. Antecedentes historicos de la liga de las naciones (Madrid: Real Sociedad Geográfica, 1919).

Merle, Marcel. Pacifisme et internationalisme (París: Coün, 1966).

Meron, Theodore. 'The Martens Clause, Principles of Humanity and Dictates of Public Conscience', 94 American Journal of International Law (2000), 78–89.

Mesa Garrido, Roberto (con la colaboración de Julio González Campos y Enrique Pecourt), 'Notas para la historia del pensamiento internacionalista español: Algunos problemas coloniales del siglo XIX', Revista Española de Derecho Internacional XVIII (1965), 380–414.

Miaja de la Muela, Adolfo. 'In Memoriam: José de Yanguas Messia (1890–1974)' 2 Revista de instituciones europeas, 1 (1975), 5–10.

Miaja de la Muela, Adolfo. 'Les principes directeurs des règles de compétence territoriale des tribunaux internes en matière de litiges comportant un élément international', Collected Courses of the Hague Academy of International Law 135 (1972), 1–96.

Miaja de la Muela, Adolfo. 'Una satira española contra los iusinternacionalistas del siglo XVIII: la lección cuarta de 'los eruditos a la violeta'', in Colección de estudios en homenaje al profesor Camilo Barcia Trelles (Santiago de Compostela: Ed. Universidad Compostelana 1945), 101–131.

Miaja de la Muela, Adolfo. 'Una satira española contra los iusinternacionalistas del siglo XVIII: la lección cuarta de 'los eruditos a la violeta'', in Colección de estudios en homenaje al profesor Camilo Barcia Trelles (Santiago de Compostela: Ed. Universidad Compostelana 1945), 101–131.

Miaja De la Muela, Adolfo. Internacionalistas españoles del siglo XVI. Fernando Vázquez de Menchaca (Valladolid: Talleres tipográficos Cuesta, 1932).

Miaja De la Muela, Adolfo. Las ideas fundamentales del Derecho de Gentes en la obra de Fray Serafín de Freitas (Madrid: Imprenta la RAFA, 1933).

Mieville, China. Between Equal Rights, A Marxist Theory of International Law (London: Historical Materialism, 2007).

Miguel Alonso, Aurora/ Alberto Raya Rienda, La colección de tesis doctorales de derecho de la universidad central, 1869–1883, Cuadernos del Instituto Antonio de Nebrija 13 (2010), 55, 56.

Mirkine-Guetzevich, Boris. 'Ius Gentium Pacis', Revista de Derecho Publico I (1932)

Mollin, Volker. 'La singular historiografía de la guerra de los 10 años en Cuba (1868–1978)' EHSEA 15 (1997), 205–269.

Moore, John Bassett. (ed.) A Digest of International Law as Embodied in Diplomatic Discussions, Treaties and other International Agreements, International Awards, the Decisions of Municipal Courts and the Writings of Jurists, and Especially in Documents Published and Unpublished, Issued By Presidents and Secretaries of State of The United States, The Opinions of the Attorney's General and the Decisions of the Courts, Federal And State (Washington, D.C.: Govt. Printing Office 1906).

Moore, John Bassett. History and Digest of the International Arbitrations to which the United States has been a Party (Washington: Government Print Office 1898).

Moradiellos, Enrique. 'El mundo ante el avispero español: intervencion y no intervencion extranjera en la Guerra Civil', in Santos Julia (ed) República y Guerra en España (1931–1939), (Madrid: Espasa Calpe 2006), 305–310.

Moradiellos, Enrique. 'The Allies and the Spanish Civil War' in Sebastian Balfour/ Paul Preston (eds) Spain and the Great Powers in the Twentieth Century (London: Routledge 1999), 96–126.

Moradiellos, Enrique. Neutralidad benevola. (Oviedo: Editorial Pentalfa, 1990).

Muller, Jan Werner. A Dangerous Mind: A Carl Schmitt in Post-War European Thought (New Haven and London: Yale University Press 2003).

Neff, Stephen C. Justice among Nations. A History of International Law (Cambridge: Harvard University Press, 2014).

Neff, Stephen. 'Jurisprudential Polyphony: The Three Variations on the Positivist Theme in the 19th century', in Pierre Marie Dupuy/ Vincent Chetail (eds) The Roots of International Law (Leiden: Martinus Nijhoff 2014), 301–34.

Neila Hernández, José Luis. 'La política exterior de la españa republicana (1931–1936): excepcionalismo y normalidad historiográfica', Studia Historia Contemporanea 22 (2004), 47–83.

Neila Hernández, Jose Luis. 'La sublevación y la improvisación de una política exterior de Guerra, 1936–1939', in J. Tussell, J. Aviles & R. Pardo (eds.) La política exterior de España en el siglo XX (Madrid: Ed. Biblioteca nueva, 2000), 263–297.

Neila Hernández, José Luis. España y el Mediterraneo en el siglo XX. De los acuerdos de Cartagena al proceso de Barcelona (Madrid: Silex, 2011).

Niemela, Pekka. 'A Cosmopolitan World Order? Perspectives on Francisco de Vitoria and the United Nations', Max Planck Yearbook of United Nations Law 12 (2008) 301–334.

Nino, Antonio. 'Politica de alianzas y compromisos coloniales para la regeneracion internacional de España', in Javier Tussell/Juan Aviles/Rosa Pardo (eds.), La Politica Exterior de España en el siglo XX (Madrid: Biblioteca Nueva, 2000).

Nussbaum, Arthur. A Concise History of the Law of Nations (London: Macmillan, 1947).

Nuzzo, Luigi. 'Memoria, identità e uso pubblico della storia: l'invenzione del derecho indiano', Forum Historiae Iuris, Artikel vom 15 (2013).

Nys, Ernest. 'Introduction', in Francisco de Vitoria, De Indis et de Iure Belli Relectiones, The Classics of International Law (Washington: Carnegie Institution, 1917).

Nys, Ernest. 'Le droit des gens et les anciens jurisconsultes espagnols' (1914) extract reprinted in G. van Hecke (ed.) L'Espagne et la formation du droit des gens moderne (Leuven: Aedibus Peeters), 66–82.

Nys, Ernest. 'Les publicistes espagnols du XVI siècle et les droit des indiens', 21 Révue de droit international et de législation comparée 21 (1889), 532.

Nys, Ernest. 'Review of S. de Freitas: Justification de la domination portugaise en Asie', Revue de droit international et de législation comparé 15 (1883), 198.
Nys, Ernest. 'The Codification of International Law', American Journal of International Law 5 (1911), 871–900.
Nys, Ernest. 'The Development and Formation of International Law', American Journal of International Law 6 (1912), 1–29.
Nys, Ernest. 'The Development and Formation of International Law', American Journal of International Law 6 (1912), 279–315.
Nys, Ernest. Le droit de la guerre et les précurseurs de Grotius (Bruxelles et Leipzig: Muquardt, Merzbach et Falk, 1882).
Nys, Ernest. Les droits des indiens et les publicistes espagnols (Bruxelles et Leipzig: Muquardt, Merzbach et Falk, 1890).
Nys, Ernest. Les origines du droit international (Bruxelles: A. Castaigne, 1894).
Obregón Tarazona, Liliana. 'Completing Civilization: Creole Consciousness and International Law in Nineteenth-Century Latin America', in Anne Orford (ed) International Law and Its Others (Cambridge: Cambridge University Press 2008), 247–264.
Obregón Tarazona, Liliana. 'Noted for Dissent: The International Life of Alejandro Alvarez' Leiden Journal of International Law 19 (2006), 983–1016.
Obregón Tarazona, Liliana. 'The Colluding Worlds of the Lawyer, the Scholar and the Policymaker: A View of International Law from Latin America', Wisconsin International Law Journal 23 (2005), 145.
Obregón Tarazona, Liliana. 'Writing International Legal History: An Overview', Monde(s) Histoire, espaces, relations 7 (2015), 95–112.
Obregón Tarazona, Liliana. Construyendo la region americana: andres bello y el Derecho internacional in Yolanda Gamarra (ed) La idea de América en el pensamiento ius internacionalista del siglo XXI (Zaragoza: Instituto Fernando el Catolico 2010), 65–86.
Obregón, Liliana. "Between civilisation and barbarism: Creole interventions in international law." Third World Quarterly 27 (2006), 815–832.
O'Connell, Mary Ellen and Lenore Vander Zee, 'The History of International Adjudication' in Cesare P. R. Romano, Karen J. Alter, and Chrisanthi Avgerou (eds.), The Oxford Handbook of International Adjudication (Oxford: Oxford University Press, 2013).
Oppenheim, Lassa. 'The Science of International Law: Its Task and Method', American Journal of International Law 2 (1908), 313.
Oppenheim, Lassa. International Law (London, New York: Longmans, Green, and co., 1905).
Orford, Anne. 'Scientific Reason and the Discipline of International Law', European Journal of International Law 25 (2014) 369–385.

Orford, Anne. 'The Past as Law or History? The Relevance of Imperialism for Modern International Law' in Emmanuelle Jouannet, Hélène Ruiz-Fabri and Mark Toufayan (eds.), Tiers Monde: Bilan et Perspectives (Paris: Société de Législation Comparée, 2017).

Orue y Arregui, José Ramón. Derecho internacional privado (Madrid: Editorial reus, 1ª ed. 1928, 2ª ed. 1932, 3ª ed. corregida y aumentada, 1952).

Orue y Arregui, José Ramón. Preceptos internacionales en la constitución de la República española (Madrid: Editorial Reus, 1932).

Orue y Arregui, José Ramón. 'Regionalism in the International Organization' Collected Courses of The Hague Academy of International Law 53 (1935) 1–95.

Orue y Arregui, José Ramón. Sociedad de Naciones (Madrid: ed. Góngora, 1923)

Ozsu, Umut 'Agency, Universality, and the Politics of International Legal History' Harvard International Law Journal—online 52 (2010), 58–72.

Padeldorf, Norman P. 'The International Non-Intervention Agreement and the Spanish Civil War', American Journal of International Law 31 (1937), 578–603.

Padelford, Norman J. "Foreign Shipping During the Spanish Civil War." American Journal of International Law 32 (1938), 264–279.

Padelford, Norman J. 'Closure of the Office of the Permanent Delegation of Spain to the League of Nations', American Journal of International Law 33 (1939), 563–566.

Padelford, Norman J. 'Remarks', Proceedings of the American Society of International Law 31 (1937) 154.

Padgen, Anthony. 'Gentili, Vitoria and the Fabrication of a Natural Law of Nations', in Benedict Kingsbury and Benjamin Straussman (eds.), Roman Foundations of the Law of Nations: Alberico Gentili and the Justice of Empire (Oxford: Oxford University Press, 2010).

Palacios Morini, Leopoldo. Los mandatos internacionales de la sociedad de naciones (Madrid: Sobrinos de Sucesora de M. Minuesa de los Ríos, 1927).

Pando, Juan. Un Rey para la esperanza. La España humanitaria de Alfonso XIII en la Gran Guerra (Madrid: Temas de Hoy, 2002).

Pastor Ridruejo, José Antonio. "Francisco de Vitoria y la modernidad de sus enseñanzas: ius ad bellum y ius in bello", in: Ignacio de la Rasilla / Yolanda Gamarra (eds.), Historia del pensamiento internacionalista español del siglo XX (Cizur Menor: Thomson Reuters Aranzadi 2012), 79–87.

Paulus, Andreas. 'The International Legal System as a Constitution', Jeffrey L. Dunoff/ Joel P. Trachtman (eds.) Ruling the World? Constitutionalism, International Law, and Global Governance (Cambridge: Cambridge University Press 2009), 69–112.

Payne, Stanley G. Falange. Historia del fascismo español, (Paris: Ed. Ruedo Ibérico, 1965).

Payne, Stanley G. Fascism in Spain, 1923–1977, (Madison: The University of Wisconsin Press, 1999).

Payne, Stanley G. Franco and Hitler, Spain, Germany and World War II (New Haven: Yale University Press 2008).

Pecourt García, Enrique. 'El pensamiento internacionalista del prof. Miaja de la Muela', Estudios de derecho internacional. Libro-homenaje al prof. A. Miaja de la muela (Madrid: Tecnos, 1979), 49.

Pedersen, Susan. The Guardians: The League of Nations and the Crisis of Empire (Oxford: Oxford University Press, 2015)

Pereira Castañares, Juan Carlos. 'España y Latino-América, Un siglo de relaciones (1836–1936)' Mélanges de la Casa de Velazquez 97 (1992), 30.

Pereña, Luciano. (ed.) Corpus Hispanorum de Pace. Volumen Indices I-XXV (Madrid: Consejo Superior de Investigaciones Cientificas, 1987)

Pereña, Luciano. 'La tesis de la paz dinámica', in Luciano Pereña (ed.) Francisco de Vitoria, Relectio de iure belli o paz dinámica. Escuela española de la paz. Primera generación (1526–1560) Corpus Hispanorum de Pace Vol. VI (Madrid: Consejo Superior de Investigaciones Cientificas 1981).

Pérez Delgado, Tomás. 'Francisco de Vitoria: institucionalización de su memoria en Salamanca (1926–1936)', in Estudios históricos salmantinos. Homenaje al P. Benigno Hernández Montes (Salamanca: Ediciones Universidad de Salamanca, 1999), 539–571.

Pérez Delgado, Tomás/Antonio Fuentes Labrador 'De rebeldes a cruzados. Pioneros del discurso legitimador del movimiento nacional. Salamanca julio-octubre de 1936' Studia Historica 4 (1986), 235–266.

Perez Gil, Luis V. 'El primer decenio de España en la sociedad de naciones (1919–1929)', Anales de la Facultad de Derecho de La Laguna 15 (1998), 199–215.

Perez Perdomo, Rogelio. Los abogados en América Latina: una introducción histórica (Bogota: Universidad Externado de Colombia, 2004), 74–80.

Pérez, Rafael García. 'La idea de la 'Nueva Europa' en el pensamiento nacionalista español de la inmediata posguerra 1939–1944', Revista del Centro de Estudios Constitucionales 5 (1990), 203–240.

Pérez-Caballero y de Posada, José María. Discurso sobre el derecho de intervención, (Madrid: Universidad Central, 1850).

Perez-Luño, Antonio Enrique. 'Natural Law Theory in Spain and Portugal', The Age of Human Rights Journal 1 (2013), 1–24.

Peters, Anne. 'Humanity as the Alpha and Omega of Sovereignty', European Journal of International Law 20 (2009), 513–544.

Picavea, Ricardo Macias. El problema nacional Hechos, causas y remedios (Madrid: Biblioteca Nueva, 1899).

Pierantoni, Augusto. Storia degli studi del diritto internazionale in Italia (Modena: Carlo Vinzenzi, 1869).

Pike, David Wingeate. Franco and the Axis Stigma, (London: Palgrave MacMillan, 2008).

Pilar Hernando/ Carlos Petit. 'Miaja de la Muela, Adolfo', Diccionario de catedráticos españoles de derecho (1847–1943) (Madrid: Universidad Carlos III de Madrid. Instituto Figuerola de Historia y Ciencias Sociales, 2011).

Portero, Florentino. 'Spain, Britain and the Cold War' in Sebastian Balfour and Paul Preston (eds.), Spain and the Great Powers in the 20th Century (London and New York: Routledge, 1999), 210–228.

Posada, Antonio. La sociedad de naciones y el derecho político (Madrid: Editorial Caro Raggio, 1925).

Pound, Roscoe. 'Mechanical Jurisprudence', Columbia Law Review 8 (1908), 605–623.

Pound, Roscoe. 'The Scope and Purpose of Sociological Jurisprudence', Harvard Law Review 24 (1911), 591.

Pound, Roscoe. Philosophical Theory of International law, Biblioteca Visseriana Dissertationum, Ius international ilustratum 1 (1923), 89.

Pradier-Fodére, Paul. Traité de droit international public européen et américain (Paris: Pedone 1885).

Preston, Paul. Franco. A Bibliography (London: Harper Press 1995).

Preston, Paul. The Politics of Revenge. Fascism and the Military in 20th Century Spain,, (London: Routledge, 1995).

Preston, Paul. The Spanish Holocaust. Inquisition and Extermination in Twentieth Century Spain (London: Harper Press, 2012).

Preuss, Lawrence. 'State Immunity and the Requisition of Ships during the Spanish Civil War: I. Before US Courts', The American Journal of International Law 36 (1942) 37–55.

Preuss, Lawrence. 'State Immunity and the Requisition of Ships during the Spanish Civil War: I. Before the British Courts' The American Journal of International Law 35 (1941), 263–281.

Primo de Rivera, José Antonio. 'Discurso de la Fundación de Falange Española' in Jose Antonio Primo de Rivera, Escritos y discursos. Obras Completas 1922–1936 (recopilación de Agustín del Río Cisneros) (Madrid: Delegación Nacional de la Sección Femenina de F. E. T. y de las J. O. N. S., 1959), 189–198.

Puyol Montero, José María. 'Joaquín María Fernández Prida', Diccionario de catedráticos españoles de derecho (1847–1943) (Madrid: Universidad Carlos III de Madrid. Instituto Figuerola de Historia y Ciencias Sociales, 2011).

Puyol Montero, José María. El plan republicano en la facultad de Derecho de Madrid (1931–1934), Cuadernos del Instituto Antonio de Nebrija 7 (2004), 197–234.

Puyol Montero, José María. Saldaña Garcia Rubio, Quintiliano (1878–1938) Diccionario de catedráticos españoles de derecho (1847–1943) (Madrid: Universidad Carlos III de Madrid. Instituto Figuerola de Historia y Ciencias Sociales, 2011).

Quintana Navarro, Francisco. España en Europa 1931–1936. Del compromiso por la paz a la huida de la guerra (Madrid: Nerea, 1993).

Quintano Ripolles, Antonio. 'Cien Años de Derecho internacional', Revista General de Legislación y Jurisprudencia 100 (1953), 134–197.

Raventós Noguer, Manuel. 'La Asociación Española de Derecho Internacional y Legislación Comparada', Revista general de legislación y jurisprudencia 77 (1928), 315–332.

Raymond, John M. / Barbara J. Frischholz, 'Lawyers who Established International Law in the United States, 1776–1914', American Journal of International Law 76 (1982), 802–829.

Redondo, Juan Carlos Jiménez. 'La política del bloque ibérico: las relaciones hispanoportuguesas (1936–1949)' Mélanges de la Casa de Velázquez 29 (1993), 175–201.

Remiro Brotons, Antonio. 'El discreto encanto—y desencanto—de la Revista Española del Derecho Internacional (1948–1978)', Estudios de Derecho Internacional. Librohomenaje al Prof. A. Miaja de la Muela Vol.I (Madrid: Ed. Tecnos 1979), 123–140.

Remiro Brotons, Antonio. Civilizados, barbaros y salvajes en el nuevo orden internacional (Madrid: McGraw-Hill 1996).

Renouvin, Pierre/ Edmond Preclin/ George Hardy, La paix armée et la grande guerre (1871–1919) (Paris: Presses Universitaires de France, 1960).

Reus, José. 'Recension de Teodoro Ortolan, 'Reglas internacionales et diplomatie de la mer, París, 1856', Revista general de legislación y jurisprudencia 5 (1857), 407–408.

Reus, José. Recensión de Mr. Laurent, 'Historia del derecho de gentes y de las relaciones internacionales, París 1857', Revista general de legislación y jurisprudencia 5 (1857) 128.

Riaza Martinez-Osorio, Roman. 'El primer impugnador de Vitoria' in Gregorio López (ed) Conferencias pronunciadas en la cátedra Francisco de Vitoria de la U. de Salamanca 27 y 28 de enero (Salamanca: AFV, 1932), 21.

Riaza Martinez-Osorio, Roman. 'La interpretación de las leyes y la doctrina de Francisco Suárez', Revista de Archivos, Bibliografía y Museos 385 (1925).

Richard, Anne-Isabelle. 'Competition and complementarity: civil society networks and the question of decentralizing the League of Nations'. Journal of Global History 7 (2012), 233–256.

Richards, Michael. After the Civil War. Making Memory and Re-Making Spain since 1936 (Cambridge: Cambridge University Press, 2013).

Richards, Mike. 'The Material Reality of Power' in Helen Graham and Jo Labanyi (eds.) Spanish Cultural Studies: An Introduction. The Struggle for Modernity, (Oxford: Oxford University Press, 1995), 173–182.

Riquelme, Antonio. Elementos de derecho público internacional (Madrid, Impr. Santiago Saunaque, 1849).

Riva Espiga, Angel. La civilización moderna ha influido en el derecho internacional? (Madrid: Universidad Central, 1853).

Rivera Garcia, Carlos. La Sociedad de Naciones: su valor positivo y juridico y el problema de la paz (Madrid: Ed. Reus, 1927).

Rivier, Alphonse. 'Notice historique sur l'Institut de droit international, sa fondation et sa première session', Annuaire de l 'Institut de Droit International 1 (1877).

Rivier, Alphonse. Note sur la litterature du droit des gens avant la publication du J. B. ac P. (Brussels: Bruylant, 1888).

Robledo, Ricardo. 'La difusion del pensamiento moderno en la universidad de Salamanca a fines del siglo XVIII', Historia Constitucional 6 (2005), 427–450.

Rodriguez Roa, Fernando. 'España en el Rif', Revista de Derecho Internacional y Politica Exterior 5 (1909–1910), 70–93.

Rodriguez, Manuel. Mares territoriales (Cadiz: Impr. Rodríguez de Silva, 1905).

Romero, Francisco. 'Spain and the First World War', in Sebastian Balfour and Paul Preston (ed.) Spain and the Great Powers in the Twentieth Century (London: Routledge, 1999), 32–52.

Root, Elihu. 'The Basis of Protection to Citizens Residing Abroad', American Journal of International Law 4 (1910) 517–528, 521.

Root, Elihu. 'The Declaration of the Rights and Duties of Nations Adopted by the American Institute of International Law', Proceedings of the American Society of International Law at Its Annual Meeting 10 (1916), 1–11.

Root, Elihu. 'The Need of Popular Understanding of International Law', American Journal of International Law 1 (1907), 1–3.

Ross, William G. 'Constitutional Issues Involving the Controversy Over American Membership in the League of Nations, 1918–1920', American Journal of Legal History 53 (2013), 1–88.

Rossi, Christopher R. Broken Chain of Being: James Brown Scott and the Origins of Modern International Law (The Hague: Kluwer Law International, 1998).

Rousseau, Charles. 'La Non-intervention en Espagne', 19 Revue de droit international et legislation comparée 19 (1938), 217.

Ruiz, Julius. Franco's Justice. Repression in Madrid after the Spanish Civil War, (Oxford: Oxford University Press, 2005).

Sabau, Pedro. 'De la organización, progreso y estado actual de la sociedad humana' Revista general de legislación y jurisprudencia 3 (1855), 62–85.

Saldaña. Quintiliano. La Justice pénale internationale, Collected Courses of the Hague Academy of International Law 10 (1925), 223–396.

Sánchez Covisa, Remigio. Derecho Internacional Público (Madrid: Gongora Eds. 1896).

Sanchez-Mejia, María Luisa. 'Tradición histórica e innovación política en el primer liberalismo español' Revista de Estudios Politicos 97 (1997), 277–289.

Sangro y Ros de Olano, Pedro. 'La unión católica de estudios internacionales', in Estudios Internacionales (Madrid: Publicaciones del Grupo Español de la Unión de Friburgo, 1934), 9–26.

Santos de Oreyta, Antonio. Tratado de derecho público universal (Amsterdam: 1758).

Sarmiento, Augusto. 'Lecturas inéditas de Francisco de Vitoria: bases para la edicion critica' Scripta Theologica 12 (1980), 575–592.
Sayre, Francis Bowes. 'The Passing of Extraterritoriality in Siam' American Journal of International Law 21 (1927), 70–80.
Saz Campos, Ismael. 'The Second Republic in the International Arena', in Sebastian Balfour/ Paul Preston (eds.) Spain and the Great Powers in the Twentieth Century (London: Routledge 1999), 73–95.
Saz Campos, Ismael. Fascismo y Franquismo (Valencia: Publicaciones de la Universidad de Valencia, 2004).
Saz Campos, Ismael. 'La política exterior de la segunda república en el primer bienio (1931–1933): una valoración', Revista de Estudios Internacionales 6 (1985), 843–858.
Scelle, Georges. 'La guerre civile espagnole et le Droit des gens', Revue Generale de Droit International Public 45 (1938) 265.
Scelle, Georges. 'La guerre civile espagnole et le Droit des gens' Revue Generale de Droit International Public 46 (1939), 197–228.
Scelle, Georges. 'Le Droit Constitutionnel International', in Mélanges Carré De Malberg (Paris: Sirey, 1933), 503.
Scelle, Georges. La traite negrière aux Indes de Castille (Paris: L. Larose & L. Tenin, 1906).
Scelle, Georges. Precis de droits de gens: principes et systematique (Paris: Editions Sirey, 1932).
Schmitt, Carl. 'El concepto de imperio en el Derecho internacional' (trad. de Javier F. Conde) Revista de Estudios Políticos 1 (1941), 83–101.
Schmitt, Carl. 'La justificación de la ocupación de un nuevo mundo (Francisco de Vitoria)', Revista Española de Derecho internacional 2 (1949), 13–44.
Schmitt, Carl. The Nomos of the Earth in the International Law of the Jus Publicum Europaeum (translated by G. L. Ulmen) (Candor, NY: Telos Press Publishing, 2006).
Schmitt, Carl. Cambio de estructura del Derecho Internacional, Revista de Estudios Políticos, separata (1943), 1–36.
Schmitt, Carl. Der nomos der erde im völkerrecht des jus publicum europaeum (Berlin: Duncker & Humblot, 1950).
Schmitt, Carl. Donoso Cortés in gesamteuropäischer Interpretation, (Cologne: Greven Verlag, 1950).
Schmitt, Carl. La defensa de la constitución, (trad. M. Sánchez Sarto) (Barcelona: Ed. Labor, 1931).
Schmitt, Carl. La Teoría de la Constitucion (trad. F. Ayala) (Madrid: Editorial Revista de Derecho Internacional Privado, 1934).
Schmoeckel, Mathias. 'Lassa Oppenheim (1858–1919)', in Jack Beatson and Reinhard Zimmermann (eds) Jurists Uprooted: German-Speaking Emigré Lawyers in Twentieth Century Britain (Oxford: Oxford University Press, 2014), 583–599.

Schwartz, Daniel. 'The Principle of Defense of the Innocent and the Conquest of America: Save Those Dragged Towards Death', Journal of History of International Law 9 (2007), 263–291.

Schwarzenberger, George. 'The Standard of Civilization in International Law', Current Legal Problems 19 (1955), 212–234.

Schwebel, Stephen M. 'Review of Sir Gerald Fitzmaurice and the World Crisis: A Legal Adviser in the Foreign Office by Anthony Carty and Richard A. Smith', American Journal of International Law 97 (2003), 992–994.

Scott, James Brown. 'History of the Organization of the American Society of International Law' Proceedings of the American Society of International Law at Its Annual Meeting I (1907–1917), 23–39.

Sela Sampil, Luis. 'Brown Scott, internacionalista', Revista de legislación y jurisprudencia 75 (1927), 632–636.

Sela y Sampil, Aniceto. 'Los procedimientos de enseñanza en la Facultad de Derecho internacional de la Universidad de Oviedo: Derecho in internacional Público y Derecho Internacional Privado', Boletín Oficial de la Institución Libre de Enseñanza XXVI (1902), 223–234.

Sicilianos, Linos-Alexander/ Thomas Skouteris (eds.) 'Symposium—The European Tradition in International Law: Nicolas Politis,' European Journal of International Law 23 (2012), 215–273.

Simma, Bruno. 'The Contribution of Alfred Verdross to the Theory of International Law', 6 European Journal of International Law 1 (1995), 33–54.

Skouteris, Thomas. 'The Force of a Doctrine', in Fleur Johns, R. Joyce & S. Pahuja (eds.), Events: The Force of International Law (London: Routledge, 2011), 69–80.

Smith Herbert A. 'Some Problems of the Spanish Civil War', British Yearbook International Law 18 (1937), 17–31.

Snow, Freeman. Cases and Opinions on International Law with Notes and Syllabus, (Boston: The Boston book company 1893).

Somek, Alexander. 'Kelsen Lives', European Journal of International Law 18 (2007), 409–451.

Souto Paz, Jose Antonio. 'Las libertades públicas en la Constitución de 1869', Revista de Derecho Político 55–56 (2002), 107–158.

Stunz, Joseph. 'Natural Law Thinking in the Modern Science of International Law', American Journal of International Law 55 (1961) 951–958.

Sueiro Seona, Susana. 'La política exterior de España en los años 20: una política mediterránea con proyección africana', in Javier Tussell/Juan Aviles/Rosa Pardo (eds.), La política exterior de España en el siglo XX, (Madrid: Ed. Biblioteca Nueva 2000), 135–157.

Swain, Geoffrey. 'Stalin and Spain, 1944–1948', in Christian Leitz and David J. Dunthorn Spain in an International Context, 1936–1959 (New York-Oxford: Berghahn Books 1999), 245–264.

Tamayo Barbena, Ana María. 'España ante el Pacto Briand-Kellogg', Cuadernos de Historia Moderna y Contemporanea 5 (1984), 187–231.

Tams, Christian. 'League of Nations' Max Planck Encyclopedia of Public International Law (2006).

Tapia, Alberto Reig, 'Aproximación a la teoría del caudillaje en Francisco Javier Conde', Revista de Estudios Políticos 69 (1990), 61–81.

Téllez Aguilera, Abel, 'La proyectada Ley de Prisiones de 1938 y la figura de D. Federico Castejón Historia de un conato legislativo' Revista de Estudios Penitenciarios 157 (2014), 9–31.

Thomas, Hugh. The Spanish Civil War, (London: Penguin Books, 1977), 980–984.

Togores, Luis Eugenio/ Jose Luis Neila, La Escuela Diplomática: cincuenta años de servicio al Estado (1942–1992) (Madrid: Ed. Escuela Diplomática 1993), 55.

Toledano, Eustaquio. Historia de los tratados, convenios y declaraciones de comercio entre España y las demás potencias. (Madrid: Est. Tip. de J. Casas y Díaz, 1858).

Tomas Ortíz de la Torre, Jose Antonio. 'L'établissement de l'enseignement officiel en Espagne du droit international' Annuaire de l'association des auditeurs et anciens auditeurs de l'Académie de droit international de La Haye 40 (1970), 122–132.

Tomasoni, Matteo. 'La Gran Guerra llega a España: la revista Los Aliados y la causa aliadófila. Propaganda y debate político en un país neutral' Rubrica Contemporanea 3 (2014), 71–88.

Tommissen, Piet. 'Miroir de Carl Schmitt', Cahiers Vilfredo Pareto16 (1978), 220–275.

Torres Campos, Manuel. Elementos de Derecho Internacional Público (Madrid: F. Fé, 1890).

Torres Campos, Manuel. Nociones de bibliografía y literatura jurídica de España (Madrid: Impr. Ancha de San Bernardo, 1884), 135.

Trias de Bes y Giro, José María. 'La Organización Internacional. Discurso leído en el acto de su recepción como académico de número contestación del Académico de número Excmo. Sr. D. José de Yanguas y Messía' (Madrid: Imprenta Viuda de Galo Sáez, 1947).

Trias de Bes y Giro, José María. 'Règles générales des conflits de lois', Collected Courses of The Hague Academy of International Law 62 (1937), 1–93.

Trias de Bes y Giro, José María. Conception Du Droit International Privé d'après La Doctrine et la Pratique en Espagne, Collected Courses of the Hague Academy of International Law 31 (1930) 623–708.

Trias de Bes y Giro, José María. Règles générales des conflits de lois, Collected Courses of the Hague Academy of International Law 62 (1937) 1–94.

Triepel, Heinrich. 'Les rapports entre le droit interne et le droit international', Collected Courses of the Hague Academy of International Law 14 (1923), 227–332.

Triepel, Heinrich. Völkerrecht und landesrecht (Leipzig: Verlag, 1899).

Trubek, David/ Yves Delazay/ Ruth Buchanan/ John R. Davis, 'Global Restructuring and the Law: Studies of the Internationalization of Legal Fields and the Creation of Transnational Arenas', Case Western Reserve Law Review 44 (1993–1995), 407.

Truyol Serra, Antonio. 'Esbozo de una sociología del Derecho natural', Revista de estudios políticos 24 (1949), 15–38.

Truyol Serra, Antonio. 'The Jus Gentium as Universal Order' 18 Spanish Yearbook of International Law 18 (2013–2014), 1–9.

Truyol y Serra, Antonio. 'Don Antonio de Luna García (1901–1967)', in Estudios de Derecho Internacional Homenaje a D. Antonio de Luna (Madrid: Instituto Francisco de Vitoria, 1968)

Truyol y Serra, Antonio. 'El Derecho de gentes como orden universal', in A. Mangas Martín (ed), La Escuela de Salamanca y el Derecho internacional en América. Del pasado al futuro (Salamanca: AEPDIRI 1993), 17–25.

Truyol y Serra, Antonio. 'El objetivismo ético de Francisco Suarez y su influencia en la historia del pensamiento', Actas IV Centenario de Francisco Suarez (1548–1948) (Madrid: Dirección General de Propaganda, Madrid, 1949) 107–209.

Truyol y Serra, Antonio. 'La filosofía jurídica y social en la crisis del mundo medieval', Revista Internacional de Sociología V (1947), 135–153.

Truyol y Serra, Antonio. El derecho y el Estado en San Agustín (Madrid: Editorial Revista de Derecho Privado Madrid, 1944).

Truyol y Serra, Antonio. Fundamentos del Derecho Natural (Barcelona: F. Seix, 1949).

Truyol y Serra, Antonio. Histoire du droit international public (Paris: Editions Economica, 1995).

Truyol y Serra, Antonio. Historia de la Filosofía del Derecho y del Estado, vol. 3 (Madrid: Alianza Editorial, 2004).

Truyol y Serra, Antonio. Los principios del derecho público en Francisco de Vitoria (selección de textos, con introducción y notas), (Madrid: Ediciones de Cultura Hispánica, 1946).

Ureña y Sanz, Rafael. 'Nuevas orientaciones del principio de intervención, Revista de Derecho Internacional y Politica Exterior' 5–6 (1909–1910), 1–70.

Vagts, Detlev F. 'International Law in the Third Reicht', 94 American Journal of International Law (1990), 661.

Van Wynen Thomas, Ann, and A. J. Thomas. "Non-intervention and the spanish civil war." Proceedings of the American Society of International Law 61 (1967).

Varela, Javier. 'Crisis de la conciencia nacional en torno al 98', in A. Morales Moya et al (eds) Historia de la nacion y del nacionalismo español (Barcelona: Galaxia Gutenberg, Circulo de Lectores 2013), 543–562.

Vec, Milos, 'De-Juridifying 'Balance of Power'—A Principle in 19th Century International Legal Doctrine' in Nico Krisch et al. (eds) ESIL Conference Paper Series Conference Vol. 1 (2011), 1.

Verdross, Alfred. 'Le fondement du droit international'. Collected Courses of the Hague Academy of International Law 16 (1927), 247.

Verdross, Alfred. Derecho internacional público (traducción, bibliografía y notas adicionales de A. Truyol y Serra) (Madrid: Editorial Aguilar, 1955).

Vernet, Paula María. 'Decolonization: Spanish Territories' Max Planck Encyclopedia of Public International Law (2010).

Viejo y Harrassarry, Julian. 'El contexto de recepción de Grocio a mediados del siglo XVII en la Monarquía Hispana', Espacio, Tiempo y Forma IV (1998), 265–280.

Vilar, Juan B. 'Aproximación a las relaciones internacionales de España (1834–1874)' Historia Contemporánea 34 (2007), 7–42.

Wadlow, René. 'Salvador De Madariaga: Conscience of the League of Nations', The Federalist Debate 1 (2009), 38–40.

Warren, Charles. History of the Harvard Law School and of Early Conditions in America (New York: Lewis Publishing Company, 1908), 371.

Watson, Alan. Legal Transplants: An Approach to Comparative Law (Athens, The University of Georgia Press, 1974).

Wehrli, Yannick 'Latin America in the League of Nations: Bolívar's Dream Come True?', in Claude Auroi/Aline Helg (eds.) Latin America 1810–2010. Dreams and Legacies (London: Imperial College Press, 2011), 67–81.

Weisbrod, Carol. 'Minorities and Diversities: the 'Remarkable Experiment" of the League of Nations' Connecticut Journal of International Law 8 (1992–1993), 359.

Wertheim, Stephen. 'The League of Nations: A Retreat from International Law?', Journal of Global History 7 (2012), 210–232.

Wharton, Francis. A Digest of the International Law of the United States Taken from Documents Issued by Presidents and Secretaries of State, and from Decisions of Federal Courts and Opinions of Attorneys-General (3 volumes) (Washington: Govt. print. Office, 1886).

Wheaton, Henry. 'History of the Law of Nations in Europe and America from the Earliest Times to the Treaty of Washington' (New York: Gould Banks, 1842).

Wheaton, Henry. Elements of International Law with a Sketch of the History of the Science (London: B. Fellowes, Ludgate Street, 1836).

Wheaton, Henry. Histoire du progrès du droit des gens en Europe, depuis la paix de Westphalie jusqu'au congrès de Vienne: avec un précis historique du droit des gens européens avant la paix de Westphalie (Leipzig: F.A. Brockhaus, 1841).

Whitton, John Boardman. 'La règle pacta sunt servanda', Collected Courses of The Hague Academy of International Law 49 (1934), 147–276.

Wilcox, Francis O. 'The League of Nations and the Spanish Civil War', Annals of the American Academy of Political and Social Science 198 (1938), 65–72.

Wolf, Eric R. Europe and the People Without History, (Oakland: University of California Press 1982), 366.

Wright, Quincy. Review of 'The Spanish Origins of International Law -Francisco De Vitoria and His Law of Nations', American Journal of Sociology 41 (1936), 539–540.

Yanguas Messia, José. El hispanoamericanismo en Ginebra (Madrid: 1923)

Yanguas Messia, José. España y la Sociedad de Naciones (Valladolid: Universidad, 1919)

Yanguas Messia, José. La expansión colonial en Africa y el estatuto internacional de marruecos (Madrid: Imprenta Alianza Tipográfica, 1915).

Yasuaki, Onuma. 'Japanese International Law' in the Interwar Period-Perspectives on the Teaching and Research of International Law in the Prewar Japan', The Japanese Annual of International Law 29 (1986), 26–47.

Zapatero, Pablo. 'Legal Imagination in Vitoria. The Power of Ideas', Journal of the History of International Law Volume 11 (2009), 221–271.

Zolo, Danilo. Cosmópolis: perspectiva y riesgos de un gobierno mundial (Barcelona: Paidos 2000).

# Index

www.ingramcontent.com/pod-product-compliance
Ingram Content Group UK Ltd.
Pitfield, Milton Keynes, MK11 3LW, UK
UKHW041844031026
15587UKWH00003B/1000

9 789004 343221